MY UNFORGOTTEN SEATTLE

MY UNFORGOTTEN SEATTLE

Ron Chew

International Examiner Press, Seattle

Book design by Debbie Louie
Cover design by Jeff Hanada and John D. Pai
Typefaces are Adobe Garamond, Gill Sans, MingLiu and Minion

24 23 22 21 20 5 4 3 2 1

Printed and bound in the United States of America

The *International Examiner* is a 501(c)3 nonprofit organization. It is the oldest and the only nonprofit pan-Asian American newspaper in the United States. The *Examiner* also publishes the *Pacific Reader*, the only Asian American review of books in the country. The International Examiner Press is devoted to publishing works by and about Asian Americans in the Pacific Northwest.

International Examiner
409 Maynard Avenue South #203
Seattle, WA 98104
iexaminer.org

ISBN 978-0-295-74841-2

To my parents and
my children

Contents

Foreword

CAREY QUAN GELERNTER

TWENTY-FIVE YEARS AGO, WHEN I told Ron Chew I wanted to write an in-depth profile of him for *The Seattle Times*, he balked. He protested that he wasn't interesting, or important, enough.

He was always urging us at *The Times* to write about the doings of the Wing Luke Museum, which he directed. But a feature about *him*? Suddenly he was reticent.

He'd spent more than a decade as editor of the *International Examiner*, the Asian American community paper, telling other people's stories.

Though he didn't like the appellation, others often referred to him as "an ID institution." Whenever *The Times* sought a source about the Chinatown/International District, or even broader Asian American issues, Ron came to mind. Reporters knew his knowledge of and passion for the people and the place went deep. He could always be counted on for a quote both pithy and on-point.

But now he was making news himself. Since he'd taken

1

over at a struggling Wing Luke three years earlier, he'd been turning heads in the staid white-wine-and-white-people museum world. The Wing Luke was attracting national attention for pioneering a model for museums that engaged and collaborated with their communities, where, as Ron put it, "Bringing people together is more important than what's on a wall."

The first exhibit under his new philosophy, *Executive Order 9066: 50 Years Before and 50 Years After*, focusing on the Japanese American internment during World War II, had been wildly successful. Its emotional power came from the precious objects and voices of families who'd been incarcerated: their diaries, scrapbooks, photos of camp life, taken despite official bans; furniture and art they'd crafted from scraps. They brought their heirlooms to the museum and shared their painful stories because they knew and trusted Ron.

As that exhibit went on to travel on loan to other museums around the country, the Wing Luke was debuting another blockbuster: *The First 100 Years: Reflections of Seattle's Chinese Americans*, drawing from a four-year oral history project that Chew had led that recorded the memories of 75 early immigrants.

As one politician and activist, Velma Veloria, explained it, seeing their lives as worth showcasing in a museum changed the way people in the community felt about themselves. "The Wing Luke has become a people's museum," she said, "and if anybody tried to take that away now, the whole Asian American community would put up a battle."

In the end, Ron agreed to the profile, partly because he couldn't really argue that he wasn't newsworthy but even more, because it would benefit the budget-strapped Wing Luke. Ron is notoriously frugal, and there's no better deal than free publicity—even if the price was baring a bit of his soul.

So *Seattle Times* readers learned some things about Ron, a baby-boomer child of Chinese immigrants who worked nearly round the clock, first in a laundry, then his father as a waiter, his mother in garment sweatshops. About his insular childhood almost entirely restricted to Chinatown/ID and Beacon Hill, where years of redlining and restrictive covenants had channeled the Chinese. About underachieving in Seattle schools that had little knowledge of or sensitivity to the experience of a child entering with neither English skills nor knowledge of mainstream white culture. About coming of age during the civil rights movement and embracing the nascent Asian American movement. About being shut out of the old boys' network that was journalism of the 1970s, winning a discrimination complaint against the University of Washington that led to broadened opportunities for others but short-circuited his own ambitions for a journalism career, changing his life course.

Now 26 years after that 1994 profile, Ron has bared a whole lot more of his soul in *My Unforgotten Seattle*, his voluminous memoir. He starts his story more than a century ago, in the small village in southern China that his grandfather left, armed with false papers, for an easier life in America; "I'm not ashamed to say I am the grandchild of an illegal immigrant."

In one of the most compelling parts of his memoir, he takes us behind the scenes of the politics, personalities, and philanthropic machinations it took to raise $23 million to buy and renovate the historic East Kong Yick Building as the Wing's permanent home. Skeptics abounded, but it opened in 2008. The grueling "Little Engine That Could" campaign would also take a great physical and psychological toll on him.

Woven into his story are the stories of many dozens of people he met and lived and worked alongside for five decades. Among the moving portraits are those of his parents: his father, the most popular waiter at the venerable Hong Kong Restaurant, who though friendly and always getting the best tips, never groveled, always maintained his dignity; Ron idolized him and continued to work for years as a part-time busboy, in part to be with him. And his salty-tongued mother, whom he patiently helped with the English language lessons she could never quite master, and who never really understood what he did but still bragged about him to her friends.

In the 1994 profile, he'd shared his hope that once he set the museum on its way to building a larger permanent home, he could return to writing. He missed "the hustle and bustle of journalism," he said. "I'm a journalist who took a major detour into the museum field."

But journalism changed. Seattle changed. As Ron notes in his memoir's introduction, anyone who's lived here for any length of time can barely recognize the place it has become, as the tech explosion has fueled rampant and dizzying development and gentrification.

It dismays him that many newcomers to Seattle have little or no idea of the history and people who came before them.

Ron has always been about preserving foundational voices and stories and passing them to the next generations.

With *My Unforgotten Seattle*, he has written his memories of the community he has identified with, been shaped by, and helped shape, for 67 years.

Seattle would not have been the same without him. This history will add to that legacy by deepening our understanding of the city.

Carey Quan Gelernter was a journalist for four decades in California, Texas and Washington state, most of that time as a reporter and editor for The Seattle Times.

A Note About Chinese Translations

I AM THE DESCENDANT OF immigrants who came from Taishan (台山) County in the Republic of China. It was formerly written as "Toisan" or "Hoisan." It's one of four counties in Guangdong Province (廣東省) in southeast China.

In this manuscript I chose to refer to the region as "Hoisan" and my Chinese dialect as "Hoisanese" (台山話) or *Hoisan wah.* My spellings mirror how my parents, who were natives of the region, spoke. Cantonese is closely related to Hoisanese, but there are many differences. Mandarin is even more dissimilar.

Throughout the manuscript, in my phonetic translations of Chinese words, I adhered to Hoisanese pronunciations rather than more popular Cantonese or Mandarin approximations that appear in Chinese American literature.

I made this choice because I wanted to remain true to the spirit of those who came before me, including my parents and the early pioneers.

Because there are so many different ways that Chinese words—including surnames—appear when Romanized, I added traditional Chinese characters in parentheses to add meaning and clarity.

A special thank you to Fred Yee, who helped import Chinese characters into the manuscript using an application on his mobile phone. Sadly, he died about a week after finishing. Cai Zeng provided additional characters.

Introduction

IN EARLY FALL OF 2016, I left my house on Beacon Hill to start my 5 a.m. run. I donned my usual attire: a long-sleeved t-shirt, a neon-yellow windbreaker, gloves, sweatpants and a bright headlamp. My two sons slept. As busy as my life had become, I appreciated this time alone. Movement gladdens and centers me. I escaped.

The streets looked abandoned. I saw no walkers, moving vehicles or lit windows. A brisk wind whipped past me, scattering dry leaves along the sidewalk. I looked over my shoulder to see the first rays of orange light the sky.

I reached the southeast corner of Spokane Street and Beacon Avenue South. I ran on a dirt and gravel trail along the edge of the Jefferson Golf Course, surrounded by bushes and shrubs and a lane of trees. I felt like I was entering a secluded forest. This pleasant illusion evaporated when the first early morning golfers arrived, wheeling bags behind them. For now, it was wonderfully peaceful.

My mind drifted back in time. I remembered when roads

were dirt and gravel. There were few cars, no traffic jams. I knew all my neighbors. Friends sent handwritten letters. Cell phones, the Internet, personal computers and social media didn't exist. The downtown skyline was dominated by the Smith Tower. I didn't feel uneasy about going anywhere late at night. The only major league sport in town was Big Time Wrestling, staged for naïfs like me.

On my return jog, cars and buses began to fill the streets. Car horns, exhaust fumes and pedestrians hurrying toward bus stops broke my reverie. The sun rose. It was bright. The wind died down. An old station wagon rattled by. I smelled weed. A sprinkle of rain touched my face. I shivered. I needed to hurry home to make breakfast for my kids and get ready for work.

I thought about the murder of Donnie Chin, founder and director of the International District Emergency Center (IDEC). He had been a friend most of my life. It had been a year since his death. He was a native son of Seattle like me, immersed in Chinatown activities and shaped by the civil rights movement. He was 59, a few years younger than me. His chronological age belied his eternally youthful appearance. I still hadn't accepted that he was gone.

Donnie worked as a self-taught street medic in Canton Alley. On July 23, 2015, he was killed in the crossfire between rival gangs. Responding to reports of trouble at a nearby hookah lounge just before 3 a.m., he drove his car along Eighth Avenue South, where he was struck by a sudden hail of bullets. I remembered the hysterical morning phone call I received from our friend Dean Wong. The news media reported that an unidentified person driving a red Chevrolet HHR had been shot and transported to Harborview Medical Center. *That was Donnie's vehicle. Please, let it not be Donnie!* The heartbreaking news was soon confirmed for both of us.

As I neared my house, gloom continued to wash over me. After a year of waiting, Donnie's killers had still not been identified. As the days and months stretched on, I knew that justice might never come. I longed for this nightmare to end.

I sprinted past the Beacon Hill Library, its glass and slate-shingle facade glittering in the early morning sunshine. I made a last turn for home. I quickly showered and dressed. Dark thoughts dogged me for the rest of the day. I shut my office door so I wouldn't have to talk to coworkers. I couldn't find peace. I wondered why Donnie had to die.

In the week immediately after this run, I decided to write this book. Donnie's passing reminded me of the fragility of life. His death awakened the memory of another friend, Gene Viernes. He and fellow activist Silme Domingo were gunned down on June 1, 1981, at the cannery union hall in Pioneer Square. Gene moved here from Wapato, a small town in central Washington, to work with Silme on union reform and to protest against repression in the Philippines. I thought I had come to terms with their deaths. Maybe I hadn't.

In the year-and-a-half following Donnie's passing, a raft of Donnie's older activist peers died in swift succession. Tsuguro "Ike" Ikeda passed on December 2, 2015, Wilma Woo on January 26, 2017, Ruth Woo on July 13, 2016, Rachel Hidaka on July 28, 2016, Bob Santos on August 27, 2016, Charles Z. Smith on August 28, 2016, Frank Fujii on October 3, 2016, and Al Sugiyama on January 2, 2017.

The collective loss left me reeling. Ike, Auntie Wilma, Auntie Ruth, Rachel, Uncle Bob, Charles Z., Frank and Brother Al were community heroes who steered Seattle from its stolid neglect into a new era of racial inclusion and social consciousness. I feared they would be forgotten, like wax figures shunted to the darkened corner of a museum gallery.

Where were the people I grew up with? I didn't see them on the Hill. I didn't bump into them in Chinatown. They resettled in places we once considered a separate universe—North Seattle, Shoreline, Everett, Bellevue, Issaquah, Maple Valley, Kent, Skyway, Burien, Federal Way and Tukwila. I reconnected with them on Facebook, not in person.

The "hood" was no longer *my* hood. I felt like a ghost transported to the future. I was lost. I woke to discover "Notice of Proposed Land Use Action" signs everywhere. Skinny new homes and tall apartment buildings—made with bland earth tone panels and flat windows—cast jarring shadows over the aging bungalows and ramblers. I felt claustrophobic.

I struggled to find parking. SUVs, full-sized pickup trucks, camper vans and boat trailers packed both sides of the road. Travel became an unsettling voyage along narrowed streets, new bike lanes and pop-up construction sites.

My new neighbors, young professionals, arrived all at once. They snatched up older homes, replacing rusty wrought iron railings with wood balusters. They tore up front lawns to make space for ornamental potted plants, stone statuary and little garden benches. Along Beacon Avenue South, I saw roving bands of older homeless people begin to camp under bus shelters, surrounded by black trash bags full of their possessions.

The world I knew was nearly gone. I felt as if I had just watched an ice floe break apart, the pieces sliding into a rising crest of vast, nameless ocean. Seattle would never be the same again. I was witnessing a kind of climate change, certain and irreversible. I acutely tasted my own mortality.

I recalled the words of Henry Chin, a wizened old-timer who lived in the Republic Hotel in Chinatown. I interviewed him in 1990 when he was nearly 90. In a poignant moment, he puzzled aloud over why he was still alive. He said his friends were all gone. He made me realize that most of us don't acquire new friendships when we become aged. We die lonely.

In early September 2016, I began writing this memoir to pay homage to the city I once knew and the people and places that defined its character for me and a generation of peers. I went to my basement to scour personal papers, diaries from the 1970s and 80s, letters and other documents stored in dusty, neglected cardboard storage boxes. I found stacks of old newspaper clippings and sepia-tinted newsletters.

On August 27, 2017, I drove to the University District to find the exact location of the old hand laundry that my father and his brother operated in the 1950s. My cousin Ben came along. We were joined by the Lukes and the Lees. Their families also ran laundries in the area. We walked up and down University Way N.E., poking our heads into faintly recognizable doorways and alleys, trying our best to resurrect names of people and businesses.

My father's former laundry—at 1316 N.E. 43rd Avenue—is now Samir's Mediterranean Grill. Ben and I chatted with the owner, Samir Alawar. He was an effervescent 61-year-old refugee from Lebanon who remodeled the space in the 1970s. Ben and I then went to look for the old house in which I spent my first year or two of life. Ben's family lived there, too. It was three blocks away, at 4134 Brooklyn Avenue N.E. When we arrived, it was gone. It had been demolished to make way for a five-story apartment building. Our hearts sank.

Later that day, I looked through a 1963 Chinese business directory at the Wing Luke Museum. It listed 24 Chinese laundries in Seattle. Six were in the U District. They were a forgotten piece of Seattle.

I was reminded that our history is built on the precarious foundation of what is remembered, acknowledged and disclosed. In the new Seattle, I still had much to discover of my own past. My work was not yet done.

In fall of 2019, nearly three years after I began, I had completed the bulk of my interviews, research and writing. I was ecstatic. I felt liberated. As a former journalist, my worst night terror was that something bad would happen to me or my notes before I had a chance to submit my story for publication.

CHAPTER I

Chinese Exclusion Act and First Arrival

M Y STORY STARTS, AS ALL personal stories do, with the stories of others who came earlier. My paternal grandfather boarded a steamship to Seattle more than a century ago. If he hadn't come here, my life two generations later might have begun and ended quietly in a small Chinese farming village near my grandfather's place of origin. I might not have attended college, experienced financial opportunity or chased the American Dream. To my grandfather, I am indebted.

I never met *Ah Yeh* (阿爺), the Chinese term my mother used whenever she spoke about him. He died eight years before I was born. When I was young, I wasn't thoughtful enough to seek answers from the elders. When I got older, they were gone. Lingering questions haunt me.

My parents didn't talk about our family's immigration history. They didn't want to expose us to the scrutiny of government officials. My mother was afraid we might be deported. My parents called the police the *luk yee* (綠衣) or "the people wearing green clothes." To Chinese immigrants, city police were like immigration officers, easy to spot in their olive drab uniforms. The police station was the *luk yee fong* (綠衣房) or "the room with the people wearing green clothes."

I grew up under this cloud of silence, with no mention of my grandparents. I thought my father and mother were the first to arrive in the U.S. My grandparents—if they were even still alive—were phantoms, without names, faces or shapes. In school, white students shared tales of wise and quirky grand-parents. Asked about mine, I responded, "I never met them." I turned away, ashamed.

One Thursday after high school, I arrived home as my father was putting away several bags of groceries in the refriger-ator. It was his day off. I had just learned about the Chinese railroad workers in my social studies class. My curiosity had been stirred.

"Did your father ever come to this country?" I asked awk-wardly. I didn't know my grandfather's name. I had never seen his picture.

My father pivoted toward me and said, "Yes." He paused, then added, "He passed away quite a while ago. He worked in Alaska. In the salmon cannery."

"How about your mother?"

He paused again. "No, she never left China as far as I know."

That was all. He didn't invite further conversation. He left the kitchen right after he put everything away.

On Sunday, March 27, 1988, when I had reached the ripe age of 35, I inquired again. This time, my father was more willing to talk. We had visited Lakeview Cemetery on Capi-tol Hill, where my grandfather was buried. Our family—my parents, my sister Linda and brothers Tom and Harvey—had gone to pay respects. There, I asked my father what year my grandfather came to this country. He didn't remember. He told me he would look it up after we got home.

Back at the house, he asked me to come to the basement. I sat with him. He pulled out some old papers written in Chinese. He put on his black-framed glasses and began telling me a story of the past, his finger stopping at Chinese characters for specific dates, places and names.

The following week, he wrote out on a sheet of blue-lined notebook paper a simple family tree of the Chew clan, beginning with my grandparents. The names of relatives were all in Chinese. The tree included the names of "paper" relatives who were not in fact related to us; they had bought fabricated identities as a pathway to America. Their names were written in red ink to distinguish them from actual relatives, whose names were written in black.

Many years later, I am now able to breathe life into *Ah Yeh's* name from this opening conversation with my father, old photographs and other stories shared in later years by my father and mother, my older cousin Sen Poy Chew, and Chinatown elders. I retrieved my grandfather's immigration papers from the National Archives at Sand Point in Seattle. They are filled with tantalizing details, both true and made up, referencing people and places in my father's home village and Seattle.

I'm grateful I've been able to recapture as much as I have. I embrace it as part of my history. It tethers me to two worlds: Seattle and China.

Here's what I know.

Chew Quay Fong (趙桂芳) was my paternal grandfather's name. He was born in 1877 in the village of Fow Seck (浮石) in the Hoisan (台山) District of Kwangtung Province (廣東省) in the People's Republic of China. He was the only son of

15

Chew Jung Man (趙仲文), who lived from 1845 to 1903. His wife, a Chin (陳), lived from 1844 to 1926. Jung Man also had two daughters. One married a Woo (胡); the other married another Chin.

The village of Fow Seck has been home to the Chew (趙) clan for over 600 years. Fow Seck translates as "floating rock," referencing the harsh topography. To the north, Fow Seck is filled with hills. To the south, there are farms, swamps and tidelands. More than 1,000 residential homes are built along narrow lanes. Almost half of the village population moved elsewhere to earn a better living. Those who left sent money to support families back in China and build new schools and roads in places that were once destitute.

Quay Fong grew up in relative comfort as a young boy. He had an education, a rare luxury in that era. But with unstable family finances, he left his homeland at the age of 34, becoming a sojourner like many Hoisanese (台山人) before him.

My grandfather's boat ticket was purchased by his doting mother, who believed that her only son might have a better future overseas, untethered from a dwindling inheritance in the village. He made a final decision to move to Seattle after marrying a woman from the Woo clan. Many members of the Woo and the Chin clans had already made their way to Seattle in the late 1800s.

Gaining admittance into America was not easy. In the 1870s, the United States had undergone a widespread economic depression. White mobs savagely attacked the Chinese pioneers recruited to build railroads and work in the gold mines and agriculture. In 1882, the U.S. Congress, yielding to anti-Chinese fervor, passed the Chinese Exclusion Act. This law, signed on May 6 by President Chester A. Arthur, made it illegal for Chinese workers to immigrate to the United States. It was the first federal law banning a specific ethnic group. In effect for 10 years, it was reauthorized in 1892, then made permanent in 1902.

Undeterred, Quay Fong set sail for America, arriving at the Port of Seattle on April 15, 1911. He petitioned to enter as a "returning citizen." He was held in an immigration detention cell until his hearing. Before coming, he memorized coaching papers. Although this was his first time in the U.S., Quay Fong told authorities that he was born at 208 Occidental Avenue South in Seattle's Pioneer Square in 1877—five years before the Exclusion Act. Because the Great San Francisco Earthquake and Fire in 1906 destroyed all the Chinese immigration records, there was no way to disprove his claim. Quay Fong was one of countless immigrants to take advantage of this serendipitous event.

Quay Fong told authorities that he lived in Seattle for two or three years before his family moved to Portland. He said that his father, Chew Hing Ying, died in Portland in 1881 and that his mother had brought him back to China two years later.

Quay Fong claimed that he first returned to the U.S. via Port Townsend on July 14, 1897, arriving from Victoria, B.C., on the SS *Rosalie* steamship. His name wasn't on the regular arrival book in 1897. But he produced a "red ink indorsement" from the Chinese inspector at the Customs Service dated January 3, 1903.

Supporting Quay Fong's story was an affidavit from Woo Gen, one of Seattle's early Chinese pioneers. Woo was a partner in the Wa Chong Company, a general merchandiser and the largest labor contractor in Washington state at the time. Woo stated that Quay Fong's father was managing partner in Hing Ying Grocery, a local business where the Woo family also lived.

Two other witness statements—from Samuel Coombs,

a respected local historian who testified in many civil suits, and M.G. Conrad, a salesman for Centennial Mill Company—were also presented to immigration authorities. Appended to the affidavit from Woo Gen was a black-and-white photo, stamped October 23, 1905. According to the affidavit, "The annexed photograph is a true and correct likeness of said Quay Fong."

After enduring a rigorous interrogation, Quay Fong was officially admitted on May 23, 1911. Like other Chinese immigrants, he immediately sought refuge and support in Chinatown. He moved into a tiny one-room Chinatown apartment in the East Kong Yick Building (東公益樓), a hotel on South King Street where the Wa Chong Company was headquartered. Later, Quay Fong moved to another apartment building around the corner on 668 Weller Street.

Through Chinatown connections, my grandfather easily found work butchering salmon in Alaska's flourishing canneries. At the end of the canning season, he returned to Seattle, where he worked as a dealer in the gambling clubs and as a restaurant cook. In his spare time, he spent time at the Yee Yuen Association (怡源號), a club for members of the Woo clan, also located in the East Kong Yick Building.

As was common for Chinese immigrant men, my grandfather went back to China to visit and conceive children. When his four sons—Kin Hong (乾亭), Hung Hong (同亭), Soo Hong (紹亭) and Lee Hong (利亭)—finished their basic schooling, he petitioned for each of them to come to Seattle. Even though they were all born in China, his sons had the right to come here because my grandfather had been affirmed by U.S. authorities as a U.S.-born citizen.

Quay Fong first brought his two eldest sons, Kin Hong and Hung Hong. He submitted a petition to immigration officials on September 24, 1924. The two arrived in Seattle on the SS *President Madison* steamship on January 28, 1925. They were detained at the immigration station until their lengthy hearing on February 5, at which time they were allowed to settle.

After briefly attending classes for foreign students, Kin Hong and Hung Hong started the Willie Dan Laundry in the Terminal Sales Building in downtown Seattle. They served the many single men in nearby hotels. Kin Hong and Hung Hong also worked summers in Alaska in the salmon canneries. They both returned to China in 1929 to marry before returning to Seattle the following year. Their wives remained in China. The Chinese Exclusion Act barred women from coming to the U.S.

When Kin Hong returned in 1930, he brought my father Soo Hong on the return journey. My father joined his older brothers at their laundry, now located between the Terminal Sales Building and the Oxford Hotel, near First Avenue and Stewart Street. My father worked and attended school at the same time. Unlike his older brothers, my father was able to master conversational English, which allowed him to interact more easily than his brothers could with the outside world.

Because of the Great Depression, Hung Hong returned to China in 1930 to live with his wife in Fow Seck. He stayed for several years, choosing village life over trying to make ends meet in the ravaged economy of Seattle. Hung Hong came back to America in 1933, bringing his youngest brother Lee Hong with him.

With the arrival of Lee Hong, all four of my grandfather's sons were reunited with him in Seattle. None of my grandfather's three wives—Woo, Mark (麥) and Eng (伍)—ever stepped foot on American soil. They lived out their lives in Fow Seck.

Quay Fong had two daughters, Nging Choon (迎春), born

in 1903; and Nging Yi (迎意), born in 1924. Nging Choon married a Chin, who left China to work in a New York Chinatown restaurant, and gave birth to a child in China, from which the family thread continued. Nging Choon passed away in 1982. Nging Yi died at age two or three in China.

My grandfather passed away in 1945 after suffering a stroke and being hospitalized. He was spared the pain of being told that his youngest son, Lee Hong, had been killed in combat in World War II earlier that year. Lee Hong's mother in China was also not told about her son's death, until many years later.

Every year, during the Ching Ming Festival (清明節), my family and I go to Lakeview Cemetery to pay respects to my grandfather. He is buried beneath a barren grave marker bearing only the name "Chew Quay Fong" and the year "1945." With a trowel, we clear the overgrown grass around the marker and scoop out a divot of soil to nestle a pot of flowers. We take turns bowing our heads three times.

Today, I'm not ashamed to say that I am the grandchild of an illegal immigrant. I believe, as my parents did, that the San Francisco earthquake was a cosmic occurrence brought about to correct a man-made injustice. My parents said, *"Ga hen yu ngan hai,"* meaning "the heaven has eyes" (天有眼).

When I hear fearmongers condemn Mexican and Central American immigrants seeking refuge in the U.S., I reflect on the words of Dr. Martin Luther King, Jr.: "One has not only a legal but a moral responsibility to obey just laws. Conversely, one has a moral responsibility to disobey unjust laws."

CHAPTER 2

My Father

I N PHOTOGRAPHS OF MY FATHER—taken in boyhood, as a young man and as a mature adult—he has a lean face, square brow, strong nose, firm jaw, pursed lips, steady gaze and matter-of-fact expression. It's hard to read what's on his mind from the pictures.

By the time I became conscious of my father's appearance—at age five—he had only a fringe of hair above his ears that wrapped around the back of his head. My mother referred to him as *gong-how low* (光頭佬) or "baldy." I asked my father why he didn't have hair on the top of his head. He responded with a smile: "Bad people who didn't like me pulled it out." My mother commented that a startling number of men in the U.S. were bald. She blamed the polluted air and Western diet.

I idolized my father. He was a stable, predictable influence, never overbearing or judgmental. He was there when I needed him. He wasn't there when I wanted to be alone. It helped that we were naturally alike in temperament and attitude: low-key, quiet and simple in our needs. I felt secure and happy around

21

him, even if we weren't exchanging many words.

But I knew little about my father's earlier life until I entered my 30s. By then he was old. I feared losing him. Haltingly, I began asking him basic questions. *How did he meet my mother? Where was he born? Why did he come to Seattle? What did he do before he became a waiter? How did he learn English? Where did he go to school?*

My father seemed both surprised and delighted that one of his children was curious enough to ask. As I gathered details, I scribbled notes to remember what he said.

My father Soo Hong Chew (趙紹亨) was born on September 5, 1916. He was the fourth of his grandfather's six children. He was the third of four brothers. His mother was my grandfather's third wife, a woman from the Eng clan. My father completed his basic education in China. He considered himself lucky. Many villages in Hoisan didn't have their own schools.

My father left for America at age 13. This was typical of males of his generation. He was ready to join his father. He said goodbye to his mother and packed a few essentials into a canvas sea bag and a suitcase. The inside seam of the sea bag was marked in black ink with the characters 趙佬, identifying it as his. He called the suitcase *Gim San Thleng* (金山箱), or "Gold Mountain" case.

My father arrived in Seattle on October 18, 1930, on the SS *President Taft* steamship, accompanied by his older brother Kin Hong. The trip took 20 days. The first thing my father saw when he landed was the 38-story Smith Tower. The skyscraper was the tallest building on the West Coast. Coming from a place with few tall structures, he looked on in awe.

He was first taken to the immigration station at First Avenue and Union Street. He was confined to a dormitory-style jail cell with other Chinese arrivals. He waited three weeks for a hearing. In China, he learned the English alphabet, but he didn't speak a word of English. Through a Chinese interpreter, Quan Foy, he was grilled about his family members, neighbors and the location of specific places in the village, such as the school, his house and the rooms and doors inside the structure. The officials compared his answers to those of his older brothers Kin Hong and Hung Hong, who served as his witnesses, to make sure they matched. My father had memorized coaching papers given to him in advance of the hearing.

Some details didn't square. On October 31, a "Board of Special Inquiry" was convened to decide whether to admit my father. In the end, Chairman G.H. Mangels stated, "There is some confusion in the record as to just where in the home village the applicant's house is, and as to points of the compass, but such differences as exist are not sufficient to overcome the great amount of corroborative testimony in the case." He made a motion to admit my father. The motion was seconded by Mrs. Lucy J. Harris and approved.

My father, grandfather and uncles were relieved. My father had squeaked through. He was officially admitted on November 1, 1930. My father was issued an identification certificate on November 29. He was required to carry it with him everywhere. He began his new life as a U.S. citizen.

My father reminded me that before World War II, there were few Chinese women in the U.S. The laws just didn't permit it, except in rare cases. "Remember, I didn't have a mother," he explained. "I'm on my own. I left my mother in China. I had to cook for myself, clean up after myself and find work to support myself. It was very different back then."

My father first lived in the back of the Willie Dan Laundry, managed by his brother Kin Hong, while attending Pacific School to learn English. He was there for one year before attending eighth grade at Central School. He completed his sophomore year at Broadway High School in 1934. He adopted the English name Gregory, or Greg for short. "Soo Hong" was challenging for non-Chinese to pronounce. "Soo" by itself sounded like "Sue," subjecting him to taunts from other kids. Teachers didn't understand that the characters for "Soo" and "Hong" were joined together for meaning.

As a newly arrived teenager, my father witnessed the Great Depression. He said that he and his brothers survived because they worked for themselves: "Business was dropping, but we were just able to make it. We never went to the breadline. If you don't have anything to eat, you can get some food there."

In 1934, at the age of 19, he opened the Continental Hand Laundry at 1118 ½ Third Avenue in downtown Seattle. It was on the ground floor of the Northern Life Tower, a 27-story art deco office building built in 1929. It is now known as the Seattle Tower. His brothers Hung Hong and Lee Hong also worked there.

My father said it took very little capital to start. He needed several irons, ironing tables, shelving and a place to do business. The washing was sent elsewhere. He had saved money from working several summers in the canneries in Cordova, Alaska, as a "topper," filling the cans before they were sealed and cooked. Running a laundry was demanding: ironing, starching and patching garments nonstop, morning to night. At 15 cents a shirt—or two shirts for 25 cents—he didn't make much.

In 1937, my father returned to China to marry my mother. Because of restrictive immigration policies, she stayed in Fow Seck when he came back to Seattle in 1939. When the U.S. entered World War II in 1941, he closed the laundry. After receiving a deferment, he became an electrician at the Harbor Island shipyards, working on destroyers.

My father's younger brother Lee Hong also had a job at the shipyards. He was in his second year at the University of Washington, studying electrical engineering, when he was drafted and sent overseas. "He got a deferment once, but then the war gets pretty bad and they need more manpower," my father explained. "I got a second deferment and didn't have to go. My father was sick at the time, and one of us had to stay back here and take care of him. I was married, and Lee wasn't. That makes a difference. He would be first in line to go."

Lee's death in combat in Italy, shortly before the surrender of Germany, deeply affected my father. The sorrow never left. The two were very close.

After the end of the war, my father's job at Harbor Island ceased. For a time, he, Hung Hong and another individual ran the Hilltop Grocery in the Montlake neighborhood. After it closed, my father went to work at the Century Chinese Laundry, a large "wet wash" laundry owned by David and Frank Luke at 5101 Ballard Avenue N.W. in the neighborhood of Ballard. That establishment—and Star Laundry (明星洗衣館) at 160 12th Avenue—handled the washing and pressing for many of the 20 Chinese hand laundries in Seattle.

By the summer of 1948, my father teamed up with Hung Hong to start Campus Laundry in the University District. Football great Hugh McElhenny and basketball icon Bob Houbregs were regular customers.

In 1949, my father returned to Fow Seck to visit. He finally brought my mother back to Seattle in 1950. Seven years earlier, the odious Chinese Exclusion Act had been repealed by the U.S. Congress.

My parents started life together in a two-story home at 4134 Brooklyn Avenue N.E. My father and Hung Hong bought the 40-year-old house for $12,000, with a down payment of $6,000. It had a coal-burning furnace and a hot-water radiator system. My family shared the basement and first floor with Hung Hong's family. They rented out the second floor and attic to students at the UW, which provided an additional source of income.

In 1952, my father began a long career as a waiter in Chinatown at the Hong Kong Café. The restaurant was started by owner Sam Yee in 1947 as a coffee shop. It grew into a flourishing *chop suey* house. The name changed to Hong Kong Restaurant (香港酒家). We always called it *Heng Kong Lau* (香港樓), or the "Hong Kong Building."

My father welcomed his change in employment. He told me, "If you work in the restaurant, you go to work at a certain hour and you go home a certain hour."

Hung Hong continued to operate Campus Laundry with Second Auntie and their growing brood: children Sen Poy (善培), Won Ping (婉萍), Benjamin (善斌) and Won May (婉美). To earn extra money, the elder son Sen Poy worked as a waiter at the Moon Light Café on First Avenue in downtown Seattle and later at Moon Temple in the Wallingford neighborhood while he was in high school. He also worked at the Hong Kong Café until 1954, about a year after entering college.

In the summer of 1955, my father and Second Uncle sold the house on Brooklyn Avenue N.E., and our families went their separate ways.

By then, Chinese hand laundries were faltering. Many garments were made of synthetic, wrinkle-resistant fabric which didn't require ironing. Household washing machines and dryers had become commonplace.

My father bought a washer and a dryer for our Beacon Hill home in the 1960s. But my mother didn't trust the washing machine to do a thorough job of cleaning. She scrubbed all the clothes by hand in a large concrete utility sink with two tubs before placing the clothes in the washer for a spin. She often chose not to use the dryer, instead hanging wet laundry on a nearby clothesline and allowing it to drip dry over the cement floor in the basement.

In my early teens, my father taught me how to iron shirts with our new electric iron, a General Electric model with a black-and-white braided cord. Instead of using the built-in spray function, my father used a small metal spray can with a blower. It came from the laundry. My parents hated seeing us in wrinkled garments. During high school, a typical reprimand from my father was, "Ronald, you're not going out of the house dressed like *that*, are you?"

Many years later, one of the first life skills I taught my first son, even before he reached adolescence, was how to iron clothes and use the old metal sprayer I had inherited.

My father worked at the Hong Kong Restaurant until 1983, serving as head waiter during most of those years. Sam Yee sold the restaurant to investors in 1984 for a substantial sum. Many restaurant staff were let go. Business plummeted and it closed.

I never understood how my father endured his demanding schedule. He tended to errands in the morning, left for work by 10:30 a.m. and didn't return until 9 or 9:30 p.m. On busy days, he finished after 11 p.m. He worked six days a week. Thursday was his one day off. Sometimes, he worked seven days a week, putting in an additional shift in the cocktail lounge as a bartender. This meant he was at the restaurant until 2 a.m.

He never said much about his work. I found out from others who knew him when he first came to America that he was "disgusted" over the lack of opportunities for Chinese immigrants. By nature, he was a private person who tried to make the most of unpromising situations.

When I entered junior high and began working as a busboy at the restaurant, I saw how much my father was respected. Regular diners insisted on having him as their server, even if it meant waiting an extra 20 minutes. He was beloved by co-workers, restaurant management and others in Chinatown.

My father wrote letters and dutifully sent money to his mother in China. My mother complained that he didn't do it often enough. He never expressed any desire to visit China. He was a practical man. China was his past. His wife and children were in Seattle. His spirit was here. He rarely mentioned his mother. She passed away in 1981 at age 90.

Today, some old-timers in Chinatown hail me on the street as the son of "Fourth Uncle" (*Thlee Sook* 四叔). That was my father's nickname when he worked at the Hong Kong Restaurant. I see how much I look like my father in his later years. I've got the same sharp features and lean body. I have the same wraparound fringe of hair. The genes pack a potent punch, like gravity yanking airborne objects back to Earth. We become our parents.

In moments of forgetfulness, a few elders mistake me as *Thlee Sook* himself. I don't bother to correct them. I smile. I take it as a compliment.

CHAPTER 3

My Mother

URING THE MANY YEARS OF marriage between my father and mother, I rarely saw either of them express—in words or deeds—affection for each other. They never once said, "I love you." They never once bought a gift for each other. They didn't celebrate Father's Day or Mother's Day. They didn't recognize each other's birthday.

This only began to seem strange to me after I discovered television and Western concepts of romance, dating, and idealized white American married life. When my mother watched television with us as kids, she expressed her disgust at mild displays of adult couples kissing or caressing. She exclaimed, *"Kwee moh lai mow!"* ("They have no manners!") After squirming, she would order us to switch the channel. Lack of decorum (冇禮貌) wasn't tolerated.

I saw my father kiss my mother only once in my lifetime. I was about nine years old. He had come home early from work in a happy mood. He was beaming as he walked up the stairs from the basement garage. My mother was in the kitchen in a full-length floral apron, stir-frying Chinese greens in a pan over a hot burner. As my father came into the room, he suddenly bent down and kissed my mother on her forehead before heading toward the bathroom. His gesture startled her. It startled me, too. My mother laughed awkwardly, cursed in Chinese and wiped the kiss off her forehead with the back of her hand. She scolded my father for his audacity. She was flattered, embarrassed and a little angry.

I never did learn the reason for my father's uncharacteristic gesture.

My parents' stoic relationship grew especially rocky when the difficulties of shepherding their four American-born children through the wearisome teen years tested their patience and commitment to each other. Their marriage survived, but the two seemed like strangers in the same household. I wondered if they were ever close.

After my parents both retired and I was an adult with my own small children, I queried my mother about her life. *How did she meet my father? What was China like? How did she adjust to America? What was it like sewing for a living?* She sat in a recliner in the living room. I sat next to her on a sagging sofa covered by a threadbare chocolate-colored slipcover. The television, set at low volume, was tuned to a televangelist's sermon. It droned in the background. Her stories spilled forward like floodwaters rushing through the breach in a dam. She spoke with great emotion. I began to see her pride and sorrow.

My mother was born Wee Gam Har (衛金霞) on September 14, 1918, in the small village of Ai Gong (大綱) in the Hoisan District. The Wee (衛) village was located not far from my father's village of Fow Seck. My mother said it was similar to the distance between Beacon Hill and West Seattle.

My mother told me that her father, Wee Tep Gong (衛

緝光), grew up as a low-class herdsman, performing menial chores like shoveling cow dung. Scorned by neighbors, he escaped his fate of landless poverty by following relatives to Canada. He worked in Vancouver's Chinatown. He saved his money and became a partner in an import-export store called Kwong Cheng Hai (廣昌泰).

Tep Gong went back to China to marry at the relatively late age of 28. His bride was Lee King Len (李琼連). Tep Gong took on the married name Ging Fook (景福). He returned to Vancouver to continue working. After finally achieving financial success, he went back to China to start a clothing business and construct two buildings in Canton City. Japanese planes destroyed the structures during the Sino-Japanese war.

My mother was the youngest of three children. She had two older brothers: Wee Wun Hong (衛煥堂) and Wee Wun Yu (衛煥堯). Her family grew up in relative comfort. Her brothers had the benefit of a good education outside the village. My mother, however, attended only a few years of grade school in her village. "My father was very old-fashioned and stern about how girls should be raised," she explained.

Her father believed that it was a waste of money to educate a girl. Females were regarded as extra mouths to feed. In agrarian China, women often couldn't perform the same backbreaking physical labor as the men and were confined to housework and child-rearing. Once grown, females would be married off to families in other villages. Their children wouldn't carry the same surname.

As a child, my mother heard fellow villagers talking about an unwanted baby girl who was brought to the woods and smothered under a pile of ashes. This incident haunted her.

My mother's maternal grandmother had bound feet, which hampered her activity outside the home. My mother recalled the awful stench when her grandmother's deformed feet were cleaned and rewrapped in new binding cloth. "That's the way it was," my mother said, sighing. "Back then, the small, dainty steps of the bound-foot female were considered desirable."

My parents married on June 2, 1937, through a brokered arrangement between my mother's father and my father's mother. My father had been living and working in Seattle since 1930. The two had never met. They had no choice in the matter. In old China, marriages were negotiated on the basis of wealth, social status and the auspicious alignment of birthdates of the potential bride and groom.

On her wedding day, my mother left Ai Gong in an early morning procession for my father's village. She arrived in a bridal sedan chair. She overheard two women gossiping about her soon-to-be mother-in-law. "Pity the poor girl that's getting married into the family," one woman said. "She'll learn what a temper that woman has." My mother quietly sobbed underneath her veil. The only escape from her fate would have been to flee or to commit suicide. During the wedding ceremony, my mother lifted her veil, changed into a red skirt and poured tea for relatives. She kept her head bowed, quietly brooding over her future.

Soon, my mother settled into her role as dutiful daughter-in-law to her new family, trying hard to keep in check her independent and strong-willed spirit. She hated her tiny, congested living quarters. That was rectified when she was moved to a larger living space.

Before she married, my mother cared for her nephews. After marriage and her move to Fow Seck with her two maids, she began serving my father's extended family. When my father returned to Seattle, she became a typical "Gold Mountain widow," surviving on money sent from my father.

It was a terrible time. China and Japan were at war. Japanese troops stormed into Ai Gong on horseback in bands of 20 to 30, dust and suffering rising in their wake. They plundered food, raped young women and killed civilians. The Chinese villagers tried in vain to slow their advance by digging ditches and tearing up roads. At times, they fled from the village with only the provisions they could carry. My mother strapped precious jewelry to her body. They hid in dank mountain caves. They tried to find dry spots where moisture wouldn't drip onto their bodies. My mother developed terrible rashes.

On one return trip from the caves, my mother and another young woman spotted a group of soldiers approaching. My mother thought for sure she was going to be killed. But as they neared, she realized from their uniforms that they were Chinese soldiers. "Don't be afraid, miss," one of them said. "We're from the Chinese army. We heard that the Japanese have caused great trouble in this region. We're here to help. Go home." My mother flung herself to the ground, kneeling in gratitude and relief.

My mother told me that the Japanese incursions traumatized her mother, a sensitive soul. After one frightful encounter with soldiers, she became ill and lost all sense of reality. She died shortly after that incident.

With the relaxation of immigration laws following World War II, my father filed a petition for a non-quota immigration visa to bring my mother to this country on March 19, 1948. After two years of legal wrangling and the exchange of required documents, my mother prepared for the journey to the U.S. She pored over her coaching papers for 30 days. All her answers had to square with those of my father.

She arrived in San Francisco on the SS *President Cleveland*. She was interrogated on February 6, 1950. Like my grandfather, my father and my uncles, she was asked about her parents, relatives and the location of houses in Hoisan. She said that her father, Wee Ging Fook, was still living in Ai Gong village and her mother, Lee King Len, had died seven years earlier.

The following day, my father was questioned at the immigration station to see whether his story matched that of my mother. He said that every two or three months, he sent $100 to $200 in U.S. dollars back to China to support my mother and his family. At the end of the interview, my father was asked, "Have you anything further you wish to state on behalf of your wife's application?" My father responded, "No, I haven't, although I'd like to get her out as soon as possible."

My mother spent 10 miserable days in detention. The food was strange. There was never enough. She ate diced meat, eggs prepared two different ways and cabbage with butter on the side. She had never tasted butter. A Chinese woman explained to her what the mysterious substance (*ngow yu* 牛油) was. My father also brought cookies (*beng doy* 餅仔).

While there, my mother befriended a woman who, like my mother, was married to a laundryman. She had been held for several months and was sinking into deep despair. Her husband, a Lee, had been arrested, accused of cheating on his taxes. When my mother was released, she felt a sharp stab of sadness for this fellow immigrant whose fate remained in limbo. My mother never found out what happened to her.

My mother moved into the University District house occupied by my father, his older brother Hung Hong and his older brother's family. Second Auntie, Gam Goon (陳金娟), had arrived in Seattle in 1948, two years before my mother. My mother and Second Auntie both worked at the laundry to supplement the meager income that our families took in. Life was busy and chaotic.

My mother was not prepared for the ordeal ahead. She didn't speak English. She had been separated from my father for 13 years. They didn't know each other. They couldn't agree on many little things, and they were both headstrong. My mother was cantankerous, loud and direct. My father was understated, reserved and indirect. When fights became heated, he went outside and sat quietly in his car. My mother would fling open the bedroom window to pursue the argument, cursing in salty Hoisanese slang until her emotions were fully spent.

My uncle Hung Hong intervened. He brought home a huge batch of *gai geuk* (雞腳), or chicken feet—a delicacy in China—and urged my mother to indulge freely. "Don't worry," he told her. "I can get a lot more if you like." Two live poultry shops in Chinatown, Quong Wah (廣華雞鋪) at 661 South King Street and China Poultry Company (中國雞鋪) at 715 South King Street, gave the chicken feet away for free. My mother boiled them in a pot of water until the skin on the bones turned gelatinous, adding a sprinkle of salt before feasting. Hung Hong also introduced her to *lee thloon* (蘆筍), or asparagus, an unfamiliar vegetable bursting with a distinctive flavor. My mother instantly fell in love with it.

My mother and Hung Hong's wife, Second Auntie, both helped out at the Campus Laundry, ironing and matching the finished laundry with orders placed by customers.

By 1952, my father left the laundry to work full-time as a waiter at the Hong Kong Restaurant. Even with a better paying job, family finances were tight. After all of us children entered elementary school, my mother set off to work at Seattle Glove Company, a warehouse at 519 12th Avenue South, on the outskirts of Chinatown. My father gave her the English name Norma. She sewed cuffs onto heavy duty work gloves, earning $1.25 an hour. The blue-and-gray gloves were sold under the Big "B" Boss label as "rubberized" and "washable," and stamped "Made in U.S.A."

Mrs. Josie Bravo, a Filipina coworker, lived three houses down the street from us, at 2319 20th Avenue South. Her husband Maurice was a cook at the downtown Frederick & Nelson tearoom and Paul Bunyan Kitchen. Their daughter Edna was six years younger than me. From our living room window, I saw her tiny figure marching off to school in the morning. Sometimes, my father drove her. The Bravos were regulars at the Hong Kong Restaurant.

My mother studied diligently for the citizenship test, enlisting the help of my siblings and me to rehearse answers and practice proper pronunciations. She learned that *Jor-gee Vah-sing-ton* was the first President of the United States. To remember the word "Philadelphia," she made a tiny smudge mark on her hand to remind herself of the Hoisanese slang term for "dirty," *leh feh*. It was through little strategies like this that she was able to pass. On February 18, 1963, my mother and 42 others took their naturalization oaths in Seattle before U.S. District Judge William T. Beeks.

My mother sent money back to China to support her fatherless nephews and their families as well as her own father, who fled to Hong Kong after the Communist takeover of China in 1949. For a time, he was homeless, living on the streets. Once, he barely escaped from a burning residence. He wrote to my mother, pleading for help after he had been robbed of all his possessions, including his wallet and his glasses, while using a public restroom.

After four years at the Seattle Glove Company working under a kindly Japanese American supervisor, my mother was shocked to find the shop suddenly closing.

She found another job at Farwest Garments. There, she was

paid by the piece instead of hourly. The two-story Farwest plant was located at 1100 Poplar Place South, just off Rainier Avenue South, a five-minute drive from our Beacon Hill home. The company, run by James Theodore "Ted" Shanahan, supplied nylon-lined jackets for Sears and JCPenney. Again, her supervisor was a Japanese American woman. All the seamstresses were either Chinese or Japanese American. She stayed at Farwest for several months before that shop closed, too.

She found steadier employment at Seattle Quilt Manufacturing Company. It was located in a six-story red brick building at 310 First Avenue South. She was stationed on the third floor. She worked on down-filled garments. They were heavy, slippery and unwieldy. At first, she sewed hoods. Later, she sewed collars, cuffs and pockets. The pace was fiercely demanding. When she started, she earned $1.60 an hour. Her salary increased annually in five- and ten-cent increments. By the time she left in 1977—the year the business closed—she earned nearly two dollars an hour. My father took her to the unemployment office for her first time.

While she was at Seattle Quilt, she began a second shift in the evening at another downtown factory, Roffe, from 4 to 9 p.m. Eventually, she transitioned to working full-time at Roffe, where she stayed for nearly 10 years. This was her favorite factory. She felt the treatment of workers there was the fairest. Management provided one donut per person in the morning, a perk my mother declined. She thought that eating donuts would make her fat. At Thanksgiving, each employee received five dollars to buy a turkey.

The six-story Roffe factory building was located at 808 Howell Street near the old Greyhound bus terminal in north downtown. There, she sewed tiny one-inch square labels onto ski jackets, finish work that required an exact stitch count. The owner, Sam Roffe, told my mother that he preferred precision to speed. At Roffe, as at all her earlier places of employment, she was one of the most skilled and productive workers. She boasted to us about the handsome cash bonuses she received at Christmas time. She didn't tell coworkers how much she received, afraid she might invite taunts of favoritism.

I marveled at her stamina. From Monday to Friday, she worked two jobs, from seven in the morning until nine at night, before returning home to prepare dinner for the family at 10 p.m. She sometimes worked Saturdays, too. She never took a day off for sick leave or vacation. When she went to the dentist to have a tooth removed, she went back to work that same day with a small cotton ball tightly wedged between her teeth to stem the bleeding.

Twice, she injured herself. At Seattle Quilt, she sliced off a layer of skin on her hand. She was rushed to an emergency clinic, where she received a painful tetanus shot. It took two weeks before the injury began to heal. Years later, at Roffe, she impaled her finger with the needle of her powerful industrial sewing machine. Again, she was rushed to a clinic for a shot. She refused to return for a second shot. Following the accidents, she returned to work the next day, her injured fingers heavily bandaged.

I developed my love of storytelling from my mother. I sometimes didn't understand what she was saying. The Chinese vocabulary was often too advanced and she made reference to places and events in China that had no meaning for me. But her dramatic flair kept me engaged and kindled my own interest to explore further.

At night, after she put us all to bed, my mother sat alone at the kitchen table with her frayed *muk ngwe*e (木魚), or "wooden fish song" booklets. She bought them in bookstores in Vancouver, B.C.,'s Chinatown. The songs or poems, born in the Chinese countryside, spoke of epic tragedies and small daily sorrows, longing, loyalty and hope. In rising and falling cadence, she chanted for hours. I heard her in my sleep. The passages touched something very deep in her memory and imagination. She wept as her voice echoed through the house.

If she had lived in another time and had had the benefit of a formal education, she might have been a poet or writer. As it was, she worked with her hands in a country that she took many years to embrace as her own.

In 1988, my mother returned to China after an absence of 38 years. She went to pay respects to her father, mother and other ancestors and to visit the offspring of her late nephews. It was a solo journey.

In advance of her trip, my mother wrote four letters to officials in the government of Deng Xiaoping, asking for the return of her father's former homes. She complained that the property had been wrongfully seized during the Cultural Revolution. She recounted the story of her father's rise from poverty, adding that during the Japanese invasion of China, he contributed a large sum to support the Chinese resistance. A village authority finally wrote back to her that she was free to repossess the buildings. She was elated.

During her trip, she received an earnest greeting from several local officials. She told the families staying in the houses that they were free to continue with current arrangements. "My life is in America now," she said. "My children are all there. I will be returning to the United States to live." My mother explained that she came to pay respects to the deceased and to see the family members and offspring of several late nephews.

My mother felt the poignant welcome of people she hadn't seen in years. Like her, their hair had turned white and their backs had withered. She greeted villagers she didn't know at all, but who knew her as the wife of a Gold Mountain man in Seattle and the daughter of a Vancouver Chinatown merchant who once served as village chieftain. The grandnephews she supported through money she sent from America called her *Muk-Lan* (木蘭), the woman warrior of Chinese folk legend. She made pilgrimages to gravesites to burn incense and make offerings of roast pork and alcohol.

After she came back to Seattle, her daily mood changed. She complained about the way of life in China. Her nose had rebelled against the outdoor cesspools and absence of flush toilets. She was disgusted by the flies hovering over her food. She was shocked that villagers still dried clothing on the ground under the porch.

She didn't say it, but her eyes told the truth: *Fa Key* (花旗)—the "land of the flowery flag"—had become home. America was where her children lived, and America was where she would live out her remaining days. She had made peace.

CHAPTER 4

Earliest Memories

I WAS BORN AT SEATTLE General Hospital at 909 Fifth Avenue on May 17, 1953. I am the third of four children born to my mother in Seattle. My father was 36; my mother, 34.

My birth certificate says I'm Ronald Alpha Chew. *Ah-lon-no* or *Ah-lon* is what my mom called me. It's as close as she ever got to replicating the sound of my English name. I never heard her say my middle name.

She also called me by my Chinese name *Jick-Ping* 植平. At an early age, she taught me to write my full name 趙植平 (*Jew Jick-Ping*). It wasn't until many years later that I learned *Jick* means "cultivate" and *Ping* means "peace." My sister Linda (*Thlew-Ping* 小屏) was born in 1950. My older brother Tom (*Jin-Ping* 振平) followed in 1952. I came next. My younger brother Harvey (*Hep-Ping* 協平) arrived two years later. A miscarriage in 1960 ended the dream of more children. I think my mother was responsible for our names. The Ping character (平) expresses one of her deepest desires.

I saw our English names in the glossary of a *Better Homes*

and Gardens handbook on a dressing table in our house. Linda's name was underlined. Maybe our names came from there. I'm not certain. If they did, I would credit my father.

When I was barely a year old, I was bitten by a rat. That's my earliest memory. It happened in the family home in the University District. I don't remember much. My mother provided the details. The dividing line between what she told me and what I experienced is hazy.

According to my mother, I slept on the floor on blankets. My sister slept in her own crib. My older brother slept in my mother's bed. The house was infested with rats. They scampered about at night, emerging from crevices and hidden corners in the kitchen. When my mother switched on the lights, the rats dashed back to their hiding spaces. She chased and slapped at them, wielding the bottom of her slipper.

One day, my mother heard me screaming loudly and urgently from the bedroom. She ran to me and was stunned to find a huge rat with its teeth embedded in my forehead. Tears streamed down my face and my mouth was frozen open, trying to push out another shriek that refused to come. Overriding her strong fear of rodents, she grabbed the rat and crushed it to death in her hands. The rodent's blood splattered all over my head. She cleaned me, washed her hands and examined my forehead. The attack left a big mark. Fortunately, I healed rapidly, without any permanent physical scars.

From that day on, my mother shut the bedroom door during our afternoon naps and at night to deter the rats from making their way from the kitchen to her children.

I hated the dark. I feared hearing the tell-tale chittering and the sound of little feet racing over floorboards. There were a few mice in the basement of our new home on Beacon Hill. There were more in my Chinatown apartment after college.

My mother told me that as a toddler I gave her another moment of fright when I picked up one of her hair curlers and stuck it into an electrical outlet. The current hurled me across the room, and the room was filled with a burning smell. I wasn't hurt. I have no memory of that event.

My mother believed that the University District house was haunted. She awakened during the night to find an invisible cold hand pressing down on her, preventing her from moving. She said my father dismissed that claim as fantasy. This irked her. "Why don't you believe me?" she asked him in Chinese. "Why would I make this up?"

My mother couldn't wait to leave that house.

In 1955, we rented a home at 4202 Sunnyside Avenue North in Wallingford, where my brother Harvey was born. Shortly after that, we moved to a rental in southeast Seattle at 3215 Rainier Avenue South close to Massi's Aquarium, a long-time Seattle business with a big pole sign.

While we were living there, my mother found out the hard way about the peculiar American tradition of Halloween. She shared the story many times.

My father was on a busy dinner shift at the Hong Kong Restaurant when trick-or-treaters arrived at our house. My mother heard rowdy voices outside. She pulled aside a corner of the curtain and saw a group dressed in bizarre masks and ghoulish costumes. They pounded on the front door. They laughed. She thought they were a band of thieves. Nearly hysterical, she ran to the telephone and called the restaurant. The person on the other line told her that my father couldn't come to the phone—he was busy with customers. My mother pleaded to talk to him, explaining the situation. The person on the phone chortled. "Didn't your husband tell you, Fourth Auntie?" he said in Chinese. "Today is Halloween. The custom is that you have to give out candy. Otherwise the visitors might throw eggs at your windows."

My mother was relieved. My siblings and I were with her in the house. She was comforted that we were safe. But she also felt foolish. She had much to learn about American customs.

Even as we got older and Halloween was no longer a mystery to my mother, we didn't celebrate. When trick-or-treaters came to our door, we were instructed not to open it. The lights outside the front door and back door were turned off, as were most of the house lights. We hid inside.

My siblings and I were not permitted to go trick-or-treating. My mother was afraid someone might poison us or try to snatch us. We pouted. She bought Chinese treats—*san ja beng* (山楂餅) or *moy* (梅)—to appease us. But it wasn't the same thing as American candies.

We felt shortchanged. We wanted to be set loose. My siblings and I usually found a way to sneak out of the house without my mother's knowledge. We waited until she migrated to the living room to get on the phone with one of her sewing factory friends. During her interminable chats—she was what my father pointedly called *cheng hee* (長氣), or long-winded—we knew her mind would be intently focused elsewhere.

We tiptoed to the basement and exited the house through the garage. Hearts beating wildly, we followed other neighborhood kids to the Promised Land of lighted front doorways.

We didn't have costumes, but we knew it didn't matter. We were kids, and we wouldn't be turned away. One year, we used pillowcases as trick-or-treat bags. They held a lot more candy than brown paper bags. We never strayed more than a block or two from home. We dashed back home periodically to make sure our mother was still on the phone. We didn't want to face her steely wrath. Surprisingly, we never got caught.

CHAPTER 5

Childhood on Beacon Hill

I N 1958, WE MOVED INTO a new split-level brick house on a
vacant lot at 1919 South College Street. It was perched on
the southwest corner of 20th Avenue and South College
Street, in the north end of Beacon Hill. The house number
1919 was auspicious; in Chinese, it is a homonym for longevity.

In that same year, Hung Hong's family also bought a new
home on Beacon Hill, a little south of us, on 7510 Beacon
Avenue South.

By the 1960s, redlining, or the use of restrictive covenants
barring people of color from buying land, was swept aside by
the open-housing movement. Families like ours started re-
locating to Beacon Hill. Our neighbors were Japanese, Filipino
and African Americans. Italians had settled there a generation
earlier. Beacon Hill was sometimes called "Garlic Gulch."

We didn't know one another's traditions, but we got along.
We didn't lock our doors. If there was discord, it was hidden
inside the home. I never felt unsafe outside alone, even at night.

The streets around our house were simple dirt roads sprinkled with gravel. After a heavy rainstorm, the roads turned sloshy. Heavy trucks left behind deep grooves. One snowy winter, Cindy Chu, a neighbor whose father worked as a cook at the Hong Kong Restaurant, rounded up a few of us to build a massive six-foot-wide snowball which we pushed into the middle of College Street.

During grade school, we played hopscotch, drawing a rectangular court on the sidewalk with a piece of chalk. We played with a coin or a beaded keychain. I used the silver name bracelet I wore to grade school. We had a small, red Radio Flyer wagon to pull one another up and down the sidewalk.

When I got older, most of the kids on Beacon Hill got red roller derby skateboards. My two brothers and I each got one. They didn't last long. After a week or two of launching ourselves down pitched driveways, the metal wheels became pockmarked and wouldn't turn. We abandoned them in the garage.

None of us ever got a bicycle. If I wanted to ride, I had to wait in line to borrow a small bike from a girl up the street. When it was my turn, I circled the block several times before plunging down the steep hill on College Street. I loved feeling my heart pound and the wind rush through my hair.

Harry, a Japanese American boy across the street, came over to play on a new swing set my father assembled on the red patio in our front yard. He was a bit of a bully, much bigger and stronger than I was. He never picked on me, but he seemed to always get into fights with other kids in the neighborhood. After he got into trouble, his father beat him. We heard his whimpers from the house.

"Did you know that you're going to hell if you think bad thoughts, Ronald," he told me as we swung side by side, each trying to go higher than the other.

"What do you mean?" I asked.

He told me that after you died, your soul ascended to heaven or it went below and burned forever in the terrible fires of hell. "For example," he explained, "if you're greedy and you keep thinking about getting a big elephant, that's a bad thought. You'd better not think about that, otherwise you're going to hell."

As I tried to digest this odd suggestion, he came back at me. "You're not thinking about getting a big elephant, are you?" He looked me in the eye. I didn't know how to respond. He had planted an image in my brain. As we continued to swing, he kept warning that I was going to burn in hell.

I was thoroughly bewildered. I thought Harry knew more than I did. My fear lingered for a day or two. I finally concluded that his concept of heaven and hell didn't make any sense. I could do without his religion.

Before and after school, I plopped down on my stomach and elbows in the living room several feet in front of a black-and-white Zenith television with tapered legs. Every five minutes, I had to get up to fuss with the rabbit-ear antennas and the "vertical hold" or "horizontal hold" dials. I ignored my mother's repeated warnings that I would go blind from sitting so close.

We watched Stan Boreson (a genial accordion-playing Scandinavian), J.P. Patches (a clown who lived in the mythical City Dump), Captain Puget (a ship captain who sang sea chanteys and introduced Pacific Northwest history), and Wunda Wunda (a princess-like storyteller). I loved the unscripted horseplay between J.P. Patches and the man who played Gertrude, the telephone operator, and the "cartoon breaks." After school, I ran home to catch *The Adventures of Superman*, starring George Reeves.

The busiest part of Beacon Hill was the "Junction," the

wide intersection where 15th Avenue and Beacon Avenue South crossed. My place of shelter—the public library—was in the middle. There were two gas stations (Richfield and Shell), the Beacon Theater, Pacific National Bank (one of the first bank branches on the Hill), a corner grocery store called Tom Boy Market, a Japanese American optometrist, a barbershop and Owen's Pharmacy. Near the Junction was Perry Ko's South China Restaurant (華南酒家), a *chop suey* house with a smoky bar called the Dragon Room Lounge.

After school, I stopped at Owen's Pharmacy for comics and candy. When I opened the front door, a little bell chimed. The pharmacist, a soft-spoken man with a mustache and white coat, looked up and smiled. His name was Bob Ohashi. He prepared prescription refills. The comics were in several spinning wire display racks. I pored over my favorites—*Adventure Comics* (featuring the Legion of Superheroes), *Action Comics* (Superman), and *Harvey Comics* (Richie Rich, Casper the Friendly Ghost and Baby Huey).

My candy picks were Big Hunk, Cracker Jack, Red Hots (a cinnamon-flavored candy), cinnamon toothpicks, Tomoe Ame rice candy and long strands of red licorice. I bought packs of Topps bubble gum, which came with Major League Baseball trading cards. I wanted a full set of the New York Yankees players. They were my favorite team. Yankee home games were broadcast on TV on the weekend. But cards for slugger Mickey Mantle, pitcher Whitey Ford and catcher Elston Howard proved elusive. I eventually gave up in frustration.

Mantle was my hero. I had saved a July 30, 1965, *Life Magazine* cover article that I discovered on a side table in the waiting area of the Hong Kong Restaurant. Titled "Mantle's Misery," it cast him as a brave hero from humble origins. At age 33, he was in his 15th year with the Yankees. He limped on chronically damaged legs nearly depleted of cartilage, legs requiring thick wraps. I rooted for him when I saw him come up to bat on TV.

When I was about 10, I acquired a Mickey Mantle card printed on the back of a box of orange-flavored Jell-O powder. My mother made Jell-O whenever someone was sick and couldn't eat solids. The Mickey Mantle card was among a small stash of treasured baseball cards clipped from the back of Jell-O boxes.

The number 3 bus, an electric trolley, was the main public transit line from Beacon Hill to downtown. Dozens of loud Chinese women crowded the buses. They worked in Pioneer Square sewing factories and crab-packing plants near the waterfront. They wore bulky ski jackets and brightly knitted gloves and hats, and they toted lunches packed with large plastic thermoses. The crab workers wore sturdy rubber boots. When they came home, non-Chinese passengers edged as far away from them as they could, recoiling from the fishy odor clinging to their bodies. The trolley line ended at Beacon Avenue and South Spokane Street, near the fire station.

Among the crab cannery workers was my Second Auntie, Gam Goon, who had lived with us in the University District house when I was an infant. Her husband Hung Hong died in 1962. She worked in the cannery to support her family, which included four children, two born in China and two in Seattle. Hung Hong was only 54 when he passed away.

The grand civic event of my childhood was the Seattle World's Fair in 1962. It was called the *Century 21 Exposition.* The fair included a new science pavilion and the Monorail. The 605-foot-tall Space Needle supplanted Smith Tower as the city's architectural jewel.

My father took us to the world's fair shortly after it opened. I was in the fourth grade. I was dazzled by the futuristic science displays and carnival rides, including the Wild Mouse (a roller coaster), Skyride (cable cars transporting passengers high over the fairgrounds) and bumper cars. I was disappointed that we didn't get to take the elevator up to the top of the Space Needle.

We dined on snacks inside the Food Circus, an old armory building gussied up to look like a giant festival tent. I tasted cotton candy for the first time. Outside, we roamed through the Fun Forest amusement park. There were games like Skeeball, balloon darts, and Knock Over the Milk Bottles. I desperately wanted to play so I could win a big stuffed animal, toy or candy treat. My parents gave me a few coins. I tossed one inside a circled area on a table, winning a yellow stuffed teddy bear. I was ecstatic. I named it Lucky.

I was shocked that my folks let me play. Neither gambled. They shunned the Chinese lotteries, even eschewing casual games of *mahjong* with friends. My mother had friends whose husbands were gambling addicts who squandered their hardearned restaurant wages behind closed doors in Chinatown.

My mother sternly warned that if she ever caught me gambling—she used the Chinese term *oo bok* (賭博)—I would be severely punished. "When your grandfather was a young boy, his mother caught him betting with Chinese coins," she recounted. "She beat him, until his behind was red. He never ever gambled again." Her words stayed with me. I never learned to play *mahjong*. I have never purchased a lottery ticket in my life.

We took home a 13-inch ceramic Space Needle souvenir from the fair. It became a permanent fixture on our fireplace mantel. I kept several *Century 21 Exposition* silver dollar tokens, used as currency at the fairgrounds, in a secret hiding spot in my bedroom along with a batch of old silver dollars from my mother. I saved a copy of the ubiquitous sky bluecolored official world's fair guidebook.

Down the hill from our house, toward the east, Beacon Hill dipped into Rainier Valley, an adjoining neighborhood of ramshackle homes and small businesses along Rainier Avenue South, the main thoroughfare slicing through the Valley. At the corner of College Street and Rainier was a small IGA grocery. I went there to buy ice cream, popsicles, cap guns, Greenie Stickum Caps and red balsa gliders propelled by a rubber band.

Further down Rainier Avenue South were two adjacent stores: Tradewell, another grocery, and Pay 'n Save, a drug store with huge blue-and-green block letters spelling out its name. My friends and I called it "Pay 'n Lose." I went there for the latest vinyl records—45 rpm singles or the more expensive long-playing albums. I picked up the latest free copy of the "Big 40" song hits leaflet, distributed by radio music station KOL, 1300 AM.

My one steadfast companion was a plastic pocket-sized AM transistor radio. It had a long thin strap, and it came in a black fake-leather carrying case. I wrapped it in an old white handkerchief from my father. It was usually tuned to KOL, KJR or KYAC, which aired the latest chart hits.

I also followed live broadcasts of the Seattle Rainiers, our marquee sports franchise, a minor league baseball team in the Pacific Coast League, and the Seattle Totems, a professional hockey team that played in the Seattle Civic Ice Arena. I listened to Garner Ted Armstrong sermonize about the imminent disaster facing civilization during the half-hour broadcast, *The World Tomorrow*.

The Rainiers played at Sick's Seattle Stadium, one-half-mile down the hill from us. The ballpark occupied a full block along Rainier Avenue South and McClellan Street. As a rare treat, my father took us to see a game. We climbed up to the cheap wooden bleachers, gingerly leaning back into our seats so that we wouldn't accidentally catch a wood sliver in our behinds. A paperboy stationed by the entrance to the bleachers hawked the evening edition of the *Seattle Post-Intelligencer* (*P-I*). On hot summers, when we opened our living room windows for air, we could hear the PA system announcements of line-up changes, the sharp crack of the bat on well-hit baseballs and cheering fans.

As my mother learned to drive, my father took her to the empty Sick's Stadium parking lot on Sunday mornings to practice. I imagined the fear in my father's face and the white-knuckled grip of his hand on the door handle as he handed the car keys to her. She became one of the few Chinese garment workers on Beacon Hill with a driver's license. Other women came to the house before the sun rose, piling into the car for a ride to Chinatown, a short bus ride away from the sewing factories in Pioneer Square.

My father also helped me learn to drive. I took a summer driver's education class at Rainier Beach High School. When we drove to the Department of Motor Vehicles office on Rainier Avenue South to take my test for a permanent license, I was so nervous that I got involved in a fender bender with another vehicle. I was terrified. We both pulled over to the side of the road. "Stay here, Ronald," my father directed. He got out and walked over to the other driver. He opened his wallet and offered a few $20 and $10 bills to pay for the damage. The other driver took the money and left. My father got back into the car. I was relieved. But I also felt awful. I knew how little he made as a waiter. My father didn't chastise me. He simply said, "Let's go, Ronald. We're late. We need to get your license."

On Sundays, when my mother enjoyed a day off from work, she took all of us kids on leisurely drives up and down Beacon Avenue South in her big red Chevrolet four-door sedan. We passed by the Jefferson Golf Course on our left as we headed south. Wire fencing and tall, lush trees framed the outer edge of the neatly trimmed green fairways. On our right, we passed a water reservoir, a golf clubhouse, a lawn bowling green and the Veterans Administration Hospital.

Traffic was sparse, especially south of the Beacon Avenue Junction. The street was divided by a wide gravel median strip, which allowed my mother to dip in and out of traffic. She drove well below the speed limit, incurring the wrath of those behind her. They honked their horns and rolled down their windows to scold her. "Ignore them," she sneered in Chinese. "It's dangerous to drive too fast. They can always go around me." Inspecting the speedometer, I pointed out to her that she was only going 15 mph.

My brothers and I rolled down the back windows and threw wet wads of paper into the open windows of empty parked cars along the street as my mother drove. We kept score. We never got caught.

With the arrival of spring. I couldn't wait to strip down to my ragged t-shirt and shorts and go outside. Near our back porch, a tall rhododendron bush exploded with bright red blossoms in late April. I climbed the steep rockery surrounding the yard, pausing to whiff the pink carnations and yellow daffodils that my father had planted between the rocks. One big rock with a flat ledge served as a make-believe fortress.

I scoured for ants, especially the big red ones. I used a popsicle stick to dig under the crabgrass sprouting between rocks. I trapped the ants in an old Skippy Peanut Butter jar and fed them bread crumbs. My brothers and I put the jar in the freezer to test how long the ants could survive. I also used a jar to catch bees as they hovered over the dandelions. Even if I got stung, I didn't ever experience much swelling or pain.

We found earwigs in the basement. We called them "scissor bugs." Linda kept a few as little pets in her room, housing them in a plastic toothbrush case. She named one Scissory. She took them outside for walks and fed them bits of dandelion.

All summer, my knees had big, bloody scabs. I was forever injuring myself. Even long pants didn't shield me. I managed to imprint them with permanent grass stains and rip through the thick knee patches that my mother sewed on.

On hot days, I would lie on my back and breathe in the sweet scent of grass. I stared up at the heavens, watching the white clouds drift across the deep blue sky. I looked for the shapes of animals and human faces. I dreamed about riding a rocket ship on an expedition to outer space. I wondered if two-headed aliens with big brains lived on distant planets. I fell asleep, hypnotized by the slow dance of clouds and cooled by a soft breeze.

A long dirt alley between College and Bayview Streets connected our property to that of our Chinese, Filipino and African American neighbors. We dubbed the alley the "Jungle." It was filled with shrubs, untamed blackberry bushes and tall grasses. Drivers unfamiliar with the neighborhood tried to take a shortcut through the alley only to find their tires churning in the mire of wet earth hidden below.

My father mowed the lawn every other Thursday. He handled the push mower; I emptied the grass trimmings from the canvas catcher bag into a cardboard box. I dumped them in the Jungle and tamped them down with my feet. I also dug the weeds out of the sidewalk cracks with a trowel and edged the lawn with a heavy pickaxe.

The growing number of cracks in the sidewalks around our house mirrored the steady aging of Beacon Hill. When we first moved in, the sidewalk had few imperfections. The concrete had been poured into uniform chalk-white squares. But as the seasons came and went, the sidewalk turned dull gray, stained by foot traffic, bird droppings, bicycle tire tracks, ground-in dirt and small pebbles. Weeds and grass appeared in the seams.

By my late teens, the sidewalk cracks had devolved into a massive web of interlocking tributaries. Near our garage, the concrete buckled and broke off in little wedges, creating a perilous walking surface. I patiently scooped out the weeds, trying to restore orderliness to the sidewalk. The growth stubbornly returned after several days of rain.

My parents thought it was hopeless. They told me to focus on removing dandelions and weeds from the lawn and crabgrass from the rockery. The grass already had brown patches and bald spots.

But I couldn't let the sidewalks go unattended. I wanted them to return to the way they looked when we first moved in. Year after year, I spent hours crouched over the cracks on the pavement with a trowel and a cardboard box, the sun beating down on me while I worked. After I finished, I vigorously swept the sidewalks clean with a stiff broom. I cared, even if no one else did.

CHAPTER 6

Chinese Foods and Medicine

M Y MOTHER RULED THE KITCHEN. When she donned her kerchief and apron, I just got out of her way, unless she called for an extra set of hands. I ate traditional Hoisanese foods, similar to what my mother had in China. She prepared dishes from fresh, preserved and canned ingredients bought in Chinatown. I never saw a cookbook in our home.

For breakfast, my mother made a huge pot of boiled egg or rice noodles (水麵), wontons (雲吞湯), glutinous rice dumplings (*youn fun hong* 圓粉湯), or rice porridge (*jook* 粥). For lunch, we ate the leftovers from breakfast. If we got hungry before dinner, we snacked on toast, cookies or fresh fruit.

I especially looked forward to fresh wontons on Saturday mornings. The wonton skins were purchased at Tsue Chong Noodle Company (聚昌麵廠) in Chinatown. At home, my mother made the filling from mashed pork, green onions, Chinese mushrooms, shrimp and egg yolk. She scooped a tiny bit of filling onto each skin with a chopstick before folding, twisting and sealing the corners with a dab of egg white. I became pretty adept at swiftly folding a large quantity of the wontons while the broth, seasoned with pork or chicken bones, simmered over the stove.

Our Hoisanese pronunciation of "wonton" was *voon hoon,* very different from how Cantonese and Americans say it. The Chinese characters mean "cloud" and "swallow." The wontons were so delicious that I could imagine a heavenly cloud gliding down into my tummy.

The *youn fun hong* was cooked in the same savory broth as the wontons. Diced green onions and pieces of Chinese radish (蘿蔔) went into the soup. I helped my mother knead the *youn fun* into little balls before dropping them into the boiling broth. We bought the raw *youn fun* on Saturdays from an old Chinese woman who lived in an apartment in Canton Alley behind Four Seas Restaurant (四海酒家). My mother and the lady haggled loudly before settling on a price.

Jook, another breakfast standard, was prepared from leftover rice in the refrigerator. The porridge was thick and very filling. Added to the broth were chicken gizzards, pork, green onions and canned gingko nuts (*bak gwah* 白果). I helped my mother crack open the gingko shells and peel the thin layer of brown skin from the yellow nuts.

Dinner was the heartiest meal of the day. It consisted of white rice, stir-fried greens, steamed meat and soup. Typically, I ate three or four heaping bowls of rice. I always went to sleep with a very full stomach.

The rice was boiled in a heavy metal pot on the stove. Water was either added or scooped out so the kernels wouldn't become too firm or mushy. We bought our rice—Texas longgrain—in 100-pound burlap sacks at Wah Young Company (華洋公司). It was stored in a big lard tin in the garage.

The stir-fried vegetables were cooked at a very high heat in a frying pan with Wesson vegetable oil, diced green onions, minced garlic, mashed ginger and a sprinkle of Morton table salt. My mother alternated between Chinese broccoli, American broccoli, *bok toy* (白菜), cauliflower, string beans, mustard greens, bitter melon, asparagus, watercress, zucchini and cabbage. She often added a dash of fermented shrimp paste (*hom ha* 鹹蝦), *ow see* 豆豉 (crushed spicy, fermented black soybeans) or *foo nwee* 腐乳 (small cubes of bean curd fermented in wine). Occasionally, she sprinkled a pinch of *mei ding* 味精 (monosodium glutamate) from a small jar near the stove.

Other regular dinner dishes included vermicelli noodle (*thlie foon* 細粉) with dried shrimp (*ha mai* 蝦米); bell peppers (*lat dew* 辣椒) with fried pork skins; curry chicken (*ga-lee gai* 咖喱雞) with potatoes; and pigs' feet (*gee geuk* 豬腳) with bean curd sticks (*foo juk* 腐竹).

We ate fish once a week, usually rock cod. My mother pan-fried it with black soy sauce, garlic, ginger and green onions. It was tasty, but a chore to eat. There were many needle-thin bones. My gums often got pricked. We also ate canned salmon, which my father bought in Chinatown. The salmon—pink or sockeye—came in six-ounce cans with a bright red label. My siblings and I fought for the pieces of skin and crumbly bones.

Twice a month, my mother made fried chicken wings (*jow gai yick* 炸雞翅). The night before frying, she marinated the wings in dark soy sauce and crushed garlic. I helped her coat the wings with a layer of Swans Down Cake Flour just before they were dropped in the frying pan. I stood by the stove watching the chicken sizzle and pop, waiting to get a few juicy wings as she lifted them out of the oil with a pair of chopsticks.

Some dishes were steamed under a lidded pot on a back burner of the stove. These included "white cut" chicken (*bok tet gai* 白切雞); taro (*wu how* 芋頭) with pork; preserved fish with minced pork (*hom ngwee gee ngook beng* 鹹魚豬肉餅); Chinese sausage (*foong cheng* 風腸); and minced pork (*ngook beng* 肉餅) with salted egg (*hom on* 鹹蛋), preserved turnip (*how toy* 頭菜) or shrimp paste. My favorite was dried squid with oyster sauce (蠔油魷魚). The squid came in big flat pieces. After steaming, the squid was pulled into thin strips and smeared with oyster sauce. The soft bone in the middle of the squid was removed. I savored the chewy texture and slightly salty taste.

We never had dessert with meals. I didn't learn what it was until I began eating school lunches.

Every weekend, my father brought home discarded pieces of very fatty pork and pork bones from the restaurant. I chopped off most of the fat with a butcher knife. The remaining meat was put into small plastic bags and placed in the freezer. It provided stock for the large pots of flavorful soup.

There was always fresh fruit in the kitchen. I snacked on oranges, apples, pears, plums, peaches, persimmons, bananas, watermelon, cantaloupe and grapes.

Oranges were my mother's go-to fruit. They were stacked high in a large serving bowl on the kitchen table. They filled the produce bins in the refrigerator. My mother stocked up when they went on sale. In the store, she squeezed them and weighed them in her palm to find the juiciest ones. She made fresh-squeezed orange juice for us at least once a week, extracting the juice in a plastic hand juicer with a ribbed center and spout. She herself preferred to peel the oranges and consume them whole, sometimes two or three at a time. My mother didn't catch winter colds. She said it was because of the oranges.

Growing up, I didn't know the English word for persimmon. My mother called it *thlee dwat*. In early winter, she bought persimmons when they were extremely ripe and spooned out

59

the pulp to each of us as we lined up to her in the kitchen. The fruit tasted like the Gerber prune baby food I was fed when I was very young.

In our front yard, we had three small fruit trees—apple, pear and plum. I knew I had eaten too many plums when I found myself sprinting to the bathroom. For fertilizer, my mother fermented a smelly concoction of leftover shrimp shells and scraps of greens in a jar in the corner of the kitchen sink.

My mother had a vegetable garden under the fruit trees. She dug out a long patch of lawn, put in fresh soil and grew *bok toy*, zucchini, green onions and garlic. By early spring, she was outside on the weekends, a straw hat strapped over her head, paddle hoe in hand, clearing weeds and loosening the soil for planting.

After harvesting the *bok toy*, my mother boiled it in a vat of water over the stove. She took the dripping *bok toy* outside to the clothesline, carefully spacing out the stalks so they could dry quickly. This *toy gwan* (菜干)—dried *bok toy*—was stored in large glass jars, to be used in later months for soup.

One year, during the first weekend in August, my mother was working quietly in her garden when the Blue Angels, six Navy demonstration planes, roared into view overhead. She crouched in terror under the pear tree, unable to move. Her mind flashed back to the wartime attacks on her village in China. Gathering herself, she ran back into the house through the kitchen. I heard the banging of the screen door snapping into place. "Why are there warplanes outside?" she asked me, her voice trembling. I reassured her that America was not at war. I told her that the planes were performing for Seafair. I explained that it was part of the summer festival, just like the hydroplane races she had seen on TV.

I had rarely seen her so rattled. Even though she now

understood, she stayed inside the house each summer when the Blue Angels performed. Her fear infected me. Even now, when friends invite me to stand with them on their roof or back porch to watch the Blue Angels, I decline.

Our kitchen cupboards were crammed with Mason jars of all sizes filled with dried vegetables, herbs, spices, dried shrimp, *wun ngee* 雲耳 (a type of fungus that translates as "cloud ear"), *ong goo* 冬菇 (black mushrooms), *hoong doe* 紅棗 (red dates), *ho see* 蠔豉 (dried oysters), *baak hop* 百合 (dried lily bulbs), *bow ngwee* 鮑魚 (dried abalone) and *foo jook* (bean curd sticks).

My mother added these ingredients to different soups: lotus root, tofu, sea cucumber, winter melon, bitter melon, mustard green and egg flower. The soups were used to treat *gnit hee* (熱氣) or "hot" elements in our system. Foods were deemed "hot" or "cold," depending on how they stimulated certain organs.

Once a month, my mother made an herbal soup called *thlee mei hong* (四味湯), or "four flavors soup." It was supposed to counteract all the Western junk food we put into our bodies. There were four main ingredients: Chinese yam (*wai san* 淮山), dried lily bulbs, dried wolfberries (*gau ghee* 枸杞) and lotus seeds (*len ghee* 蓮子). She used pork bones to flavor the broth. It was soothing to eat.

She made winter melon soup (冬瓜湯) when we got sick. She added *toy gwan*, pork bones and a sprinkle of salt. The soup helped treat *gnit hee.*

I didn't care for the bitter melon soup (苦瓜湯). I preferred steamed bitter melon stuffed with minced pork; the bitterness was less overpowering. My mother insisted that bitter melon was good for our skin.

Every Thanksgiving and New Year, my mother made a jumbo pot of sea cucumber soup. We called it *hoy tam hong* (海參湯). It was an expensive delicacy. The sea cucumbers were immersed in a large jar of water on the kitchen counter for about a week. Every day or two, we took the large, slimy carcasses out to scrape the surface indentations with a spit rod and plastic mesh scouring pad before putting them back in the jar with fresh water to continue soaking. The soup was cooked with winter melon, Chinese mushrooms, chicken gizzards and pork. I loved the deep, rich flavor and the unusual sponginess of the sea cucumber.

Once a year, my mother prepared a pot of ginseng broth. She believed it strengthened our young immune systems. She steam-cooked it inside a clay pot (*oon go lai* 燉高麗) for many hours. She added white meat from a freshly cut chicken to sweeten the bitter, woody flavor of the ginseng. For several days before and after consumption of the ginseng broth, she restricted us to certain foods.

The term we used to refer to a common cold was *seng fung* (傷風), which translates as "wind injury." I caught a lot of "wind injuries" when I was little. If we were sick, my mother steamed or boiled foods rather than frying them. If our colds got worse, she forced us to drink bitter concoctions made from herbs and dried ingredients in the mason jars.

Packaged Chinese medicines were kept in the kitchen and bathroom. The most popular was Po Chai Pills (*bo dai yuan* 保濟丸), almond-colored pills resembling birdshot packed in small, clear containers. We swallowed the pills with water. They treated stomach problems and diarrhea. When I had a nasty bout of stomach flu and couldn't stop vomiting, they were the only thing that provided relief.

Kam Wo herbal tea (甘和茶) was another standby. It came packed in square, paper-wrapped bricks and made a foul-tasting brew. One time while suffering from a severe bout of flu for nearly a week and unable to shake the high fever and chills or keep any food down, I gave in to my mother's entreaties to try the tea. Within minutes, I felt much better. A warmth spread quickly throughout my body, beating down the fever and making it possible for me to eat again.

For muscle aches and severe strains, my mother applied Tiger Balm (*mon gim yu* 萬金油), a thick salve which came from a round, gold container, or Wood Lock Medicated Oil, a liniment dispensed out of a small bottle. Both provided quick and effective relief. Both emitted a very pungent smell. I waited until evening before applying them.

There were concoctions inside the kitchen cabinet that I didn't ask about, mainly because I just didn't want to know. There was a closed jar on a top shelf filled with baby mice soaking in alcohol. I assumed it was a health tonic or medicine.

I asked my mother about some dried ingredients in a small cupboard just above the stove. She told me they were deer testicles and deer antlers. "Yuck!" I cried. "Please don't make me eat that!" She laughed, explaining that these were very expensive because of their potency.

During the Dragon Boat Festival (龍船節)—the fifth day of the fifth month of the lunar calendar—my mother prepared a huge batch of *doong* (粽), a concoction of glutinous rice stuffed with fatty salted pork, dried shrimp, salted egg, peanuts and Chinese sausage, wrapped in fragrant bamboo leaves. My friend Dean Wong, noting the shape of the *doong*, jokingly referred to them as "Chinese hand grenades."

In China, this festival commemorates the suicide of a legendary Chinese poet and patriot. It was celebrated with colorful dragon boat races in the river. My mother recalled seeing these races as a young girl. She had learned from female elders how to prepare *doong*. She revived this tradition after she began her own family on Beacon Hill.

Preparing *doong* was an elaborate affair. My mother made several trips to Chinatown to gather ingredients. She spread them out across the top of our green Formica table with chrome legs. She expanded the table by adding a leaf section in the middle. The bamboo leaves, purchased at Kwan On Wing (均安榮), were left to soak in water for several hours in white plastic buckets.

My mother, sister Linda and I took turns wrapping the *doong*. Our mother did most of the work. She was fast and artful. Each of her *doong* looked like a pyramid. Linda and I were slow. Our *doong* turned out lopsided. We made a mess, spilling rice and other ingredients. We had to use extra leaves and string to keep our little bundles from splitting apart.

My mother cooked the *doong* in several large pots filled with boiling water. The cooking went on for a full day.

When my siblings and I were very young, we didn't have an appetite for *doong*, so my mother prepared less than a dozen, mostly for herself and my father. In elementary school, my brother Tom finally asked, "What is the thing you make with leaves and sticky rice?" My mother explained, adding with a smile, "I thought you didn't like it." Tom implored her to make another batch. He said he, Linda and I could pool our money and give her a few dollars for the ingredients. My mother revved up her *doong*-making operation after that.

Every year, my mother made over 100 *doong*, counting them out into separate piles for our family and friends in the neighborhood. Next door, Mrs. Chinn could barely wait for my mother to deliver a bag of *doong* to her house. Our refrigerator was stocked for weeks with this tasty, homemade "convenience food," which we could reheat quickly over the stove.

Until the last two decades, this Dragon Boat Festival tradition was kept alive in Seattle by women like my mother. *Doong* were made only in the home. Now it's a popular food item in Asian stores and restaurants. It's no longer restricted to a season or a tradition. You can enjoy sticky rice wrapped in bamboo leaves any time.

When I was growing up, no food was wasted. Broccoli and cauliflower stems were stir-fried together with the florets. After dinner, my mother gathered leftover food from our plates into a bowl so she could eat it later. My mother and father gnawed on pork and chicken bones to extract the succulent marrow after they were used for soup stock.

My mother reminded me that people in China went to sleep hungry every night. Her heart ached every time she saw a malnourished child with a protruding stomach on TV during famine relief drives. She remembered beggars in China scavenging through rotting piles of waste, looking for a few edible scraps. "You are so lucky to live in America and enjoy so much food," she often said.

She and my father, raised in a climate of scarcity, couldn't fathom the Western concept of dieting—*jai oo* (制肚). My mother said dieting was silly. She encouraged us to eat until we were satisfied. We didn't count calories or restrict fats or starches. Linda, Tom, Harvey and I were thin. I'm sure it had something to do with our mother's knowledge of food, healthy home-cooked meals and all the fruit we ate.

CHAPTER 7

Surviving Elementary School

MY WORLD OPENED UP AFTER I began school at Beacon Hill Elementary School in 1959. The school, a classic turn-of-the century building with high ceilings, large windows and wide hallways, was located about four blocks from my home. It was a short walk, but an uphill climb.

The first four years—kindergarten, first, second and third grades—were not easy. I was shackled by my halting command of English, my mother's strict edict to "be quiet and not talk back to the teacher" and my naturally shy nature. I daydreamed. My mind drifted and raced. I couldn't sit still. It wasn't until I was deep into adulthood—in my 40s, raising two boys of my own—that I began to suspect that I had ADHD or attention-deficit hyperactivity disorder.

I was also sickly. I missed many days of school. I suffered from painful ear infections; I couldn't hear well. I had a bloody nose nearly every day. I suffered debilitating migraine headaches. If I sensed one coming on, I looked for a quiet, dark space to hide. At home, I crawled under my blankets, willing myself to sleep so that the nausea and hammering throb would be gone when I awoke.

One summer, my parents sent us to Bible class at Seattle Chinese Baptist Church (CBC). The red brick structure with mullioned windows and a white cross on the roof was at the corner of 10th Avenue South and South King Street. We attended weddings and funeral services there. The pastor was Paul Fong. Succeeding him was Rev. Paul Szeto, who helped erect a new church on Beacon Hill in 1976. Decades later, I worked with Rev. Szeto's daughter Melissa at the Wing Luke Museum.

Linda and Tom attended most of that summer's classes, but I went only once or twice because I was sick for weeks. I only remember learning that Jesus, a white man with long hair, a beard and flowing white robes, was the son of God. I was jealous when Linda and Tom returned from church with ice cream. Tom brought home a little money pouch with leather braiding that he had made.

That summer, I alternated between lying in bed shivering feverishly under a mound of blankets and sitting on a green, cracked-vinyl chair in the kitchen, a bowl of my mother's winter melon broth in front of me, the bright sun streaming through a set of thin floral curtains.

My father took time off from work to take me to the doctor. His car had an extra cardboard box lined with old newspapers in case I threw up during the drive. My two saviors were Dr. Ernest Ching (錢永富), a Chinese American from Hawaii with a medical office on the second floor of the Governor Apartments, a white terracotta building in Chinatown; and Dr. Charles Kaplan, a pediatrician on Brooklyn Avenue N.E., not far from our earlier home in the University District.

I preferred Dr. Kaplan. He had a big, warm smile and reassuring manner. I got a free balloon or small toy at the end of the visit, after my shots. Dr. Kaplan and his family dined at the Hong Kong Restaurant every other weekend. My father was his waiter. Dr. Kaplan always ordered the "long rice," the vermicelli noodle we called *thlie foon*. It was his favorite. Every December, we received a holiday card from him. Every May, he sent me a birthday card. My mother trusted and adored him.

I struggled to keep up in elementary school. Chinese, not English, was spoken at home. I barely knew what was going on. I never raised my hand. When I was called upon, I froze in my seat. My mouth clamped shut. My teachers puzzled over what might be wrong with "Ronald."

During the first week of kindergarten, we were asked to sketch a picture or build something with wooden blocks. I decided that it would be fun to build a house. I stacked blocks to make four walls, then added two windows and two doors. Before class ended, the teacher came around, asking each of us to describe our creations.

"Can you please tell the class what this is, Ronald?"

I wanted to say that I had built a house, but I didn't know the English word.

Long silence. No response.

My teacher tried another question: "Can you tell us where the front door is, Ronald?"

This time, I was puzzled by the question. I interpreted it literally. I knew what a door was, but how could I say which was the front and which was the back? These were just blocks.

More silence.

The teacher again: "Where is the front door, Ronald? Please tell the class."

By now I was totally embarrassed by the attention of the other kids, paralyzed with fear.

Another long silence.

Mercifully, the teacher moved on to the next person.

That's how it was. I couldn't wait for my mother to come pick me up at the end of the school day and walk me home.

My sister Linda faced a similar rough transition. On the first day of kindergarten, all the students in her class were asked to grab their name card from the front blackboard and tell others who they were. "Hmm," Linda thought. "I don't know how to speak. I don't know how to read. I don't know how to write. What do I do?" She waited until everyone else had claimed their names, then she pulled the last card from the blackboard, correctly assuming that it bore her name. Linda adapted much more quickly than I did. She was clever and tenacious. She soon became an excellent reader.

My adjustment continued to be slow. In first grade, I couldn't figure out where I was supposed to go after first period home room class. I was afraid to ask for help. Petrified, I hid for a long time in the lower-level restroom. I stayed until the final bell rang to signal the end of school.

Once, I got caught running through the hallway, egged on by a few other boys who were racing me to the front door. My forward momentum was suddenly halted by a male administrator who grabbed me by the collar, jerking me backward. "Hey, no running in the school," he shouted, angry because of what he perceived as overt flaunting of school rules. The other boys had vanished. I tried to say that I wasn't the only guilty party, but before I spoke, he kicked me in the behind with his hard leather shoe and I went sprawling. "Don't ever do this again," he said sternly, fire in his eyes. He walked away. I wasn't hurt, but I dreaded that the incident would be reported to my parents and that I would get into even more trouble at home.

On another occasion, in either kindergarten or first grade, my mother came into the school looking for me, waiting to walk me home. She usually stood outside, but this time she entered the building because my last class had run late. When she finally spotted me, she asked why I was late. A white administrator came forward and interjected, "Is this your mother?" I said yes. "Can you please tell her that if she wants to come inside the school, she needs to speak English?"

My mother, seeing the school official, smiled, trying to be friendly. "What did he say?" my mother asked me in Chinese. I didn't respond to either my mother or the school authority, but my face turned red. I grabbed my mother's hand, pulling her to the front door. "Let's go," I begged. Outside, my mother again asked me, "What did that man say? Did you do something bad?" I told her it was nothing. But from that day forward, I made sure to leave class as early as I could so that my mother wouldn't come inside the school. That incident made me deeply ashamed to be Chinese.

By the second grade, even though I still lagged behind, I was cagey enough to find the correct answers to test questions by peeking at the work of a few bright students when the teacher wasn't looking. I remember the inky smell of the purple-colored exams, freshly printed on a ditto machine, as they made their way down each row. Each student would take one sheet and hand the stack over their shoulder to the person behind them. Cheating allowed me to get by for a while. But this was unsustainable. Grades depended on verbal participation, and I never spoke in class. I also got caught copying. After a teacher loudly admonished me in front of others, I never did it again.

I did find moments of joy. In either the first or second grade, my art teacher allowed students to draw anything they wanted to as long as the images came from real life. We used colored pencils. I decided to draw an apple tree. I thought this would be easy. I first drew the outline of a tree and a person standing next to a ladder. Then I used brown to color in the tree trunk and branches, red to draw some big ripe apples, green to depict some grass on the ground and a mixture of other colors to complete the ladder and human figure. I was so pleased with my accomplishment that I took it home with me after class.

For the rest of the term, I made the same sketch over and over. Each succeeding image got sharper, more precise. "Don't you want to draw something else, Ronald?" my teacher asked me one day. I shook my head. The act of drawing the same picture over and over was soothing. I accumulated a stack of these images at home. I showed them to my mother. She asked the same question as my teacher. I shrugged. I didn't know how to explain what I was feeling.

Through the fourth grade, I squeaked by, earning Cs and a few Bs and Ds. The passing grades masked how badly I was lost and how much of a nightmare school had become for me.

I didn't have friends. I was ruthlessly teased by non-Chinese kids. They called me "Chew, Chew" and "Chewing Gum" and "Choo-Choo Train." The boys never once called me by my first name. At times, I wished that I was Smith or Johnson.

I wanted badly to be accepted. *Was I an American?* Some kids didn't think so. My mother didn't think so either. She said we were Chinese. Americans were white and black people. That's what I learned on TV, too. Chinese were "foreigners."

What color was I? I knew African Americans were black and European Americans were white. What about me? During the Cold War, when the People's Republic of China was isolated from the West, I heard many references to "Red China." I thought we might be red-skinned people. No one told me I was yellow.

Then I saw racist caricatures of Chinese as "yellow bellies," "yellow-skins" and "The Yellow Peril." A light went on. *We were yellow.* On TV, I heard American Indians called "redskins." *They were red.* I didn't want to be yellow. I wondered how Indians felt about being red.

When I looked at the skin tone of my classmates, I didn't see anyone who was actually white, black, brown, red or yellow. Everyone was a shade in-between. When I was issued a box of Crayola crayons, one was labeled "flesh." It was a peach color. I didn't see anyone with that skin tone. If I sketched a white person, was I supposed to use the "white" crayon? That would have been silly to do on white paper. If I was doing a self-sketch, should I use the yellow crayon?

One day, my teacher asked students to describe their religion. I didn't know what to say. Was I a Christian? Was I a Baptist? Was I something else?

My mother made daily entreaties to *Seung Ai* (上帝), or God, and *Yeh Thlew* (耶穌), or Jesus. But she also prayed to *Kwan Yin* (觀音), the Goddess of Mercy. She never talked about heaven or hell like the kids in school did. I asked my father, "What religion are we?" He responded curtly, "We don't have a religion." The way he said it sounded cold and grim, as if our family hadn't been endowed with any soul. He didn't offer any further explanation. I felt let down. I was unsure what to tell the teacher the next day.

I wondered: If we didn't have a religion, why did we go to the Chinese Baptist Church? Who was that porcelain laughing Buddha with the five children that sat so prominently on our fireplace mantel? Who were all these Buddha figures that adorned the lunar calendars on our kitchen wall? Were those religious icons? Was I a Buddhist?

I didn't rely on my parents for answers to these basic mysteries. I simply handed them my year-end report card. They didn't attend parent-teacher conferences. My father couldn't take time off work, and my mother couldn't communicate with the teachers. To this day, I wonder how my fellow Chinese American classmates coped and whether they had an easier time than I did. But I never found out because we never talked.

I dreaded the weekly "show-and-tell" time. Students brought a favorite object from home to share a story with the entire class. I envied one Japanese American student who, week after week, came with a new toy or cool gadget. I had nothing. Once, my older brother Tom made me a musical instrument to take to school, fashioning it out of a few spare pieces of wood and different lengths of rubber band. In private, I had many hours of fun with it. But when it came time to pull it out of my paper sack to show the other kids, I balked after seeing what my Japanese American classmate brought that day. I told the teacher that I forgot to bring my toy.

By the fifth grade, we began to study nutrition and diet. My teacher used a food pyramid chart to discuss the four basic food groups: milk, meat, fruits and vegetables, and grains.

Class, let's find out if you have a balanced diet. What did you eat for breakfast, lunch and dinner?

I thought to myself: "Rice. Chinese dishes. Fermented soybean paste. Dried bean curd. White radish. Bitter melon. Lotus root soup." *But what were the English words?* I didn't see pictures of these foods on the chart.

I began to lie. If a white kid ahead of me had bacon and eggs for breakfast, that's what I had. If someone else had toast and jam, I had toast and jam. If another kid had pancakes, I had that, too. I didn't even know what pancakes were, but lying became much easier than trying to explain.

In fifth grade, the teacher led the class through a discussion of jobs. *What did our parents do? How did they earn a living? What did we want to do when we grew up?* Other kids said their parents worked in offices, at the post office or The Boeing Company. My father was a waiter in Chinatown. My ears turned red when I told the class that he served Chinese food and cleared tables. I felt a strong kinship with a Chinese American girl whose father also worked in a Chinese restaurant—as a cook. At least I wasn't alone.

I envied students whose mothers were homemakers. That seemed to carry status. My mother worked in a run-down sewing factory, shuttered from the view of passersby. I was embarrassed to admit this. Not knowing how to describe her job to the class, I asked my father. He pulled out an employment form and pointed to the words "power machine operator." The next day, I came to class armed with that lamentable euphemism. I got tongue-tied. It would have been better if I had simply told the class that my mother sewed garments.

During lunch period, I discovered many new foods: chili con carne, macaroni and cheese, sloppy joes, cottage cheese, pizza, lasagna, and toasted cheese sandwiches. I was repelled by the odor of cheese. It reminded me of two instances when I accidentally drank spoiled milk from our refrigerator. My favorite lunch offerings were hamburger, meatloaf and fried chicken. The school lunches usually came with milk (which I never drank), a small dessert (which I usually ate), and a slice of buttered white bread, which I gave to a kid who shadowed me, looking to see what he could scavenge. He didn't bring a home lunch or have money to buy anything.

If I brought lunch from home, it was a plain sandwich with chopped ham or baloney in the middle of two slices of white Wonder Bread. If the sandwich was cut diagonally and placed tidily inside a waxed bag, I knew my father had packed it. We always had a fresh loaf of Wonder Bread on the kitchen table. TV ads told us that the bread "Builds Strong Bodies 8 Ways!"

Later the number was upped to 12. My lunch might include a few pieces of leftover fried chicken and a small bag of Lay's Potato Chips or Fritos Corn Chips. The chips were from a multipack with a free plastic dinosaur.

My father began buying Kellogg's Pop-Tarts from the grocery store. They came in a variety of flavors, two to a pack in foil wrappers. I loved the flaky biscuits with fruit filling. Strawberry was the tastiest. We heated them in the toaster for a quick snack.

Every Monday, my teacher walked down the aisles in the classroom, stopping to peer inside the ear canal of each student. "Clean" or "dirty" was the pronouncement, depending on the amount of ear wax she spotted. My ears were always "dirty." I had drainage issues. My mother never cleaned our ears. We didn't have cotton swabs.

A Chinese American classmate named Trina was lauded for her stellar aural hygiene. She was also a model student. Many years later, I learned from her younger sister that their mother made all the kids lie down on the couch and cleaned their ears with a gold-colored spoon.

During the first few years of school, I dressed in long-sleeved flannel shirts and stiff corduroy pants or jeans, none of which fit me because of my thin frame. My mother had a nickname for me: *mah-low doy* (馬騮仔)—little monkey. My father punched extra holes in my belt with an awl from his basement tool box. I stuffed wads of notebook paper in my back pockets to round out my concave butt.

I wore hand-me-downs from my older brother. My younger brother Harvey, in turn, received my old clothes if they had survived the wear-and-tear of my rough play. If I had the good fortune to get a new pair of pants, they were several sizes too big. My parents didn't want to spend money on clothing I might outgrow in less than a year. I rolled up the cuffs at the bottom, using small safety pins to keep the hem cinched.

In kindergarten and first grade, I didn't wear underwear. At home, we wore pajamas. We were comfortable enough without an extra layer underneath. But when I sat down in the hard-back wooden school chair with the flip-up desk, the zipper from my pants chafed against my crotch. I wanted to go home and slip back into my soft PJ's for the rest of the day.

By the time P.E. emerged as a regular course, my brothers and I were properly outfitted with cotton briefs. It was a relief to move around with a soft layer of protection. I felt like I fit in with my classmates.

Every other Saturday, my mother cut our hair in the basement with a pair of black electric clippers. Lining up for our turns, my brothers and I sat on a small metal folding chair with a Mickey Mouse image on the back. To keep the clippings from scattering all over our bodies, she first wrapped an old linen sheet tightly around our necks, securing it with a clothespin. After she finished, she used a vacuum cleaner hose on us before we went upstairs to wash up, dunking our heads under the water faucet at one of the small washstands in the bathroom.

We each received the same haircut—a typical Chinese bowl cut. But by the mid-1960s, boys were letting their hair grow long and applying hair products like Brylcreem and Vitalis to add luster. They sported Beatles mop tops and wore skinny drainpipe pants. I wanted to be like them. But my mother felt it was wasteful to spend money on a barber.

I was ashamed to be in school for the first few days after a haircut. I pleaded with my mother: "Don't cut it so short!" She ignored my complaint. If she tried to style it, the cut looked even worse. I was better off with the dreadful rice bowl cut.

My father began taking me and my brothers to several Filipino barber shops in Chinatown. One was the Liberty Barber Shop. It was directly across the street from the Hong Kong Restaurant in the Eastern Hotel. It was run by Florencio Della. Customers sat and flipped through the latest stack of *Life, Look, Hot Rod* and *Playboy* magazines while they waited. The Chinatown barbers—old, gruff men from the old country—weren't much better than my mother. They were adept at military-style crew cuts and flat tops.

We took weekly baths. There was a showerhead over the bathtub, but we never turned it on. On days when we didn't bathe, we washed our faces, underarms, hands and feet in the wash basin with soap and water. We washed one foot at a time. I stood on a wooden stool, tightly gripping the edges of the sink with one hand while I lathered up with the other. We couldn't go to bed with dirty feet.

Although I struggled in school, it didn't become apparent that I was having any problems until the arrival of progress reports. I didn't tell my parents what I was studying, and they never asked. The report card at the end of spring quarter was the only thing they were interested in. *Did I get A's, B's, C's, D's or F's? Did I pass or did I fail?*

In third grade, my grades were awful. My low reading skills and my silence in class were noted in my report cards. My mother heartily scolded me. She compared me to my siblings, who were earning excellent grades. "What's wrong with you? You need to try harder! You need to study more. You must be lazy. Are you stupid?"

When I didn't respond, she flew into a rage, taking off one of her brown Chinese house slippers—she called them *thlat hai*—and whacked me in the ear. Then she hit me several times on the butt with the bamboo end of a chicken feather duster, the *gai mo thlow* (雞毛掃). I cried. Yanking me by the ear, she pulled me outside, drew a chalk circle on the red patio outside our kitchen and ordered me to stand inside the circle. She returned to the house, and she locked the door. I stood outside for about 10 minutes, whimpering and crying, feeling sorry for myself, and hoping the Japanese American neighbors across the street wouldn't see me. I felt like an awful failure.

My mother was the disciplinarian. If I talked back to her or got into a fight with Harvey, she pulled the *gai mo thlow* from a closet in the living room and came after me. I tried to run away, but she was usually too quick for me. I lived in fear of the almighty feather duster. I discovered a safe haven—the crevice under an old bed in the middle bedroom. Once, I squeezed under the bed when my mother began reaching for the *gai mo thlow*. She couldn't get to me. I wouldn't come out. She threw up her hands. She began to laugh hysterically. Her anger dissipated. She said I was getting too clever for her.

On Sunday evening, February 9, 1964, the Beatles appeared for the first time on *The Ed Sullivan Show*. As our black-and-white TV warmed up, Linda clicked the knob to Channel 7, cranked up the volume and adjusted the rabbit ears. Tom, Linda and I perched forward on the sofa. Ed Sullivan begged the screaming young fans to settle down and be courteous as he introduced another opening act. Linda began to bounce and make dance moves with her arms. When the "Fab Four"— Paul McCartney, John Lennon, George Harrison and Ringo Star—performed "All My Loving," the young female audience exploded into fits of shrieking, clapping and gyrating. Linda reacted the same way. My mother came out of the kitchen to see what was going on. I divided my attention between the Beatles on the screen and my sister's uncharacteristic frenzy.

That year, I began to develop more self-assurance. I didn't dread school anymore. I made a few friends. I occasionally spoke out in class. The breakthrough took place in sixth grade, my final year at Beacon Hill. My teacher was Miss Muraka-mi. She was young and pretty. She had a beehive hairdo and a sweet personality. Miss Murakami had the patience to spend extra time with me and explain to me the little things that my racing mind couldn't follow during her lectures. I felt lucky that she was my Spanish language instructor. She seemed to know instinctively that I wasn't failing for lack of trying. I crept out of my shell.

For the first time, I enjoyed P.E. and running around out-side on the school grounds. Occasionally, P.E. was held in a small, free-standing building outside the school. There, we practiced square dancing, moving to the taped instructions of a twangy male caller telling everyone to "do-si-do with your partner." I dreaded these sessions. I was clumsy and out of step. I preferred playing soak 'em, a game of dodgeball using a large, soft ball. There, I was skinny and fast and was usually among the last players still "alive" at the end.

I began to enjoy class writing assignments. For one paper, titled "School and Homework," I playfully wrote, "My opinion of school is that teachers give too much schoolwork and not enough recess period. I'd say about ¾ of school should be re-cess. There should only be homework once every two months at the most…At recess I would give absolutely no square danc-ing. Every day would be choice day."

I wrote a short story titled, "The Cannibals," a first-per-son narrative about a terrifying camping adventure. I was cap-tured by several strange-looking men who chased me down with knives and swords, tied me to a tree with rope and took me to an open fire, intending to make me their "next supper." The story ended: "I began to feel the pain of the knife in my whole body. Then I suddenly woke up and found myself under my bed. I realized that this was all a dream, and I hadn't gone camping yet. But I decided not to go camping after all."

That year's class had the opportunity to take an overnight camping field trip to Camp Casey, an old army fort site on Whidbey Island. Students were excited. Nearly all of them went. My mother refused to sign the permission slip for me. She thought it would be dangerous and unsanitary for me to sleep outdoors where I might be attacked by wild animals and exposed to strange diseases. I was very disappointed. I was embarrassed to be left behind.

In sixth grade, I volunteered to raise the flag on the school grounds on Saturdays. I thought it would be fun to do. But I had to ask my mother for permission. I knew she would say no. *How would I even explain the point of this ceremony to her?* I decided not to tell her. On Saturday mornings, I sneaked out of the house when she wasn't there or if she was preoccupied during one of her many long-winded conversations on the phone. I slipped out through the basement garage and ran as fast as I could to the entrance of the school. Hoisting the flag, I then tied the rope securely to a tall metal pole, then dashed back home. My mother never found out I did this.

Miss Murakami was my favorite teacher at Beacon Hill. Melancholy crept over me as spring approached. For the first time, I didn't want school to end.

She gave me A's and B's for my last quarter in all my classes: Spanish, spelling, handwriting, arithmetic, social studies, science, art and music. My self-esteem skyrocketed. I was happy that I wouldn't have to deal with the wrath of my mother when I brought my report card home.

Miss Murakami signed my yearbook, "Study hard. *Felicidades y parta bien, Señorita Murakami.*" I stared at the note all summer.

CHAPTER 8

The Search for a Jock Strap

I ATTENDED THE SEVENTH, EIGHTH and ninth grades at Asa Mercer Junior High School. It's now called Mercer International Middle School. The school was much further from my home than Beacon Hill Elementary. It was a brisk 35-minute walk from my house, past the Jefferson Park Golf Course and the Veterans Administration Hospital.

In the morning, my father drove my siblings and me, along with several other neighborhood kids, to school in his old, green Chevy. On cold days, the engine took at least 10 minutes to warm up. The underpowered vehicle chugged slowly up the hill, huge plumes of white smoke billowing from the tailpipe. The other kids included Sherrie and Alan Chinn from next door and Karen from another house further up the block. One or two kids squeezed into the front seat and four or five kids jammed into the back. There were no seatbelts. The car had a defroster, but it was useless. There was a small rag to wipe the foggy windshield so my father could see where he was going. We took turns wiping away the thick condensation.

Although I was still a gangly, introverted kid, I had finally adjusted to the routine of public school and could focus well enough to pass most of my classes with decent grades. I didn't participate in any after-school activities. I started working at the Hong Kong Restaurant as a busboy when I was 13.

At Mercer, I took the usual mix of junior high courses: arithmetic, algebra, English, music, geography, metal shop, wood shop, U.S. history, Washington state history, science, typing, junior choir, art, music and P.E. Nearly all the instructors and administrators at Mercer were white. In fact, I don't recall taking a single class from anyone who wasn't white.

My music teacher was Mr. Smith, an intense young man with an explosive temper. He introduced me to musical symbols and simple piano melodies. But without a piano at home, I didn't retain much. I hated junior choir because my voice was stuck in the ungainly transition from soprano to crackling baritone. I didn't want to take part in the singing exercises. Most other boys felt the same way. On several occasions, Mr. Smith got so frustrated at the lack of class participation that he thundered at the top of his lungs and angrily pounded his fist on the top of the piano. He was visibly shaking. He fought to recompose himself. I was surprised that the piano—or his hand—didn't crack.

My music class went on a field trip to see a "school concert" performed by the Seattle Symphony at the Opera House. The Symphony was led by Milton Katims. I clearly remember all the students clapping at the wrong moment—during the end of a movement—believing that the concert had concluded. Katims, furious, stopped everything, pivoted on the rostrum and sternly lectured us about the need to wait until his arms were at his side before applauding. He scared and embarrassed us. We felt very stupid. I vowed never to return on my own.

I chose Spanish for my foreign language class because other students said it was easier to learn than French, German or Russian, the other options. I had several different instructors, none of whom appeared to be native speakers. I don't recall having any Latino classmates. Our learning aid was *Hoy Día*, a monthly Spanish language news publication issued by Scholastic Magazine. Each student got a Spanish name. Mine was Reynaldo. At Mercer, my younger brother, Harvey, who took French, became "Henri." From Harvey, I learned a few French phrases, like *Je m'appelle Henri* and *J'ai mal à la têt*.

I was puzzled why Chinese and Japanese language classes weren't offered. I didn't see the value of learning French, German or Russian unless a person planned to move overseas. *What was the point of learning something you wouldn't use?*

My comfort with school increased after I developed two very close pals there, Michael and Edmund. Michael was a jovial but serious black kid from the neighborhood, mature for his age. He had an easy laugh which usually came out as a series of chuckles. Edmund was a slender, low-key Native American from the Blackfeet Nation who also lived on Beacon Hill. He had brown skin and long, straight, dark brown hair which flopped over his eyes. He was quiet, sensitive and introspective. I thought it was a curious coincidence that his last name was Brown when everything about him looked brown, too.

Every day after school, Michael, Edmund and I walked home together, stopping at the Beacon Avenue Junction to buy candy at Owen's Pharmacy. I leafed through the comic books; Michael pored over the body-building magazines. In the two years that the three of us hung out together, we rarely spent time inside one another's homes. Still, we were very close, playing baseball and football in the streets. I knew that Michael's father had left—I wasn't sure what the circumstances were.

Michael became the prominent male figure in his home, keeping his younger siblings—James, Kerry and Brad—in check. They all became part of the gang that played in our front yard.

One day after school, as Edmund and I met up on Rainier Avenue South, he told me that his family had decided to move back to the reservation in Montana. This was the middle of the school year. "Give me your address and phone number," he said. "I want to stay in touch." I didn't believe he was going. "No way," I said. "You're lying. How can you leave just like that?" Edmund said, "Hey, it's true. I didn't even know myself." We walked in silence. As I turned on College Street to go to my house, he pleaded with me again, "Give me your information. I'm going away." I didn't know what to say. He was one of my few friends and I couldn't accept that he was leaving. I never heard from him or saw him again.

I blossomed in my final year at Mercer. I was still terribly shy, but at least I didn't freeze when my name was called in class. I contributed two pieces to a creative writing magazine in my eighth-grade class. The magazine editor was Marilyn Tokuda, a popular, outgoing classmate I would come to know much better in high school and college. I was flattered when Marilyn told me she loved my writing. One piece was a humorous satire titled "Will Somebody Hold My Peanut Butter Sandwich," and the other was a scary tale about a haunted attic that led into a peaceful garden.

The scary story I had polished over and over at home, using a pocket thesaurus (*Soule's Dictionary of English Synonyms*) to create an H.G. Wells-style first-person narrative. I had purchased Wells's classic sci-fi thrillers *The Time Machine* and *War of the Worlds* through Scholastic Books. I knew his Victorian prose style and voice well.

I excelled in P.E. I usually got an A or a B. I was rail-thin and could do an endless number of push-ups, chin-ups and bent-knee sit-ups. When we did leg lifts lying on a mat on our backs, I was usually able to hold my legs up longer than anyone else. Many of the extremely skinny Asian kids like me were good in rope climbing competitions. We pulled ourselves up, hand over hand, to the top of thick ropes suspended from the gym rafters, then descended to the gym floor. I hated the rope burns I got on the way down.

During the first week of school, the gym teacher—a fit-looking white man in a flat top hairstyle, white t-shirt, gray sweatpants and white sneakers—introduced himself. He held a clipboard and draped a whistle around his neck. He barked out a set of rules. We were assigned to odd- and even-numbered "squads." We were required to dress in a clean white t-shirt, white gym shorts, sweat socks, white or black tennis shoes, and a jockstrap. This was our P.E. uniform. Every Monday, we were inspected. We were penalized for wearing dirty shorts.

"Let me show you what a jockstrap is, young *men*," he said, emphasizing the word "men." He held a sample jockstrap high above his head. He splayed open the cup with his fist, then yanked on the elastic strap that was supposed to wrap tightly around our butt. "Get one," he bellowed. "Wear it at all times during my gym class. It will protect you." During strenuous physical activity, he warned, one or both of our "balls" could pop right out of their "nutsack." This could result in irreparable harm to our "family jewels." We might not be able to have kids. His warning quieted the gymnasium. A few kids snickered.

I told my parents what I needed. I already had a few white undershirts. I could buy white shorts at Chubby & Tubby. *But where could I find a jockstrap? How could I explain to my mother what it was?* My father helped interpret. Tom had come to my father with the same request. My mother frowned. She wondered what kind of brutal contact sport we were engaged in. My parents went to the usual shopping places—Sears, JCPenney and Woolworth's. No luck with jockstraps.

I joined them on the hunt at Woolworth's. The store was at the corner of Third Avenue and Pike Street. It had a long luncheonette counter which served blue plate specials like hamburgers, meatloaf and liver and onions. The candy center sold ropes of licorice and single lollipops strung together in long clear plastic-wrapped strands. We occasionally bought a batch of fried chicken wings to take home in a white paper bag.

After we struck out at Woolworth's, we walked to The Bon Marché just one block away. The Bon—as it was called for short—was a big department store a full pedigree above JCPenney and Sears. A sales lady told us that The Bon did, indeed, stock jockstraps. They were on the third floor in the boys' wear department. My mother refused to take the escalator. She believed that it might pull her beneath the floor and crush her. I snickered. I thought it was strange that she feared the escalator more than she did the wickedly dangerous industrial sewing machines at work. My father and mother walked over to the elevators. I took the escalator.

As I prepared to step onto the third floor, the back of one sneaker got caught in the teeth of the escalator. It was a scary moment. I yanked free, but not before the escalator ripped a chunk of rubber from my shoe. I felt guilty for pooh-poohing my mother's fear. I regained my composure by the time she and my father met me. I didn't say a word.

The sales lady led us over to a table of athletic supporters. They came in three sizes: small, medium and large. After visiting the fitting room and finding that none of the sizes really fit me, we decided on the small one. It was the cheapest. We got one for Tom and one for me.

I hated the binding waistband and the scratchy, bumpy, synthetic cup. After P.E., I was relieved to change back into my cotton briefs. On my way home, I began walking instead of running. The gym teacher's health advisory scared me. I didn't want to risk dislodging one of my testicles. On hot summer days, I wondered if I was in peril because my "nutsack" was sagging lower than usual. I wondered about the cold winter days when it seemed to shrivel closer to my body. *What was happening to my testicles?* I had no one to ask.

Another lasting memory from Mercer was Alfred Hitchcock's movie *The Birds*. It was shown in segments over the course of a week or two during lunchtime in the darkened school auditorium. The 1963 psychological thriller rose to an unbearable climax with the massing of thousands of aggressive birds readying to attack a family in a quiet seaside community. It was the first horror movie I had ever seen. It was the talk of the school. I didn't want to open my bedroom closet at night. I was afraid that a flock of crows was inside ready to attack.

At Mercer and later at Franklin High, I rushed home to catch two late afternoon TV programs. The first was *Dark Shadows*, a soap opera that featured ghosts, werewolves and zombies journeying through time. The second was a musical program called *Where the Action Is*. It starred a versatile singer named Steve Alaimo, who served as host, and a rock band called Paul Revere and the Raiders. I thought Alaimo had a nice voice. I was puzzled why I didn't hear him on the radio.

Every Saturday, I watched *Big Time Wrestling* on Channels 7 and 11. The matches were hosted by announcer Ron Forsell. Sandy Barr was the referee. He had floppy hair, long sideburns and a striped shirt. I thought these studio bouts, staged at the Portland Sports Arena or the Masonic Temple, were real. I rooted for the good guys, but they lost because of stupid refereeing or predictable cheating by the bad guys. My brother Tom, who attended one of the matches at the Masonic Temple, returned home to report that the matches were "for sure" fake. He said that the contestants didn't actually hit one another.

During my last year at Mercer, I was crestfallen to find that all my close friends were assigned to go to Cleveland High School instead of Franklin, where I was headed. Over the summer, I moped. I probably wouldn't see many of my friends again. I didn't know where they lived. I didn't visit their homes and they didn't visit mine. I would have to start all over.

CHAPTER 9

Turbulent Years at Franklin High

I ARRIVED AT FRANKLIN HIGH School as a freshman in 1968, during the height of the civil rights movement. The school was a serene beaux arts structure with classical columns, white terracotta, red bricks and arched windows. It was perched on a hillside overlooking Rainier Valley, about a 20-minute downhill walk from my home. From afar, it looked like a place of retreat. But inside, a storm had broken.

In the spring of 1968, protests against segregated facilities and unfair treatment of blacks in the South spread north, reaching into my high school. On March 28, two black students were suspended after a fight with a white student. The white student escaped punishment. Two black females were disciplined for wearing "natural" hairstyles. These incidents triggered a march on the principal's office, a sit-in, arrests and demands for immediate reforms at Franklin High and at the University of Washington. Protesters pressed for an end to discriminatory disciplinary practices, the teaching of black history classes and inclusion of diverse authors in the library collection.

Three organizers of the Franklin sit-in—UW activists Aaron Dixon, Carl Miller and Larry Gossett—were convicted on July 1, 1968, and sent to King County jail, sparking violent uprisings.

National civil rights leader Rev. Martin Luther King, Jr., was assassinated in Memphis, further escalating tensions. On April 7, three days after his murder, thousands marched from the Central District to Memorial Stadium at Seattle Center to honor his legacy. I saw on TV and read in *The Seattle Times* and the *Seattle Post-Intelligencer* that the newly formed Seattle chapter of the Black Panther Party was calling for armed struggle. Those words scared me. I didn't understand what that meant for me as a Chinese person or where this was headed. I watched with trepidation and curiosity.

That summer, hardly anyone came out to dine at the Hong Kong Restaurant. On the weekends, usually the busiest times, the waiters and busboys like me sat around in the front area booths, idly waiting for customers. A brittle stillness gripped Chinatown. On some days, the manager Uncle Alvin or the owner Sam Yee sent the busboys home several hours early.

Frank Hanawalt, a widely respected school administrator, was dispatched to Franklin to bring calm. He replaced principal Loren Ralph, a conservative old-school leader who alienated parents and teachers with his response to the sit-in. Ralph told faculty members that they shouldn't expect black students to excel in science. His racist beliefs extended to Asians. At one faculty meeting, he said, "There's a lot of paperwork for all of you in the coming weeks. Find a nice Oriental girl to help you."

By outward appearances, Hanawalt looked a lot like every other white male administrator I had known: conservatively dressed, serious and stiff, with a furrowed, bushy brow and receding hairline. When he spoke at assembly, the tone of his words was surprisingly liberal and compassionate. But when I crossed paths with him in the hallway, he always looked grim. I didn't dare say a word to him.

Mr. Hanawalt addressed a message to students on the front page of the "Back to School" edition of the *Franklin Tolo,* the semi-weekly school newspaper. He noted that there were many new staff changes and that his goal was to "open up as many effective channels of communication as possible." He vowed to involve the community, parents and students "in the planning and development of the school program."

Roberta Byrd Barr, an African American, was appointed vice principal. I had seen her on television serving as moderator for a local public affairs program on KING 5 TV called *Face to Face*, on which topics like desegregation and civil rights were explored at length. She had a quiet charisma and spoke with passion and grace in a calm, melodic voice.

Despite these changes, police still patrolled the school grounds. Inside, the school seemed on perpetual lockdown. Teachers and security guards were stationed in the hallways to make sure that no one was loitering or carrying weapons. Students were not permitted to roam without a signed hall pass.

I felt on edge walking to my cream-colored locker in the dark school hallway. I didn't want to get jumped and beaten up by older students while my guard was down. This disquiet had little to do with the upheaval. I was in a new school, surrounded by gushing male hormones.

Bruce Solibakke, a popular white social studies teacher, was hit over the head with a stool in the lunchroom by a former student. He received 16 stitches and was back in class the next day. This incident shook the school. Some teachers tried to conduct their classes as if the classrooms were sheltered from the mounting tumult, but it was a transparent charade. During lessons, they were distracted. Their fear rubbed off on students.

My sophomore year was daunting. I wasn't motivated. I felt scattered. I didn't have buddies I could turn to when I didn't understand what the teachers were talking about. I kept to the back of the classroom, sitting mutely, daydreaming, waiting for the rescuing clang of the bell. I yearned for Friday to arrive.

In my English class, students were asked to research a topic, write an essay and read it aloud. I had never done anything like this before. I procrastinated. I got headaches. I was terrified.

Finally, I decided to write about the passenger pigeon. I copied my essay nearly word for word from an entry in the World Book Encyclopedia. When it was my turn, I stood nervously at the front of the room, mechanically reading my paper, never once making eye contact with the class. At one point, I heard several students giggle. I didn't look up. I marched back to my seat as soon as I was done. After I sat down, my teacher gently explained to me that I had said "passenger penguin" instead of "passenger pigeon" throughout my talk. My cheeks and ears flushed. There were more peals of laughter. I grinned sheepishly, then slumped down in my chair. I wished I could magically vanish.

A very popular instructor was Mr. Rick Nagel, a wavy-haired young social studies teacher who taught contemporary problems, and law and society. His class was in the basement, in Room 15. He carried a row of pens in the pocket of his white shirt. He clutched a piece of chalk in his hand, pivoting effortlessly between scrawling on the blackboard and talking to his class. He kept his students listening with rapt attention because he offered up case studies about slavery, civil rights and minority history.

Mr. Nagel openly criticized President Nixon's decision to order secret bombing missions in Cambodia and Laos, expanding the Vietnam War. Nixon had been elected to office in 1968 because of his pledge to end the unpopular war. But American troops continued to fight and die overseas. When the first draft lotteries took place in 1969, assigning conscription numbers to young men turning 18, the prospect of being forced to fight overseas became real. In a couple years, it would be my turn.

On October 15, 1969, the Moratorium to End the War in Vietnam, a massive teach-in demonstration, took place across the country. Franklin High offered discussions of the Vietnam War in the auditorium. Students were free to skip their regular social studies classes. A propaganda film, produced by the Defense Department, was juxtaposed against presentations by those opposing the war.

During basketball and football games and at school assemblies, most students stayed seated during the reciting of the Pledge of Allegiance to show support for the civil rights movement and to protest the war. Under the Ralph administration, students who had done this were suspended. But Hanawalt changed that policy. Like most of my friends, I chose to remain seated.

In class, Mr. Nagel handed out a sheet with information about a 1943 U.S. Supreme Court decision affirming the right of Jehovah's Witnesses to refuse to salute the American flag and recite the Pledge of Allegiance. I later learned that Mr. Nagel had put the same sheet in the mailboxes of the other teachers.

In Mr. Nagel's class, minority students, especially African Americans, spoke unguardedly about their personal encounters with racism. I felt emboldened to write an essay about the awkwardness I felt as a Chinese American navigating between two cultures. Over two decades later, I had lunch with Mr. Nagel in Chinatown. He returned the original paper to me.

Another influential instructor was Mr. Robert Maestas,

my Spanish teacher. We addressed him as "Señor Maestas." At first, I regarded him as just another foreign language instructor whose assignments I had to endure as the price of graduation.

But after protests by black students, his classroom persona transformed. He took time out from his usual rapid-fire Spanish drills to discuss the plight of Mexican American farm workers. He talked movingly about his own experiences as a Chicano. He apologized profusely for shortchanging us on the drills, but he said he believed that what was happening in the community was more important than the teaching of Spanish.

Prior to this, I didn't think Mr. Maestas was much different from the young white woman who was my Spanish teacher in an earlier grade. I had assumed, as did many other students, that he was from Spain. His skin coloring was light. He wore a suit and tie and highly polished black shoes, and he smelled of cologne. But now I saw him in a totally different light—as an American, just like me. I didn't know what to make of it.

When I met one-on-one with Mr. Maestas to discuss my grade for the term, I hoped I might get lucky and squeak by with a C. My coursework had been mediocre. I hadn't contributed during the crucial classroom conversations and drills. He began by asking me about my background as a Chinese American. I didn't volunteer much beyond saying that my parents were immigrants and that I worked in a Chinatown restaurant.

He nodded, then asked, "Ronald, what grade do you expect to get from this class?" I paused, lowering my gaze. "Maybe a C."

He grinned, then said, "How about if I give you a B. Are you okay with that?"

I took a deep breath. I didn't say a word. I tried not to smile. He waited patiently. Gathering myself, I finally blurted, "Sure, a B is okay with me."

He interjected, "If you don't think it's fair, I'm happy to raise that. To tell you the truth, I'm not sure I believe in the grading system anyway." I didn't want to get greedy. I reiterated that a B was fine. When I got my report card, I was startled to find that he had given me an A.

It didn't surprise me that several years after I had taken his Spanish class, Mr. Robert Maestas reappeared in the news as Roberto Maestas, the leader of a group of Chicanos who had taken over the abandoned Beacon Hill Elementary School, my old grade school. The group demanded that the city turn the property over to the community to develop as a service center for the growing Latino population. By this time, Mr. Maestas dispensed with his Establishment suit and tie. He allowed his thick, wavy hair to grow out. He sported a full beard. He had a colorful bandana around his head. He dressed in a black leather jacket, flannel work shirt, flared jeans and dark shades.

The one teacher with the biggest impact on me was Mrs. Alice Allen, a young, chic African American language arts instructor with a huge Afro that covered most of her forehead and the tops of her ears. I took her creative writing course as a senior. She had an upbeat teaching style. One assignment was to write a poem that included all the senses: touch, sound, sight, smell and taste. I titled my poem, "Wind." I described the wind moving through the trees, "rushing up my nostrils," producing a "sweet, flowing earthy" smell, tasting "mildly refreshing, yet somewhat hollow and transient." The prose was overwrought, yet Mrs. Allen, recognizing my effort and sincerity, wrote on my paper, "You have a nice flair for writing."

I also wrote a short prose piece about sitting in the grass against a tree as evening approached, surrounded by a breeze, birds and insects, watching "only the morose form of a moon pinned against a canvas of pure ebony." She gave me an A, writing at the top of the page, "Beautiful, Ron. You have a definite feeling for nature in all its forms. Are you city-bred?" My self-confidence grew. I composed short stories and poems over the summer.

Privately, I yearned for an imaginary kind of peace that eluded me. The social unrest, conflicts at home and adolescent blues were too much. I sank into brief waves of depression. I suffered excruciating migraine headaches. It sometimes took every particle of willpower to lift myself out of bed to go to school. Writing helped me regain my bearings.

During the height of racial tensions, Michael, the kid I had befriended at Mercer, called my house after school to make sure that my sister Linda got home safely. If I picked up the phone, we talked briefly. If my mother answered the phone, he simply hung up. If my parents suspected that a black kid was calling Linda, she would have been punished. My sister didn't want to trigger the wrath of my mother.

Linda and I felt miserable that we couldn't be truthful to our folks about the people and things that mattered in our lives. The gulf between our generations was far too wide to bridge. We kept our sadness and suffering to ourselves. We never invited friends to the house if our parents were there. When I was home, I retreated to the bedroom, shutting the door firmly behind me. This angered my mother. She didn't believe children had a right to blockade themselves from their parents in the same house.

In my final two years at Franklin, a wave of Chinese immigrant kids from Hong Kong arrived. They struggled. They couldn't speak English, and many came from homes with family conflict. There were no bilingual Chinese counselors or instructors. I saw brawls and knife-fights break out between the Chinese and the black kids in the hallways. I felt bad for the new arrivals. My peers—the ABCs (American-born Chinese)—shunned them, derisively referring to them as "FOBs" (Fresh Off the Boat) or "TCs" (Typical Chinese).

I felt caught in the middle. I worked alongside some of these foreign-born Chinese students at the restaurant. My mother worked in the sewing factory with their mothers. Still, I didn't have the same feeling of closeness with these kids as I did with my ABC friends from the neighborhood.

Among immigrants, I felt like an outsider because I was born here and spoke English much better than I spoke Chinese. But among ABCs, I felt trapped inside the culture of Chinatown and the restaurant life I was trying to escape. I wasn't quite an ABC and I wasn't quite an FOB.

At the end of one school assembly, a group of four or five of the girls from Hong Kong walked over to me. Their gaudy, outdated dresses marked them as FOBs. They tried to strike up a friendly conversation. "Are you planning to go to college?" one of them asked with a heavy accent. She smiled. I recognized her from one of my classes, but I didn't know her name. I stuttered and stumbled over my words as I explained that I was considering the University of Washington. "But I don't know yet," I said. "I haven't decided."

The girl who addressed me was quite pretty. The others were, too. They waited for me to say more, but I couldn't. I was terribly self-conscious. My heart began to race. My stomach churned. My hands turned clammy. My voice disappeared down my throat. I was rescued by the bell signaling that it was time to return to class.

I made two new buddies—Manuel Alinas and Keith Wong. Manuel was a dreamy Filipino American boy who constantly fussed with his hair and dressed in stylish shirts with wide-open collars. He had a crush on a popular Chinese American girl he never had the courage to approach. Keith, a classmate of my brother Tom, was a nutty, loquacious Chinese American kid who lived several blocks from me on Beacon Hill. Keith was thin and frail. He wore thick black-framed glasses and chukka boots with crepe rubber soles. Manuel and Keith were mediocre students. They were nonathletic like me. None of us had girlfriends. We went to Dag's, just across the street from Franklin on Rainier Avenue South, to eat Beefy Boy burgers and fries, talk nonsense and stroll home together.

Manuel and I were in the same journalism class, taught by Mrs. Barbara Nilson, advisor to the *Franklin Tolo*. Mrs. Nilson's class was dominated by rowdy seniors who tried to talk over her, ignoring everything she said. I felt bad for her because she wasn't a bad instructor. But her voice was high-pitched, squeaky and difficult to hear. I wrote one small, insignificant article for the *Tolo*. I envied Gary Iwamoto, Brian Aburano and several other excellent student reporters. They were frequent contributors. Gary was editorial page editor. The newspaper won many journalism awards.

Manuel asked me what I planned to do over the summer. When I told him I worked as a busboy at a restaurant in Chinatown, he countered, "You should come with me to Alaska instead. I'm going to make a bundle of money working in the cannery. You have to work pretty hard, but they pay you a lot."

Manuel told me he could make arrangements for me. Other classmates heading to Alaska had connections through their fathers. I thought about Manuel's offer, but I said no. I wasn't ready to leave Beacon Hill and I wasn't sure my parents would consent to my leaving. I never saw Manuel again.

Keith was my dearest friend. He made me laugh because he just couldn't stop gabbing. He knew he was a dufus, but he embraced who he was. He would ask, "Don't you think I'm silly?"

Without waiting for a response, he would flap his hands in a rapid up-and-down motion. He spent hours obsessively dissecting the box scores of all the baseball and basketball teams in *The Seattle Times* and the *Seattle P-I*. He followed obscure players who rarely made it into the lineup.

Keith and I talked a lot about music. He memorized the rank order of all the top pop singles on the music charts. I did the same thing.

My father bought a mustard-colored plastic turntable at the downtown G.O. Guy drugstore for our home. We had inherited vinyl records from the 1950s and early 60s by Frank Sinatra, Kay Starr, Guy Lombardo, Nat "King" Cole, Jane Froman, Teresa Brewer and Vic Damone. They came from an abandoned jukebox in the basement of the Hong Kong Restaurant. Keith and I bought our own 45s and LPs from Pay 'n Save. My selections included Sam Cooke, the Young Rascals, Bob Dylan, Stevie Wonder, the O'Kaysions, the Box Tops, Eric Burdon & the Animals, and Barbara Acklin.

At home, I played make-believe DJ, mixing old songs with current pop hits, suggesting that listener requests were pushing certain records up the charts. My sister helped me organize the 45s with cardboard divider cards.

Linda's favorite songs included Nancy Sinatra's easy listening tune "Sugar Town," Glenn Yarbrough's 1965 hit "Baby, the Rain Must Fall" and the gospel-influenced love ballads of Jerry Butler, a Chicago soul singer. We had several pricier LPs of Sonny and Cher, the Supremes, the Beatles and Otis Redding.

During my senior year, Keith moved on to Seattle Central Community College. I waited near the college for him to finish his last class, a sociology course taught by Peter Koshi. We then caught the bus downtown and got off near Third and Pike. We walked past the box office of the seedy Embassy

Theater and watched men in dark overcoats slink in to watch the latest triple-feature porn flicks. We ate dinner at Kentucky Fried Chicken, exchanging *The Seattle Times* and the *Seattle P-I* sports sections while we ate. Before returning home, we scoured the latest records and tapes at the Warehouse of Music at 421 Pike Street. On weekends, we attended early matinee screenings of old movies at the Colonial Theater on Fourth Avenue. Admission to double features of Clint Eastwood spaghetti westerns and Marilyn Monroe classics cost 50 cents.

When *Enter the Dragon*, the last film Bruce Lee completed before his death, premiered in 1973, Keith and I saw it together at the Coliseum. It was a big downtown theater with a distinctive terracotta facade, an ornate interior and a wide screen. We waited to get our tickets in the midst of a throng of young Asian Americans, blacks and whites. The entire audience erupted in applause as soon as the movie began. We were mesmerized by Bruce's charismatic intensity and fighting grace. For once, we had a Chinese movie character that *everyone*—Chinese and non-Chinese alike—cheered. I returned to see this movie several more times with other friends. Each time, the theater was packed.

Through Keith, I met Steve Goon, a happy-go-lucky kid with a big, sheepish grin. His family also lived on Beacon Hill. Steve was another classmate of my brother Tom. After Manuel moved away, Keith, Steve and I became a trio. On Tuesdays, we went to Skipper's Seafood 'n Chowder House on Broadway for all-you-can-eat. We got four pieces of battered, deep-fried cod in a basket and a cup of clam chowder. Keith stopped at seconds. I went on for thirds. Steve returned five or six times. Steve wasn't fat, but he was a champion eater. Steve became one of my closest friends at the University of Washington.

When the Hong Kong Restaurant needed more busboys,

Keith was hired. But he could barely hoist a full tray of dishes on his own into the kitchen. Several times, when his tray was fully loaded, dishes, glasses and teacups slid off the top, crashing to the floor as he struggled to maintain his balance. Whenever owner Sam Yee saw him carrying a huge tray on his own, his face turned pasty white. He was afraid that a costly accident was about to occur. It often did.

Nevertheless, Keith continued to work some weekends. He was pressed into service during busy days when we were short-handed.

Chapter 10

An Active Imagination

EVER SINCE I WAS LITTLE, I relished being alone. I could daydream for hours. I imagined myself as a superhero in a futuristic universe, using magical powers to battle villains and rescue civilization. I fantasized about becoming a music star, singing and playing the guitar onstage to mobs of adoring fans. Sometimes, I was a baseball star like my idol Mickey Mantle, overcoming debilitating injuries and helping win games by blasting mammoth home runs over the outfield fences. Or I was a famous painter creating unforgettable canvases filled with awe-inspiring mountains and trees and dreamy white clouds.

My secret life rivaled that of Walter Mitty.

My only ambition—if I had one—was to invent games, toys and fun activities.

When we were very young, Tom, Harvey and I slept in the same tiny bedroom. I made up stories to amuse my little brother. Two of us slept in bunk beds. After my mother turned out the lights, Harvey tiptoed over to my bed, crawled under my covers and listened to my corny jokes and riddles. I contorted my hands to create shadow puppets on the walls and lowered my voice to a creepy pitch to scare him with ghost stories. Harvey had a hard time containing his chuckling. His noises often roused my mother. If we heard her shuffling over to our room in her slippers, Harvey jumped back into his own bed, and we pretended to be asleep.

I spent many lazy afternoons on the back porch playing card games with Tom, Harvey and other neighborhood kids. We had decks of *Crazy Eights*, *Old Maid* and *Animal Rummy*. The games became monotonous, so I came up with different rules for matching and eliminating cards. I named these new games *Pocko*, *Tocko*, *Locko* and *Jocko*. We played until the porch light came on.

I also made up games using the tiny free toys that came in boxes of Tomoe Ame, a popular jelly candy wrapped in edible rice paper. Each box had four or five candies and a small toy surprise, usually a plastic or rubber car about 1 ½" long. I amassed about 15 of these tiny cars. Harvey and several other friends had their own collections, too. We named our individual cars. We took turns throwing eight of our best cars against a wall, trying to get them to land upright. Results were recorded on a sheet of paper.

I invented a tiny car game which I simply called "car stacking." We took turns stacking our cars one on top of another. Once your heap collapsed, you were out of the game. This game required a quick, light touch.

I made wrestling action figures out of small toy army men. Using a small pocket knife, I shaved off the rifle, bayonet and flat stands at the bottom. I wrapped strips of masking tape around the arms of the figures to create muscular physiques. I retreated to my bedroom to play with these action figures, inventing intricate storylines pitting scoundrels against heroes.

In the 1980s, over 20 years after I started converting my cheap toy soldiers into wrestling action figures, the World Wrestling Federation began marketing rubber wrestling action heroes to kids. I thought to myself, "Hey, they stole my idea!"

During the Christmas holiday, we pulled an aluminum tree out of storage and assembled it next to a rotating color wheel in a corner of the living room by a large picture window. We took care to avoid bending the metal branches or breaking off the silver tinsel. The tree would be reused year after year. I sat on the sofa and stared at the tree, hypnotized by the changing hues. The color wheel smelled like burning plastic. I imagined all the toys Santa might bring to our house. We played an album of Julie Andrews's favorite Christmas carols on the turntable.

I really wanted the Rock 'Em Sock 'Em Robots made by Mattel. I saw many commercials for it on TV. But I knew I wouldn't get it. It didn't matter whether we were naughty or nice. Santa wasn't coming. Every year, we each got a new shirt, pajamas or a red envelope with cash. That was all. My father and mother didn't give anything to each other. A plastic-wrapped fruit cake from Frederick & Nelson and a gift from a family friend always appeared under the tree along with several metal tins of cookies and candies.

I don't know why, but the Christmas of 1964 was different. Linda, Tom, Harvey and I each got something special. Our presents were tidily wrapped with curly ribbon bows on top, my father's signature touches. I got a Kenner's Battery-Operated Give-A-Show Projector. It came in a bright box with 15 strips of color slides, samples of favorite Hanna-Barbera TV cartoons: *The Flintstones, Huckleberry Hound, The Jetsons, Quick Draw McGraw, Magilla Gorilla, Touché Turtle, Hokey Wolf* and

Wally Gator. I was in heaven. Harvey and I ran into the bedroom with my toy, crawled into the closet, shut the pocket door and watched the cartoon strips projected onto the wall.

By high school, I had given up on Santa. I bought myself a View-Master, a toy stereoscope made of red plastic which looks like a pair of square binoculars. By inserting round cardboard discs and holding the viewer up to a light source, dramatic three-dimensional scenes appeared. It reminded me of the Give-A-Show Projector. I stared in awe at the images of the Seven Wonders of the Ancient World and dinosaurs. I hoarded my View-Master and precious slides in a wooden cigar box with a hinged lid which came from the Hong Kong Restaurant.

Many years later, after I had two boys of my own and they began collecting Yu-Gi-Oh! Cards, these warm, nostalgic moments of carefree play flooded back.

Growing up was different for my kids. They received so many toys and games from relatives that I regifted some and brought many others to Goodwill unused. I kept the ones they cherished in a white wicker trunk: Thomas the Tank Engine train cars, Dollar Tree baseball mitts, several Raymond Briggs stuffed snowmen, and Buzz Lightyear action figures.

I've told them about my modest childhood. I gave them my Give-A-Show Projector. It still works with fresh batteries. The little Tomoe Ame cars went to my younger son Kino, who was fond of model cars. When he was a toddler, I got down on my knees to play car games with him in the attic. We took turns hurling the tiny cars against the wall and tracking our scores on paper. He later amassed his own collection of die-cast model cars. He gave each a name. He stashed them all in a cardboard box under his bed, pulling them out at night to play with when he was supposed to be sleeping.

He reminds me a lot of how I was when I was his age.

CHAPTER 11

Think-A-Newspaper

EVERY SUNDAY MORNING, THE HUGE weekend edition of *The Seattle Times* arrived on our back porch, landing with an assertive thud. The pages were held together by a thick rubber band. My father was the only one who read it. I yanked out the color comics section so I could pore over my three favorites: *Superman*, *Nancy* and *Ripley's Believe It or Not*. I used a pink-colored wad of Silly Putty to pull reverse images off the pages, elongating faces like a funhouse mirror.

My exposure to *Scholastic NewsTime* in elementary and junior high school aroused my curiosity about newspapers. Looking over *The Seattle Times* comics section—and seeing my parents follow the tragic news about the assassination of John F. Kennedy in 1963—inspired me to create my own publication. I called it *Think-A-Newspaper*. I added the "A" to simulate the "ah" sound that Chinese append to the beginning of names.

Kennedy was a hero to Chinese Americans because of his advocacy for changes to restrictive immigration laws. These changes allowed Chinese mainland refugees in Hong Kong to come to the U.S. When Kennedy was assassinated in 1963, the Chinese American community in Seattle mourned. My mother wept for weeks. My father bought daily copies of *The Seattle Times* and the *Seattle P-I* to follow developments. Even though my mother couldn't read English, she grieved each time she saw front page photos, including the now-iconic images of his veiled widow Jacqueline and the funeral salute from JFK's young son John while his sister Caroline watched.

My mother never threw away those newspapers. She stacked them in a kitchen broom closet. From time to time, she would pull them out and gaze at the pictures. Tears would flow anew.

I produced editions of *Think-A-Newspaper* from age 11 to 14. My imagination surged as I made up stories and sketched fictional people and places. The newspaper included local and world news, jokes, comic strips, sports articles, scores and clip-out baseball cards. I had an audience of one: my little brother Harvey. He skipped straight to the jokes, comics and sports.

I worked quickly, completing one edition every couple of days. My newspaper office was a six-foot-long redwood picnic table in the basement. My mother bought the rough-hewn table and two matching benches for ten dollars from a man driving through the neighborhood in a big pick-up truck filled with patio furniture. I sat under a square, fluorescent light fixture, drafting the newspaper in pencil on sheets of wide-ruled notebook paper.

I created an advice column called "Ask Chubby." It was inspired by the "Dear Abby" column in *The Seattle Times.* Chubby was supposed to be a witty, irreverent teddy bear. I borrowed the name from the Chubby & Tubby store, where we shopped for housewares, clothing and tennis shoes.

One of the first editions of *Think-A-Newspaper*, dated June 10, 1964, featured a true story about a goldfish named Popsy.

My mother bought Popsy at S.H. Kress & Company, a five-and dime store at Third Avenue and Pike Street, directly across the street from Woolworth's. The beloved goldfish was the only pet we ever bought. We took Popsy home in a plastic bag filled with water. The headline screamed, "Popsy's DEATH!" The article read:

> *We did not know why he died, but we thought we gave him too much food. Tommy spotted him first. He layed motionless on the bottom of the bottle. Linda saw him but he was still breathing a little. When mother came home, we told her about Popsy's death then she threw him away.*

I drew a picture of the dead goldfish lying at the bottom of a jar, which had a metal lid punctured with air holes.

I made up several breaking stories about the assassination of Washington Governor Dan Evans. I also wrote imaginary tales about the death of the owner of Sears, Roebuck, the closure of Pike Place Market, the war in Vietnam, bizarre weather disasters, robberies and other local crimes. I was influenced by what I saw in *NewsTime* and headlines in *The Seattle Times* and the *Seattle P-I*.

The sports section in *Think-A-Newspaper* consisted of detailed baseball box scores of fantasy teams. The scores came directly from contests between Harvey and me as we squared off in the basement in mock baseball contests, playing with plastic bowling pins as improvised baseball bats and discarded toilet paper tubes instead of real baseballs. I meticulously recorded statistics, including at-bats, hits, home runs, doubles, triples, strike-outs and errors. We made up silly names for all the players; "Chubby" and "Tubby" were two we used often.

When we got too rowdy, our mother barked down to us from the upstairs kitchen landing, "What are you doing down there? Are you throwing a ball around? You're going to break a window. Stop!" I responded with a half-truth: "No, we're just playing. There's no ball here." When she came down to the basement to dust and wash the floor, she found crushed toilet paper rolls near the oil furnace and behind furniture and book-shelves. She must have known what we were doing.

In 1965, I also put out several editions of *Funny Toes News-paper*, a *Think-A-Newspaper* knock-off. Like its sister publica-tion, it was filled with jokes, puzzles, sports scores and crazy news briefs. It had an advice column called "Ask Dul." Dul was the first name of an imaginary character "Dul Wah Dat," derived from the phrase "Duh! What's that?"

This was a typical *Funny Toes* news article:

> *A boeing plan XBLX123 crashed into the empire sate building. One man came out alive and he was the pilot, his name max Mac. He said, "why did you guys put a tall building there for." He has a few stracthes.*

Another news story, titled "Fin's Cave Has Cave In," read:

> *Fin's cave had a cave in. It is located in western Seattle and this happened about 6:00 A.M. to-day. The are thirty men in there. So far proof is that ten remain alive. The cave in was caused by one of the supports came lose and the cave in start-ed. Men have been digging and digging. They say the will be freed in about 2 hours.*

Despite my early newspapering, I didn't give any thought to becoming a journalist. I was simply having fun, having found an outlet for my chronic restlessness. I enjoyed amusing my little brother. It was exhilarating to see a smile appear on his face each time one of my publications showed up on the picnic table in our basement.

CHAPTER 12

Chinatown

E VEN THOUGH I LIVED ON Beacon Hill, Chinatown felt like a second home. It was just a five-minute drive or a 10-minute bus ride away. It wasn't simply the place my parents worked. It was where we went to buy groceries, eat out, watch movies and theater performances, catch up with relatives and friends and go to church. It provided an emotional touchstone. I could relax and joke freely there, without regard to how the larger community might judge me.

My parents called Chinatown *Hong Ngin Fow* (唐人埠) or *Hong Ngin Gai* (唐人街). *Hong Ngin* (唐人) is what Chinese people called themselves; it means "people of the Tang Dynasty," a nod to China's golden past. *Fow* (埠) means port; *gai* (街) is street.

Chinatown was loud. It was alive. Shoppers scrambled in and out of stores, dumping armfuls of purchases into the back of cars left idling. People chatted gleefully, yelling at one another even though they stood only inches apart. Thin bachelor men smoked in doorways, hacking vigorously and spewing wads of phlegm on the sidewalk. Along both sides of the alleys, rusted black metal fire escapes zigzagged downward, the railings draped with wet clothes and kids peering from above. The streets smelled like a mixture of pungent fried Chinese food, gasoline and rotting garbage.

Some shop owners still used abacuses instead of cash registers. I watched their deft fingers slide quickly and lightly across the clacking beads. My mother wrangled over prices, trying to squeeze out the best deal. Transactions were handled in cash. My father and mother didn't have checkbooks or credit cards. Receipts were written with fountain pens dipped in inkwells.

I accompanied my mother into the Quong Wah poultry shop. It was owned by Chong Loo and Howard Low. Chickens squawked, and I cringed as I watched the shopkeeper grab an unlucky bird from a cage, chop off its head, drain the blood and pluck the feathers. The chicken was wrapped in butcher paper, old newspapers and string dispensed from an overhead spool. Chong Loo's daughter Maxine rang up purchases. Sometimes a chicken scrambled out the front door before its execution, and Maxine and her youngest brother Jerry chased down the bird before it was snatched up for dinner by waiters at Tai Tung Restaurant (大同飯店) next door.

There were no parking meters. Sometimes we were trapped inside a row of double-parked cars, waiting to pull out. We knew who was hemming us in because we recognized their vehicles. We bought more goods and visited a few more shops until we could leave.

We dined out as a family only several times a year, usually when hosting out-of-town guests. Eating out was a luxury. The tiny Chinese American community didn't yet have a moneyed professional class.

Our favorite restaurants were Linyen (蓮園), Eight Immortals (留仙酒家) and Little Three Grand (小三元酒家). My mother bypassed the printed menu, marching straight back into the kitchen to request specific dishes from the cook. She explained how each should be prepared and negotiated the price. We ate minced pork steamed with salted fish, shrimp paste or Chinese sausage. We ordered heaping mounds of white rice to dilute the salty taste. The sharp smell of these dishes drew frowns from non-Chinese customers. This was very different from the aroma of almond chicken or sweet-and-sour pork at the Hong Kong Restaurant.

Little Three Grand had a front counter with a row of stools where Chinatown bachelors ate pastries and drank coffee. My friend Dean Wong's dad—Yit Tow "Milton" Wong—worked there. I knew Dean from Chinatown; we became buddies at the University of Washington. Dean's mother Puey King ran a small storefront hand laundry called "Re-New Cleaners" at 505 Maynard Avenue South, next door to the Hong Kong Restaurant. We brought our bed sheets there to have them washed and pressed.

Our family came down to Chinatown during Chinese New Year. Vibrant lion dances—punctuated with a cacophony of firecrackers, drums, gongs and cymbals—attracted small impromptu gatherings in front of the stores. We visited family friends and relatives living in upstairs apartments or working at shops and restaurants. As kids, we got crisp new dollar bills, coins or lucky candy (利是糖) stuffed inside red envelopes. My parents exchanged bags of fruit and tins of cookies with others.

My parents occasionally took us to see Cantonese opera. It was performed in the second story hall of the Chong Wa Benevolent Association (中華會館), a brick building with a red tile roof and balcony at 522 Seventh Avenue South. The stage had big red curtains and oak wainscoting. A large, framed image of Dr. Sun Yat-sen and the flags of the United States and the Republic of China hung in the background. My father's restaurant coworkers acted out ancient classic tales in elaborate costumes under heavy make-up. I didn't understand much of what was going on, but I was tickled to see people I knew up on stage. There were very long intermissions between acts. We never knew if—or when—the show had ended.

I much preferred going with my mother to see Chinese films at the Kokusai Theater (太平戲院), a 490-seat movie house at 412 Maynard Avenue South. The cushioned theater seats were more comfortable than the hard folding chairs at Chong Wa. I didn't have to endure long, random intermissions. The films were in Cantonese, so I could follow the plot and a little bit of the dialogue. Occasionally, films offered poorly translated English subtitles.

The Kokusai was owned by Mr. Tadao Kitamura and his wife Mitsuye. Their four kids, Lance, Elaine, Darrell and Zen all worked there. Lance had been my classmate in elementary and junior high school. He had a happy grin, big teeth and a thick shock of unruly black hair.

The movie house opened in 1918 and was previously known as the Atlas Theater. In the 1960s, the Kitamuras renamed it the Kokusai or "International" Theater. The Kokusai alternated between twin features of Chinese, Japanese and Filipino movies. Monday and Tuesday were Chinese nights, Wednesday was Filipino night, and Friday, Saturday and Sunday were reserved for Japanese offerings.

After passing through the glass-paned front doors, we stopped at the ticket office in the lobby to pay for admission before proceeding through one of four doors into the seating area. We watched two black-and-white films from Hong Kong for $1.25 per person.

The films began right after the big red velvet curtains parted to reveal the screen. I marveled at the martial arts and supernatural ghosts flying through the air. I didn't care for the violent sword-play and the brutality of severed limbs and heads. There were moments when I had to close my eyes and turn away. My mother hated the violence as well. She came for the romantic stories of separation and heartbreak, the epic tales of filial devotion, and the heroic stories of uprisings against tyrannical rulers. She arrived with a full box of napkins in her purse, readying herself for cathartic crying sessions.

We snacked on Chinese watermelon seeds (*ga ghee* 瓜子) and homemade fried chicken wings (炸雞翅) which my mother packed in several brown paper lunch bags. I heard the steady click and clack of watermelon seeds being bitten in half by the dozens of Chinese women in the audience. The noise was distracting when the movie entered quiet tender moments. The small chestnut-colored shells of the watermelon seeds and leftover chicken wing bones were scattered all over the floor. I had to be careful where I stepped if I didn't want the bottom of my shoes coated with a disgusting combination of spilled soda pop, gum, popcorn and food waste. I felt sorry for the people who had to clean up.

On Mondays, it was especially difficult to sit still. After a weekend of bussing dishes at the Hong Kong Restaurant, my legs and feet felt tingly and sore. I had muscle cramps. I escaped to the dimly lit front lobby just to get out of my seat. There were vending machines for candy, soda pop and popcorn. But I had no money. I roamed around until a theater patron made a purchase at the popcorn machine. Then I looked to see if any popcorn was left at the bottom of the dispensing slot. I reclaimed every last piece, including unpopped kernels.

Every week, my parents stopped in Chinatown to pick up

the latest preview flier for the Chinese movies. The fliers were in a mail slot near the Seattle Kung Fu Club storefront at 658 South King Street.

In 1983, the Kokusai closed. Several Chinatown shops began selling and renting video cassette tapes of Chinese movies. Home viewing became popular. My mother bought tapes at two shops: Nam Duong (南洋行) on Seventh Avenue South and Kue Hing Company (僑興行) on South Jackson Street.

In 1985, businessman Danny Woo and a partner purchased the Kokusai. They wanted to remake the building into a multi-use six-story development with apartments, office and commercial space, and a Chinese movie house. But Woo passed away in 1987. The property was sold to Assunta Ng, publisher of the *Seattle Chinese Post* and *Northwest Asian Weekly*. The beloved Kokusai, severely damaged in a 1997 snowstorm, was torn down to make way for a new structure that has served as headquarters for Assunta's publications since 2001.

In the 1960s, the Kitamura family also ran the Raku Raku Restaurant at 416 Maynard Avenue South, next door to the Kokusai. It was one of the first Seattle establishments to serve *sushi*. In 1975, the space was remodeled into the home of the newly created International District Community Health Clinic, later renamed International Community Health Services (ICHS). I never ate at the Raku Raku. It wasn't until college that I deviated far enough outside my limited culinary upbringing to sample *sushi* for the first time.

CHAPTER 13

The Hong Kong Restaurant

A T 13, I BEGAN WORKING as a busboy alongside my father at the Hong Kong Restaurant. One day, after I arrived home from Mercer Junior High, my mother announced that my father had arranged for me to start that weekend. She said I would get valuable work experience and earn money for my education. I didn't question the decision. I simply asked, "What time?"

I spent a decade at the restaurant, continuing through the end of college. This experience left such a deep impression that even today, many of the dreams I remember upon waking take place inside the restaurant and involve my father, waiters, waitresses, kitchen workers and other busboys, many of whom have passed away. The restaurant's old phone number (MAin 2-0366) still plays in my brain on an automatic repeat track.

My father was the head waiter. The Hoisanese term for waiter is "*key hoy*" (企柏), which translates as "stand by a table." My father and the *key hoy* men spent 10-hour days on their feet, earning $1.25 an hour, without employer-provided benefits such as medical and dental coverage, retirement, sick leave and vacation. They worked until their bodies began to falter and they no longer had the strength to rush trays of food and dishes back and forth from the kitchen to the dining area.

Customers probably didn't realize the importance of tips to a waiter's livelihood. The tips were called "*fah lee*" (花利), which translates as "flowery profits." The waiters needed to take home ample *fah lee* to survive. They grumbled if a party left a few insignificant coins or no tip at all. My heart sank when I heard a waiter glance at a tip and mutter, "*Oong swee*" (冬水) or "cold water."

The Hong Kong Restaurant was located at 507 Maynard Avenue South, on the street level of the old Mar Hotel (馬氏旅館), mid-block between Weller and King Streets. By the time I started working there, the four-story structure, which once provided spartan living spaces for bachelor men, had slid into disrepair. The apartments were vacant. I went upstairs through the kitchen to a tiny room lit by a single hanging bulb to get extra supplies and dishes. I was afraid to venture anywhere else.

During the golden *chop suey* era, the Hong Kong Restaurant was a topflight Seattle business. Customers lined up outside the front door on weekends, salivating for their weekly fix of the standards: almond chicken (杏仁雞), sweet-and-sour pork (甜酸肉), *chop suey* (雜碎), fried rice (炒飯) and *egg foo yung* (芙蓉蛋). A brightly glowing vertical green neon sign with a red background hung from the building's facade. At night, you could see it from blocks away.

Just inside the front door, a counter lined with floor-mounted, chrome-and-vinyl bar stools provided seating for individual customers. The restaurant had full dining areas on three levels, a large aquarium (halfway between the first and second levels), and a dimly lit cocktail lounge called the Sampan Room.

The aquarium was nothing like the cloudy fish tanks that decades later began popping up near the entrances of Chinese restaurants as holding tanks for live king crab, lobsters and fish awaiting their end in the kitchen. The Hong Kong Restaurant tank was a true viewing aquarium filled with goldfish of various shapes and hues with bulging eyes and flowing fins, darting through carefully arranged rocks, driftwood and plants arranged over a bed of gravel.

The ceiling on the first level was lit by neon lights tracing the outline of a huge dragon. Suspended from the ceiling were several red-tasseled Chinese lanterns. On the second level, watercolor murals of Chinese landscapes by artist Fay Chong decorated walls. Freestanding red-and-black ornamental screens served as space dividers on the second and third levels.

Like me, many other Chinese American teens worked as busboys. It was a rite of passage. Some later became waiters. My two brothers Tom and Harvey also put in time. We worked on Fridays, Saturdays or Sundays, the busiest days. We began at 4 p.m. and left around 9:30 p.m. We came in earlier if there were big parties. We stayed later if business didn't die down. During the summer, we worked additional hours.

Our responsibility was to clear tables rapidly so that the next group of guests could be seated. There were two or three busboys per shift. Working as a team, we stacked dishes, teacups, water glasses and cutlery onto a large oval fiberglass tray. The used white tablecloth and dirty cloth napkins were rolled in a tight bundle and placed on top. One busboy carried the tray through a pair of saloon doors into the kitchen. Another busboy spread a clean tablecloth and put down new settings. A third busboy rushed ahead to begin clearing another table. The pace was brutal.

As we got older, some busboys—myself included—became

strong enough to carry all the contents from a table of 10 on a single tray into the kitchen. The tray, bowing in the middle, weighed close to 50 pounds. We were slight teens. Customers stared at us, mouths ajar.

We brought cash tips back to the front counter, identifying them on small scraps of paper with letters or numbers corresponding to the table they came from. That way the *fah lee* got back to the right waiters. The numbers and letters of every table are still committed to my memory, over 40 years after I left. My father routinely collected large tips from regular Japanese American and Jewish American customers.

Three men started the restaurant—Sam Yee, Ngew Chu and Henry Louie. Sam Yee was the major investor. Ngew Chu worked as a chef in the kitchen with his son Roy. Henry Louie was a bartender in the Sampan Room.

All four men were members of the Hop Sing Tong (合勝 堂), one of four tongs in Chinatown. The tongs were secret societies formed in ancient China and imported to America, operating as brotherhoods in the modern era. The Hop Sing Tong was at 512 Maynard Avenue South, directly across the street from the restaurant.

Sam, Roy and Henry were passionate about traditional Chinese music. They were stalwarts at the Luck Ngai Musical Club (樂藝音樂劇社), established in 1937 to support war relief efforts in China. Louie—we called him Uncle Henry or Lep Sook (立叔)—was an original member. After work, the merry trio—Uncle Henry, Uncle Roy and Uncle Sam—went to the club to practice on Chinese instruments until the wee morning hours.

Uncle Sam wore glasses and had a gaunt face. He wore elevator shoes and a lopsided black toupee. I never saw him without a suit and tie. He treated the busboys with kindness and my father with great respect. He had a small office in the back near the kitchen. He fretted over daily problems like broken toilets or unexpected shortages of food supplies, fresh linen or dishes. My father helped Uncle Sam maintain the financial ledgers. Uncle Sam trusted no one else with money matters.

One day, Uncle Sam enticed a few busboys to go upstairs to help catch pigeons that had broken into the hotel. He wanted to make pigeon soup, a prized delicacy. He gave us large nets. We ran around in the dark with flashlights. I had no luck. I was grossed out by the heaps of pigeon poop on the floors.

The *maître d'* was Uncle Alvin, a slight man with slicked-back hair and wire-rimmed glasses. He was neatly attired, usually in a charcoal pinstripe suit with a pocket handkerchief. He smoked and spoke in a raspy voice. His assistant Dennis was taller and astonishingly thin. He looked like a scarecrow in an oversized suit and tie. He drove a sporty Mustang.

The other regular at the front was Auntie Dorothy. Like Uncle Alvin and Dennis, she smoked. Auntie Dorothy was middle-aged and lived alone in Chinatown, at 414 Canton Alley South. Even with thick glasses, she could barely see. She dressed in fashionable but conservative long dresses. Standing behind the counter, she handled food orders to go. She had a short fuse, sternly admonishing the waiters when they made mistakes on reservations. Many years later, Donnie Chin informed me that she was killed by a car while crossing the street.

Uncle Sam's wife Sue helped Auntie Dorothy, answering the phone, guiding customers to their tables and working the cash register. She was much younger than Uncle Sam. She had a baby face, rosy cheeks and a stylish perm. She came from Yakima, where her father, Monwai Wen, ran the popular Golden Wheel Restaurant. Sue's two young sons, Kenford and Victor, hung around but didn't have assigned duties. They played and chatted with the busboys and waiters. Sam Yee's older son Bennett worked as a parking valet.

To prepare for large parties, we busboys descended a dark flight of stairs to the basement to retrieve extra chairs and round table tops. We carried the chairs up in stacks of four. We hoisted table tops up one at a time, balancing them over one shoulder while carefully negotiating our way up the creaky wooden steps. The table tops were slotted over the square tables, creating tables for 10 or 11 people.

I hated going down to the basement. It was dark, cold and damp. The concrete floor was covered with swarms of dark brown cockroaches with greasy-looking bodies. It was gross. We stomped on them, crunching their hard shells. We tried to see how many cockroaches we could flatten. Over time, I noticed the cockroaches getting bigger and developing harder shells. I understood why they outlived the dinosaurs and why it was said that they would survive a nuclear holocaust.

When I first started, I was stationed in the kitchen, sorting and drying the silverware as it came out of the dishwashing area. I hauled the clean silverware to the dining room, stashing it near the ice-making machine and tea dispensers. I also brought out large metal-framed racks of freshly washed water glasses and plastic tubs of clean teacups and dipping saucers called mustard chips.

The restaurant employed two dishwashers, Marty and Roy. They were among the many Filipino bachelors who worked in Chinatown.

Roy was the older of the two. He was hired before Marty and left before him. Roy was a taciturn, industrious man with a hard-bitten face and very bad asthma. He had a severe hacking cough. When I saw Roy begin to pause from his work to cough up blood in the year before he left the restaurant, I knew there was something terribly wrong. I heard from Marty that Roy had married and left for California. Roy soon landed in the hospital.

Marty—his real name was Marion—stayed on after Roy. He was in his 50s. He had a short crew cut and tattoos on his thick, hairy arms. He had a slow, plodding manner and a high-pitched giggle. He lived at the Alps Hotel, where he paid $42 a month for rent.

After work, he went to the downtown Coffee Corral at 3:30 a.m. for a breakfast of pancakes, toast, hash browns and coffee. In 1978, I decided to surprise him with a visit. He told me he used to drink but gave it up after his doctor told him he was "going to end up six feet under." Marty didn't follow his doctor's other stern advice about quitting smoking; he lit up a cigarette while we sat and talked at the counter. Marty told me he wanted to go back to the Philippines to find a wife but needed to save more money first. He earned $375 a month. A round-trip ticket to the Philippines cost $700. I didn't know if he ever made it back home.

Three Chinese girls from Beacon Hill helped in the kitchen, preparing wontons and cutting vegetables. They were Sherrie Chinn and Janine and Cindy Chu. Uncle Roy was Janine and Cindy's father. A younger sibling Christopher was a busboy like me.

Sherrie's father, Fred Chinn, was the younger brother of Sam Yee. Sherrie's family lived next door to us. Uncle Fred occasionally worked as a waiter at the Hong Kong, but his primary job was as a fabricator for Boeing, assigned to the lunar orbiter program. He was born in China and came to the United States when he was 16. Uncle Fred's wife, Auntie Barbara, came from a huge family in Portland. She had six sisters and five older brothers. Sherrie's younger brother Alan was the kid

I played cards with on our porch. Sherrie had a younger sister named Patty.

Sherrie, Janine and Cindy teased me and tried to mess up my work. As I dried silverware, they threw food bits at me. Sherrie had a big crush on me. When I ignored her, she pouted and pretended to cry. Once, as I entered the kitchen carrying a heavy tray of dirty dishes, she spit on my uniform. The moist shards of a fortune cookie spilled all over the floor around me.

Janine liked my brother Tom. After school, Janine, Cindy and Sherrie tried to peek inside the partially open bathroom window in our home to see if either of us was inside. They couldn't see directly into the house because the window was pebbled glass. But they tiptoed and peered over the bottom sill. If I needed to use the bathroom, I first made sure they weren't hiding outside. Janine, accompanied by her snickering co-conspirators, crooned an old popular song through the window:

> *K-K-K-Katy, beautiful Katy,*
> *You're the only g-g-g-girl that I adore;*
> *When the m-m-m-moon shines,*
> *Over the cowshed,*
> *I'll be waiting at the k-k-k-kitchen door...*

Uncle Roy and his father did most of the cooking over a row of flaming black woks in the back corner of the kitchen, their hands nimbly tossing vegetables and small slices of meat into sizzling hot oil with clanging spatulas, smoke billowing about them. Uncle Roy's mother, a tough old lady with a wise and caring demeanor, cut up vegetables and meat in another area of the kitchen. When the dirty dishes began stacking up, she took command. Even though she was quite elderly, she was fast and efficient, outpacing employees half her age.

In the 1960s, the restaurant began serving a limited menu of *dim sum* (點心) pastries on Saturdays and Sundays for lunch. It was one of the first restaurants in Chinatown to do so. We called it *cha ngow* (茶餚) or tea pastries, not *dim sum*. I never heard the term *dim sum* when I was growing up. The *cha ngow* choices were limited to *siu mai* (steamed pork dumplings 燒賣), *ha gow* (shrimp balls 蝦餃) and *hom bow* (barbecue pork buns 咸飽). *Hom bow* is now more commonly called *cha siu bow* (叉燒飽).

Uncle Roy prepped batches of *siu mai*, *ha gow* and *hom bow* on Thursdays. They were cooked in three huge wok-sized bamboo steamers. Janine recalls, "The *hom bow* were the size of hamburgers, the *ha gow* were the size of dinner rolls and each of the *siu mai* were as large as a good-sized meatball." She wasn't exaggerating. I remember getting full on just a single *hom bow*. It was a meal in itself.

By the time I got off work, my knees, ankles and feet ached. I was frequently in so much agony that I couldn't sleep. My mother rubbed smelly Tiger Balm on my legs. Dr. Kaplan told my parents that I might be vitamin-deficient and at risk of suffering deformity in my knees and legs. He said that in a worst-case situation I might have to wear leg braces. He suggested changes in my diet, but he reassured my parents that I would probably grow out of this problem.

He was right. As I moved through adolescence, the pain diminished. I grew taller and got stronger. I was able to carry heavy loads of dishes into the kitchen like the older busboys.

I frequently saw Ruby Chow at the Hong Kong, conversing with Uncle Sam. She was loud and plump, and she wore a tall beehive hairdo. I also saw Danny Woo, owner of the New Chinatown Restaurant. He had a thin build, a thick shock of neatly combed gray hair, black-framed glasses and a primly tailored suit and tie. He always sat in the same booth near the front of the restaurant, a pipe in his mouth, usually with Uncle Sam's youngest son Victor crawling on his lap. The three restaurateurs—Uncle Sam, Ruby and Danny Woo—chatted about business, then walked across the street to the Hop Sing Tong.

Unlike Sam Yee and Danny Woo, Ruby Chow had big political ambitions. She shrewdly put together a power base by hosting local politicians and civic and business leaders at her restaurant. She later ran for King County Council, becoming the first Asian American elected to that body.

In 1973, during Chinese New Year, Seattle police arrested 75 people, including Danny Woo, charging them with illegal gambling. The next day, Ruby stormed in to see Mayor Wes Uhlman, demanding that the charges be dropped. I saw Danny Woo's photo on the front page of the newspaper. At home, my mother delivered another stern warning about the hazards of gambling. The people charged were promptly released, and Danny Woo resumed his accustomed spot at the front booth of the Hong Kong Restaurant on the weekend.

Bruce "Little Dragon" Lee (李小龍) was a hero to all of us busboys. Several busboys were inspired to join the Seattle Kung Fu Club up the street. They yearned to become as good at fighting as Bruce was. They came to work griping about sore muscles and the rigors of training. As they became more proficient, they began to show off with high front kicks and back fist punches.

Bruce Lee had starred as Kato in the TV series *The Green Hornet*. He overshadowed the white lead actor who couldn't move with Bruce's style, grace and speed. Before Bruce, the only Chinese male characters on TV were servants and houseboys. One was Hop Sing, the cook on the TV series *Bonanza*. He dressed in traditional Chinese garb and sported a long queue of braided hair down his back. He spoke with a "Chinese" accent. Stereotype or not, I liked Hop Sing, as did my mother, because we didn't see anyone else on TV who was Chinese.

After *The Green Hornet*, Bruce appeared in several Hong Kong martial arts films in which the Chinese were depicted as downtrodden victims fighting back against vicious Japanese soldiers. When I watched *The Chinese Connection* with my mother—it was finally made available on American television in the 1990s—the scenes transported her back to her wartime years in China. She cheered loudly for Bruce, raising her fist and cursing the Japanese.

Uncle Henry, a young waiter, was one of Bruce Lee's work-out partners. Uncle Henry was a quiet, confident man with a strong, stocky build. He combed his hair straight back and held it in place with gobs of shiny hair tonic. He boasted about Bruce's speed and power. He said Bruce shunned classical Chinese martial arts techniques and chose instead to invent his own improvisational street style. I never saw Bruce at the Hong Kong, but I was told that he would go back into the kitchen with Uncle Henry and the two of them would break vegetable crates with forceful punches and kicks.

After the dinner crowd died down, Uncle Henry demonstrated explosive front kicks, strikes delivered with either hand, and parrying moves. He showed us how, before an attack, to keep your lead foot and back foot properly balanced and your arms tucked close to the body.

When business was slow, the busboys congregated at one of the dining tables and challenged one another to arm-wrestling matches. The waiters watched, bemused. During one match between the waiters and busboys, someone jokingly challenged my father, in his 50s, to take on Uncle Henry, who was winning handily against the younger waiters and busboys. My father wasn't a large man—he stood about 5'6", and was of medium build—but he was very strong. I saw him effortlessly lift and carry a 100-pound sack of rice into our garage.

At a booth in the front of the restaurant, Uncle Henry and my father squared off, the two locking forearms. Despite his best efforts, Uncle Henry couldn't budge my dad. They fought to a draw. At first, they went at it with their right hand, then the left. Same result. I was surprised and incredibly proud.

Several of the American-born Chinese busboys boasted about having white girlfriends—what Chinese termed *gwee nwee* (鬼女). They regarded it as an emblem of distinction, the definitive measure of personal daring, a sign of acceptance into the larger society.

One day, several older busboys led me down to the basement. They wanted to teach me how to smoke. "Here's how it's done, Ronald," one of them said. He pulled out a lighter, lit a cigarette, took a drag, then blew out a gush of smoke. Another busboy lit up, too, but he exhaled through his nostrils. They told me to try it. I said no. I wasn't interested. I was sure that if word got back to my father, he wouldn't be happy. I also didn't like the foul odor and the way the smoke clung to my clothes. It was bad enough that I came home reeking of greasy *subgum*.

The busboys thought smoking made them look cool and tough. Back then, the tobacco industry hid the dangers of smoking. It wasn't until 2005, long after the restaurant closed, that smoking was banned from eating establishments in Seattle. A few of the omnipresent round glass ashtrays, emblazoned with the Hong Kong Restaurant name, made their way to my home as souvenirs. We used them to discard bubble gum.

The restaurant job allowed me to spend precious time with my father. He was usually away when I was home. I was delighted that everyone—Uncle Sam, Uncle Alvin, the waiters, busboys and kitchen workers—looked up to him. Customers asked for him by name, knowing that he would greet them warmly and help them order dishes tailored exactly to their liking. The Kitamura family, owners of the Kokusai Theater, were among his regular customers. They came every weekend after they finished work at 11 p.m. They didn't mind waiting till my father was available.

My father served as the enforcer. If an unruly customer—usually someone who was extremely intoxicated—started making trouble, everyone searched for him. Uncle Alvin or Auntie Dorothy pressed the two-way intercom system, which connected to the kitchen, and asked in Chinese for *Thlee Sook* or Fourth Uncle to come to the front right away. My father would physically escort the troublemaker out. Several waiters carried guns to work. I would see their concealed weapons when they donned their waiter uniforms in a small changing room near the front of the restaurant. My father didn't carry a gun or use a firearm, yet he always handled delicate situations with confidence.

One day in 1970, I was shadow-boxing in my parents' garage. I had just watched Muhammad Ali outclass Oscar Bonavena on TV during his heroic return to boxing. I didn't realize that my father had stepped into the garage behind me. He moved toward me. "No," he said, smiling. "This is how you do it." He showed me how to stand, how to position my two fists and how to put the weight of my body behind my punches. He clearly knew quite a bit about boxing. This was a side of him I had never seen. I was so taken aback that I couldn't bring myself to ask where he had learned his moves.

Uncle Ming—*Ming-bok*—was the other waiter who rivaled my father for longevity at the Hong Kong Restaurant. *Ming-bok* was a short, portly man with thinning hair. His black-framed glasses, round head and large forehead gave him an owl-like appearance. He spoke little and had a stoic but bright demeanor.

Ming-bok was born in 1912 in China and immigrated to New York City in 1923. His first job was peeling potatoes 10 to 11 hours a day, seven days a week. He didn't receive any pay, but he ate for free. At the Hong Kong Restaurant, he was usually the first to arrive and the last to leave.

His wife was African American. He brought her to community events, prompting curious and sometimes derisive glances from his Chinese peers. *Ming-bok* talked to the busboys about his frequent fishing trips to Moses Lake and his litter of cats. We kidded him about the age of the old car he drove, asking whether he would ever replace it. We saw it sputtering down the street, straining to go faster than 20 miles per hour. He shrugged. He didn't do any maintenance at all. He said he hadn't changed the oil in years.

Ming-bok often went to visit his friend Lung Sing Luke, father of Wing Luke, for whom the Wing Luke Museum is named. Mr. Luke ran a small grocery store at 920 James Street. *Ming-bok* delivered bags of flat fortune cookies from Tsue Chong Noodle Company so that Mr. Luke could resell them for several cents each.

I loved the sweet vanilla flavor of the fortune cookies. I got mine free at work. The busboys periodically dipped into the five-gallon tin bucket behind the front counter to grab fistfuls of the broken ones. I sipped on Coca Cola or 7-Up with ice to wash them down. This high-octane sugar mix kept me going.

Dinner for the waiters, busboys and bar waitresses was served at 9 p.m., after the evening rush. Several large batches of food in large aluminum foil trays were placed on a flat surface in the kitchen. When the busboys heard that dinner was ready, we tore into the kitchen. By then, my stomach was growling audibly. Typical offerings were stir-fried vegetables, deep fried chicken wings, fried smelt and Chinese-style spareribs with black bean sauce. I piled my dinner plate as high as I could. We ate in the dining room, sitting amid the sea of abandoned tables left behind by recently departed customers.

It was an unspoken courtesy that busboys could grab their food before the others. The older waiters didn't eat as much as we did. *Ming-bok* was the one exception; he filled his big dinner bowl with enormous portions. Often, my father continued working, clearing tables and serving late-arriving customers. He never seemed to be in a rush. He knew he could eat later. I envied his calm. I doubted that I could ever be like him.

CHAPTER 14

A Door Opens into the World of Books

EVEN BEFORE I COULD READ, I loved to open children's books and pore over the illustrations. I marveled at the well-scrubbed, ruby-faced people in the Dick and Jane readers. I saw pristine homes, white picket fences, forest-green lawns, and litter-free streets. This jeweled world seemed so much more desirable than my own. I wanted to shrink myself and jump in.

I dreamed up stories to match the pictures and the mysterious printed words I could barely decipher. I imagined riding through Chinatown on the back of the friendly dinosaur in *Danny and the Dinosaur* or flying on Elmer Elevator's baby dragon to a hidden jungle filled with ripe persimmons.

I discovered the Beacon Hill Library on a third-grade class field trip. It was located in a nondescript storefront at the junction of Beacon Avenue South and 15th Avenue South. The space used to be a grocery store, but it was converted into a 3,300 square-foot library in 1961.

The librarian, Mrs. Norma O'Brian, told us all to sit down

on the worn tile floor and be still. A big black potbelly stove with a tall stove pipe hummed in the background. She read two simple picture books, pausing to display the bright, colorful illustrations. She showed us a wooden cabinet called the card catalog, explaining that everything was organized according to the Dewey Decimal System. She then told us how we could borrow books for free. We had to return them before the stamped expiration date inside the cover.

With the end of school around the corner, she encouraged us to join the library summer reading club. For each book you read, you earned one star. If you got at least 10 stars, your name appeared on a special list posted on the front window.

I wanted to see my name on the window. I wanted to see how many stars I could get. But I knew it would be tough. I could barely read. I checked out the easiest picture books I could find. I stuttered and faked my way through sessions with Mrs. O'Brian to claim credit for my books. I was relieved that she didn't ask many questions. She mostly smiled and nodded.

My first year in the reading club was 1962. I was in the fourth grade. I received a certificate adorned with the *Century 21 Exposition* logo and an image of the Space Needle. In 1963, the reading club theme was "Sail Around Seattle." I had never been on a boat. My certificate came with an official Seattle Public Library gold seal. I felt proud.

My parents were pleased that I was at the library. They trusted that it was safe. They were thrilled that I could borrow a lot of books for free. My mother called it the "lie-beh-lee" when she tried to pronounce the word. In Chinese, she called it "*hoo see gwon*" (圖書館).

It was ironic that I loved holding books in my hand. I was nearly illiterate. For years, my mind swirled in a dense fog as I transitioned to an English-speaking school outside my

Chinese-speaking home. Teachers shunted me off to the poorest reading groups. There, I simply kept quiet and tried not to make any trouble. That didn't deter me from staring at pictures and daydreaming.

I persisted. My vocabulary increased as I coupled images with words. My mother's gift for storytelling and my parents' love of learning pushed me past this confounding phase.

As I entered junior high and high school, peer pressure drew my vulnerable male friends into fights, gangs and drugs. A few tried to drag me in. I resisted. The library gave me a place to hide. The smell of aging books on wooden shelves wrapped me in its timeless, safe embrace.

I pulled out the same well-thumbed books from familiar niches. I buried myself in the tales of Paul Bunyan and his blue ox Babe. I followed the heroic journey of Johnny Appleseed. I applauded the cleverness of the Five Chinese Brothers. I pored over Lois Lenski's illustrations.

My favorite book was Gertrude Chandler Warner's *The Boxcar Children*. Linda told me about it. I checked it out over a dozen times. I loved the story of the four orphaned children who made a home in an abandoned boxcar. There was Henry, the older brother; Jessie, the older sister who cooked and looked after the others; Violet, the sensitive younger sister; and Benny, a cute seven-year-old who found a cracked pink cup in the dump. In the end, a kind-hearted grandfather rescues them all. The book was filled with memorable black-and-white silhouetted illustrations.

I connected the story to my own life. At times, it seemed as if my parents didn't exist because they were always working. Henry was my brother Tom. Jessie was Linda. And Benny was Harvey. I never had the chance to meet or know my grandparents. The thought that a grandfather might miraculously show up one day, plucking us out of poverty, was a delightful fantasy.

At home, my mother and father had their own special books. My mother hoarded a stack of well-worn *muk ngwee see* or "wooden fish song books" (木魚書) in her bedroom on top of a honey-colored art deco dresser with translucent Bakelite handles. She bundled the tattered booklets loosely with rubber bands so that the pages wouldn't fall out of sequence. When she had time, she pulled a book out from the pile and read aloud, usually sitting alone.

My father's books were *High School Self-Taught*, published in 1939, and *Trader Vic's Bartender's Guide* from 1947. The second book had practical use when he worked as a bartender in the Sampan Room at the Hong Kong Restaurant to earn extra money. Both were stamped in blue ink with his name and address on the inside cover.

My father bought two encyclopedia sets. First was the 1959 edition of *Golden Book Encyclopedia*, profusely illustrated in color and written for children. A few years later, he purchased the *World Book Encyclopedia*, targeted for a higher level of readers. I spent many hours leafing through these volumes, exploring foreign lands and vanished empires and absorbing facts about dinosaurs, insects, flowers and famous people in history.

An 11-volume set of the 1937 *Collier's New Encyclopedia*, pages brown and brittle from age, sat unused in our basement. The print was tiny. I guessed that the set once belonged to my late Uncle Lee, who attended the University of Washington.

Together, these three encyclopedia sets filled an entire wooden bookcase. My mother sewed an orange, patterned curtain to pull across the front to protect the books from dust.

One of the very first books I owned was *The How and Why Wonder Book of the Human Body*. When I was eight, my father asked each of us kids to choose a book from a store display table during a downtown shopping trip. I was drawn to the cover. It featured illustrations of the muscular system, a thigh bone and a cross-section of the human heart. The book—part of a series on science, history and nature—cost $1. It was a lot of money in those days. I spent many hours poring over the book. I was haunted by a sequence of images showing how a fetus developed from a fertilized embryo. Instead of unraveling a mystery, I was presented with a new one. *How were babies made?* I had no one to turn to for answers.

In the sixth grade, a weekly publication called *Scholastic NewsTime,* was distributed free in class. It included national and world news, short stories, a multiple-choice vocabulary test, science features and short fiction. The back page had jokes, brain teasers, riddles and silly verse. At the end of class, I carefully placed the *NewsTime* edition in the inside pocket of my honey-colored Pee Chee folder, sandwiching it between sheets of notebook paper for protection till I got home.

I was overjoyed because *NewsTime* came with an order form for the Arrow Book Club. I could buy my own books! I selected from a list of mysteries, sports books, and collections of jokes, riddles and cartoons. The books cost 25 to 35 cents each, discounted from their cover prices. I counted down the days till my order arrived. I wrote my name in ink on the inside cover of each book, taking great care not to damage the spines or crease corners. These were my most cherished belongings.

The Scholastic titles unleashed an insatiable hunger for peering beyond the walls of my house and boundaries of my neighborhood and Chinatown.

By then, my home life had degraded. My mother's shifting moods terrified me. She fought daily with my father. She complained bitterly about coworkers and supervisors at the sewing factory. She clashed with my headstrong sister. She scolded my brothers and me for speaking to her in English. She screamed and cried. She threatened to pack her bags for China. Whenever I wanted to escape the noise, fights, drama and uncertainty, I buried myself in books. The Beacon Hill Library was just a short walk away. I stayed for hours.

My sister developed another "public library" in our basement. It consisted of all our Scholastic books. As the library "manager," she issued renewable library cards to my brothers, a few neighbor kids and me. My brother Tom constructed several bookshelves out of discarded wooden crates nailed together into a tall stack. I covered the outside of the crates with brown adhesive vinyl wrap, purchased at Pay 'n Save, to fill big gaps and minimize the danger of splinters.

In high school, I discovered Shorey's Bookstore, a used bookseller on the second floor of a building at First Avenue and Union Street in downtown Seattle. It first opened in 1890. It was home to bibliophiles and history buffs. I spent a lot of time there. Shorey's had rooms and rooms full of books, dwarfing the Beacon Hill Library. I climbed a ladder to pull down dozens of old books from the upper shelves. I read for hours, undisturbed, sitting cross-legged in the aisles, a stack of titles next to me.

At Shorey's I discovered H.G. Wells. There were several rows of his hardbound titles, including his science fiction classics *The Time Machine*, *The War of the Worlds*, *The Invisible Man*, *The Sleeper Wakes* and *The Island of Dr. Moreau*. I bought them for a dollar or two each. I also snatched up his lesser known and more pedantic socialist novels and essays. I consulted the public library's bound volumes of *Book Review Digest* to track down everything Wells had written. I amassed nearly 80 Wells titles, storing them in a small locking metal cabinet I bought at Woolworth's.

My favorite Wells book was *The Wonderful Visit*, originally published in 1895. I found a red hardcover rebound edition at the downtown Seattle Public Library. I checked it out a half-dozen times. It was an insanely funny story about an angel who falls by accident to Earth and tries in vain to understand the cruelties and strange customs of humans before succumbing to the first pangs of emotion himself.

In my junior year at Franklin High, I chose H.G. Wells for a language arts assignment on a favorite author. I wrote a short story, "The Cry of the Fairy," about my encounter with a "four-inch-high, pink-clothed, pointed-eared, green-cheeked" creature near the edge of the Franklin track. It was influenced by "Mr. Skelmersdale in Fairy Land," a tale in Wells's science fiction collection *Twelve Stories and a Dream*. I wrote a second short story, "Mr. Wells Objects," about a middle-aged writer cursing the materialism of Christmas. A third story, "The Christmas Present," focused on a tender farewell between high school friends "Empintel" and "Nancy Skelmersdale."

After Wells, I latched onto African American writer Richard Wright, author of *Native Son*. His books were reissued in paperback during the Black Power movement. My first Wright title was his harrowing 1961 short story collection *Eight Men*, which I read in high school. Like Wright, my personal discovery of books and the public library were my salvation. In his autobiography *Black Boy*, Wright wrote that reading became "a drug, a dope." He said it "created moods in which I lived for days." I knew exactly what he was describing.

Unlike Wright, I didn't grow up in the church under a tyrannical fear of God. I hadn't suffered hunger, brutal poverty or the lash of atrocious Jim Crow laws. But I saw unnerving echoes in what my parents had to endure every day in their low-wage jobs. I appreciated the simplicity and modernity of

Wright's prose. I bought all of his books. I dreamed I could one day write like him.

Wright led me to Upton Sinclair, Theodore Dreiser, James Baldwin, Ann Petry, Carson McCullers, Victor Hugo, Fyodor Dostoyevsky and Charles Dickens.

When I was in college, John Steinbeck enjoyed a resurgence. His books were reissued as Bantam Classics. I bought most of them. The titles I didn't buy, my brother Harvey, an avid reader like me, did. The richly descriptive, plain-spoken prose and the spare, heartfelt dialogue in *Of Mice and Men*, *The Grapes of Wrath* and *In Dubious Battle* gripped me.

At the University of Washington, I read a mix of counterculture and protest titles for my humanities courses: *The Greening of America* by Charles Reich, *Future Shock* by Alvin Toffler, *The Movement Toward a New America* by Mitchell Goodman, *Steppenwolf* by Herman Hesse, *Soul on Ice* by Eldridge Cleaver, and *Do It* by Jerry Rubin. Two books sharpened my understanding of racism: comedian Dick Gregory's *Nigger* and John Howard Griffin's *Black Like Me*. I admired Gregory's quick-witted use of humor to mock racism and his embrace of the women's movement. Griffin, a white journalist, wrote about disguising his skin tone so that he could "pass" for black.

After Shorey's closed in 1991, I hunted for other used bookstores in the city. I found Beatty Book Store at 1925 Third Avenue, across the street from the downtown Bon Marché at Third and Pine; and Horizon Books, a ramshackle house on 15th Avenue in Capitol Hill. I also frequented Comstock Books in Rainier Valley.

All those places are now gone. Barnes & Noble and Amazon have swallowed up the book market. There are few used bookstores left in Seattle. I am still sad about this.

In 2000, as a mid-career adult, I was asked to join the

Libraries for All capital campaign. The effort included a new Beacon Hill branch three times the size of the old building. I didn't hesitate. The library had sheltered me from the streets and had fed my mind.

After my father retired, he became a regular at the Beacon Hill Library. He read the daily newspapers, basking in the simple pleasure of keeping his brain active. He didn't have a chance to enjoy the new facility—it wasn't completed until 2004, eight years after he died—but it is heartening to know that we both found joy in the same space.

When my two boys were very young, I read to them daily before bed. The books came from the new Beacon Hill branch, the public library's used book sales at Magnuson Park, Goodwill Outlet and my own collection of Scholastic titles. I used these stories as a springboard to improvise Beacon Hill adventure tales which I added to the story-time mix. I inserted each of them as fantasy heroes triumphing over make-believe villains. I often had great difficulty persuading them that "papa is really tired and has to go to sleep."

CHAPTER 15

Seattle Central Community College

B EFORE I GRADUATED FROM FRANKLIN High School in the spring of 1971, I took the Washington pre-college test. It predicted a career in agriculture or forestry. This was curious. I had no interest in either. But I didn't know what I wanted to do with my life other than daydream, listen to music and write stories.

Still, college was inevitable. My parents wanted my brothers and me to get the opportunity they never enjoyed. They didn't feel the same way about Linda. "After she gets married, she will then take on the name of her husband and become part of his family," my mother announced. "She will serve them. Her children will not carry on the Chew name."

My sister was a friend of Dean Wong's sister Jeannie. When Linda began dating boys that my mother didn't approve of and going out at night, my mother called Jeannie, pleading tearfully with her to talk sense into Linda. It was painful to hear those living room phone calls. I retreated to my bedroom, but my mother's voice bellowed past the door. I could tell that it was agonizing for Jeannie to be caught in the middle of those family conflicts.

Linda wanted to be independent. Her goal was to become an office secretary. She took a retailing class at Franklin High School. At age 16, she was hired at the large JCPenney at Second and Pike in downtown Seattle. She worked there for 10 years. She started in the records department, selling 45s and LPs, and worked her way up to the teen boutique, costume jewelry and candy departments. She bought a quarter-pound bag of cashews, introducing my mother and the rest of us to a new delicacy.

One day, she finally pulled me aside and confided, "I really need to move away." Linda and my mother had had several fiery arguments. Linda shouted at her in English, "If I want to go out, that's my business. Leave me alone! I am an individual! I am an individual." She stormed out of the room, crying. My father, emerging from the basement, was asked to translate my sister's words. My mother turned her fury on my father: "It's your fault," she said in Chinese. "You speak English to them. You don't discipline them. You allow them to be disrespectful. I should take all of the children back to China before they get totally ruined by this country." Even though I hid in my room, I heard every word.

My sister was determined to go to college. But in addition to believing that Linda's proper fate was to get married off to a nice Chinese boy, my mother said it would be shameful, a loss of face, to accept help from the government. My sister didn't listen. She applied to the UW. She requested financial aid. She asked me to help forge their signatures on the forms. I copied their handwriting from tax returns. She thanked me, adding, "Don't tell Mom. She's just going to take it out on you and there will be more trouble because you're still living at home."

Years later, after discovering the connection between my family's hidden history and the Chinese Exclusion Act, I understood that their unwillingness to apply for assistance probably also had to do with avoiding government scrutiny.

I was forlorn when Linda moved away. She was responsible for taking care of me and my brothers while our parents were at work. At age 11, she began preparing dinner, skillfully replicating all of my mother's familiar dishes. She also introduced us to new foods. In high school, she made buttermilk pancakes in her home economics class and brought a stack home. They were delicious. She made crispy fried potato pancakes from a packaged mix, and French fries using fresh-cut potatoes.

My mother told Linda, "If any of your brothers are naughty, you have my permission to spank them." But Linda never resorted to punishment. She kept close watch over Harvey, the baby of the family, making sure he didn't wander far from the house and run into neighborhood bullies. Through most of his early teen years, Harvey was small and slight.

Before she left home, Linda deeded me her well-worn paperback copy of Ayn Rand's novel *The Fountainhead*. It was her favorite book. I casually flipped it open, noticed how tiny the type was and remarked, "Too many pages!" I didn't grasp why Rand appealed so strongly to my sister.

At age 19, Linda moved to an apartment in the University District. My parents disowned her and told her never to return home. My mother heard rumors that my sister was living with a non-Chinese boy. My father was dispatched up to her apartment to excoriate her. One evening, my sister was startled to find my father and Roy Chu standing on a borrowed ladder, spying through her window.

Although Linda left on non-speaking terms with my parents, a small measure of peace returned to the house. The unrestrained shouting matches between Linda and my mother had finally ceased.

Before long, it was time for me to consider college. I was scared of the big university. I didn't think I could succeed there. I decided to attend Seattle Central Community College, where tuition was only $50 per quarter. I figured I could transfer to the UW later.

I was not as eager as Linda was to exit our parents' house. I didn't know how my mother would react if I said I wanted to move out, given the terrifying emotional drama with my sister. After Linda left, I moved into her old bedroom.

At Seattle Central, I took a course in creative writing. My instructor allowed students to explore a full range of prose styles and to discover their own voice. I loved this freedom. I did well. But I also felt intimidated being among so many older students. In a course on Washington state history taught by state legislator George W. Scott, the star pupil was a white man in his 60s. He lugged a heavy brown leather attaché to class. When he snapped it open, I saw that it was crammed with books and papers. He raised his hand at every opportunity. He knew more than Scott. I never understood why he was enrolled in the class and what he hoped to learn.

During the summer of 1971, I wrote an essay about the ongoing Vietnam War for another class. I asked why the American public so eagerly expressed indignation at the death of U.S. soldiers while ignoring the slaughter of Vietnamese people. I read the paper aloud. After finishing, a slender, baby-faced Vietnamese man approached me. He walked with a pronounced limp and had a prosthetic arm. He told me his name was Do Van Du. "I really appreciate what you said," he remarked. "I'd like to have a copy of your paper." I was flattered. He was the first Vietnamese person I ever met.

He explained that he had fought as part of the U.S. Army Special Forces. In 1968, when he was just 14, he lost his arm and leg in an explosion at Lộc Ninh. After his recovery, he came to the U.S. to complete high school. He lived on Capitol Hill in Seattle. He wanted to raise money to send back to Vietnam to support orphanages there. We kept in touch between classes and became friends.

I took my first Asian American studies course. It was called "Sociology of Asian Americans." Cynthia Chan-Toyoji (later Cynthia Chan-Imanaka) was the instructor. She was born in Menlo Park, California. She moved to Seattle to pursue a graduate degree in sociology at the UW. Cynthia arrived at Seattle Central a year after the Oriental Student Union, led by Al Sugiyama and former Black Panther Mike Takagawa, organized protests demanding Asian American studies classes at the college.

Cynthia was my first Chinese American instructor. It was thrilling to see someone who looked like me and understood me. I hadn't felt this way since Miss Murakami was my sixth grade teacher. I assiduously took notes while listening to Cynthia lecture about the Chinese, Japanese and Filipino immigrants who pioneered the American West and the horrible laws and acts of violence they had to endure. I was fascinated to learn about the concept of the "marginal man"—the person who straddled precariously between two cultures.

The required readings included textbooks by Harry Kitano and Derek and Stanley Sue, which I didn't enjoy. The psychobabble was foreign and dense. I did enjoy *Roots: An Asian American Reader*, an anthology published by the UCLA Asian American Studies Center; and a newspaper called *Gidra: The Monthly of the Asian American Experience*, published at the University of California at Los Angeles. *Roots*, with its iconic black-and-white cover caricaturing the American flag, was the Bible of the Asian American movement. *Gidra* was the era's underground newspaper.

Cynthia challenged the stereotype of Asian Americans as a model minority. She raved about Bruce Lee as a wonderful, assertive male figure. She also told the class she had just discovered a new stereotype that "Asians don't sweat." Laughing, she said there was conclusive evidence to the contrary. She was right. I sat near several guilty parties. To be safe, I doubled my morning application of Right Guard.

After I completed Cynthia's class, I purchased subscriptions to *Gidra* and *Amerasia Journal,* an academic journal which, like most Asian American literature of the era, came from the UCLA Asian American Studies Center.

Cynthia made me question the cartoon shows I grew up watching. Mr. Magoo had a buck-toothed Chinese houseboy named "Cholly" or Charlie, who spoke fake broken English. Quick Draw McGraw, a cartoon horse, had a sidekick named Baba Looey, who wore a sombrero and spoke with a heavy Mexican accent. *The Dick Tracy Show* featured Joe Jitsu, a Japanese policeman who bowed and apologized by saying "So solly"; and Go-Go Gomez, a Mexican with a big sombrero who napped in a hammock. African Americans were nearly always portrayed as buffoons—either slow-shuffling dimwits or jungle cannibals instantaneously aroused to dance by music.

My friend Steve Goon's mother gave him a copy of the 1950 *Better Homes and Gardens Story Book* featuring "The Story of Little Black Sambo," illustrated by Scottish author Helen Bannerman. He kept the book as a memento and didn't realize until years later that the portrayals in this popular children's fable were offensive.

For a brief time, I sported a "Yellow Peril" button on my

jacket. I wore it as an expression of rebellion against the historical scapegoating of Asian Americans.

After a year at Seattle Central, I left with a much broader knowledge of who I was, the beginnings of a political awareness and a bolstered confidence in my study skills. But I still had no idea what kind of degree I wanted to pursue or what I wanted to do after college. I figured that would come later, after I entered the University of Washington.

CHAPTER 16

The University of Washington

THE COST OF TUITION AT the University of Washington was $144 a quarter. This was a lot of money in 1972. My father was taking in a full-time annual salary of $3,000 at the restaurant and my mother was earning less than $7,000 at two sewing jobs. My parents tucked away a little bit at a time, waiting for the day when Tom, Harvey and I would go to college. Some cash went into the bank; some was hidden in corners of the closet and dresser.

To save money, my parents wore the same clothes year after year until they became threadbare, at which point they were cut up and used as rags for cleaning windows, floors and the bathroom. They wore their Chinese household slippers until the soles couldn't be patched any more. The clothes we purchased for them every Mother's Day and Father's Day sat untouched in their original gift boxes.

My mother made jackets, pajamas, sweaters, pants and vests. She altered clothes that didn't fit us and patched holes in our pajamas. On weekends, she spent hours hunched over her Singer sewing machine in the living room. From my bedroom, I could hear the chugging and high-pitched whine of the stitching needle punching through cloth. She was surrounded by cardboard boxes filled with fabric, zippers and down fill scavenged from the sewing factory. She bought fabrics at markdown from Sears and JCPenney. A round, blue Dansk butter cookie tin held spools of thread, needles, buttons and thimbles. As her vision deteriorated, she asked me to thread the sewing machine needles.

By the time I entered the UW, I was desperate to flee this cloistered world of frugality and poverty. I understood how Linda felt. I was suffocating.

The first time I visited the UW, I thought I had entered a forested retreat in another city. I was mesmerized by the stately old trees, giant rhododendrons, sweeping junipers, mature shrubbery and trailing ivy that decorated every winding pathway through the lush, green campus. I marveled at the older castle-like buildings with stone facades, leaded-glass windows and arched doorways. The cavernous Suzzallo Library felt like a holy space, a temple of knowledge dwarfing anything the Seattle Public Library might ever offer me.

I lingered outside Smith Hall, along the Quad (Liberal Arts Quadrangle). I sat on the lawn and enjoyed the beautiful canopy of pink blossoms bursting from the branches of the famous Yoshino cherry trees in the spring. The Quad includes a large, grassy courtyard criss-crossed with red brick paths. I took my favorite history and liberal arts courses there.

Although I felt liberated being at the UW, I struggled. I knew only a few other students, and none of them shared classes with me. I receded into my quiet shell. I couldn't keep up with the outsized reading demands, even with the assistance of lecture notes.

By my second year at the UW, I had moved into an old brick apartment building at 4203 Brooklyn Avenue N.E., a few blocks off campus. I lived in unit 100, in the basement. The rent was modest—only $90 a month—and the location was ideal. But the apartment was unclean, dank and dark. The carpet was moldy. Silverfish and spiders inhabited crevices. The mattress was heavily stained with blood. I studied in the cafeteria at the Husky Union Building, commonly referred to as the HUB, or in the Suzzallo Library, under one of the magnificent vaulted ceilings. I returned to the apartment only to sleep.

In 1974, my junior year, I moved to another apartment, at 4337 ½ University Way N.E., next door to the Varsity Theater. It was up a flight of steps. I stayed for a year. I regretted the move. Although the Washington Book Store and University Book Store were just outside my door, my living space was run-down, the toilet often didn't work and the hallway was thick with the pungent odor of marijuana. The other tenants were hard-core stoners. Raucous banter and teeth-rattling rock music thundered through my walls all night. I barely slept.

One bright spring morning, right after my clock radio alarm woke me up to Minnie Riperton singing her high-pitched pop hit "Lovin' You," the phone rang. It was Marilyn Tokuda. She was one of the few Franklin High classmates I kept in touch with at the UW. "I'm in the neighborhood," she cheerfully announced. "Can I come by?" She had never seen my apartment. I told her no. I was embarrassed that my place was cramped and filthy, but she insisted. When she arrived, she sat on my lumpy bed—I didn't have a single chair—and we talked. I wanted to become a writer and she longed to become an actress. She told me she had to move to California to pursue her dream. I told her I planned to stay in Seattle. She promised to write. I did, too.

I felt fortunate to be at the UW, not fighting in Vietnam. A student deferment allowed me to escape the draft. Public opposition to the war had become fierce. No one could explain why we were in a country that most Americans couldn't even identify on a world map. But President Nixon, despite a campaign pledge to end the war, couldn't craft a politically viable exit strategy, and the U.S. troop presence continued.

During my senior year at Franklin, I had registered for the draft as all young men turning 18 were required to do. On May 24, 1971, I went down to Local Board No. 5 of the Selective Service in the Federal Office Building in downtown Seattle and filled out paperwork to get my registration certificate. On August 24, I was issued a Notice of Classification certifying me as 1-A, which meant I was available for military service. By law, I was required to keep the registration certificate and classification notice in my "personal possession at all times."

By 1972, my name was entered into a new pool of potential inductees. A lottery was held to determine who might have to go to Vietnam. I watched it on TV in the basement of the HUB. Undergraduates packed the room. The volume was turned way up. One by one, 365 pieces of paper, each corresponding to a day of the year, were plucked out of a glass jar and read aloud.

As students heard their draft numbers, they reacted by groaning, cursing or cheering. The crowd thinned. I nudged closer to the TV. Finally, I heard my birthday, May 17. It was a high number: 273. I was safe. I could stay at the UW. On July 12, 1972, I was issued a new classification card. I was now 1-H, which meant I was "not currently subject to processing for induction."

During the lottery, my mother was at the sewing factory. She knelt by her machine, praying to *Kwan Yin*, the Goddess of Mercy, that I would get a high number. My father watched the lottery on a small television in the Sampan Room at the Hong Kong Restaurant. Both were overjoyed when they heard my number. A year earlier, my brother Tom had been spared, too. His number was 327.

By the following year, an all-volunteer army had been created. My younger brother Harvey did not have to go to Vietnam either.

At the UW, conscientious objectors burned their draft cards in protest. This was against the law, but few were ever prosecuted. I never thought about joining them, despite my disapproval of the war. My family's immigration history was muddy. I didn't want to expose myself to scrutiny. I never went anywhere without my registration certificate and classification cards in my wallet. I carried them for well over 20 years after the war ended.

At the UW, I was drawn to the humanities. My courses included American literature, communications, creative writing, Eastern European history, Far Eastern history, American history, political science, women's studies, art history, astronomy and math.

In the winter quarter of 1972, I took an English class from a heavily bearded white instructor who dressed in a plaid flannel shirt, tattered jeans and hiking boots. He looked like a hippie. At the beginning of each class, we arranged the chairs into a circle. He railed against the Establishment. Our sole text was *The Movement Toward A New America: The Beginnings of a Long Revolution*, a 752-page anthology of 1960s counterculture prose collected by Mitchell Goodman. We read selections from the book and kept a journal. We wrote whatever we wanted to, in whatever form we liked. We turned in our journals every couple of weeks. The instructor scribbled a few light comments in the margins. He said he expected all his students to earn A's.

I didn't say much in class, but I wrote in my journal every day. I began crafting a play about a star-crossed young man and woman from two different worlds, barred from marrying. In a dark twist, she kills him because she can't accept this reality. After the class ended, I continued my journal. I jotted down random thoughts, stories about my parents and accounts of community events—whatever came to mind. It calmed me. Writing was like crouching near a big reflecting pond, idly tossing pebbles into the water and watching the ripples swell and ebb. I kept up my journal for 12 years.

While at UW, I continued working at the Hong Kong Restaurant, but I felt increasingly out of place. The work was a mindless grind, and I faced sporadic episodes with redneck customers who treated the Chinese waiters and busboys as faceless underlings they could order around.

On several occasions, I heard a patron call a waiter called "Charlie." There was no one at the restaurant with that name. I heard one white customer order one of the middle-aged waiters, "Get me some more tea, boy!" Another bellowed, "What's taking so long with my order, boy?" One drunken patron, impatient for his meal, yelled out, "Where's my food? Doesn't anyone here understand English?" These words, spoken like demeaning commands to a servant, made me tremble with fury. Only when customers became belligerent or a physical threat to others would they be directly challenged and asked to leave.

During the summer of 1974, I was clearing a round table on the second floor when a sun-burnt white woman in sunglasses at a nearby table waved me over: "Young man—could you come here?" There were eight others in her party. She got up from her seat, snatched me by the arm and drew me closer. She handed me her fortune cookie slip and asked, "Can you read this for me? I don't know how to read Chinese." I looked at the fortune. It was written in English. I was puzzled. *What did she want? Was this some kind of test?* I paused. Everyone at the table waited. Finally, I read the fortune aloud: "You will meet happiness in matrimony." I was met with, "Hey, he speaks English better than you do." Everyone roared in amusement. I turned and walked stiffly away. I cursed under my breath. I couldn't wait to get off work.

Despite these affronts, I continued at the restaurant because it gave me long spells with my father. I watched him proudly go about his work. It saddened me to watch him age. The creases in his jawline deepened. His eyes grew bloodshot. His back became stooped, and his step got slower and unsteady. I held my breath when I saw him carry a loaded serving tray over his shoulder, afraid that he might accidentally slip or collapse. At home, he asked me to put eye drops in both eyes while he propped his head backward on the sofa. Every winter, he caught a severe cold. His loud, phlegm-laden hacking cough lingered until spring. His gout worsened. At night, I heard him cry out in pain from his bedroom when his big toe brushed against the bedsheets. I worried he might suddenly die.

I ached with guilt at having the luxury to dawdle with intellectual pursuits at the University of Washington while my father and mother continued to toil as manual laborers during their senior years. It didn't seem right or fair. They had taken care of me. *Who would take care of them?*

Some of my UW friends stopped by the restaurant after the dinner rush to ask me for editing help. They knew I was at the *UW Daily,* the student newspaper.

Marilyn Tokuda came often. Her dad ran Tokuda Drugs, a popular neighborhood pharmacy on Yesler Way. The soda fountain attracted young people from nearby Washington Junior High. They came for soft drinks, ice cream and comic books. The business later moved to the International District, where it continued until 2005.

Marilyn asked me to edit her paper comparing the viewpoints of three writers on the topic of revolution: Jean-Paul Marat, Frantz Fannon and Jacques Roux. I made a few changes, then complimented her. "By the way, would you be interested in writing for the *UW Daily*?" I asked. "Maybe you could review plays." She smiled broadly but brushed me off. She wanted to become a Hollywood star.

Marilyn left for Los Angeles after graduation. She wrote to me about her tour with popular country music singer Mac Davis. In a January 1976 letter, she wrote, "You have great talent. It would be a shame not to be able to use it to its fullest. Who knows, some day you may even make it down to California where you can join the rest of us starving, absolutely insane, zany artists. It's tough, but so far I'm surviving." In another letter, she told me that Ken Mochizuki, a mutual friend from Seattle's Beacon Hill, had moved in as a roommate. He too was seeking to break into acting. I met Ken after he returned to Seattle, disillusioned by the dearth of roles for Asian American male actors.

DeAnne, a slender, soft-spoken woman with a tight-cropped Afro, also came to see me several times at the restaurant. She wanted to write for the *UW Daily*, but she abhorred the cliquishness and egotism of some white reporters. She was from Inglewood, California. She spoke often about her mother, whom she adored. I supported her efforts to become a writer, and she backed me after I filed a discrimination complaint against the *UW Daily* in 1975.

"Ron, to tell you the truth," she told me, looking at me fiercely in the eye, "I hate white people. I absolutely hate them and their attitude of superiority." I remember looking back at her and saying, "Uh, DeAnne, I think that's been established. How many times have you said that?" We laughed long and hard. She covered her mouth and giggled through both hands.

DeAnne came to the restaurant with handwritten drafts of news articles. We sat at one of the booths while I did my editing. She later wrote several articles for the *International Examiner*, where I had volunteered since 1975. After she graduated from the UW, she returned to California. In the summer of 1977, she traveled to Nigeria and Ghana. She began pondering an overseas journalism career after meeting a reporter for Radio Nigeria. She wrote to me in September, asking if I had been able to secure a full-time job at the *Examiner*. Unemployed and feeling out of place in Los Angeles, she wrote that she was "willing, very willing to return" to Seattle to work for me. I was sad that I had nothing to offer her.

Another student journalist I met through the *UW Daily* was Assunta Ng, an immigrant from Hong Kong. She came for college at the age of 19. I was amused that many people mispronounced her name as "nug" instead of "Eng." I admired her deft confidence and steely determination. In 1974, we teamed up to write a story exploring whether local gambling laws discriminated against Chinese and Filipino immigrants.

One day in the newsroom, a white reporter flippantly asked whether he should use the term "Red China" or "mainland China" in his story. He was a member of Young Americans for Freedom, a conservative youth action group. He said he preferred "Red China." It was apparent that he was trying to bait someone into an argument.

Assunta confronted him: "That's not right. You should use 'People's Republic of China.'"

"That's too long," he shot back.

"Well, I'm Chinese and I should know." She spoke in a

tone of annoyance, dismissively turning away from him after she spoke. She was cool and self-assured. I was proud that she spoke up.

The campus setting allowed me to meet Native Americans from outside Washington. I developed a warm relationship with Barbara Means, a deeply spiritual Teton Sioux (also known as Lakota) from Wounded Knee, South Dakota. Her cousin was Russell Means, the well-known American Indian Movement activist. She was enrolled in a Native American literature program. Over long lunches, we compared our respective cultural traditions, marveling at discovered similarities. Once, she picked me up in her old beater. The car radio was tuned to KAYO 1150, a country station. A surly redneck tune played. I wondered why she listened to that stuff, but I didn't ask. She probably would have been equally mystified over my preference for soul music. Barbara and I kept in touch for more than a decade, mostly through letters.

Barbara was steeped in the poetic stories of her grandmother, the last person in her tribe completely fluent in the Teton language. Barbara went on to become an author and storyteller. She advised best-selling author Ruth Bebee Hill, who wrote and published *Hanta Yo*, a wildly successful but controversial book tracing three generations of the Lakota tribe before the arrival of white settlers. Barbara worked as a consultant for a TV movie adaptation of the book.

At times, my personality felt splintered. My mind toggled between the vibrantly open cultural and political opportunities at the University of Washington and the rigid traditions of Chinatown and my upbringing. I didn't know where I belonged. I didn't know how to reconcile living in both.

One evening in June 1974, restless and blue, I felt an intense yearning to see my old high school. I drove down to Pay 'n Save on Rainier Avenue South, parked, then walked over to Franklin. This was my first visit back since graduation. I walked past the fence surrounding the playfield, track, tennis courts and bleachers. It was still light at 7:30 p.m. I saw a few students lingering, chatting and clowning around. I wondered if the term had ended.

I walked up the huge steps leading to the first floor of the school building. The door was ajar. As I stepped inside, my footsteps echoed loudly. I heard voices from downstairs. I walked past the administration office and up a familiar ramp leading to the library. I tried the library doors; they were locked. I wanted to see whether a few favorite titles were still on the shelves where I first found them. I continued up to the second floor, moving past the locker-lined hallway. I saw the bookroom, closed and sealed from human approach like an ancient Egyptian tomb full of treasures. Then I saw an African American cleaning woman wheeling a cart into a room not far from me. At first, she didn't see me. After catching her eye, I asked her, "Is school already out for this quarter?"

I startled her. She looked bewildered: "What are you doing here?"

"You see, I used to go to this school a long time ago," I said. "I just came back to see how the place has changed."

"How did you get in here?" she persisted. "All the doors are supposed to be locked."

"I came in the front. It's not locked."

She looked around the room she had begun cleaning, then turned back to me and said, "Today's the last day of school. And everyone's already gone. Did you want to see somebody?"

"No," I said quickly. "I just wanted to see the school again—maybe see if it's different in some ways, maybe see if it's changed."

"Well, I don't know how you got in, but you are not supposed to be in here. The janitors are down in the basement. You can go talk to them."

I thanked her and went immediately down to the first floor. I slipped out the same door I had come in. I walked slowly back to my car at Pay 'n Save and drove off. I didn't know what I had been looking for that day. Maybe I was hoping to make peace with some part of who I once was. Something deep in my gut had slipped out of alignment. I didn't know how to make things right. I wasn't sure where I was headed, but I wanted at least to affirm where I had come from.

I returned to Franklin very infrequently since that visit. The next time was for my 30th year class reunion. The following time was when I went with my son to explore the school as a possible choice for him; we decided Garfield High School was a better fit. The last time, in 2013, was to be inducted into the Franklin Alumni Association's Hall of Fame.

CHAPTER 17

Working as a Student Reporter

As a sophomore at UW, I took a news writing course from William F. Johnston, a balding man with a fringe of gray hair, black-framed glasses and a very wry sense of humor. He was a veteran journalist, having worked at the *Lewiston Tribune* in Idaho, the *Salt Lake City Tribune* and the Associated Press.

Johnston—students affectionately called him "B.J."—made writing fun and was great at teaching the essentials. He proselytized about news reporting as a noble career path. He infected me with his vision of an independent press as vital to the health of a democratic society. B.J. inspired me to become a journalist.

"Omit needless words," he would boom, a happy drill sergeant for the writing guidelines in Strunk and White's classic *Elements of Style.* He considered it the Bible of good writing. B.J. argued convincingly for using the active voice, writing with clarity and precision and properly attributing quotes and sources. He believed in journalistic objectivity.

I found my life's calling. Although B.J. tore apart my copy—as he did with all the students—I took it as good medicine. He helped me master the basics of interviewing, note-taking and news style. I learned how to listen and how to write simply and rapidly. I learned how to be open to criticism. I learned how to edit my own writing.

I applied what I learned in B.J.'s class at the *UW Daily*, where I became a regular freelance reporter. For the first time in my life, I got paid to do something that I loved. I received $20 or $30 per article. It supplemented my modest wages from the restaurant.

I spent more time at the *Daily* than I did in class. My childhood friend Dean Wong, who had also entered the communications school, reminded me of this when he came looking for me there. His passion was photography; mine was reporting. Dean had shoulder-length hair, parted in the middle, Prince Valiant style. He wore a dark green leather jacket, bell-bottom jeans and platform shoes. He carried a yellow Adidas shoulder bag with a pair of nunchaku (or nunchuck) sticks tucked inside. He purchased a set of nunchucks through a mail-order catalog, then learned to fashion his own from pieces of a broom handle and metal chain. Dean didn't say much. His large saucer eyes did most of the talking for him. He carried his sister Jeannie's Nikon camera, snapping photos of Chinatown and community events.

Dean grew up with his family in Chinatown in a cramped apartment near Eighth Avenue South and South King Street. They moved to Beacon Hill when he was in the eighth grade. While we were at the UW, he gave me a lift back to Beacon Hill in his blue, vinyl-topped 1967 Pontiac Firebird. We joked about both getting cast off plastic army men as toys from Sam Yee's family.

I scurried around campus, my skinny reporter's notebook tucked under my arm, returning to the *Daily* office just before nightfall to hammer out articles on a manual typewriter. I worked on two or three stories at the same time. I drank up to 12 cups of black coffee a day and ate packaged cherry pies from vending machines. For dinner, I bought a plain hamburger and an order of french fries to end my day.

What saved me were the Chinese meals my mother prepared when I came home on Sundays for dinner. She cut up extra pieces of boiled chicken, pork and fried shrimp and packed them in recycled Chinese restaurant take-out boxes for me to carry back to my apartment. She forced me to take more than I could ever finish by myself, so I shared this food with friends who lived near campus.

For other Chinese fare, I went to Lun Ting (蘭亭) Restaurant at 4318 University Way N.E. Its *chop suey*-style combos were much tastier and nutritious than the food on campus. The same Chin family who owned the Wa Sang Company grocery (華生) in Chinatown also operated this restaurant.

It was a grand time to become a journalist. During the Watergate scandal, *Washington Post* reporters Bob Woodward and Carl Bernstein had injected a dose of edgy excitement and heroism into a profession that had been regarded as boring, removed and mundane. I saw how reporters could be watchdogs against corruption and feisty champions for social justice.

My first article for the *UW Daily* appeared on November 1, 1973. It described a lecture by Stanley Sue, UW assistant professor of psychology, at the Wing Luke Museum.

Another early story was an interview of Marilyn Tokuda. She talked about chasing opportunities in a profession in which "the white actors have control of about 100 percent of the roles." In 1972, Marilyn produced *The Marginal Man*, a play about the history of racism against Chinese, Japanese and Filipino Americans. She achieved notoriety as the "Renton Mazda girl" in a frequently aired TV ad. "Come to Renton Mazda," Marilyn says, smiling into the camera, "and you'll be treated right." Raising her right hand, she adds, "I promise."

I wrote about a controversial new gadget on campus in the November 21, 1973, *Daily*. The headline read, "Pocket calculators: buying easier studies." I reported that some instructors wanted calculators banned from classrooms. The story included a quote from my friend Keith Wong, a senior in business: "In my opinion, it's okay for homework. Basically, it's no worse than paying someone to type your term paper. You're still doing the important part of the homework yourself, but it's faster."

I reconnected with my Vietnamese friend from Seattle Central Community College, Do Van Du. He was studying architecture at the UW. In the summer of 1972, he had returned to Vietnam to visit orphanages in Gia Định and Vũng Tàu. He was moved by the plight of children disfigured, blinded and crippled by war. During the winter of 1974, he was Northwest regional director of Aid to the Children of Vietnam, a humanitarian relief group with branches in France and the U.S. He sold Vietnamese Christmas cards to raise funds to help the estimated 500,000 homeless children. I wrote several stories to support his efforts.

By 1975, I was covering major front-page news stories. Chicano grievances with the University over hiring policies had triggered the resignation of Chicano faculty and staff and a student-led demonstration in Red Square which attracted 2,000 participants. Popular jazz instructor Joe Brazil filed suit against the music school over its refusal to offer him tenure. African American dental student Calvin Goines challenged his dismissal from the school, charging the dean with racism.

I interviewed several national activists and newsmakers, including actress Jane Fonda and her antiwar activist husband Tom Hayden; Ken Kesey, author of *One Flew Over the Cuckoo's Nest*; and presidential candidate Eugene McCarthy.

Campus organizers alerted me to major events in advance. One very good friend was an older white woman with long, flowing brown hair. She wore a colorful muumuu and suede Birkenstocks. She called herself Cassandra—no last name. She told me she was from Honolulu. She served as head of the UW Women's Commission and was elected ASUW President. I wondered if she ever attended any classes. All she seemed to do was plan events. She said she was a songwriter and an un-published author. One story was about a 13-year-old girl who was "sent off in mysterious circumstances to find out who her parents are, in a country overrun by magic."

In the fall of 1971, Cassandra decided to name the UW central quadrangle "Red Square" because she felt it looked as dreary as its counterpart near the Russian Kremlin. At the time, she was managing editor at the *Daily*. So she changed "new quad" to "Red Square" in all the stories that crossed her desk. After *Seattle Times* education reporter Julie Emery began using "Red Square," the new term stuck.

When Jane Fonda and Tom Hayden visited the UW in January 1975 to promote their new antiwar film, I was assigned to the story. Though some considered her a traitor, Fonda was a popular figure on college campuses. Hayden had achieved notoriety as a member of the Chicago Seven, a group of young radicals tried by the government on charges of inciting vio-lent protests at the 1968 Democratic Convention. Fonda and Hayden were an unlikely couple.

In 1972, Fonda visited North Vietnam and, in a famous radio interview, urged U.S. troops to cease the illegal bombing of Hanoi, the capital. Two years later, she and Hayden toured Vietnam with a camera crew, producing the documentary, *Introduction to the Enemy*, with director Haskell Wexler.

On December 17, 1974, I attended a preview showing at the Movie House, a tiny, old theater on N.E. 50th Street and University Way N.E. It later became Grand Illusion Cinema. Before the documentary began, an older gentleman tapped me on the shoulder from behind. He introduced himself as Paul Dietrichson, a philosophy professor. He told me he was very moved by my *UW Daily* articles on the struggle of Chicano farmworkers. He thanked me for writing the stories. I was touched and surprised. I naively assumed that UW professors didn't read the *Daily*.

Introduction to the Enemy was shown at Hec Edmundson Pavilion (Hec Ed). Nearly 4,000 people came. UW history professor Giovanni Costigan introduced the program. I set up shop at a typewriter in a back room where Hayden waited before going out on stage to speak. He had a serious demeanor, long hair and a craggy face. We both wore the exact same green army jacket, standard issue for student demonstrators.

I was hoping to interview him. But his schedule was too tight. We shook hands and exchanged a few words. When the event ended, I grabbed my jacket from a rolling metal coat stand and returned to my apartment, not realizing until the next morning that I had grabbed the wrong coat. It had the musty aroma of a stranger's sweat. Hayden had my jacket and I had his. His name was written on an inside label. The pockets had a few random receipts and a pen. I was miffed because I had left an old pair of glasses in my coat. Hayden had already flown out of town.

Through an intermediary, Jeff Dowd, we agreed that Hayden would keep my jacket and I would keep his. I chuckled to myself when I later saw Hayden in a television interview dressed in my army jacket. I had first met Dowd through *UW Daily* editor Dean Paton. Dowd was a member of the radical Seattle Liberation Front and one of the Seattle Seven, a group of leaders arrested and jailed following a violent demonstration at the federal courthouse in downtown Seattle on February 17, 1970. Dowd later moved to Los Angeles and became an independent movie producer.

The day after the documentary screening, I interviewed Fonda in the basement of the Masonic Temple. I was nervous. She was a famous movie star. She had won an Academy Award for her role in the crime thriller *Klute*. I was pleasantly surprised to find that she was modest and approachable. She was taller and thinner than I had imagined, casually dressed in a gray, ribbed sweater and jeans, her hair styled in a shag. Unadorned by make-up, she looked very tired. For about half an hour, we drank coffee together at a long, bare table and chatted about her film and her unlikely transformation into an outspoken antiwar activist.

In February 1975, I met Oregon author Ken Kesey. He was in town to speak at the UW on the topic "Finding Community in an Urban Environment." I went with the event organizers to pick him up at the airport. Kesey was a balding blonde hulk of a man with mutton-chop sideburns. He wore purple pants and tennis shoes. He was a bundle of wild, joyous energy, embellishing his responses to all my questions with zany quips. He rolled a joint and smoked, pointing to different signs along the highway and laughing heartily during the entire trip.

I wasn't sure when he was being serious and when he was just talking nonsense. He explained to me that he was coming to talk about "Egyptians, Venutians and Washingtonians." He told me he had been thinking about opening a beer bar that would cater to people from all walks of life, including loggers and statesmen. It would be a combined bookstore and day care center. "People want to drink and get down to it and talk to friends," he said. "This would be in keeping with the agony this nation is facing. This would be a back off from the speed vibes of the '40s that we're still hooked to."

He talked politics. He said he was optimistic: "I mean, shit, man...we've made tremendous progress in the last 10 years. We brought a President down."

"If you take the Constitution or the Bill of Rights as a revolutionary mandate, as a guardian—not just the words, but the spirit—and travel around the country putting your energy into righting the wrongs—it could be as 'in' as the peppermint twist."

He raved about listener-supported, noncommercial radio, extolling the virtues of the KRAB 107.7 FM station in Seattle. "It will always have patches on its knees and cornflakes in the side of the mouth. As long as you're scuffing, you know you're alive." He added as an afterthought: "If it does not survive, we'll plant a bomb in the Space Needle. How's that?"

I smiled. My mother was a faithful KRAB listener. She tuned into *Cantonese Time*, a weekly smorgasbord of news and popular music produced by UW students from Hong Kong who called themselves the Chinese Media Committee. My mother and her friends complained that the program was sympathetic to the Communist regime in China, but they never stopped listening.

The car detoured at a small diner in Ballard where Kesey met a few buddies. They handed him several small wrapped bundles; I assumed they contained pot or psychedelic drugs. We then headed over to the UW. I was dropped off at the *Daily*, where I feverishly went to work on my article. I finished it in less than 30 minutes. The editors wanted to include it in the next day's paper.

In April 1975, Presidential hopeful Eugene McCarthy arrived on campus to speak at a panel. He had vied unsuccessfully for the Democratic nomination in 1968 as a peace candidate. After another futile effort in 1972, he left the Democratic Party. He was gearing up to run as an independent in the next Presidential election. He still had a loyal following on campuses because of his reputation as a poet and witty intellectual. Many others had become disenchanted with him, perplexed by his decision to run again.

I rode with McCarthy to the airport following his presentation. I asked him about his candidacy. "I have unfinished business left over from 1968," he told me. "Once you become involved in politics, you feel you have to play it out to the end." He didn't explain. I didn't press him. I wondered if his heart was really in the race after so many failed attempts.

I distinctly recall the encounter with McCarthy because I had forgotten to bring something to write with. Halfway into my interview, I finally mustered the courage to sheepishly ask him, "Do you have a pen or pencil I can borrow?" He pulled a pen from an inside pocket and gave it to me. I began to scribble notes, but I lost some beautiful quotes about his poetry and his literary perspective that I might have included in my article. We arrived at the airport before I could re-ask my questions.

In 1975, I interviewed Peng Ming-min, a leading advocate of democracy in Taiwan. He was living in exile in the United States after being jailed for sedition by President Chiang Kai-shek. Through Peng, I discovered a political perspective that ran counter to the viewpoint of most of the overseas Chinese Americans in Seattle. Leaders like Ruby Chow favored Chiang's goal of reuniting Taiwan and China under the Nationalist banner. In 1996, Peng would return to Taiwan to become the Democratic Progressive Party's first presidential candidate, continuing his fight for Taiwanese independence.

The one political figure who enthralled me was Cesar Chávez, head of the United Farm Workers Union (UFW). I had written several stories about the Union's national boycotts of non-union head lettuce, grapes and Gallo wine. I wore a "Boycott Lettuce" button with the signature black Aztec eagle in the middle surrounded by a red border.

Chávez came to Seattle University in April 1975 to show-case *Fighting for Our Lives*, a new hour-long documentary on the 1973 strike by southern California grape workers. Chávez, who helped establish the UFW in 1962, was using a national boycott to try to beat back efforts to destroy his union. I met him at the press conference. Chávez, a proponent of nonviolent protests, was on one of his periodic fasts. He was a very slight figure, dressed in a simple plaid shirt, khaki pants and boots. He exuded a deep sense of spirituality—and moral authority— that kept the room full of reporters and United Farm Workers supporters mesmerized and hushed. I, too, was in awe. Chávez shifted gracefully between English and Spanish.

While I was a student reporter, Norman Mailer, Hunter S. Thompson and Tom Wolfe—practitioners of what was dubbed the "new journalism"—were creating a stir by borrowing liter-ary techniques from fiction to make reporting of current events more colorful and alive. Some of my *UW Daily* colleagues— more daring than I was—were tossing aside B.J.'s reporting edicts and testing these new approaches. I relished reading their articles, especially those of Tim Egan, the most gifted of my peers. Tim went on to write for *The New York Times* and become a celebrated author.

In my own reporting, I gravitated toward the spartan, unpretentious style I first learned from B.J. His lessons—and the lean prose of Hemingway and Steinbeck—better suited my temperament.

I had no majestic delusions about one day becoming a famed literary author. I just wanted to be a credible, competent journalist. I wanted to continue to highlight social justice concerns. I hoped to become skillful enough to reach folks who might not agree with me, but who would be open to my take on things. I still needed practice to get there.

CHAPTER 18

My Racial Discrimination Complaint

I N THE SPRING OF 1975, I applied for the position of *UW Daily* news editor for the coming fall term. This job involved assigning stories to reporters, editing copy and weighing in on story choices for each day's edition. I believed I was well qualified. I was one of the most seasoned staff members. I consistently turned in clean copy. During my three years, I wrote dozens of stories about topics on campus and in the community, many on very short deadlines. I often helped edit the articles of novice reporters and recruited minority students.

Looking ahead, I wanted to expand my repertoire of skills to prepare for a career beyond just reporting. I saw other minority students contribute stories for a term or two, then vanish from the newsroom without ever rising to positions of greater responsibility and higher pay. I didn't want that fate.

Over the summer, I waited to be contacted about my application. By tradition, the editor-in-chief selected the news editor and other members of the editorial team. That person was Larry Maloney. He had been appointed by the Board of Student

Publications. But I found out through others that Larry had already offered the news editor position to others who hadn't applied for the job. I was furious. I thought that I deserved at least the courtesy of an interview.

I filed a discrimination complaint on July 15, 1975 with the UW Staff Human Rights Office. In my letter, I explained what had happened, adding, "Minorities on the whole begin as reporters and end as reporters, without achieving the upward advancement to editorial positions many whites achieve."

My complaint was assigned to an investigator, Julie Herak, who conducted 23 interviews and reviewed *UW Daily* and university policies. She issued a report on January 23, 1976, supporting my allegations. She concluded that I was qualified for the position, but that "four persons, all white and all of whom did not apply for the position, were contacted to determine if they were interested in the position." She also found that "a white woman who had not applied for the position, and in fact, had specifically requested that she not be considered for an editorial position, was hired."

In a February 9, 1976, memo to the University, Herak pointed out that the *UW Daily* didn't have hiring guidelines, job descriptions or minimum qualifications and that there were no procedures "to assure all applicants equal consideration for the editorial staff positions." She noted that "only one minority" had achieved any of the top four editorial positions—editor-in-chief, news editor, night editor and managing editor—since the 1973 academic term.

She recommended back pay, establishment of job descriptions and qualifications, hiring guidelines, and diversification of the Board of Student Publications to address the lack of representation of women and minorities at the *Daily*.

I felt vindicated.

The Board of Student Publications immediately pushed back against the UW Staff Human Rights Office findings. It adopted a resolution stating that "the report as rendered is invalid and the process by which it was written is grievously faulty and unprofessional." The board delivered a letter to UW President John Hogness urging him to reject the settlement.

I was flabbergasted. The board hadn't even read the report or spoken to me. The members did speak with Maloney though. One of three board members who had not been present when the board voted—an African American and the only person of color on the board—criticized the resolution, calling it a "hasty and ill-informed response."

I pressed for an opportunity to speak. During a four-and-a-half-hour meeting, I finally had my chance. I told the board that my complaint had not been predicated on the question of whether Larry Maloney was a racist. "The system is what discriminates," I said, "and if the board does not recognize this—does not take steps to rectify this—there will be minority persons after me who will not be as patient as I have been."

Mayumi Tsutakawa, a communications graduate student at the UW, offered me help. She was not timid. She had chaired the UW Asian Student Coalition and had demonstrated against the construction of the Kingdome in Chinatown. She was a founding member of an Asian American arts collective called Cicada in a tiny storefront in the Bush Hotel at 623 South Jackson Street. Mayumi's father was the internationally renowned sculptor and painter George Tsutakawa.

Mayumi weighed in with a February 18 letter to President Hogness. She said she had been on the Board of Student Publications the previous year when Maloney had been selected editor-in-chief. At the time, she wrote, "Only one other minority person, also a female, sat on the nine-member board. Suffice it to say that our views were clearly overbalanced by those of the seven white, male members of the board." She argued that "minority writers who have persevered and attempted to continue to report minority news have not been rewarded."

My challenge was covered at length by the *UW Daily* as well as *The Seattle Times*, the *Seattle P-I* and local TV stations. My name and face were attached to this news story for two long years. Critics branded me a malcontent who was unqualified for the job. One former editor and frequent *UW Daily* columnist warned that if the UW Staff Human Rights Office's recommendations were implemented, "the independence of any future *Daily* editor to choose and direct the paper's staff and determine its editorial policies will be in serious jeopardy."

Among my stern critics was Don Pember, a highly respected UW professor and a member of the Student Publications Board. He considered my legal challenge a threat to the First Amendment right to freedom of the press. He argued that affirmative action had no place in a free and unfettered newsroom. In a piece in *The Seattle Times*, he wrote, "Mistakes, including errors involving bias, should be placed on the shoulders of Board members. These mistakes then could be corrected four or five months later when a new editor is chosen."

My simple demand for fair treatment—the standard by which working journalists guided their own dealings with news sources—apparently didn't matter inside the profession. Pember's logic made no sense to me.

Pember's printed remarks sparked an indignant letter to Hogness from Terry Tafoya, president of Indians into Communications. His organization published *Northwest Indian News*. Tafoya was a former *UW Daily* staff member. Terry charged Pember with "trying to cloud the issues" by claiming that "affirmative action is in direct conflict with freedom of the press." "The right of minority people to freedom of expression is inherent in the freedom of the press," he countered. "We feel freedom of expression for minority people does not presently exist within the *Daily* structure."

Although the UW chapter of the Society of Professional Journalists and other individual *UW Daily* staff members wrote letters on my behalf, it was a lonely and emotionally draining battle. While I waited for my case to be settled, I continued to work as a *Daily* reporter. I tried to keep up a cheery front and ignore the side conversations of those who questioned my motives, but it took a toll.

Finally, Alvin Ulbrickson, Vice Provost for Student Affairs, conferred with the UW's senior assistant attorney general. They arrived at a settlement package which included $1,200 in back pay and directed the Student Publications Board to "remedy weaknesses in the *Daily's* hiring practices." I accepted the settlement after mulling it over for a day or two.

By then, I was eager to leave the university. I was still a few credits short of earning my bachelor's degree. Ironically, all I was lacking was a reporting requirement, which could have been fulfilled by interning at any number of local newspapers, including several throwaway shopping news publications. I had already been freelancing for the *International Examiner*. But the Communications Department said my work at the *Examiner* didn't count. It was only published twice a month and didn't make the list of sanctioned publications. I continued to take classes at the UW, hoping that this decision might change. It didn't.

My mother found out about my discrimination case from my father. She confronted me at home one weekend, asking why I hadn't told her. I didn't have a suitable answer. I remained silent. "I understand why you did this," she said. "I know about discrimination. That is the way it is in America. But the *bok gwee lo* (white devils 白鬼佬) have more power than you. Remember that they are going to find a way to attack you. You are not safe. I have been so worried that I can't sleep at night. You have to be very careful from now on."

She was probably right to be concerned. I received an anonymous hate-filled racist phone call at my campus apartment. I hung up right away. A stranger on a bus who had seen the news coverage of my case came up to me and asked if I was the one who had accused the *UW Daily* of racism. When I said I was, he began to lay into me with an expletive-laden rant. I quickly moved away and stepped off the bus.

My father didn't ask me many details about my case, but he told me he was proud of me for speaking up. On the weekends, when I was with him at the restaurant, he made a point of calling me over to introduce me to his regular customers. One was a ruddy-faced sports writer at *The Seattle Times*. "This is my boy Ronald," he said, placing one hand on my shoulder. "He's studying to be a newspaper reporter." His unconditional support kept me strong.

Around this time, I decided to leave the Hong Kong Restaurant. It wasn't the same place I knew from the old days. I didn't know whether this change in attitude was because of physical changes in the restaurant or because of the person I had become.

The veteran waiters like my father and *Ming-bok* were still there, but most of the younger men had moved on. The interior had been remodeled. A drop ceiling with nondescript recessed lights replaced the colorful neon dragon that had presided over the dining room for decades. The booths were freshly reupholstered. The round tables were outfitted with Lazy Susans. The waiters were issued new red uniforms. The glazed ceramic serving platters, plates, teapots, tea cups, saucers and other dishware were usurped by unbreakable synthetic tableware, including unadorned stainless-steel serving platters and teapots.

In August 1976, the restaurant hired a new 25-year-old chef from Hong Kong, Wing-kai Tse. *Dim sum* emerged as a new, trendy Chinese delicacy. Tse knew how to make over 100 different kinds of *dim sum*. He quickly set about expanding the menu of *dim sum* choices to 40. The restaurant morphed away from its original identity as an old-style *chop suey* house.

I was very hesitant to tell my father that I didn't want to work at the restaurant any more. I had been there for 10 years. It was the one place I could be with my father. He spent more time there than at home. I felt I had failed. I was leaving college without a degree. I didn't have another job lined up.

We were at the restaurant after most of the dinner customers left when I told him. We sat at a table on the second level, away from the front area where the other waiters lingered. I heard the clang of silverware against dishes and water glasses as an empty table was cleared. It was quiet otherwise. I told my father I had been at the restaurant for a very long time, since I was a child, and that the experience meant a lot to me. "But it's time for me to move on," I said. After I finished, he looked me straight in the eye, nodded his head, then smiled. He gently patted my hand. "I knew this day was coming," he said. "There's nothing for you here. This is my world. You go out and make your own."

I sighed deeply. I felt sad.

The UW and the restaurant vanished behind me like a puff of smoke. I had to make a new life.

I began to hunt for a full-time job. I applied for writing positions at *The Seattle Times*, the *Seattle P-I*, Metro Transit, the city of Seattle and King County. Nothing panned out. Without a degree—and having been cast as a troublemaker because of my discrimination complaint—I was not a very marketable job applicant, especially in a thriving profession that supplied an abundance of other well qualified, ready candidates for every job opening.

Still, I was more than a little surprised that no one wanted to interview me. I had been one of the most prolific reporters at the *UW Daily*. I had also produced stories for several other publications as well, including the *International Examiner* and *Northwest Access,* an independent tabloid produced by minority students. I had a huge portfolio filled with hundreds of printed articles, but it apparently wasn't enough to overcome my reputation as a troublemaker.

I had not thought about the power and reach of authority figures at the UW like Pember. I won my case, but speaking out negated all I had accomplished as a reporter in the eyes of prospective employers. I had backed myself into a corner. I didn't have a degree. My outspokenness cost me strong professional references. Backed into a corner, I watched my career aspirations crumble.

CHAPTER 19

The *International Examiner*

L EFT WITH LIMITED OPTIONS AFTER leaving the UW, I invested my workaholic habits and passion for writing into the *International Examiner*.

My first encounter with the *Examiner* was in 1975 when Mayumi Tsutakawa recruited me as a volunteer. At the time, I was reporting for *UW Daily*. "How would you like to do a story for this new newspaper in Chinatown?" she asked. "I think you know some of the activists who are involved in it. I've got a couple story ideas here, but, well, truthfully, you can write about whatever you like."

From among the sheaf of papers in her hands, I extracted a short press release about two Filipina nurses facing unfair deportation. Several Filipino activist organizations in China-town—a neighborhood that everyone now began calling the International District or the "ID" in recognition of its multi-ethnic character—had taken up their cause. The story caught my attention because it coupled my interest in social justice with writing hard news.

I interviewed Bob Yamagiwa, a legal services *pro bono* attorney representing the nurses, and Ben Rafanan and Zenaida Guerzon, two Filipino leaders at the International Drop-In Center (IDIC). This story drew me from campus straight back into the heart of the community I had known since childhood. But now I was rediscovering it through a new, mature set of eyes, armed with a budding political understanding born of my time on campus and my newly honed journalism skills.

My article appeared in the November 1975 edition of the *Examiner*. That edition included news about a protest over the lack of affordable housing, planning for a new children's park, construction of an information kiosk in Hing Hay Park and an art auction to support the Wing Luke Museum. There was a feature about the International District Emergency Center (IDEC) written by Donnie Chin. He explained that IDEC—supported with supplies from a "free people's health clinic" in the ID—was formed to provide swift emergency medical care "before trained units arrive," train Asian American youth in emergency services, teach them street survival skills, and offer in-depth tours of the neighborhood.

Under Mayumi's editorship, I discovered an intense emotional connection to my identity as an Asian American and a sense of purpose as a journalist. I became friends with Donnie Chin and other social service and housing activists. I embraced their causes. I felt I could make a difference.

The *Examiner* had been launched in June 1974 by Larry Imamura and Gerald Yuasa. Imamura, a native Seattleite, graduated with a degree in interior design from Washington State University. He opened an office furniture store in a former Safeway grocery at 409 Eighth Avenue South, on the corner of South Jackson Street. He used $5,000 of his own money to leverage a loan from Seafirst National Bank, now Bank of

America. Yuasa, originally from Spokane, was assistant branch manager at Seafirst's International District branch.

Both believed that a newspaper could help boost lagging commerce in the International District. Larry asked a friend he knew through the U.S. Army Reserve, George T. Cox, to manage the newspaper. The *Examiner's* first office was in the back of Imamura's store, Officemporium.

At the time, the neighborhood was in deep peril. In 1973, a giant concrete sports stadium called the Kingdome was built, driving property taxes skyward and forcing aging hotels to shut down. Public officials pitched other large-scale projects—including a multimodal transportation hub at Union Station, a King County work-release program at the Immigration and Naturalization Service building and a garbage-burning plant—without considering the cumulative impacts on the International District. Asian restaurants and mom-and-pop businesses faced loss of parking and ruinous traffic congestion.

As a nonprofit newspaper, the *Examiner* differed from the archetypal commercial newspapers I learned about in my communications classes. It highlighted concerns overlooked by the mainstream press. It wasn't afraid to take sides and advocate for the neighborhood. While the *Examiner* kept an eye to its finances, it wasn't ruled by big advertisers or moneyed interests.

In 1976 and 1977, I wrote several exposés on the sewing factories. From my mother, I knew that working conditions were abominable and that the two unions—the United Garment Workers Union and Upholsterers International—didn't support worker concerns. There was no Chinese interpretation, even though the majority of workers didn't speak English. At one meeting, the Chinese women didn't even know whether they were being asked to approve or reject a contract offer.

The unions were headquartered at the Labor Temple in

downtown Seattle. I went there to find answers. Their offices were in small rooms with dark oak doors with frosted glass. At the United Garment Workers Union, I asked an official how they planned to address the issues of non-English-speaking workers like my mother. He told me that that translation was unnecessary. As we spoke, an older white woman looked up from a stack of papers on her desk, frowned, then snarled, "Who are you? Who sent you here? Are you a Communist?" I reiterated that I was a reporter from the *International Examiner*. She told the other official that he shouldn't say anything more, then asked me to leave.

I was dismayed but not surprised that nearly a century after the Knights of Labor drove Chinese American workers from the city, union antipathy to immigrants still flourished in the Labor Temple in the heart of progressive Seattle. But now the Asian American community had a newspaper to say that some things were wrong.

My articles sparked a complaint to the National Labor Relations Board and an investigation by the Seattle Women's Commission. In September 1976, the United Garment Workers Union finally agreed to allocate $200 to translate its new three-year contract into Chinese. On November 14, the Chinese Information Center hosted the first ever conference of Chinese garment workers, gathering to discuss working conditions and legal issues.

At the end of 1976, Mayumi left to work as a feature writer and copy editor at *The Seattle Times*. She became the first Asian American woman reporter in a major metropolitan daily newspaper north of San Francisco. She stayed at *The Times* for six years.

I took over as *Examiner* editor. In the December 1976 edition, Mayumi bid farewell to readers. She offered a "New Year's toast to a better *Examiner*," adding that "donations for the Ron Chew aspirin and Alka Seltzer Fund" could be sent directly to the newspaper office.

By then, I accepted that I might never work in mainstream media because of my discrimination case at the UW and my lack of a college degree. At the *Examiner*, I could still live out my dream of becoming a reporter and editor, even if I didn't make money. I reasoned that headaches came with any job. I was cursed by migraine headaches anyway.

To support myself financially, I took on random side jobs such as monitoring parking lots in the International District and stapling and folding brochures in a print shop.

In 1977, I found a full-time job outside the *Examiner*. The Coalition for Quality Integrated Education (CQIE), a citizen's group supporting the voluntary desegregation efforts of the Seattle Public Schools, hired me to prepare *In Touch*, a tabloid disseminated to parents through the school district. I worked in an elementary school portable in Seattle's Wallingford neighborhood. In the February edition of the *Examiner*, Judi Nihei, editor of the "District Notes" column, crowed: "Truth is stranger than fiction! Ron Chew has finally gotten a job in his field!"

I asked friends—writers and graphic artists I knew from the *UW Daily* and the *Examiner*—to be my volunteer staff at *In Touch*. DeAnne, who had supported me throughout my discrimination ordeal, prepared a story about a conference at Garfield High School on youth who were developing their own curriculum. Evelyn Iritani wrote about the confusion and discontent spurred by the magnet school program. Barbara Means contributed a piece about the possible elimination of the Indian Heritage High School Program. I stayed at CQIE for six months before the grant supporting my position expired.

CHAPTER 20

Alaska Cannery Workers Association

WHEN I JOINED THE *EXAMINER* in 1975, the Alaska
Cannery Workers Association (ACWA), a legal
advocacy group formed by Asian American and
Native American cannery workers, had just taken over the
newspaper from Larry Imamura and Gerald Yuasa.

In March, Nemesio Domingo, Jr., ACWA director, bought
the *Examiner* for the token sum of one dollar. The newspaper
was moved across the street from Officemporium to the ACWA
office at 416 Eighth Avenue South. Nemesio put out a call for
volunteers to Mayumi and others at the UW communications
school. Mayumi then approached me.

ACWA's paramount goal was reform of the Alaska canneries. Asian Americans had been the backbone of the labor
force for generations. My grandfather and father worked there.
When Nemesio and his brother Silme went to Alaska, they
were horrified by the unsafe conditions, segregated bunkhouses
and job discrimination. They and other young coworkers filed
class-action lawsuits in 1973 against the biggest cannery firms

in Alaska: New England Fish Company (NEFCO), NEF-CO-Fidalgo, Wards Cove Packing Company, Columbia Wards Fisheries and Bumble Bee Seafoods.

Because they had been blacklisted from their union, Local 37 of the International Longshoremen and Warehousemen's Union (ILWU), Nemesio and Silme established the ACWA office in the ID to pursue their efforts. Working with attorneys, they took depositions from potential class-action members, including many Filipino old-timers in nearby hotels.

ACWA was inspired by Tyree Scott, an African American electrician. He founded the United Construction Workers Association (UCWA) in 1970 to challenge discrimination by local unions and establish apprenticeship and training programs for minorities. As a *UW Daily* reporter, I covered a UCWA press conference in February 1975. The UCWA had just shut down a national construction project on Rainier Avenue South and was demanding that work not begin again "until a majority of the workforce is composed of Third World workers."

At the UCWA event, I met Michael Woo, a square-jawed young organizer with Chinatown roots. His mother worked at the Tuck Shing Trading Company (德星公司) on South King Street; his father ran gambling establishments. I was surprised to find him working at a black organization. He worked at NEFCO with Nemesio and Silme Domingo, key plaintiffs in the ACWA lawsuits. Michael counseled them to follow the UCWA strategy of pursuing legal recourse through Title VII of the 1964 Civil Rights Act. He helped the Domingo brothers find the office on Eighth Avenue South.

With the *Examiner* headquartered at ACWA, I began working in the hub of the International District, interacting with dozens of young Asian American activists and learning about the neighborhood. The ID became my second home.

Next door, at 414 Eighth Avenue South, was the Wing Luke Museum. It was staffed by Peg Marshall, a weaver who devoted countless unpaid hours as director. Peg was tall and angular with a cheerful disposition. She had deep wrinkles on her face and hands and a sing-song voice. She came by often to chat. Just north of the museum was the Asahi Printing Company. The proprietor was Peter Ishigaki, a Japanese immigrant and Kendo enthusiast. He provided printing services in English and Japanese.

Immediately south of the ACWA office were the Locke Family Association (駱氏宗親會) and Hen Sen Herbs (天生藥行). In between was a door that led down into Bruce Lee's basement martial arts studio. The herbal shop was operated by Hen Sen Chin, a small man with a wise, knowing manner and an encyclopedic knowledge of Chinese medicine. He had been at the same corner since 1950, serving white patients desperate for medicinal alternatives after Western treatments had failed. On the fourth floor of the building was the headquarters of the Hip Sing Association (協勝公會), a Chinese tong.

In those days, I saw a lot of both Nemesio and Silme at ACWA. They darted in and out for meetings. The two were very different. Except for his corny jokes, Nemesio was business-like, solemn and methodical. He had a pile of wavy hair and looked geeky behind his big glasses. Silme, the younger brother, had long hair, dressed flamboyantly and laughed easily. Silme sometimes nodded off in the middle of a conversation, taking a quick nap slouched inside the storefront window.

Nemesio and two young women—Terri Mast and Julia Laranang—staffed the office. Silme recruited Julia to serve as the office manager after meeting her at a UW protest against martial law in the Philippines. Julia grew up in South Seattle. Both her father, Basilio Laranang, and stepfather, Monico Tugadi, worked in the Alaska canneries. From age 13, Julia participated in the Filipino Youth Activities Drill Team. She was steeped in community traditions.

Terri, a young white woman who worked as a cook in an Alaska cannery, joined the ACWA staff a short time later. Terri had been a shipping clerk at Seattle Art, a major art supply company in downtown Seattle. Terri was involved in the anti-martial law movement, helping silk-screen t-shirts and doing research for the lawsuits.

Nemesio served as "publisher's representative" for the *Examiner*. He watched over the paper's microscopic budget and doled out token checks of $10 to those who contributed articles, photos and art.

He was especially proud of the deal he had made to acquire the newspaper. "It was only a dollar," he would brag. But I reminded him that if Mayumi and I and others hadn't stepped forward, the paper wouldn't have had much of a future.

The work at the *Examiner* was much more demanding than at the *UW Daily*. I had to do everything: answer phones, attend community meetings, respond to letters, sell ads, find volunteers, assign and write stories, edit, proofread, design, paste up copy, and deliver newspapers. There was barely time to breathe. I skipped meals. I ignored my appearance. But I was making a lot of new friends. My work felt richly satisfying. Every small task had a purpose. I was learning. Maybe this was the career I had been preparing for all along.

Shortly after I became editor, Mrs. Nilson, my high school journalism teacher, mailed in a subscription to the *Examiner* along with a handwritten note congratulating me. It felt nice to be remembered, even though I hadn't been one of her stellar pupils. She remained a faithful subscriber.

I worked with Terri and Julia in the front area of the cold, dank ACWA office. Peering through the large glass storefront, I saw customers going in and out of the Four Seas Restaurant. I waved to those I knew. The ACWA folks called the Dynasty Room their "conference room." They went there for free ice water and maraschino cherries.

In the back, past a set of double doors, was a storage space with leftover newspapers, picket signs, old leaflets and an offset printing press. Upstairs was a partitioned mezzanine with a low ceiling. People crashed there for the night if they had too much to drink at the Dynasty Room or were visiting from Eastern Washington.

When toilets overflowed in the Don Hee Apartments above, our ceiling leaked. We positioned plastic waste baskets over half a dozen spots to keep water from soaking into the thin mildewed carpet. I wore a sweater and coat over a long-sleeved flannel shirt. Tim Otani, a UW student volunteer, traded jokes with me around the theme of "How cold is it today?" Even with the electric baseboard heaters cranked up, my puffs of breath were visible.

The ACWA office was the unofficial drop-in center and mail pick-up address for groups fighting against the Marcos dictatorship in the Philippines and for Women in Trades, which was battling gender discrimination at Seattle City Light. The Committee for Corrective Action and the International District Youth Council, both formed in the early 1970s after the Kingdome construction, received a steady trickle of mail, but they had disbanded before I began working there.

The office also served as headquarters for an International District farmers market, coordinated by Mark Della, a young activist. In the summer of 1976, ACWA created the program with funding from the Hunger Action Center. On Saturdays, Filipino farmers from Kent, Puyallup, South Seattle and Wapato sold fresh seasonal produce and fruit from parked trucks near Hing Hay Park.

One day, Julia found a note taped to the front door when she came to work. It was from "Friends of the Weather Underground." The note said there was a package behind the dumpster at the side of the building. The Weather Underground was a domestic terror group which planted bombs to express its opposition to the U.S. government. Alarmed, she waited for Silme and Gene Viernes. They went to check, retrieving a stack of the group's newspapers. Curiously, a local radio reporter called the office later to inquire about the incident. Julia wondered: *How did he find out?* No one from ACWA had told him.

When the Asian Multi-Media Center closed in 1979, ACWA stored the group's equipment. The center, located in a second-story office building on Rainier Avenue South, had provided workshops in photography, silk screening, drama and graphic design since 1973.

At ACWA, I met Gene, a self-described "Wapato farm boy." He was a plaintiff. He saw me working with my knitted gloves on. He shook his head, asking wryly, "Gosh, Ron Chew! How can you type?" He brought in a long portable space heater and placed it at my feet. Right away we became friends. We were both history geeks and straight-laced hicks—he from the countryside and me from Beacon Hill. He swooned over—and briefly dated—a Filipina immigrant named Aurora from urban Manila who mended his torn jeans. They broke up after he learned that big city and rural values don't mix well.

I always felt closer to Gene than to Silme. By nature, Gene and I were both introverts who liked observing people from afar and carefully analyzing situations. Silme gravitated toward the limelight. Silme was cool. He wore tinted sunglasses, leather jacket, tight bell bottoms and platform shoes. His hair was stylishly cut to shoulder-length, covering his ears and swept neatly across the forehead. He looked ready to go out and party.

Gene was raised in the tiny farming town of Parker, four miles north of Wapato. Silme was born and raised in Killeen, Texas. He attended Ballard High School in Seattle's North End. I didn't know where any of these places were, including Ballard, which I had never visited.

Even though Gene was quiet, he was high-strung. He did handstands and cartwheels in the office. He was explosively strong, the result of manual labor. During high school, he loaded vegetables and fruit in warehouses onto semi-trucks. He also picked vegetables in the field. The summer before he began working in Alaska, he rose early to ride his bike five to six miles daily each way to work at one of his uncles' farms. He had not yet started 10th grade.

Gene often looked as if he had dashed out of the shower without bothering to dry or comb his hair. He wore a white painter's cap, a faded jean jacket or torn sweatshirt, and jeans with holes in the knees. His clothes looked like discards from friends. He hated dressing up. I did, too. Gene griped about people he regarded as money-oriented—"too bourgie." In 1980, during the inauguration party at the Seattle Hilton for the newly elected board of the cannery union, Gene borrowed a sport coat and a pair of slacks. He complained that he looked like "an ice cream cone."

Gene showed me some wrestling holds, impressing me with his quickness and dexterity. He competed on his college wrestling team. I had participated in intramural wrestling at Franklin. We both took up running. Like Dean Wong, Gene had a set of nunchaku sticks, which he twirled rapidly in the air, then seized under his armpits. Gene produced ear-splitting belches to shatter the stillness of the office and lighten the mood. He and Julia erupted into hilarious make-believe monologues in the broken-English accent of the *manongs*. They sounded just like the old Filipino men.

I encouraged Gene to write a seven-part series on the history of Asian laborers in the Alaska canneries. It appeared in the *Examiner* in 1977. We received many requests for back issues of that series. Under my gentle coaxing, Gene became a regular writer for the paper.

Gene began expanding his series into a book. I agreed to be his editor. In one scribbled note, Gene told me he wanted to include recent photos "embodying the humanness, deepness of Filipino personalities and life experiences." He began writing a preface and introduction, but stopped after he realized that he didn't know the difference between the two. I confessed that I didn't know either. The project waited for a time when we could apply ourselves to the project. We were both very busy. That time never came.

Silme and Gene emerged as natural leaders within the clique of college-educated activists who migrated to the International District. They were the first to offer opinions. Silme talked people over to his side, using logic, wit, charm and doggedness. He was a great storyteller. Gene won people over by referencing history. He walked around with a stack of dog-eared books under his arm, an eclectic mix of Asian American titles and obscure local publications.

In those days, I did my newspaper work on a small, brown manual typewriter with mechanical keys. It had a red-and-black ribbon and a carriage that rose and groaned loudly when I typed capital letters. I edited with pen and pencil. The revised copy was taken to Franklin Press on Capitol Hill to be retyped on a phototypesetting machine that spun out long strips of type for layout. The *Examiner* was the first ethnic newspaper in the region to adopt this "modern" technology. There was one big drawback. If there was a mistake, everything had to be retyped.

The strips of type were cut up with X-Acto knives and pasted onto layout sheets with wax. This painstaking process required a sharp eye and a steady hand. Even though I consumed five to eight cups of black coffee a day, I never had a problem pasting in the tiniest of corrections, including single lines of 8-point type. Coffee made my heart race, but it didn't make my hands tremble.

The owner of Franklin Press, Jim Behrend, a bearded, ruddy-faced, fiercely partisan Democrat with workaholic tendencies, taught Mayumi and a few others of us from the *Examiner* the rudiments of newspaper layout. Mayumi asked Jim if we should use a different typeface for each headline. A polite German gentleman, he just said, 'Yah, you could do that, but it would be a little wild-looking.'"

The *Seattle Sun*, an alternative weekly founded by Nick Licata (later elected to the Seattle City Council), and *Seattle Gay News*, one of the oldest gay publications in the U.S., also assembled their publications at Franklin Press.

After a few years, Jim entrusted me with a key to the shop. On some mornings, I arrived to find him sleeping on the floor next to the printing press, snoring, curled up under a threadbare blanket after working all hours to meet an impossible delivery deadline for campaign fliers. I took care not to wake him as I looked for a place to begin my work.

But it wasn't Jim Behrend who shepherded the *Examiner* into the computer era. It was Greg Tuai, a Franklin High graduate who had returned from Yale University, where he had studied bioengineering. He looked at the manual typewriters and shook his head. "These are obsolete," he pronounced. At a liquidation sale, Greg found some computers made by Morrow, one of the first computer manufacturers. The computers used 5 ½" floppy disks. He donated the computers to the *Examiner*, setting us up on what Greg described as a "thoroughly user-hostile word processing program" called WordStar. We tiptoed into the 21st century.

Ironically, Greg's father Liem Tuai, a former Seattle city council member who ran unsuccessfully for Mayor in 1974, supported construction of the Kingdome. During the November 2, 1972, groundbreaking ceremony, he was jeered as an Establishment sell-out by young Asian American activists like Nemesio, Silme, Mayumi and Michael Woo.

In the early days, I handled most of the newspaper distribution myself. I didn't mind. I loved talking to the elderly residents and shopkeepers. They beamed when I arrived with the latest issue. Gene sometimes helped. As a macho over-achiever, he took at least two or three giant bundles at a time, walk-running from door to door to complete deliveries as fast as he could.

Julia asked Rod Mamon, an ACWA member, to bring a stack of newspapers to the Tsue Chong Noodle Company. He returned with the stack. Julia asked Rod what happened. "I went over to the address you gave me, but they told me there was no one named Sue there." We all broke up with laughter. Julia explained that "Tsue Chong" was not a person.

During the day, I swigged cup after cup of black instant coffee, a bad carryover from my days at the UW. I snacked on broken fortune cookies, purchased in bulk from Tsue Chong. By noon, my stomach growled, pleading for real food. If I had time, I joined the ACWA gang in a lunch outing.

Once, Gene and I agreed to meet at the Luna Café at 502 South King Street. The restaurant, operated by Marceline and

Vannie Nerida, served American breakfast fare, burgers and chili as well as Filipino dishes. I usually ordered a bowl of noodles or pork *adobo*. As I approached, Gene stepped out, a grimace on his face. "What's wrong?" I asked. He paused briefly before saying, in a somber voice, "I don't think I'm hungry anymore." I waited. In his most serious deadpan voice, Gene said, "Some guy just barfed all over himself inside. I don't think I want to eat lunch anymore, Ron Chew. Let's go back to the office and do some work."

As I began to develop my own staff at the paper, I spent much less time with Nemesio, Silme, Terri, Julia, Gene and the rest of the ACWA crowd. They began going down to the Pioneer Square office of the ILWU, intent on claiming control of the union. I often had the whole ACWA office to myself.

I saw Silme and Gene when they stopped by to produce fliers for the Rank-And-File Committee, which they formed in 1977 to support election of reform-minded candidates for union positions. I helped with editing, proofreading, layout and design. Gene did the printing on the offset printing press in the back office.

Silme and Gene urged me to go up to Alaska to work as a writer-organizer and document the movement for racial equality and labor reform. They pointed out that Filipino American author Carlos Bulosan had done that for Local 37 back in the 1950s when Chris Mensalvas was union president. They showed me Local 37's 1952 Yearbook, produced by Bulosan to defend the union against McCarthy-era attacks. It was beautifully designed and the prose was eloquent. They wanted to produce something similar.

Bulosan passed away in 1965. When Silme and Gene approached me about going to Alaska, Mensalvas was living at the Downtowner Apartments, an eight-story building at Fourth

Avenue South and South Jackson Street. I heard him speak once at a May Day rally in Hing Hay Park in 1976. He was a tiny, old man. Terri knew him. She had been dating his son Chris, Jr. She listened to the elder Chris recount union history when he and other ILWU elders gathered for dinner and wine.

I met Chris, Jr., when he dropped by ACWA to see Terri. He often came with Gene. He was a cannery worker like his father and a gifted artist with a quiet demeanor. After he showed me some amazingly intricate and colorful drawings he had done, I asked him to illustrate for the *Examiner*. In 1977, he contributed an iconic image of the Kingdome as a villainous figure holding a bundle of cash in one hand and a pickaxe in the other, chipping away at hotels in the International District. The drawing accompanied an article marking the one-year anniversary of the stadium's opening.

"Ron, we need someone with good writing skills who also understands the broader perspective of our work," Silme said. "If you go up there, you can write firsthand about the terrible conditions."

I thanked him, but I gave a firm no. "Silme, be serious," I said. "I'm no Carlos Bulosan. I don't have that kind of talent. Besides, I'm Chinese. You should find a Filipino to help you."

Silme and Gene dismissed my remark. "It doesn't matter that you're Chinese," Silme said. "This is a multiracial movement. Let us know if you change your mind. We'll help arrange it. Besides, you can make pretty good money during the season. It's way more than what you make doing what you do for the *Examiner*."

I laughed. "That's assuming I don't gamble it all away before I get back, right?" I had heard that Filipino gangs controlled high-stakes gaming in Alaska. I recalled my mother's harsh edict about betting.

I never took Gene and Silme up on their offer. I wanted to continue my career in community journalism. I was just beginning. I sometimes wonder what would have happened if I had followed them.

Eventually, Nemesio and Silme urged me to look for another space for the newspaper. Silme said they weren't sure whether they would keep the ACWA office. Gene pulled me aside one day at the International District Community Garden. He had become heavily involved with the Union of Democratic Filipinos, a leftist revolutionary group opposing the declaration of martial law in the Philippines under Ferdinand Marcos.

I knew the group by its acronym KDP, which stood for *Katipunan ng mga Demokratikong Pilipino.* The KDP was founded in the Bay Area in 1973, but its tentacles reached deep into Asian American activist circles in Seattle. Silme and Gene were rising stars. In addition to fighting for democracy in the Philippines, KDP members supported low-income housing, affirmative action, and immigrant and workers' rights. The KDP was dedicated to a socialist revolution in the United States.

Gene respected my independence, but he reiterated what Nemesio and Silme had already told me: "I think it's time for the *Examiner* to move out on its own. You want to preserve your freedom to print whatever you want. There's going to be a lot of pressure from the KDP for you and the paper to serve as the publicity arm for the movement. I think you want to be separate from all of that."

I appreciated Gene's candor. I began to see less of him as his life became even more hectic with union organizing, attending KDP study circle meetings and traveling between Seattle and Wapato, where he went faithfully to check in with his large extended family. I continued to help him edit and design leaflets. He dropped off his drafts and news stories for the *Examiner.*

Over time, I met other KDP "comrades" from California. They called me a "middle force." They asked for help in "mass-lining" political messages. Silme spoke about "particularizing" issues. They poo-pooed other non-KDP activists as "ultraleftists." When they used jargon, I had a general idea what they were talking about, but I wasn't always sure. I had no interest in participating in Marxist-Leninist study.

Once, I overheard a discussion about one ACWA member exhibiting unacceptable "lumpen tendencies." I whispered to Gene, "What the hell does that mean?" He chuckled. "Too much drinking and partying," he said. "Not good behavior."

In 1978, the KDP activists put forth a slate of recommended reform candidates for cannery union posts. They included Silme's father Nemesio Domingo, Sr., for vice president, Gene for secretary-treasurer, Silme for dispatcher, John Hatten for trustee, and at least half a dozen others for the executive board.

I agreed to help design the election brochure. Gene gave me the text and several images. "Where's the rest of the photos?" I asked. "I'll need pictures of everyone." We faced a tight printing deadline. Neither of us had a camera. We didn't have time to take pictures and get to a darkroom to develop prints. This was before the advent of smartphones with digital cameras.

"Here, I've got an idea, Gene," I said. "There's a photo booth at Woolworth's downtown. Why don't you ask folks to go there to take black-and-white head shots?" It turned out to be a fast, cheap solution. We got the pictures we needed, including those of John Hatten and several executive board member candidates. The entire reform slate swept to victory.

I finally took Gene's advice about unhitching the *Examiner* from ACWA. In April 1979, I moved the paper into the Jackson Building at 318 Sixth Avenue South. In 1980, the *Examiner* incorporated as a nonprofit organization. A new era had begun.

CHAPTER 21

Discovering Other Political Causes

EVEN THOUGH JOURNALISM HAD BECOME the center of my life, I didn't shy away from participating in civic affairs. I didn't think there was anything wrong with stepping outside the newsroom and working with others on social and political causes.

I wasn't a revolutionary like many of the activists I knew. Nor did I identify as a Democrat, Republican or independent. I was less concerned with ideology, party or movements than in working on small projects with tangible outcomes. Seeing the direct results of my efforts left me with the warm glow of making a positive difference in the lives of people around me

At ID community meetings, I saw the prickly divide between young activists and older, buttoned-down leaders. The favorite slogan of the activists, borrowed from Chairman Mao Tse-tung, was "Serve the People," shouted as the coda to a roster of demands. The conservative leaders rolled their eyes, folded their arms and appealed for compromise. I kept my mouth shut and took notes, adhering to my reporter role. I found it ironic that my activist friends spoke on behalf of immigrants like my mother. She had fled Mao's China and hated the Communists. Her brother had been a victim of the Chinese Cultural Revolution.

The only person I knew who truly abided by the "Serve the People" mantra was International District medic Donnie Chin. He actually *did it* every waking moment. For many others, those words slipped out of their vocabulary as their idealism wavered.

I entered community service in the late 1970s. By then, the political tide had shifted to the right. Anti-poverty programs started under President Lyndon B. Johnson were dismantled. This change fully asserted itself with the election of Ronald Reagan in 1980. Federal dollars for civic engagement, construction and social services under the Model Cities Program dried up. The Comprehensive Employment and Training Act (CETA), which supported public service jobs in the International District, vanished.

Many of my peers left the low wages and grind of nonprofit work. Some became yuppies. I held out. At the same time, I distanced myself from others who hardened their radical political stances, accusing others of joining the "petty bourgeoisie."

I had been deeply affected by Richard Wright's essay in his 1949 collection *The God That Failed*. I had found it in a small, obscure bookstore in the University District. Wright described his abandonment of the Communist Party (CP) after a decade as a card-carrying member. Wright had first joined because of the CP's unyielding embrace of the working-class movement and its fervent denunciation of racism. But eventually he found that any rigid ideology is flawed. He wanted to reclaim his independence as an artist, answerable only to his conscience rather than an "official mood."

After I read Wright's piece, I felt validated. I didn't need to pledge unquestioning loyalty to any ideology.

I floated from cause to cause. I volunteered for the International District Improvement Association (InterIm), Neighborhood House, Denise Louie Childcare Center, Chinese for Affirmative Action, Seattle Rape Relief, Coalition on Government Spying, and groups supporting the United Farm Workers Union and anti-apartheid efforts in South Africa. I served on the board of Alternatives for Women, an early job training and employment service for low-income women of color in the Rainier Vista housing project. I helped write press releases and design fliers, brochures and posters. I usually drifted away after a year or two, restless to dock somewhere fresh.

The Coalition on Government Spying was formed after it was revealed in 1974 that Seattle police had secretly gathered files on hundreds of social justice and minority activists. Mike Kozu, a perennial ID organizer, told me he had seen a photo of me at a demonstration in one of the files. "You should request your file," he said. I never did. I assumed the police spied on everyone, especially journalists. My only curiosity—which quickly passed—was whether I was wearing Tom Hayden's green army jacket.

In addition to the *Examiner*, I contributed to *Northwest Passage*, a monthly underground tabloid published by a collective of writers. In the late 1970s, I met Doug Honig, Michelle Celarier and Bill Patz, three editorial board members. Michelle had read my *Examiner* stories on the Alaska Cannery Workers Association lawsuits and the fight for Chinese garment workers' rights. She wanted to reprint them.

Michelle, Bill and Doug invited me to their newspaper office on Capitol Hill at 1017 East Pike Street. As I waited inside for them, I suddenly heard the creak of bed springs from an apartment unit just above my head. It was loud and rhythmic. I then heard the moans and screams of a couple passionately making love. During a pause, a toilet flushed several times. The cycle of sounds resumed. It was embarrassing. It seemed to go on forever. When the trio arrived, the sounds had finally abated, much to my relief. By then, my ears were hot and my face was bright red. I wondered if they had to endure these sounds all the time.

In 1977, I joined the steering committee of the Pacific Northwest Chapter of the National Committee to Overturn the Bakke Decision (NCOBD). The NCOBD was formed in response to a reverse discrimination case involving Allan Bakke, a white student who applied unsuccessfully for law school at the University of California, Davis. Bakke claimed that he was rejected in favor of less qualified minorities. His case, argued before the Supreme Court in October of 1977, was a major test to see whether programs benefiting underrepresented racial minorities would survive a constitutional challenge. Activists feared that the hard-won civil rights gains of the 1960s and '70s might be torched.

The NCOBD set up shop at the ACWA office. As the one working journalist in the NCOBD, I agreed to head up the publicity committee. KDP members had taken up the cause as a priority. I attended planning and strategy sessions that stretched into the late evening. I found myself swept along by the energy and commitment of others. This was the first time I had ever worked at the center of a protest movement.

I reunited with my former Spanish teacher Roberto Maestas at NCOBD organizing meetings. Since leaving Franklin High, he had become executive director at El Centro de la Raza. He spent the first trying years repairing broken windows, upgrading the electrical system and repainting the interior with colorful murals. He established a food bank, emergency services, Head Start, job training and senior programs at the old school.

El Centro was part of the NCOBD coalition, as were a number of minority and women's organizations. I was thrilled to work alongside Maestas and his peers Larry Gossett, Bob Santos and Tyree Scott. I learned a lot by observing them.

I hadn't worked with Larry or Tyree before, but they dazzled me with their natural organizing talents and political savvy. Larry and I both attended Franklin High, but he was eight years older than me. His younger sister Theresa was in my class. Larry came from the Central Area Motivation Program, the hub of anti-poverty programs in Seattle for many years. Tyree, an electrician and leader of the United Construction Workers Association, was my senior by 13 years. Both were masters of inspirational rhetoric at rallies. Behind the scenes, they helped channel our inexperienced and diverse group toward consensus after heated—and sometimes pointless—exchanges. Uncle Bob lobbed well-timed goofball quips to defuse tense conflicts. He knew that distraction has its uses.

Our chapter organized a week of educational programs in February 1978. We put on a well-attended National Day of Protest on April 8. We marched from Hing Hay Park to the federal courthouse downtown. Picket signs and fliers were stored in the back of ACWA's office. Shortly after the Supreme Court's mixed decision on June 28, we organized a press conference and a second demonstration at the federal courthouse.

Leaders of the NCOBD came from the Line of March, a Maoist organization based in Oakland. They praised my writing skills, asked me to join their movement and write for *Frontline*, a biweekly news publication advocating for a working-class revolution in America. I quietly declined. I remembered Richard Wright's essay. I prized my independence.

In 1981, Maestas, Uncle Bob, Larry and Native American leader Bernie Whitebear formed the Minority Executive Directors Coalition (MEDC) to fight for racial and social equity across ethnic communities. They called themselves the "Four Amigos." At MEDC meetings, Maestas patted me on the back and crowed about how I was once his student at Franklin High.

Craig Shimabukuro was one of the more colorful Asian American activists of that era. He moved from Los Angeles in 1979 to become director of the Employment Opportunities Center (EOC), a job referral agency in Southeast Seattle. He sought me out. He wanted to find out what was happening in town. He parked his motorcycle outside the *Examiner* office and tromped upstairs wearing a crumpled black leather jacket and black boots, his motorcycle helmet in one hand, a Marlboro cigarette in the other. With his long black hair, walrus mustache and thick, black-framed glasses, he looked like a cartoon character from the 1960s.

Craig loved to reminisce about his part in street protests outside the 1968 Democratic national convention in Chicago and in the Native American uprising at Wounded Knee, South Dakota, in the early 1970s. My friend Barbara Means was at Wounded Knee too, but she told me she was sickened and disillusioned by the violent confrontations.

Craig left the EOC to join the Washington State Commission on Asian American Affairs (CAAA) as an outreach worker. He later worked at the American Friends Service Committee and the International District Housing Alliance. He loved hanging out with Donnie Chin, admiring his unbounded devotion to community service.

Craig invited me to dinner at Quong Tuck Restaurant. He launched into a monologue about his disgust with Ronald Reagan, the inherent corruptness of electoral politics and his misty dream of a Communist revolution in the U.S. As he worked himself up into a froth, his legs jiggled. I pulled him away from the precipice by cracking a joke. It worked, and he threw his head back and cackled. I didn't have much to add to our one-sided conversation since my goals were rather pedestrian: get enough ads and stories to fill the next issue of the *Examiner*.

I didn't like it when Craig talked about armed struggle. I didn't like it when others did, either. When they discussed the violent overthrow of the capitalist system, I winced. I didn't believe in bloodshed, no matter how noble the cause.

I thought about my friend Barbara. I thought about Diana, an older African American woman I met during my work with the NCOBD. Diana had participated in the SNCC (Student Non-Violent Coordinating Committee) protests in the Deep South during the 1960s. I also reflected on Martin Luther King, Jr., and his wise words:

> *Returning hate for hate multiplies hate, adding deeper darkness to a night already devoid of stars. Darkness cannot drive out darkness; only light can do that...Hate multiplies hate, violence multiplies violence, and toughness multiplies toughness in a descending spiral of destruction.*

As militant as he was, Craig was also lighthearted. He kidded me about my intense distaste for cheese. He poked fun at his own long-winded nature and propensity to perspire. In a warm room, he mopped sweat from his brow and pushed his glasses to keep them from sliding down his nose.

"Sweat doesn't bother me," I reassured him. "Just keep the cigarette smoke and the cheese away."

CHAPTER 22

IDEA, Enter the Jogger and Garamond

I N 1976, I JOINED THE International District Economic Association (IDEA). It was formed in 1973 by a small band
of business leaders and professionals who wanted to restore
economic vitality to the neighborhood. IDEA's two signature
events were an annual summer festival and a year-end holiday
party. The festival became IDEA's enduring legacy. The holiday
party faded away.

The core members were Tomio Moriguchi, chairman
of Uwajimaya, the largest store in the ID; Bertha Tsuchiya,
a partner at Luke's Pharmacy; Raymond Chinn from Wa
Sang Groceries; Glenn Chinn, director of Merchants Parking Association; Bill Ishii, a certified public accountant; and
Shigeko Uno, manager of Rainier Heat & Power Company,
which owned the Bush Hotel and several other properties.

Tomio, Bertha and the others welcomed me to their group
because of my role at the *Examiner*. I wanted to meet more
people in the ID, especially the old hands who knew more local
history than I did. The *Examiner's* founders Larry Imamura

and Gerald Yusua had preceded me as IDEA members. I stayed with the group through the late 1980s.

I was the youngest one in IDEA. I considered the others my mentors. The only person close to my age was Glenn, a soft-spoken transplant from the East Bay in California. He was Mayumi Tsutakawa's husband. The two met in 1972 while working on the Summer Youth Program for the city of Seattle. They married in June 1975. Glenn chaired IDEA's monthly meetings. He was the only out-of-towner. When he suggested changes that others didn't like, Shigeko would object firmly, "That's not the way we do things here, Glenn." After a while, Glenn figured it out. The others had a shared past.

IDEA meetings were often held at Sambo's, a national 24-hour breakfast and pancake house in the SoDo area, just five minutes south of the ID. The restaurant was similar to Denny's. I felt uneasy about patronizing it. By late 1970s, the term "Sambo" was widely recognized as racist and offensive to African Americans. After protests against the restaurant chain, it closed in 1982. I was relieved that IDEA meetings moved back to the ID.

The first summer festival took place on June 5, 1976. It was held at the Nippon Kan Theatre, the performance hall for the Japanese American community from 1909 until its closure in 1942. Ed and Betty Burke purchased the building in the late 1960s and were trying to restore it. Ed suggested holding the event at his site. Across from the Nippon Kan, a small public park featured an ancient four-ton granite lantern and newly-planted Mt. Fuji cherry trees, gifts from Kobe, Seattle's sister city. Ed designed fabric banners with stenciled Japanese characters, placing them on bamboo poles outside the Nippon Kan.

Later that summer, the Chinatown Seafair Festival, a separate event sponsored by the Chinatown Chamber of Commerce, was held on August 6 and 7 in Hing Hay Park. The festival featured a similar array of activities—food, martial arts and arts and crafts—but with a stronger Chinese flavor.

The following year, IDEA moved the summer festival down the hill to Hing Hay Park. This provided a showcase for a freshly-painted mural on the south facade of Bush Hotel. The mural, created by artist John Woo, included colorful images of Asian laborers and a long, flowing dragon at the center. Food and information booths lined the streets around the park.

The festival grew in small bursts. In 1979, Steve Goon added a fun run at my suggestion. We were running buddies, both living at the Evergreen Apartments at Maynard and Jackson. In a moment of endorphin-induced zeal, I turned to him and said, "Why don't you put together a little running event for all of us nutty joggers in the ID?"

Two years earlier, Jim Fixx had sparked a fitness revolution with his best-selling book *The Complete Book of Running*. Practically everyone I knew jogged. I ran in white tube socks, a white cotton t-shirt, gym shorts, JCPenney sneakers and a red elastic headband. In hot weather, I traded the t-shirt for a favorite ribbed tank top I bought for 50 cents at Wigwam Stores on Empire Way, now Martin Luther King, Jr. Way South.

My regular running partners were Steve Goon and Ruthann Kurose. Steve and I started out at the Evergreen Apartments. Our first destination was Ivar's Fish Bar, where we stopped for greasy French fries to power the rest of our run along Alaskan Way and through the streets of downtown.

In June 1990, Steve got busy operating his own small business, which he named The Financial Pages. It was in a kiosk on the third floor of Westlake Center, near the food court and across from the Monorail terminus. He sold money-themed novelty gifts such as board games, drinking glasses, silver dollar coasters and colorful ties. I ran solo from the apartment, using Westlake Center as my turnaround point so I could visit him. Steve's dad sat at a table near the kiosk, drinking coffee and reading the newspaper. His dad's refrain: "Help me find a girlfriend for Steve!"

My most memorable run to Westlake Center took place on Saturday, July 25, 1992, when I accidentally encountered Presidential hopeful Bill Clinton, in town for a rally. The streets were clogged with thousands of people.

The crowd was dispersing. I saw Clinton dip into a car just east of the Bon Marché. But a few minutes later, he stepped back out. The people behind me surged forward. I was hemmed in. To my surprise, Clinton walked straight at me, flanked by security officers. He was dressed in a dark suit and yellow tie. With TV cameras trained on me, he offered his hand. I felt obligated to shake it. He said, "I hope you'll vote for me." Tongue-tied, I simply nodded. The person next to me held a "Free Bosnia-Herzegovina" sign. Clinton pivoted to him, wagged his finger and said, "I'll be putting a statement out on that tomorrow. I think you'll like it." Clinton moved away and shook more hands before finally departing.

As I jogged back to my apartment, I felt newly motivated to follow the outcome of the November 3 match-up between Clinton, President George H.W. Bush and independent Ross Perot. *Had I just shaken the hand of the next President?*

I ran regularly with Ruthann in the 1980s while she was an aide to Congressman Mike Lowry. Her office was on Rainier Avenue South near Chubby & Tubby. We went to Myrtle Edwards Park, jogging along the trail near Elliott Bay, or up at Greenlake, following an unpaved path around the outer perimeter of the lake. My runs with Ruthann continued on and off for about five years.

Martha Choe, who worked downtown as a vice president at the Bank of California, sometimes joined us. Martha ran in four grueling Hood-to-Coast relays in Oregon. I loved watching her easy, loping stride. She and four close friends secretly called themselves the "leopard ladies," donning matching Lycra costumes and dark sunglasses during team relays. Martha later went on to serve two terms as the first Korean American member of the Seattle City Council.

There was one local race I never missed. From 1985 to 1992, I participated in the annual Pratt & Chew Holiday Classic, a four-miler held in November at either Gasworks Park or along the Burke-Gilman Trail. It was a fundraiser for the Emergency Feeding Program of Seattle-King County. One year, it attracted over 1,300 participants. Pratt & Chew was the downtown accounting firm established by my brother Harvey and his partner Charlie Pratt. Harvey was race director. I didn't register for any other events except an occasional Seafair Torchlight run with Steve.

Bob Santos, who lived down the street from us at the Freedman Building, was a serious runner. He liked my idea of an ID summer festival run. Bob had tackled the Seattle marathon. When he was living on Beacon Hill, he ran daily with a springer spaniel that belonged to Theresa Fujiwara, a social worker at Asian Counseling and Referral Service (ACRS). Uncle Bob stopped by her house in the early morning while she slept, opened the door with an extra key, and brought the dog with him on his run. She left a glass of orange juice for him. Sometimes, Uncle Bob met a few young activists like Susie Chin at the Jefferson Park Tennis Courts to run as a group.

After initially balking, Steve relented. He got advice from Bill Roe, founder of Club Northwest, a runners group in Seattle. I helped Steve hand out brochures. Mayumi's cousin Laurie

Tsutakawa, an artist at Cicada Gallery, created an "Enter the Jogger" race t-shirt, featuring a playful red dragon in sneakers on the front. KISW-FM, a local rock-and-roll station, was the event sponsor.

The summer festival and fun run were scheduled for June 9. A week earlier, the Seattle Supersonics had just won their first and only National Basketball Association championship by beating the Washington Bullets. Thousands of ecstatic fans embraced the team at a downtown victory parade on June 4. People screamed and cheered. Cars honked. I went to see it, but Steve decided to celebrate quietly by enjoying a solo meal at Ying Hei Restaurant (燕喜樓). He was nervous. He still had an event to execute in a few days.

I participated in the fun run because I wanted the t-shirt. The run went from the ID across the 12th Avenue South bridge to Beacon Hill Playfield, where the route turned back toward the finish in the ID. The event went smoothly. Unfortunately, it was never repeated. It was more work than any of us had imagined. No one else wanted to take it on.

IDEA also organized an annual Christmas party. In its early years, it was held at the Nippon Kan Theatre. Later, it moved to the GMC Truck Center on Sixth Avenue South, next to Uwajimaya, the ID's best-known Asian supermarket. We went door-to-door to solicit contributions. We asked each restaurant for $50 worth of food in exchange for $25 cash. No one turned us down. The party became a must-attend event for city council members and political wannabes.

In 1994, a new nonprofit, Chinatown-ID Business Improvement Area (CIDBIA), supplanted IDEA. I dropped out. The CIDBIA had the advantage of having paid staff and stable funding derived from taxes levied on area businesses and property owners. After IDEA dissolved, the pig roast at the

International District Community Garden became the go-to annual event for political glad-handing.

In 1979, I began doing part-time editing, design and writing for McDonald "Don" Sullivan. He had been hired a year earlier as the first executive director of the newly-created Seattle Chinatown-International District Preservation and Development Authority (PDA). The agency was created by the city of Seattle to spur restoration and revitalization of the ID. Its first big project was a $3.5 million remodel of the old Bush Hotel into a multi-use community center.

Don, the son of missionaries, was born in Shanghai and spent his boyhood in China. He had an extensive background in real estate development. Because Don was an outsider to the ID, he leaned on me for advice after meeting me through the *Examiner*. I told him to stop using the term "Orientals," explaining that it was derogatory. I recommended that he hire Julia Laranang as his office manager. I also suggested that the PDA, later rebranded as SCIDpda, print its annual report as a paid supplement in the *Examiner*. This helped bring desperately needed revenue to the paper and fostered a close bond between our two groups.

As plans for the remodel of the Bush Hotel proceeded, Julia found an old brochure on the Bush Hotel. I marveled at several photos of the hotel in its heyday. In one image, the words "Modern, Fireproof" and "Low Rates" were visible high on the west facade of the building, crisply painted in a beautiful classic typeface. The lettering was still there, but barely visible. "Julia, make sure you keep those words and that nice typeface up there on the facade," I urged. "I like it a lot. It's part of the character of the building." She laughed and agreed.

She knew I was a typeface aficionado. At ACWA, I would proselytize about which type styles were classy and readable and which were tacky and difficult for the roving eye to decipher. Garamond was my favorite. I was an outspoken fan of classic serif faces. I preferred them over modern, blocky sans serif faces.

Jim Behrend at the Franklin Press tried to wean me off of Garamond. He bought a bundle of new type fonts for his shop's typesetting machine. He wanted to put them to good use. "Why don't you try Clarendon?" Jim implored. "Nah," I said. "Too modern." "Okay, how about Goudy Old Style?" "Nah," I responded. "I don't like the italic." He rattled off half a dozen other typefaces. I spurned them all. Jim threw up his hands and walked away.

Silme, Gene and others at ACWA knew about my ardent love affair with Garamond. I helped them design many fliers, brochures and newsletters. I always insisted on Garamond. "Do what you like," they would say. They didn't care.

The words were, indeed, repainted on the Bush Hotel, but in a modern typeface. I was peeved. I thought it was a bad decision. I whined to Julia. I also complained to Gene and Silme about it. They humored me, accepting my fussiness over typography as our private joke. I don't think anyone else noticed.

CHAPTER 23

Danny Woo Community Garden

I
N 1975, BOB SANTOS, DIRECTOR of the International District Improvement Association (InterIm), and Donnie Chin scoured the neighborhood for volunteers to help build a new community garden on the hillside near Sixth Avenue South and South Main Street.

I was one of dozens who heeded the call. Gene, Silme and the folks at ACWA shut down the office. I stopped typing my stories and joined them on the five-minute walk up to the hillside. Many of my close friends—Lorraine Sako, Gary Iwamoto, Susie Chin, Jeff Hanada, Steve Goon—went there, too.

This project spoke to my heart, not to any ideological calling. We were building a terraced garden for Chinese, Japanese and Filipino seniors living in apartments in the International District. Many had been farmers. They were living out their remaining years confined to small urban spaces without the opportunity to work the soil and summon life from it. That seemed so unjust.

The property for the community garden had been donated

by restaurateur Danny Woo and his wife Wilma. The Woo family owned the New Chinatown Restaurant, a large *chop suey* place, from the 1950s until 1975. It was on the corner of Sixth Avenue South and South Main Street, up a long flight of stairs. It was like the Hong Kong Restaurant, only bigger, accommodating parties of over 400. It featured live jazz. The New Chinatown parking lot was across the street from the restaurant, on a small sliver of land covered with gravel and overgrown by blackberry bushes.

After the restaurant closed, Danny Woo agreed to turn the vacant lot over to InterIm to create a space where low-income ID residents could grow their own vegetables. In return, Inter-Im would pay the property taxes.

I was 23 at the time. I had been working at the Hong Kong Restaurant for 10 years, carrying hefty trays of dishes and moving heavy tabletops and stacks of chairs. I felt fit and strong. But I was surprised by how challenging the work on the garden turned out to be.

Working in loosely supervised shifts over a period of several months, volunteers helped lay the foundation for the garden. We unloaded railroad ties from trucks and moved piles of dirt, gravel and fertilizer by wheelbarrow. We leveled the ground with shovels and rakes.

A wheelbarrow filled with gravel was nearly impossible to move, especially for someone of my slight build. I could barely inch it forward. The railroad ties, carried by crews of one or two people at each end, were huge and awkward to maneuver into their proper places, since the hillside had not yet been terraced. When seasonal rains came, the area became one big, muddy, formless bog.

A pickup truck dumped horse manure from an Eastside riding farm at the top of the hill. The stench was unbearable.

At times, no one seemed to be in charge. Common-sense safety rules were not followed. Unfortunately, young men like to impress others with their physical prowess. I nearly lost my left hand when a railroad tie was stacked on top of another tie before I could move my fingers out of the way. "My hand!" I shouted. Mercifully, there was an indentation between the two ties. I eased my hand out, suffering only minor bruises to my fingers. The other guys carrying the railroad tie with me had already moved away and didn't hear my cry of distress. I was shaken. I took a 15-minute breather.

Uncle Bob celebrated the development of the garden by organizing an annual summertime pig roast. He had hosted a similar event at his South Seattle home for years. He simply moved the event up to the Main Street hillside, making it a bigger party. A live pig was purchased at a farm in Auburn, butchered and prepared for roasting on a spit over an open fire pit. Volunteers were enlisted to turn the pig during the night. The wee hours of the morning became a tradition of uproarious storytelling.

The next day, when the pig was ready to consume, a potluck was held for elderly residents, garden volunteers and the community. It was a gigantic feast. Danny Woo, his wife Wilma, daughter Teresa and son Curtis brought refreshments to keep the volunteers going through the night, prepared a salad for the potluck and helped carve slices of roasted pork. Everyone contributed dishes, including the residents.

By noon, there was a long, noisy line stretching along the top of the garden. Seniors came first. City council members and candidates dropped in to schmooze.

Every year, Uncle Bob, the emcee and community garden visionary, took a moment to acknowledge the contributions of the Woo family and the volunteers who helped build, maintain and expand the garden as it blossomed into a treasured spot in the neighborhood.

Today, the 1.5 acre site is still the largest green space in the International District. There are 100 plots serving 70 gardeners. The residents grow mustard greens, Chinese lettuce, chives, green beans, chayote, scarlet runners and mugwort. The garden includes an entry gate, children's garden, chicken coop, outdoor kitchen and fruit tree orchard. There are picnic benches, public art and walking trails.

After I came to the International District to live in 1986, I often visited the garden, rediscovering a place to escape and think through problems. Later, after I became a parent, I initiated my two young boys and a few of their friends to the pig roast. They took shifts turning the pig over the fire. They met Uncle Bob. One hot summer, armed with shovels and picks, they helped restore a section of retaining wall.

The pig roast continues every July even though Uncle Bob and Danny Woo are gone.

On September 26, 2019, InterIm hosted a party in the garden to announce the formation of Friends of Danny Woo. The garden was reintroduced to a new generation. Pradeepta Upadhyay, InterIm director since September 2014, announced, "We remain committed to preserving Uncle Bob's precious legacy and keeping the land fertile for our connected generations to play and learn about gardening, sustainability, and the history of our community."

CHAPTER 24

Milwaukee Hotel Fire Watch

I<small>N</small> O<small>CTOBER</small> 1976, <small>THE CRISIS</small> over the lack of decent, affordable low-income housing in the International District came to a head with the looming closure of the five-story Milwaukee Hotel (美利和記旅館) at 668 South King Street. The hotel, badly damaged by a fire in 1975, housed 50 low-income immigrant families and single men.

The Milwaukee Hotel had once been an architectural crown jewel. It was built in 1911 by legendary Chinese pioneer Goon Dip (阮洽) to house visitors flocking into town following the 1909 Alaska-Yukon-Pacific Exposition. He reserved the top floor as his personal residence, watched over by a white bodyguard. His furnishings included porcelain, silk, cloisonné and carved teak.

Goon Dip came to America in 1876 at the age of 14 from the village of Seung Gok. Although he arrived penniless and started as a houseboy, he later amassed a fortune as a cannery labor contractor, becoming honorary Chinese Consul for the Pacific Northwest. He was a partner in the Hirst Chichagof

217

gold mining company in Alaska and in the Marconi Company, an automobile battery manufacturing company in Seattle. He was a member of the Seattle Chamber of Commerce and headed up the Kong Yick Investment Company (公益實業有限公司), which built two hotels on South King Street. He passed away on September 12, 1933, at the Milwaukee Hotel at the age of 71.

I often heard tales about the hotel and Goon Dip. Steve Goon's father Clifton, a pharmacist, was Goon Dip's grandson. Both were proud of their family history. Both inherited Goon Dip's round face, smooth brow and grinning visage. Steve told me that he and his siblings spent their childhood in the hotel watching *My Three Sons* on a small black-and-white television in the back of the Goon Dip Company (阮洽公司) office. Today, that space is occupied by a Vietnamese *phở* café.

Clifton told me he didn't know his grandfather very well because he grew up in Portland and Goon Dip was usually away, often in Seattle. He recalled Goon Dip as a heavy-set man. "He would have a shot of whiskey, and he would let us dip our fingers into the whiskey," he reminisced, relishing that memory. Clifton was just 13 when Goon Dip passed away.

One evening when Clifton was watching NBC's *Tonight Show Starring Johnny Carson,* he learned that there was a mountain in Alaska named after Goon Dip. The mountain was on the northern end of Chichagof Island. It isn't very tall. According to the U.S. Geological Survey, Goon Dip Mountain rises only 1,601 feet in elevation, making it the 2,151st highest summit in the world. Still, it bears his grandfather's name. He shared this tidbit with Steve, who in turn told me. Half in jest, I proposed, "Hey, let's go up and visit." He agreed. But we've never made the trip.

Clifton took over management of the Milwaukee Hotel

from his father Daniel, after Daniel passed away in 1959. Clifton collected rent and handled repairs to the aging structure as best he could. He was also busy as a pharmacist. He owned the Rex Drug Store in Pioneer Square. He later worked at Bonney's Drugs and Owen's Pharmacy.

In 1965, Jordan Wong and Donald Louie bought the Milwaukee Hotel. The new owners didn't see eye-to-eye. They allowed the once-stately edifice to tumble into ruin.

In 1970, the city passed a law restricting occupancy of buildings without adequate fire escapes and sprinklers. With the coming of the Kingdome, many old hotels in the ID, including the Milwaukee, were targeted for closure. The International District Housing Alliance (IDHA) and InterIm organized protests at City Hall, urging Mayor Wes Uhlman to allocate at least 200 units of new housing to the ID through Section 8 of the federal Housing Assistance Program.

Meanwhile, the two groups fought to keep the Milwaukee Hotel open. They recruited over 100 volunteers to wall off a deteriorated section of the building, haul away 14 tons of debris, repair light fixtures and make safety upgrades. Tyree Scott brought his UCWA members down to help. IDHA organized a 24-hour fire watch, a condition set by Seattle Municipal Court Judge Barbara Yanick to keep the hotel in operation.

The fire watch was staffed in two-hour shifts around the clock. Greg Della coordinated the schedule. Fire watch volunteers included Andy Mizuki, Bob Santos, Susie Chin, Melvin Inouye, David Della, Dan Rounds, Rick Furukawa, Donnie Chin, Dicky Mar, Maxine Chan, Doralinn Jung, Lorraine Sako, Michael Woo, Cissy Asis, Dale Borgeson, Gene Viernes and Silme Domingo.

Steve Goon, who at that time worked as a teller at the Chinatown branch of Rainier Bank, took on a graveyard shift on the weekends. He lamented to me, "It's sad to see this happening. Maybe our family should have found a way to hang onto the building."

I volunteered for a fire watch shift, too. I chose either 4 to 6 a.m. or 6 to 8 a.m. I sometimes did a double shift if the person who was supposed to follow me didn't show up. Michael Woo shared those two undesirable slots with me. His uncle, Paul Woo, was a Milwaukee Hotel resident who worked across the street as a waiter at Linyen Restaurant.

I was living in Gene's old apartment on Capitol Hill. On my way to Chinatown, I stopped by the 7-Eleven on 15th Avenue to purchase a cup of hot black coffee from the vending machine. This precious stimulant kept me awake.

The Milwaukee Hotel was cold, drafty and eerily hushed. I stationed myself in a vacant apartment off the first floor landing. A window faced out onto South King Street. I got up to patrol the creaky, dark halls every so often with a flashlight, checking for signs of smoke seeping from under the cracks of doors. All I saw were cockroaches and mice. I sat in my chair, nursing my coffee and trying to stay alert. I read newspapers and books. My shifts were uniformly uneventful. After I was done, I headed straight to the *Examiner*.

One day, Bob Santos discovered a blank, red journal in the hotel "under a pile of junk." He started writing entries in what was to become the Fire Watch Journal. He offered daily observations about the District. This entry from Uncle Bob—the very first—was dated May 1, 1978, at 6:04 a.m.: "History will document that the people of this hotel stopped the negative trend of hotel closures by saving the Milwaukee Hotel from the court-ordered closure."

I contributed to the journal, as did others. It lessened the boredom. I left messages for other volunteers. We shared goofy jokes, community news and gossip. Some wrote more than others. Some doodled. Gary Iwamoto studied for his UW bar exam during his 2 to 4 a.m. shift. As a journalist, I couldn't resist the temptation to write often.

On June 2, 1978, I penned this entry during my 6 to 8 a.m. shift:

> It has been said, for many of us who are active in the social life of the District or who work here, that this is our roots, even though we may not live here. That's true. We feel a belonging, influenced by our parents, our parents' parents, or our culture.
>
> My friend's great-grandfather, Goon Dip, used to own the Milwaukee. And my friend tells me, from what he was told, that the hotel used to be a grand hotel, one of the finest in town. Would be good if all the hotels for our elderly could be that way. No?

In another entry, I shared that the *Seattle Sun* was preparing to publish a story on Bob Santos, describing him as the "unofficial mayor of the International District." I had just seen the soon-to-be-published story at the Franklin Press, where both the *Sun* and the *Examiner* were assembled. That title stuck and became his shorthand description.

Tim Otani, a volunteer at both the *Examiner* and the International District Emergency Center (IDEC), took the Friday 10 p.m. shift. He, Donnie Chin and a few others converted two vacant rooms into a darkroom for *Examiner* photographers.

One day, Tim was at IDEC, just up the street from the

hotel, when a call for assistance came in. Donnie and Tim raced over to the hotel. They discovered that one of the residents—a man Tim had met during his fire watch shift—hung himself with electrical wire in the hallway outside his apartment. The suicide victim's face was blue. Tim was unnerved. "For two weeks after that," Tim said, "when I was at the hotel, I didn't look left, I didn't look right. I just looked straight ahead."

Greg Della had the unpleasant task of cleaning an apartment occupied by an elderly white resident with a small black mutt. His place was filled with feces. "Why don't you take your dog out for a walk every now and then," Greg pleaded.

Bob Santos wrote the final journal entry on November 14, 1978, marking the last day of fire watch. A fire alarm system had been installed. Uncle Bob thanked the volunteers: "It was a chore, but you were all lovely. We'll take the journal to InterIm and Ron can do what he thinks is fair."

Eventually, InterIm and IDHA gave up trying to keep the Milwaukee Hotel open. In late 1979, after unsuccessful negotiations to acquire it from the owners, they helped the remaining 35 tenants find housing elsewhere in the ID.

The Milwaukee Hotel—a cornerstone of the early history of Chinatown and the poster child of the community's low-income housing struggle in the 1970s—sat shuttered and lifeless for nearly three decades.

In 2003, James Koh, a private developer with a vision for restoring economic life to the ID, bought the Milwaukee Hotel, the Mar Hotel (which once housed the Hong Kong Restaurant) and the Alps Hotel (next door to the Mar Hotel). He spent the next decade renovating the vacant apartments and storefront spaces in all three buildings, luring a new generation of tenants to the neighborhood.

CHAPTER 25

Uncle Bob Santos

I GOT TO KNOW BOB Santos during construction of the community garden and the Milwaukee Hotel housing struggle. Everyone called him "Uncle Bob." Student activists starting out in community work looked up to him as their inspiration and mentor. He fashioned the International District Improvement Association into the command center for preservation and redevelopment of the International District.

Filipino elders knew Uncle Bob's dad, "Sockin' Sammy" Santos, a winning prizefighter; they rooted for him in local fighting arenas in the 1920s and '30s. After Sammy lost his eyesight from years of bruising contact in the ring, Uncle Bob stayed with his dad, a resident at the N.P. Hotel on Sixth Avenue South. His apartment, unit 306, was conveniently located across from the elevator. Arm in arm, Uncle Bob guided his dad to restaurants, pool halls and other favorite hangouts. Uncle Bob learned the neighborhood from his father.

In 1968, during the height of urban unrest, InterIm received start-up money from the Model Cities Program. In

1972, Uncle Bob came on as executive director. He began a memorable tenure there. Not only did he lead efforts to develop the community garden and preserve the Milwaukee Hotel, he also helped secure funding for a health clinic, a mental health agency, a community-run parking lot under the I-5 freeway, a daycare center, a community center in the Bush Hotel and the International District Village Square. He uplifted the quality of life in the ID.

I first met Uncle Bob in 1973, in his office on South Jackson Street. I came to interview him for a story for the *UW Daily* about the impact of the Kingdome on the ID. He sat at his desk, dressed in a casual pullover sweater and khakis. He shook his arm and cursed loudly into the phone: "What kind of bullshit is that?" Other pungent phrases followed. He abruptly hung up and, in one easy motion, he swiveled in my direction. His demeanor brightened. "Hey, guy!" he said, extending his hand. "What's up? Are you from the U-Dub? Have a seat, guy." I was, needless to say, taken aback.

I never did learn the source of his anger—whether it was an insensitive public official or an ally with whom he had just had a testy spat. But over the years I had other opportunities to witness his fiery temper. Uncle Bob didn't kiss up to those he didn't like, despite his congeniality and patience at building political coalitions. He was a kindly uncle, but ornery, too.

Uncle Bob's arch rival was Ruby Chow. "Auntie Ruby" was a powerhouse in Chinatown because of her domineering presence on the board of Chong Wa Benevolent Association and the relationships she had cultivated with politicians at her restaurant on Capitol Hill. She dismissed the term "International District" as a meaningless way to describe an area that she regarded as "Chinatown." In turn, Uncle Bob mocked Ruby as a do-nothing community advocate. Each had a healthy squad of followers. Uncle Bob proudly—and effectively—carried the banner for "International District."

Uncle Bob knew how to work a crowd. I saw him speak at meetings of elderly residents at the International Drop-In Center at 610 South Weller Street and at the cannery union hall on South Main Street. He was good at exhorting feisty Filipino American residents like Al Masigat, Leo Lorenzo or Sam Figueros to stand up and be heard: "No one can force you out of your homes," he would assert. "But we need all of you and your friends to pack the City Council hearing and let the officials know that they've got to act on behalf of *your* interests."

Uncle Bob was insatiably social, as likely to be spotted in a local karaoke bar as at a political rally or a Seattle City Council hearing. He clowned and joked, offering up painfully corny puns, followed by "Get it?," an impish grin, a chuckle, and then "Just kidding!" Over the years, Bob's ability to connect with people allowed him to dissolve barriers, cultivate allies and open up neutral ground to bargain with those in seats of power.

Uncle Bob was a devoted fan of the *International Examiner*. During the early 1980s, when federal cuts decimated many nonprofit agencies, he quietly negotiated for funds to hire "trainees" to backfill jobs that were lost. Thanks to Uncle Bob, I worked as a CETA "trainee" for InterIm for two years. My job was to serve as editor of the *Examiner*. He was my boss, but he allowed me to run the paper as I saw fit. He respected my judgment. He saw the paper as an essential cornerstone of the community.

In May 1979, when the *Examiner* was limping through a financial drought, Uncle Bob initiated a special column titled "InterIm's Corner." This paid column was a thinly disguised strategy to deposit a few dollars in the newspaper's kitty. "But here's the deal," Uncle Bob told me. "I can't type. If I write a story and I can't get someone at InterIm to type it for me, you've got to do it for me." I told him that that wouldn't be a problem. By the time I was done editing, I would have to re-type the final piece anyway.

InterIm's office was located in the Bush Hotel, on the corner of Maynard and South Jackson in a space formerly occupied by United Savings and Loan. A long teller counter divided the room. When I delivered a bundle of newspapers, Uncle Bob popped up from his corner desk, walked over to greet me and eagerly peeled a copy from the top of the pile. "What's happening in the world, Ron?" he asked while leafing through the issue. I responded, "I don't know, Uncle Bob. You tell me." I relied on him to give me news tips.

Once, when I was working on a story about a proposed large-scale transportation project at Union Station which would severely impact residents and small businesses in the ID, he called me at my office.

"Hey, if you're free, why don't you join me in the bar at the Four Seas this evening? I'm going to be meeting with a couple officials who can give you an inside scoop. They get pretty talk-ative after they've had a few drinks."

"Thanks for the offer," I responded. "But I don't drink. Maybe you can give me their names and I can contact them later."

On another occasion, Uncle Bob called me at the *Examiner* to tell me about a party at a private residence that evening. He said there would be a lot of good food, music and dancing. "You really should come," he implored. "You're a bachelor guy, aren't you? There's a couple of nice young ladies who are new to the community, and you can help introduce them to what's going on. By the way, do you dance? You know, women love to dance, but most guys don't."

"Sorry to disappoint you, Uncle Bob, but I'm one of those guys who doesn't dance," I said. "Besides, I'm busy tonight. I've got to put the paper to bed and get it off to the printer." Uncle Bob responded: "What? You don't dance? That's no good! Okay. I just thought...If you finish up early, come hang out."

Uncle Bob wasn't easily deterred. A week later, he invited me to Bush Garden for karaoke. "The Bush" was an old-fashioned, family-style Japanese restaurant on Maynard Avenue South. Karaoke in Seattle got its start in the bar of the Bush. That bar was also his living room. Uncle Bob was a regular, known for his smooth renditions of Frank Sinatra standards like "New York, New York" and "My Way." When he sang "The Lady Is a Tramp," he changed "tramp" to "champ." Activist Cherry Cayabyab's favorite Uncle Bob rendition was "Through the Eyes of Love," the theme song from the movie "Ice Castles." He agreed to sing it at her wedding.

Uncle Bob once nudged reluctant ID activist Jamie Lee onto the stage to join him in singing "You Are the Sunshine of My Life" at a going-away party for Greg Garcia, director of WAPI (Washington Asian Pacific Islander) Community Services, a nonprofit substance abuse rehabilitation program for Asian Pacific Islander youth. This was the only time Jamie ever stepped on stage at The Bush.

But I was more bull-headed than Jamie. I turned down his invitation: "Remember, I told you before that I don't drink, Uncle Bob. Well, sorry to disappoint you again, but I don't sing either."

A brief time later, when I came to drop off the latest edition of the *Examiner*, he praised a few stories in the previous edition: "Keep up the good work, guy!" I thanked him. He added, "I'm still puzzled at how you're able to get all this inside information. You don't drink, you don't dance, you don't sing. Shit, how are you able to meet people and find out what's going on?"

We shared a hearty laugh. We had two distinctly different personalities. At my core, I am an introvert. I prefer an early bedtime and the company of my books and a few low-key friends. Uncle Bob, on the other hand, was a party animal. What drew us together is that we both believed in the same things. We both found our dignity and voice under the sheltering spirit of our fathers.

One day in 1986, Uncle Bob invited Gary Iwamoto and me to his apartment. He didn't tell us why until we got there. The size and layout of his place was very similar to mine. It even smelled the same. I heard the familiar rumble of cars from the street. I asked if he had rodents. He seemed unperturbed: "Yep. I got a few of those mousies running around. They're annoying, but that's the way it is when you live down here."

He urged us to sit down. He said he had started writing a book about his life and the ID. He handed me a blue-lined tablet with 29 pages of writing. It began: "Macario Santos was born in 190_ in San Mateo, Rizal Province, in the Philippines. He left home at an early age looking for adventure." Gary and I took turns reading. "That's my dad," he said. "This is as far as I got. I'll find out the date. But I wanted to know what you thought of this. I need advice from some writers."

The three of us met on and off over the next several months to help Uncle Bob craft an outline. I stored notes from these discussions on a 3.5-inch floppy disc and printed them out on the dot-matrix printer at my apartment for our meetings. Unfortunately, we got too busy and ended up shelving the book after working on it for a year.

But that wasn't the end of the project. Uncle Bob used my notes to produce a script for a one-man show, *Uncle Bob's Neighborhood*, which he performed in 1994 at the Theatre Off

Jackson, a 75-seat community space on Seventh Avenue and South Jackson, housed beneath the Wing Luke Museum. It was a humorous retelling of the community fight against the construction of the Kingdome. The title was a spoof of the popular PBS children's program *Mister Rogers' Neighborhood.*

In 2000, Uncle Bob, in between jobs, revived the book project. Gary became his close collaborator, researching, fact-checking and helping ghost-write sections. Uncle Bob's book, *Hum Bows, Not Hot Dogs,* was published by the *International Examiner* in 2002. He took the title from a sign used at protests against construction of the Kingdome.

After I had become the parent of two toddlers, Uncle Bob came by the Wing Luke Museum where I served as executive director. He handed me a one-page sheet. At the top, it read "'Max the International Child' by Uncle Bob." I quickly read it over. It was the opening chapter of a children's fable about a young boy born to a father from the Philippines and a mother from Japan. Max lives in the International Settlement. He watches Mr. Lee steam *hom bows,* eats noodles at Mrs. Nguyễn's place, goes to Mrs. Luna's café for *lumpia* and gets *sushi* at the Mikado Restaurant.

"Could you read this to your kids?" he asked. "Maybe there's another book here. Let me know." I told him I would add it to my next bedtime story session. I thanked him. Uncle Bob was at it again. He was looking for a new challenge and an opportunity to influence the next generation.

Chapter 26

Higo Variety Store

THE SECOND MAJOR HOME OF the *Examiner* was on the second floor of the Jackson Building, a two-story, sand-colored brick structure at the corner of Sixth Avenue South and South Jackson Street. On the street level beneath the *Examiner*'s new space was Higo Variety Store, an old-fashioned five-and-dime with a display window fronting Jackson Street.

Higo was run by three Murakami siblings—Aya, Masa and Kay. Their father Sanzo started the store in 1907 in the Presley Hotel on South Weller Street a few blocks away. In 1932, Sanzo moved his business to the newly-constructed Jackson Building he had financed. It was one of the few structures built during the Great Depression. He leased storefront space to several businesses and the upstairs office cubicles to professionals. The building became a bustling pillar of Japantown, or *Nihonmachi*.

During World War II, the Murakamis were incarcerated along with other Japanese Americans from Seattle. Higo closed. They resumed the business in January 1945 upon their release after the war's end. Tragically, Sanzo died of a heart attack a mere eight days after their return.

I discovered the Higo store in the 1960s. It looked like a set from *The Twilight Zone*, frozen in time. The big storefront display never changed, but the sun-bleached walls had turned pink. The cracking linoleum floor tiles squealed underfoot. Everything had a gray, uneven pallor. The place smelled like mothballs.

In the 1970s, Seattle had four other Japanese American emporiums: Tobo Imports, Shiga's Imports, Uwajimaya and Fuji 10 Cent Store. Tobo and Uwajimaya were in the International District. Tobo was operated by George Y. and Yoshi Suzuki. Shiga's was on University Way N.E. Its owner Andy Shiga was a colorful antiwar activist and University District leader. Tsuyoshi and Aya Horike operated Fuji 10 Cent Stores in the Wallingford, Greenwood and Queen Anne neighborhoods. In the early 1980s, Tobo and the Fuji 10 Cent Stores closed. Uwajimaya, Shiga's and Higo continue to thrive.

After the *Examiner* moved into the Jackson Building in 1979, I dropped in often at Higo. I couldn't resist its charm. The store was a treasure hunter's paradise. Anything I needed or wanted I could find for cheap. The store had four long aisles of cabinets, tidily crammed with stationery, colorful pens and pencils, calligraphy sets, kimonos, fans, mousetraps, slippers, hair care products, shoe polish, candy, fabric, sewing kits, wind-up toys, clothes, dolls, puzzles, imported dishware, cookery and tea sets.

I bought many orange boxes of Tomoe Ame rice candy and Hershey milk chocolate bars. During a frenetic last-minute search for Christmas cards, I discovered a batch of musical cards hidden on a back shelf, the edges brown from age. They had probably been there for years. One friend made a special long-distance phone call to thank me: "Wow, I've never received a card that plays music when you open it! Very cool. I couldn't stop opening and closing it."

The second floor of the Jackson Building was subdivided into tiny units that once served as medical and dental exam rooms. There were still two dental practices when the *Examiner* moved in. Several attorneys and accountants also had offices there. The *Examiner* was across the hall from the Merchants Parking Association.

The Murakami sisters Aya and Masa ran the store downstairs and their brother Kay handled repairs and other chores. An office, kitchen and dining area stood in the back, separated from the store by a Japanese doorway curtain. Aya was quiet. So was Kay. Masa was chatty and full of nervous energy.

Kay walked the halls several times in the evening to make sure no light bulbs were out, offices were locked, restrooms and toilets were working and no unwanted strangers were lurking. After I got off work, I ran into him browsing through magazines and books at Magazine City, a popular downtown spot. I went there for the latest paperback copies of books by Ed McBain, a prolific author of the 87th Precinct mysteries. There, Kay and I caught up on events of the day.

After Kay passed away in 1982, I helped Aya and Masa lug heavy boxes around in the back of the store. When an overhead fluorescent tube began to buzz and flicker, I climbed on a ladder to change it. I spent a lot of time talking to them and discovered their curious minds, knowledge of history and fierce commitment to the store their father had started. They were saddened by the rapid assimilation of third-generation Sansei and the loss of Japanese language fluency.

They were deeply spiritual. I knew they visited the Nichiren

Buddhist Temple near the Seattle Glove Company, where my mother had worked. But I wasn't sure whether they were Buddhist. They seemed like very free thinkers. They sometimes talked to me about the paranormal—ghosts, the afterlife, other worlds, the inexplicable. "Are you a Christian?" Masa asked me. I told her that I didn't belong to any church. "I guess you never know what's on the other side until you get there," she said. I agreed.

I later discovered that they had a huge number of books on Seichō-no-Ie, a New Thought faith that emphasizes the deep connection between spirituality, divine thought and health.

The store was their life. They were always there, except when they took off to travel. They told me about wondrous historic sites in Europe, South America, Africa, China, Russia and Mexico. They said each journey expanded their understanding of others, in turn deepening their spirituality and belief in our common humanity. They came back refreshed, eager to settle back into the routine of running the store.

The Murakamis were among the first inmates to return to Seattle after World War II from Camp Minidoka in southern Idaho. "We were lucky," Masa told me. "A lot of the Issei and Nisei didn't have anything to come back to because they sold everything when they went off to camp." Pointing toward the Jackson Loan Company, a pawn shop next door to Higo, she explained, "The folks over there took care of the store for us while we were gone. We owe them a debt of gratitude. Without them, we wouldn't have been able to start up again."

Aya added, "When we went away to Minidoka, we made sure to save a crowbar and a hammer. When we came back, we pried the plywood off the front of the store and we were back in business again."

The folks Aya and Masa were referring to were a Jewish

family, Julius Blumenthal and his half-brother Maurice Zim-mer. They watched over the boarded-up business and paid bills for the Murakamis in their absence. In return for that act of kindness, the Murakamis never raised their rent, allowing the pawn shop to survive despite its dearth of business. For years, I faithfully delivered copies of the newspaper to Julius, stationed behind the pawn shop counter, and never once saw a single cus-tomer enter the faintly lit space. From Aya and Masa, I learned about the bond of friendship.

Aya passed away in 1999. Masa continued to work at Higo, joined by her good friend Esther Matsuda, until they were too old to keep things going. The store finally closed in 2003, after 75 years of business, out of concern for Masa's safety.

Paul Murakami, a cousin of the Murakami sisters, helped clear out much of the store's huge inventory. Kimonos were donated to the Japanese Queen Court. Some items went to the Wing Luke Museum and the Ayame Kai Guild. Much of the remaining merchandise—toys and dishes—were boxed up and stored in a warehouse in the Jackson Building. It's now a hidden time capsule.

In 2004, an old friend of mine, Binko Chiong, and her husband John Bisbee, an architect, reopened the store. They renamed it Kobo at Higo. This was their second store. Their first—Kobo—is located on Capitol Hill and features the work of Northwest artists and small studio artisans from Japan. Kobo at Higo carries similar work and also hosts community programs. It includes a small museum of old objects from the original store.

During the remodel of the store, John found a small box of colored drinking straws that had fallen through a crevice between the cement floor and a wooden cabinet. It was iden-tical to the straws he got as a child when his mother served him Ovaltine mixed with milk. The box featured an image of Mother Hubbard and a hinged cardboard door opening to a cellophane window, revealing the colored drinking straws inside. On the package was written, "Old Mother Hubbard went to the cupboard to get her dog a bone."

John said that in that moment, the taste of Ovaltine rose in his throat.

Masa attended the opening of Kobo at Higo on November 20, 2004. By then, she had moved to Nikkei Manor, an assisted living facility in the International District. Esther came, too. Both had failing memories. When John tried to explain to Masa that he and Binko were reopening the store, she thought that they were new employees. She responded, 'Have you talked to my sister? Is it okay with her?'" Masa forgot that her sister was gone.

I went over to shake Masa's hand. I hadn't seen her in years. She looked confused, but she perked up when she saw me approach. She remembered my father and the Hong Kong Restaurant, one of her favorite eateries. My heart warmed.

Masa died peacefully in her sleep on January 29, 2010.

John and Binko lovingly restored a small garden behind Higo. It had been started by Chiyo, the second oldest Murakami sister. She died from tuberculosis in 1937 at the age of 22. The garden included a pear tree which still bears fruit a century later. The restored garden has since become a community gathering place.

One day, Bob Santos asked to meet with John to discuss using Chiyo's Garden for a reception for InterIm. They met at Kaname Izakaya, the Japanese restaurant next door to Higo, also in the Jackson Building. They drank green tea, sitting in a mahogany booth salvaged from the old Jackson Café.

The booth jolted Uncle Bob's memory. He and his father

used to eat breakfast at the Jackson Café on Saturdays. Uncle Bob's dad flirted with Ruby, the waitress. She always remembered their orders. "I can see my dad and me sitting in this booth," Uncle Bob told John, his eyes tearing, his voice catching. "Wow. Thank you for preserving this memory."

CHAPTER 27

The Egg Capital of the
International District

THE MOVE TO THE JACKSON Building above Higo began
a new chapter for the *Examiner*. Operating an arm's
length away from ACWA, I felt more secure about
pursuing independent journalism.

In our first year, we crowded inside a single 200-square-
foot room. Later, we settled into two adjoining offices, rooms
126 and 127, and a third unmarked storage room down the
hall. Our rent was only $90 a month, including utilities. When
we got behind, Masa reassured me: "Pay me when you can."
She said she liked the paper's mission and its support of the
community.

Our offices had solid oak doors with pebbled glass panes
on top. From the outside, they looked like a private detective's
suite lifted from the 1930s. Inside, cast iron steam radiators
provided heat, clanging and hissing throughout the day. Each
room had a wash basin with running water. The space was insanely cramped. A tan, vinyl-covered loveseat offered the only
guest seating. Visitors simply stood and talked while I worked

at my primitive computer. File cabinets, stacks of old newspapers and Asian American publications filled every corner. In the summertime, a noisy window-mounted air conditioner roared in the background. I had to yell to be heard.

Despite our modest footprint, the *Examiner* office was a busy community hangout. People stopped by to suggest story ideas and to find other Asian Americans of like mind. We learned the news from them. The Internet, social media and cell phones didn't exist. Our visitors included student activists seeking a path into community service, left-leaning political crusaders, angst-ridden artists, ethnic identity-seekers and geeky intellectuals.

Ken Mochizuki, my staff writer, marveled at the large number of "eggs"—eccentrics, iconoclasts, wayward souls—who came by. The term "egg" was derived from Sherwood Anderson's short story collection *The Triumph of the Egg*. I recommended the book to Ken after he asked me to review his unpublished manuscript *Beacon Hill Boys*. I suggested that he check out another Anderson book, *Winesburg, Ohio*, the rendering of a fictional small town as seen through the eyes of an aspiring writer, once young, now past 60. All the characters in Anderson's two works were what the author called "grotesques," a "long procession of figures," "amusing" and "beautiful," earnestly seeking life's elusive "truths."

I thought of the International District as a distinctive place much like Winesburg, Ohio. The people who paraded through our offices were its characters.

Ken and I used the word "egg" to describe anyone who had trouble adapting to social norms. Those with eggish tendencies gravitated to our office. We didn't use the term as a pejorative. Eggish people were colorful, fun, idiosyncratic, random, astute, spontaneous, hilarious. But by nature, they couldn't accept the way things were. They were skeptics, cynics and change agents. They agonized. They complained. They whined. The *Examiner* was a basket full of eggs. Ken and I were eggs. Uncle Bob and Donnie Chin were surely eggs. I boasted to Ken that the *Examiner* was the egg capital of the International District, maybe even all of Seattle.

Like Ken and me, most *Examiner* contributors had grown up on Beacon Hill. We were like members of the same clan. We were reared by stern World War II era blue-collar parents. We lived in split-level *Brady Bunch*-era homes with moss-infested lawns. We played in gravel streets and vacant lots and went to the same schools and churches. We patronized the same chain department stores, family grocers, *chop suey* restaurants and Japanese American auto repair shops.

Ken had returned home after limited success as an actor in Hollywood. Although he grew up on College Street about a block away from me, we didn't meet until he joined the *Examiner*. We probably romped in the same wooded areas. He was born in 1954, a year after me. His birthday was May 18, and mine was May 17.

Other Beacon Hiller boys included Gary Iwamoto, a columnist and occasional reporter; Dean Wong, chief photographer during the latter part of my tenure as editor; and Jeff Hanada, an illustrator who worked at Boeing as a graphic designer. Jeff sketched the calligraphy for the *Examiner* masthead. At Mercer Junior High, I was a classmate of Jeff's older brother Gary. Ann Fujii, a frequent news contributor, was the cousin of Marilyn Tokuda, my friend from high school. Ann's father, artist Frank Fujii, taught at Franklin when I was a student there.

Female staff with Beacon Hill roots included Karen and Kathryn Chinn, sisters whose mother worked alongside mine sewing outerwear jackets at Seattle Quilt Manufacturing

Company. They both majored in communications at the UW. Karen worked as the advertising sales manager. Kathryn wrote features.

Karen was very eggish. She had a childlike curiosity about everything. She started all of her sentences with "Gosh!" She had no inhibitions about asking ridiculous questions. I never understood how her mind made associations. After work, I dropped her off at her mother's house on Beacon Hill, a few blocks from my parents' house. During the ride, she talked to me about the chemotherapy she had received for non-Hodgkin's lymphoma in high school. She felt lucky to be alive. "You know, Ron, I'm not afraid to speak my mind because for me, every day I'm alive is a gift," she said. "I want to enjoy every moment."

Karen moved to New York City to pursue her dreams. She and several others started *New Asian Times* in 1988. She served as its advertising manager. The monthly publication folded after only a few issues. She went on to work as executive director of the Asian American Arts Alliance. In the summer of 1989, she met and fell in love with Philip Lee, cofounder of Lee & Low Books, an Asian American publishing company specializing in multicultural children's titles. They married in 1991. She gushed to me about how happy she was to have found him.

Sally and Sara Yamasaki were another sister duo at the paper. Sally rivaled Karen for exuberance and gab. She loved to ask questions, often stringing four or five together, barely pausing to breathe or wait for a response. I discovered that Sally's husband Dan Benson was the younger brother of Ray Benson, a classmate of mine at Franklin High. Ray and I were in a math class together. He was my only white friend in high school.

Lorraine Sako also grew up on Beacon Hill. She was an artistic soul with glowing empathy for others and a rascally nature. She wrote stories and drew illustrations for the *Examiner*. I met her in 1979 at the UW. Although Lorraine's primary interest was landscape architecture, she took a class in Asian American studies from Peter Bacho which whetted her appetite for community work. Like Dean and me, she shared a very close relationship with Donnie Chin.

Lorraine told me that her father Sam had worked for Aluminum & Bronze Fabricators. He designed the guardrails in the Kingdome. He also fashioned the brass handrails for the Nordstrom store several doors away from an apartment I lived in during my final year at the UW. On hot days, I used to go inside the store and run my hands along the handrails because they looked so cool and shiny.

Georgene Kumasaka, a Franklin High School classmate, had been a regular contributor to the *Franklin Tolo*. I envied her and other Asian American students whose bylines appeared in the paper. I even saved a 1970 edition of the *Tolo* with her reviews of Lillian Hellman's *The Little Foxes* and Nathan Teitel's *The Initiation*, two Seattle Repertory Theatre productions. It felt somehow ironic to become her editor.

Diane Wong, the second director of the Washington Commission on Asian American Affairs, was another freelancer. She sent me articles from San Francisco on national topics after moving there in 1980 to work for the Chinatown Youth Center. Two years later, she became editor of *East/West News*, a prominent Chinatown newspaper. Her mother was a seamstress at Skyway Luggage. She and my mother were friends. Diane was married to Gary Locke, a member of the Washington State House of Representatives with a brilliant political future. Gary grew up on Beacon Hill and attended Franklin High, three years ahead of me.

Three siblings in the Mano family—Mark, Leslie and

Charlene—also contributed to the *Examiner*. Mark was a reporter, Leslie coordinated an arts column and Charlene did illustrations. Their great-grandfather, Frank Niroku Shitamae, had operated the N.P. Hotel, where Bob Santos's father lived. Charlene's grandmother and grand-aunts grew up in the hotel.

Sumi Hayashi, a versatile writer-photographer, was raised in the Central Area, where her parents ran the Madison Plaza Pharmacy. Her husband Carlos Smith helped distribute the *Examiner* and volunteered at the International District Emergency Center, working with Donnie Chin and Dean Wong. Carlos's father, Charles Z. Smith, later rose to prominence as the first African American Washington State Supreme Court Justice. Guy Tsutsumoto, the *Examiner's* bookkeeper during the early years, was another local whose family ran a pharmacy, State Drug Company, just outside the International District.

Vicki Woo, a Japanese American, was unusual even among us eggs. She was older and had a young daughter. The rest of us weren't even thinking about marriage or parenthood. What drew Vicki to the *Examiner* was an intense curiosity about her Japanese American roots. She was close friends with Yuri Takahashi, a member of the Asian Pacific Women's Caucus. But she didn't know—until learning about Yuri's fatal cancer—that Yuri was married to a man named Jim. Vicki was frustrated by how indirect and private Japanese Americans were. "Who is this person named Yuri?" she asked. "I don't really know."

In 1989, Vicki left Seattle to attend law school at McGeorge School of Law in Sacramento. I wrote a letter of recommendation for her. Vicki told me that her kids Jay and Holly didn't want her to leave Seattle, but she felt she needed to escape her comfortable environment, force her children to grow, and develop her own identity and career. I was happy that her work at the *Examiner* had helped build her confidence to take this step.

Serena Louie, the business manager, was at the *Examiner* for a long stint—from 1982 to 1994. She kept track of finances, sold ads and answered the phone. She had no interest in attending community meetings. When she was done at the office, she went home. She had a carefree manner, a wry sense of humor and a wild laugh that went on forever. She wore a hunter green Nike hoodie, jeans and white sneakers. She played basketball in the Asian American community leagues and was a drummer for the Seattle Chinese Community Girls Drill Team.

Sandra Goong, who preceded Serena as business manager, had recruited Serena to replace her. They were friends from basketball and drill team. Sandra fearlessly made cold calls to prospective advertisers, weathering the many rejections with a casual shrug. She left the paper after a year-and-a-half for a better-paying banking job downtown but continued to join us for lunch. Serena and Sandra kept everyone in stitches with their offbeat banter.

Michelle Kumata, who started working for the *Examiner* as her senior project in high school, was a prolific and talented graphic artist whose illustrations graced the pages of the paper for years before she left to do similar work for *The Seattle Times*. She had a coy sense of humor. Michelle called me "Uncle Ron," as did many other younger volunteers. During newspaper production, she said, "Uncle Ron showed me the finer points of paste-up. Check under your shoes for lost pieces of copy."

Sue Chin, a freelancer, had previously worked for the city of Seattle, staffing the International Special Review District Board. She wore cable-knit sweaters with jeans and sported a pixie haircut which accentuated her broad smile and rosy cheeks. She looked like a female version of the logo character on the Sunny Jim peanut butter jar. She and Serena traded risqué gossip. I relied on Sue to turn in clean copy that required little editing. She eschewed material possessions, living modestly in a trailer in North Seattle.

At several junctures when the *Examiner* ran very low on cash, Sue made financial contributions, relying on money she received from the sale of her late father's commercial building in southeast Seattle. Her only stipulation to me was that she get no recognition for her gifts.

Sue's gesture taught me a lesson which guided me years later in my career as director of the Wing Luke Museum. *Fundraising follows passion.* Sue, like others at the paper, was there because it fostered a sense of community among a circle of people who believed in the same things she did. When individuals feel rooted in a cause, they will easily decide to give, often with little prompting.

I met Brian Lock, who grew up in the small south Puget Sound town of Shelton, during my final year at the *Examiner*. He sold ads. He and I had much in common. I had grown up in the *chop suey* environment of the Hong Kong Restaurant; Brian in the Ming Tree Café (明樹餐館), his dad's restaurant, which served loggers in Mason County. Even though Brian was more than a decade younger, we became lasting friends. We had the same low-key temperament and a high disdain for pretense. Serena gave him the nickname "Brain Lock" after she saw a piece of mail with his name misspelled.

Not all *Examiner* contributors were locals. Some were transplants. David Takami, a freelance writer who spent three years in Japan, had worked as an editor for the English language *Japan Times*. Bob Shimabukuro had served as editor for *Pacific Citizen*, the newspaper of the Japanese American Citizens League (JACL). Alan Chong Lau was a visual artist and poet-writer from California. They added a broader lens to our conversations and work.

Stan Shikuma and Tracy Lai were a husband-and-wife team from California who alternated as advertising sales coordinator. They met at UC Berkeley as student activists, moving to Seattle in 1981 after Tracy decided to pursue a graduate degree in multicultural education at the UW.

Stan grew up in Watsonville, where his father farmed strawberries, raspberries and blackberries. Tracy was born in San Francisco's Chinatown but was raised in Los Altos. Tracy was involved in an unsuccessful effort in 1977 to prevent the eviction of the low-income tenants in San Francisco's International Hotel, where her aunt lived. The International Hotel struggle, which ended in a dramatic clash between 3,000 protesters and 400 riot police, mirrored the Milwaukee Hotel struggle in Seattle.

Whatever the job at the paper lacked in financial compensation was more than made up for by the time I got to spend with my tribe of fellow eggs and activists. I gained many close, lifelong friends whose sensibilities matched mine and whose talents I enlisted for future shared endeavors.

One day, I saw one of the ubiquitous pink "While You Were Out" message slips for me pinned on the cork bulletin board above Serena's work area. It was addressed to "Ant-eater." "What's this?" I asked. Serena said a man had called—it sounded like an elderly gentleman—but she had a difficult time understanding him because of his heavy Filipino accent. She finally surmised that his name was Mr. Francisco. "But he kept asking for the ant-eater," Serena said. "I'm not sure what he wants. Can you call him back?" I burst into laughter. It was Emiliano Francisco, the crusty publisher of the *Filipino American Herald*. He probably wanted to come by to trade tips about where to get ads. "'Editor'—that's what he said, Serena!" I said. "He was asking for the editor!"

From that moment on, I was known by Serena and others at the *Examiner* as "the ant-eater." We began to address Serena as "Serena Louis" after she received a letter mistakenly referring to her by that name.

Serena teased me about my limited palate. Sometimes, I bought a plain French baguette from the grocery store down the street and nibbled on it for hours, washing it down with sips of boiled water from the small electric water pot. I had kicked my coffee addiction. I now drank hot water all day. Serena quipped, "You might feel right at home in prison." I thought about it. "You're right, Ms. Louis! And I'd probably make more money as an inmate, too! How can I get in?"

Serena, Ken and I tried to one-up one another over the frugality of our families. We were crazy, cheap Asians. Ken said Japanese Americans rinsed out and saved Wonder Bread bags and empty plastic condiment cups. "That's nothing," Serena bragged. "My grandma reuses paper towels by hanging them up to dry and using them again." I chimed in: "Hey, my mother does that, too." I pointed out that a corner of our kitchen dining table was piled with disposable Styrofoam bowls that were used again and again after washing. Serena and I both commented that the "practical" Chinese didn't take the protective plastic wrap off of newly purchased lamps: "There's dang plastic wrap all over stuff in the living room. That way, you don't have to clean."

Serena had another thing to crow about: "We couldn't afford snow boots so we'd take Wonder Bread bags and strap them on tight over our regular shoes with a couple rubber bands so that we could go play and have warm, dry feet! Much cheaper than five pairs of snow boots for the Louie kids!"

We discussed the bargain basement in the big Sears store on First Avenue South near South Lander Street in the industrial area now known as SoDo. All the Chinese shopped there. This part of town was sprinkled with warehouses, surplus shops and manufacturing plants. Getting there necessitated a teeth-rattling car ride over old railroad tracks to a building with a lofty clock tower visible from far away. Chinese called it the *see-lop fong*, or the "garbage room."

Penny-pinchers came to paw through clearance merchandise—clothing, accessories, shoes, appliances and power tools—heaped on large tables. Prices were marked down several times. If you weren't careful, you might get elbowed in the eye. I saw tug-of-wars erupt between shouting people vying for the same bargain item. It was almost as amusing as Big Time Wrestling.

CHAPTER 28

Fine-cut Rice at Ying Hei Restaurant

I N MY DAYS OF BLITHE freedom as a community journalist, lunch hour was my favorite time. I reserved the noon hour to eat with close friends and peers who, like me, were drawn to the nonprofit work in the International District. Later in my career, as a professional fundraiser, lunch became something very different. Lunch became a responsibility—a time for dress-up appointments with donors, corporate leaders and important public officials.

I never went to the Hong Kong Restaurant. It felt awkward to go back as a customer to the place where I had been a busboy for so many years. My father, *Ming-bok* and Auntie Dorothy were still there. It made me sad to see them still laboring on their feet in their old age. It sank my spirit.

I gravitated toward restaurants that were homey and cheap. I didn't like spots that catered to tourists or people with fussy gourmet tastes. My preferred lunch spots were Kau Kau (巧巧孖結), King Café (天子飯店), Linyen, Luna Café and several Japanese American hole-in-the-wall diners.

Kau Kau was the only restaurant that served barbecued pork and roasted meats. It started as a Polynesian-style restaurant downtown on Second Avenue in 1959 and moved to Chinatown in 1974. It offered classic *chop suey* fare: fried rice, *chow mein*, sweet-and-sour pork, egg rolls, almond chicken and deep-fried squid. I ordered the juicy barbecued pork with rice. My friend Gene Viernes got the rice platter with shrimp and lobster sauce, gobbling all of it down in minutes.

Silme Domingo favored King Café. He picked everything on the limited menu. If I was in a hurry, I asked for three steamed *hom bow*—a single order—at the front counter from Mrs. Fannie Lew, the owner, then hustled back to work. For only $1.50, my stomach was satisfied until dinner time.

I sometimes ate alone at Linyen. It was never busy. I went there because Ken Woo, the cartoonist for the *Examiner*, was the waiter. He made sure the rice plate combo I got was plentiful. I liked Ken's quirky humor. We discussed ideas for upcoming cartoon strips.

My favorite Japanese American diners were Ma's Café, Puget Sound Café, Crescent Café and the 300 Restaurant. They served daily specials of white rice, Asian-style vegetables, stewed meat and Langendorf white bread for $2. The 300 outlasted the others. I went there on Friday for its famous stewed oxtails over white rice. The diner got its unusual name from its original address: 300 14th Avenue South. It was run by Mrs. Tsuruko Nakano, an elderly white-haired woman, and her son Terry. When it moved to 1825 South Jackson Street, the tiny café bolstered the number of seats from 13 to 24.

I took "field trips" with the ACWA gang to Royal Fork Buffet on 15th Avenue on Capitol Hill for the all-you-can-eat buffet. The line started with diced fruit, dinner rolls, salads and mashed potatoes, followed by the more desirable items:

meatloaf, fried chicken, ham, and roast beef. I returned for second and third helpings to get my money's worth. It was nearly impossible to work—or even stay awake—when I returned to the office. I needed several cups of coffee to restart my brain.

After the *Examiner* got settled in the Jackson Building, we discovered Ying Hei Restaurant at 664 South King Street. It opened in May 1977 in a storefront previously occupied by Little Three Grand Restaurant and later Sun Ya Restaurant (新雅). The front facade was bright green, with the trace outline of a curved pagoda rooftop above the name. Ying Hei was open daily from 11:30 a.m. to 10:30 p.m.

We hit the jackpot. The food was reliably delicious and cheap. We never had to wait. No tourists. It became our default lunchtime destination. We went there practically every day. It was the *Examiner's* private dining club.

As the hands of the wall clock arched toward the noon hour, Serena turned to me and said, "Hey dare, Ronnie! *Hwee hek lunchee!*" (去吃嘛治) Translation: "Let's go eat lunch!" I looked up from my work. "Is it time already?" Serena: "Yep." I turned to Ken: "Usual?" "Sure," he said. No further discussion. "Okay, let's go." We shut down the computers and turned on the phone answering machine. A few friends and volunteers in the office walked to the restaurant with us.

The Lee family ran this modest business. The father, Kam Lee, was the cook and the mother, Bik Lee, the cashier and kitchen helper. The eldest daughter Jeannie, the one who spoke English, was the waitress. Her younger sister Angela and younger brother Chris scampered about, sometimes vanishing upstairs to the vacant second-level banquet room used for storing extra chairs.

Kam Lee, a slight man with a booming voice, first immigrated to Seattle with his father in 1966 from 49 South Village

(四十九南村) in Hoisan. Kam's wife and Jeannie joined them in 1974. By then, Jeannie was 12. The family lived in the Kong Yick Apartments at 707 ½ South King Street. Prior to starting Ying Hei, Kam Lee was a cook at the South China Restaurant. He showed others how to make fried egg rolls, preparing the thin outer crepes by deftly swirling a layer of batter in a frying pan with his fingers and lifting the crepes out as they cooked.

Our usual eating spot was a booth near the front of the restaurant, just past the bright orange counter where old Chinese men sat on stools drinking coffee, smoking and eating.

The dining room walls were decorated with four classic Chinese carved wood panels. The largest framed image featured 100 horses. But it was hard to appreciate the fine detail under the sheath of plastic wrap covering them.

Jeannie, still a teenager when she started, knew our favorite dishes by heart. She didn't waste time on menus unless there was an unfamiliar face in our party. We knew all the dishes and prices. The Ying Hei Special Rice was my standard. It featured a mixture of available stir-fried vegetables and meat, usually chicken slices.

Ken's go-to dish was the black bean *chow mein* with beef. He preferred the Hong Kong-style crispy noodles. His second favorite was what we termed the "off-white" dish: rice with squid and cauliflower. After trying nearly every dish on the menu, we experimented with unusual combinations; hence, the "off-white" dish.

When Ken couldn't decide what to order, I asked, "Do you want volume or flavor?" He wrinkled his brow in mock reflection before answering. A preference for volume meant the *chow mein*. A vote for flavor meant the "off-white" dish.

I went through a similar ritual with other members of our party. I tried to guess what might tickle their palate, picking from each person's favorites. We were all very predictable. Serena had the "fine-cut" chicken curry over rice. Dean liked the scrambled eggs with pork on rice. Michelle ordered the combo plate special with *chow mein* and sweet-and-sour pork. David chose the *chicken chow mein* with crispy noodles; sometimes, he'd go for the curry chicken like Serena. Greg Tuai favored the black bean chicken dish with peppers and onions. Whatever her choice, Elaine Ito—yielding to her frugal nature—ate only half her lunch, boxing up the remainder for dinner.

Among the Ying Hei regulars, the term "fine-cut" quickly migrated into our daily vocabulary, used to add emphasis and punch, as in "What a fine-cut mess he's created for himself."

Shortly after moving to Seattle, Bob Shimabukuro joined us at Ying Hei for his inaugural lunch with the *Examiner* crew. Bob is a soft-spoken, reflective soul. He was puzzled as to why I was ordering for everyone. When he heard Ken saying he was going to have the off-white or *lo fan* dish, he peered through his thick glasses and asked, "What's that?"

Serena giggled, "You'll see when it comes out."

Jeannie stood at the side of our table, bemused, sometimes tossing in a cavalier suggestion herself. This routine always started out our lunch on a cheery note, eliciting loud peals of laughter from everyone at our table and bewildered glances from uninitiated diners at other tables. The Chinese men at the orange counter paid no heed.

During lunch, Donnie Chin came by to pick up food to go. He often left his meal selection to Jeannie and Mr. Lee in the kitchen. While he waited, Donnie stopped by our table and shared information about recent robberies, fires or emergencies. He wore his khaki uniform and carried his police scanner, one ear attuned to the staccato rhythm of the radio dialog.

If Dean Wong was with us, Donnie trash-talked him.

Donnie started by saying, "Goddamn, fuck you. You're a piece of shit." He called Dean "Wrong Wong" or shook his head and commented, "That boy needs to get his act together." Dean sighed, shrugged or shook his leg. An uninitiated bystander might think that Donnie had just publicly degraded Dean for no good reason. He hadn't. He had great respect for Dean, as did Dean for Donnie. If Maxine Chan stopped by, her way of expressing endearment was to shout: "Eat shit and die!" By comparison, Karen Chinn's pet swear word was a tame "Boogers!" which Lorraine and I adopted when hailing each other: "Boogers to you!"

When Donnie heard something of interest on the radio, he dashed off in mid-sentence, before his food was ready. His order was kept warm until he returned.

Dean felt especially at home at the Ying Hei because of his childhood memories of the restaurant when it was the Little Three Grand and his father worked there. Dean's dad arrived from China in 1922 and was a U.S. Army cook during World War II. Dean accompanied him on trips to Capitol Hill to pick up donuts and pastries for the Little Three Grand in his father's light blue 1955 Chevy.

We faithfully adhered to our Ying Hei routine until February 1996, when the family sold the business. We were very sad to see it go. By then, I was working at the Wing Luke Museum, welcoming newcomers to the neighborhood at other lunch spots. Ying Hei Special Rice became a quaint memory.

The new owners continued the business as a Chinese restaurant. They removed the plastic wrap from the wall art.

CHAPTER 29

Quong Tuck Restaurant

THE QUONG TUCK RESTAURANT (廣德酒家) was the activist community's favorite dinner and evening hangout. If, during the course of a single day, I made it to Ying Hei for lunch and Quong Tuck for an evening meal, my stomach would be happy and I'd be caught up with friends and all that mattered in my small universe.

The Quong Tuck Restaurant—often referred to simply as "Q.T."—was steeped in Seattle's pioneer past. The Quong Tuck Company (廣德號) was established as an import-export firm in 1890 by legendary Chinese labor contractor Chin Gee-Hee (陳宜禧). He dispatched Chinese laborers to construct local railroad lines and regrade downtown streets. The firm was first located at Second Avenue South and Washington Street in old Chinatown. In 1910, it moved to 721 South King Street, where it stayed until it was converted into a restaurant.

Quong Tuck Restaurant owner Danny Woo was the grand-nephew of Chin Gee-Hee. He worked at Quong Tuck when it was still his grandfather's business. In 1975, Danny and his wife Wilma reopened the unused storefront—closed for years—as a modern restaurant. As they cleaned out the space, they discovered huge bales of Chinese workers' clothing, tea cups, rice bowls, winnowing baskets, trunks and family photos. They were donated to the Wing Luke Museum, ensuring that a vital piece of the community's past would be saved.

Woo asked local architect Joey Ing to design the restaurant. The main dining area featured a row of cozy oak booths with high backs and plush orange seat cushions. The ancient Quong Tuck sign hung over the space. A large wooden herbal chest, Chinese scrolls and images of the Chinese kitchen god added to the decor. The mezzanine level included a second dining area, a bar and several video gaming tables. After work, the Chinatown regulars filed upstairs, taking their usual tables. Some folks sat for hours, nursing their beverages and playing Pac-Man, Space Invaders and other video games until they ran out of quarters. There was a TV at the bar and a dart board in the back of the room.

The day-to-day operation of Q.T. was managed by Wilma—everyone called her "Auntie Wilma"—and two grown children, Curtis and Teresa. I attended Mercer Junior High with Trina, a third child. She worked at *UW Daily* while I was there. She moved to Berkeley, California, after college.

Danny, hobbled by poor health as he aged, perched in a chair at the front of the restaurant, calmly smoking his pipe and welcoming customers. He didn't say much. Sometimes, he barely moved. Each time I saw him, he appeared even more frail and shrunken. He reminded me of the stereotypical wooden cigar store Indian common decades ago.

The restaurant billed itself as the only ID eatery offering "American cuisine." It offered huge, juicy prime rib sandwiches, pork chops, burgers, fries, and desserts like cheesecake and apple pie. Occasionally, Auntie Wilma prepared stewed oxtails, giving the 300 Restaurant a run for its money. The Q.T. stayed open until 4 a.m.

I went upstairs to watch friends play video games before coming back down to eat in one of the booths. It was quieter there. I ordered the prime rib or pork chops. The entrées came with rice and veggies, usually zucchini and onions sautéed in oil and butter. I was not a big dessert person, but it was here that I developed my love for apple pie with a flaky crust.

The restaurant had a call list of folks who wanted to know if oxtails or short ribs were offered as lunch specials. Several attorneys—Rod Kawakami, Mike Leong and Kathryn Bannai—were at the top of the list. They worked in a suite of offices a few blocks away. They were trying to overturn the conviction of former Seattle resident Gordon Hirabayashi, who had defied incarceration orders against Japanese Americans during World War II.

One regular was Susie Chin, the receptionist at the ID health clinic, later renamed International Community Health Services. By the late 1970s, the tiny clinic was deluged with a wave of Vietnamese refugees. She was so busy tending to six phone lines and the mob of walk-ins that she didn't have time to eat or take a restroom break. After she got off, she headed directly to Quong Tuck to grab a meal and unwind. There, she learned to drink hard liquor. She had Wild Turkey straight up.

Susie sat upstairs with Uncle Bob, Bernie Whitebear and Bernie's youngest sister Laura Wong. Bernie founded the United Indians of All Tribes Foundation. He was the most prominent Native American leader in Seattle. I didn't know Bernie very well, but Laura was a dear friend.

Laura's mother Mary Christian Hall Wong was a fabled storyteller and member of the Sin-Aikst tribe, part of the

Confederated Tribes of the Colville Reservation. Mary's first husband, Bernie's father, was Filipino. Bernie's original last name was Reyes. Laura's Chinese last name came from her mother's second husband.

Laura added "Whitebear" to her name to honor Bernie after he passed away. She shared fond memories of her parents' *chop suey* restaurant along Pacific Avenue in downtown Tacoma. Laura mastered traditional methods of coiling and twining to create beautiful Native American baskets with a contemporary flair. She sold them at the prestigious Santa Fe Indian Market and the Heard Museum Guild Indian Fair & Market in Phoenix. After I became director of the Wing Luke Museum, she donated baskets to support our fundraising auction.

One day, Bernie came to Q.T. with Native American actor Will Sampson, who starred with Jack Nicholson in the 1975 movie *One Flew Over the Cuckoo's Nest.* Bernie introduced Sampson to Laura and the regulars. Sampson was in town for the annual Seafair pow-wow, hosted by Bernie's agency. Laura recalled with a laugh, "He was so tall that he was taller than us even when he was sitting down. He pulled out a piece of paper and sketched a picture of a Native person. Just like that, in no time flat. It was amazing."

Other Q.T. regulars included the *Examiner* gang I ate with at Ying Hei. I also saw Tim Otani, Michael Flor, Sue Taoka, Arlyne Sevilla and other young Asian American activists there.

Auntie Wilma was everyone's "second mom." Tim Otani said Wilma "always welcomed you back 'home.' It was like the TV show *Cheers*, a place where everyone knew your name." In 1984, the bar at Q.T. was recreated as a theatrical set for Northwest Asian American Theatre's annual "Community Show-Off" fundraiser. Curtis Woo made a guest appearance as the bartender during this riotously funny event.

If I needed to reach someone for a story in the *Examiner*, I left a note for Auntie Wilma, Teresa or Curtis. It was more likely that I would find them there in the evening than at home.

During his carefree bachelor days, Michael practically lived at Q.T. He played Space Invaders, dined on prime rib, and drank beer, gin and tonic, or martinis. He first met Auntie Wilma at the New Chinatown Restaurant in the early 1970s, where he'd go on weeknights after his UW classes. Wilma introduced him to martinis. They talked all evening. Michael followed Auntie Wilma to Q.T. after the New Chinatown closed.

Gary Iwamoto was another Q.T. faithful. He drank Budweiser or scotch—and sometimes Wild Turkey, like Susie. Gary often closed the bar at 2 a.m. He played all the video games: Donkey Kong, Asteroids, Ms. Pac-Man, Missile Command, Gorf, Galaga, Frogger and Space Invaders. Tim Otani was considered the master of Space Invaders.

Some friendships at Q.T. blossomed into marriage. Sue Taoka met her future husband, Richard Mar, during her first visit. Uncle Bob brought her for a drink. Everyone in the community knew Richard as Dicky. They saw Dicky sitting alone. Uncle Bob made introductions. Dicky took out a photo of a sailboat and asked Sue if she wanted to buy it. They began talking. "Who would have thought a pick-up line like that would stick?" she now reflects.

Dicky's father was Dewey Mar. He was in charge of Chinese movie nights at the Kokusai Theater. As youngsters, Dicky and his brothers Kenny and Tommy helped in the projection booth. Kenny was in my class at Mercer Junior High and at Beacon Hill Elementary School. Tommy, a volunteer photographer at the *Examiner* in the 1970s, was a good friend.

When Sue and Dicky decided to get married, they opted for a simple party. Bernie Whitebear invited them to use Daybreak Star Cultural Center, a Native American lodge in Discovery Park with a splendid view of Puget Sound. It was also the headquarters of the United Indians of All Tribes and Bernie's headquarters. Bernie had spearheaded a nonviolent takeover and occupation of the property in 1970 after most of the land was surplused by the government. The lodge was completed in 1977. Not only did Bernie offer up Daybreak Star for Sue and Dicky's wedding party, he also bought salmon directly off the fishing boats and helped prepare the fish over a fire for the event.

I had been to one other wedding at Daybreak Star. It was the union of my friend Barbara Means and her husband Russ Adams on February 4, 1978.

As young activists around me started getting married and settling down, Q.T.'s business plummeted. Only diehards like Uncle Bob and a few others continued to come. Danny Woo tried to resuscitate the business by adding Chinese American cuisine, but that idea went nowhere. Curtis joined the Seattle Police Department and Teresa enrolled in computer school at Boeing. In 1985, the restaurant closed. In January 1986, the Crystal Shrimp Restaurant opened in its place.

Auntie Wilma turned to babysitting and knitting. She designed and knitted custom Christmas stockings for her extended family, which included special Q.T. patrons. Wilma raised money for Donnie Chin and IDEC by knitting miniature Seattle Seahawks and UW Huskies stockings.

Every summer, I looked forward to seeing Wilma, Teresa and Curtis at the pig roast in the International District Community Garden. We always had a lot to catch up on.

CHAPTER 30

Donnie Chin

D ONNIE CHIN WAS THE EYES and ears of the neighborhood. He knew every Chinatown street and alley, every building, hotel room, restaurant, store and back room. He also knew all the residents as well as the troublemakers who drifted through. He was the neighborhood's advocate and protector. It was his life.

Donnie grew up in the Central District, but Chinatown beckoned. He moved there as soon as he was old enough to be on his own, and he never left. Dean Wong met Donnie on the corner of South King Street and Maynard Avenue South when the two were about seven or eight years old. Donnie scolded Dean for having a few Japanese American friends. Donnie was angry about the Japanese invading China during World War II. Like so many kids, he blurred the distinction between Japanese and Japanese Americans.

When I met Donnie—probably a decade later—he was grown up. I was bussing dishes at the Hong Kong Restaurant. I saw him sauntering up the street in long hair, khaki garb and army boots. He had been radicalized by the Asian identity student movement. He was swept up in the new crusade to preserve the International District and improve the quality of life for its low-income residents.

His family ran the Sun May Company (雙美古董店), a small Chinese gift shop at 672 South King Street. Every inch was filled—floor to ceiling—with imported knick-knacks, kung-fu shoes, Chinese quilted jackets, vintage signs, collectible toys, puzzles, books and magazines. Donnie's parents, Don and Myra Chin, originally opened the Sun May in 1962 as a basketry shop.

Myra, a stocky woman with big glasses and a round, permed hairdo, sat on a stool at the front counter. There were glass-paned wooden cabinets topped with old neon signs directly behind her. Donnie's mother was a Mar, the younger sister of Jimmy and Howard Mar, two brothers who ran Yick Fung & Company (益豐號), an import-export shop, one of the oldest continuously running businesses in Chinatown.

Donnie's father Don, an assertive, nattily dressed elder, helped establish the Chinatown Chamber of Commerce in the 1950s. He was also a founding board member of InterIm. I watched him on the street corner welcoming groups of visitors and at the International District Emergency Center (IDEC) with Donnie. Father and son would sit at IDEC in silence facing each other on opposite sides of a room, no more than 10 feet apart, barely exchanging a word, both strong-willed and proud. Often, it appeared that the two were mad at each other. I didn't dare ask what was up.

In 1967, Donnie and Dean, still in junior high school, created Asians for Unity with the goal of helping keep the neighborhood safe by patrolling its streets. They cleared out an abandoned apartment on the west side of Canton Alley, put up new walls and a staircase and converted it into their headquarters. Empty boxes and junk were moved into the basement of the Sun May Company.

The International District Emergency Center (IDEC) was born. Locals came to call it "The Center" or "I-D-E-C." Non-native Seattleites referred to it as "Eye-deck," a shorthand I've never used. Donnie trained to become a medic so he could better respond to incidents of street crime and fire and medical traumas, as well as to better provide volunteer support for community events.

A heavy metal door with a security alarm was installed at the front of IDEC headquarters. Inside, the walls were painted bright red. Donnie covered them with old posters for Asian American Heritage Month, Asian movies and community causes. He hung a Chinese lion dance head near his desk and draped a long windsock in the shape of a goldfish over one wall. The heart of IDEC was the radio room, where Donnie monitored police and emergency response calls. He kept fire helmets, flashlights, emergency medical kits, tools and army field rations near the door. Donnie reserved the white fire helmet for himself. Other volunteers used yellow helmets.

The upper level of IDEC became Donnie's private living space and residence. He rarely invited visitors up there. He used a sewing machine to make beautiful decorative pillows for women he was especially fond of, sewing the covers from scraps of silk embossed with Asian characters.

Donnie was also on a crusade to rescue and preserve history. He salvaged old signs, immigration and business documents, letters, restaurant menus, photos and the ordinary effects of daily life. He wasn't above snatching abandoned objects and papers on the sly from a recently vacated hotel room, a failed restaurant or a Chinese association office. He turned over much of his stash to the Wing Luke Museum after I became its director. His one caveat: "Remember, Ron, you didn't get none of this stuff from me."

He showed me a few rare Chinese American books tucked in a corner of Sun May. He gave me a copy of a classic 1913 Chinese American phrase book that authors Frank Chin, Shawn Wong and Jeffrey Paul Chan pointed to as evidence of the racism endured by early Chinese immigrants. Typical phrases included, "How long will we be kept in quarantine?," "The mob couldn't break into the cell," "If he breaks in you may use force," and "Have you heard about the murder?" I also saw in print the Chinese character combinations that Hoisan-ese immigrants used, including my parents—words like candle (洋燭), holiday (大日子), butcher shop (牛肉鋪) and oven (麵包爐). My first language was affirmed.

In 1977, Bob Santos tapped Donnie's sister Connie, three years younger than Donnie, to head up the new Denise Louie Child Care Center. It was named in memory of a 21-year-old Seattleite tragically gunned down in a gang shootout while she was dining in San Francisco's Chinatown. Connie worked with volunteers to convert a vacant portable building next to the Chinese Baptist Church into a facility serving 20 kids. It opened on June 19, 1978, as one of the first multilingual Asian American daycare centers on the West Coast.

Donnie and Connie—many of us referred to the two of them in the same breath—were a spunky brother-sister team. I saw either one or both of them at nearly all community events I attended as a reporter for the *Examiner* in those early years.

At one point, I asked Donnie to produce a monthly blotter for the *Examiner*. He firmly said no. A day later, he called to say, "When do you need it? If it helps you fill space, hey, no problem." We decided to call it "District Watch." It was a compilation of recent police, fire and other emergency incidents. He scribbled it in longhand on blue-lined notebook paper. I typed up as much of it as I had room for, cleaning up the grammar, rough street language and profanity.

Donnie and I chatted almost daily in Canton Alley because I parked my car in a lot near IDEC. He was always immaculately dressed in the same wrinkle-free khaki uniform, his big wire-rimmed glasses sliding down his nose. He had an impish grin that spread widely and quickly over his face when he became amused.

Our conversations always started the same way. "What's going on, man?" he'd ask. I would respond, "Not much." He would nod, pause, bob his chin, swiveling his head quickly to the left and right to see if anyone else was nearby. Then he wound up for a profanity-laden tirade about "fools, idiots and knuckleheads." He named high-profile community leaders, elected officials and activists. He fumed about apathetic bystanders who tuned out crimes on the street and the hardship of poor ID residents ("They didn't see nothing, right?").

I would let him rant. After a few minutes, he flamed out, concluding with a heavy sigh. His cynicism was somewhat contrived, a bit of a show. He wasn't as pessimistic as he tried to appear. Beneath his tough-guy artifice, he was unabashedly sentimental and soft-hearted. He took more time than anyone else I knew to mentor young people trying to find an emotional bridge to the ID. He loved the kids and let them hang out at IDEC and follow him around.

On March 9, 1984, when members of the Guardian Angels, a controversial street patrol group founded by anti-crime activist Curtis Sliwa, offered to establish a presence in the International District, Donnie Chin pushed back hard. Four members of the Guardian Angels, dressed in their signature red berets and t-shirts, squared off against Donnie and other community members at a meeting at the Bush-Asia Center. Folks from the ID said in unison: "Thanks, but no thanks." Donnie was direct: "It takes time to build up trust. If you think you're going to come down here and get the support of the community after a couple of sessions with us, you're crazy." After the meeting, which I covered for the *Examiner*, he told me he had one word to describe the Angels: "Fools." The Guardian Angels never set foot in the International District again.

About two weeks prior to his murder, I spoke to Donnie about retirement. It was one of countless Canton Alley conversations between the two of us over the years. We weren't talking about retirement for ourselves, but about the growing number of peers who ended their careers, falling into the welcoming embrace of Medicare and Social Security. The two of us hadn't reached that stage yet. I asked him how long he intended to continue at IDEC.

"You're not a young man anymore, Donnie," I lectured him. "What you do is way more dangerous than what I do. You should get someone else to go out on these runs for you."

Donnie shrugged, not responding to my suggestion, except to say that he had worked with many a "knucklehead" who had come and gone during his time in the District. He wondered where the next generation of leadership would come from: "A lot of these kids you see these days, Ron, I saw them when they were little and they were running around at I-D-E-C. Now, all they care about is money. It's sad." He shook his head and sighed. *Who would lead IDEC after Donnie?*

Newcomers to the nonprofit community realm had to pass the infamous "Donnie test." He didn't want people to use the ID as a launching pad for selfish gain. He hated fancy titles, thick portfolios and lists of past accolades ("Who gives a fuck?"). He eschewed community honors and refused to walk on stage to be recognized ("An award ain't good for nothing except covering a hole in the wall and keeping out the draft.").

Pauline Zeestraten, the first director of the Chinatown-International District Business Improvement Area (CIDBIA), was one outsider who passed the "Donnie test." A native of the Netherlands, Pauline worked closely with Tomio Moriguchi, Raymond Chinn, Dan Mar, Sue Taoka, Pauline Lau, Jan Johnson and several others to create a nonprofit self-taxing organization to replace IDEA in the 1990s.

In her first year at CIDBIA, Pauline wore hiking boots to work because she had to clean grease and lard from filthy Chinatown alleys. She didn't mind. Pauline's parents were small farmers back in the Netherlands, raising livestock and crops like wheat, barley and sugar beets. Pauline fit in right away. Donnie spent many hours hanging out at CIDBIA with Pauline, sharing news and gossip. He invited Pauline and her assistant Carolyn Hyman into the inner sanctum of IDEC to watch the September 11 terror attacks on his small black-and-white TV.

Another non-Seattle native who passed the "Donnie test" with flying colors was Sue Taoka. She came to Seattle in 1979 to attend law school. As a nonprofit community leader, Sue oversaw the development of the International District Village Square. Donnie quickly grew to trust and respect her. Like Pauline, Sue hailed from a farming background. Her parents had a vegetable farm in Hudson, Colorado. Uncle Bob called Sue a "pig-tailed country girl."

A third outsider Donnie came to trust was Jamie Lee, a California native who grew up in southeast Ohio. Jamie met Donnie at a Canton Alley barbecue in 2014 four days after she was hired by Seattle Chinatown-International District Preservation and Development Authority (SCIDpda) to work on public safety issues. Donnie hosted free summer barbecues, grilling hot dogs from Grocery Outlet and serving them in tortillas. Fortuna Café set up a table and sold fried chicken, *chow mein*, egg rolls and sticky rice. Donnie welcomed Jamie—as he had Sue and Pauline—by warning her about unsavory characters in the area, alerting her to drug-dealing hotspots and sharing derisive tidbits and jokes about "fools" he detested.

In 2009, the Wing Luke Museum began sponsoring Jam-Fest in Canton Alley every July in conjunction with Donnie's barbecues. Mini-rickshaw races were held, with battery-powered plastic toys from Donnie.

Since Donnie's death, there have been times when I've passed through Canton Alley or Maynard Alley and spotted someone ahead of me who looked like Donnie, in khaki-colored clothes with the same physical build. My heart jumps each time. I take a few deep breaths to regain my bearings.

Often, when I see the bright strobe lights or hear the shrill siren of emergency, fire or police vehicles converging in the ID, I also have to catch myself. *No, Donnie is not going to be there. He's gone.*

I wonder if this was how a phantom limb feels. I miss him every day. I still feel his presence.

CHAPTER 31

Alan Chong Lau

A TRADEMARK OF THE *EXAMINER'S* success has been its finely textured Asian American arts coverage. Much of the credit belongs to the paper's longtime arts editor Alan Chong Lau, a self-effacing poet and visual artist now represented by Art XChange Gallery in Seattle.

In the early 1980s, Alan's *State of the Art* section and *Arts Etc.* column began proudly covering new artists and community events not deemed worthy enough to be covered by mainstream press. In addition to lifting unrecognized visual artists out of the shadows, he launched *Pacific Reader*, a full literary supplement devoted to Asian American authors. He pays special attention to independent publishers and alternative media. For four decades, he has been the Pacific Northwest's premier champion of Asian American artists and writers.

Alan was born in Oroville, California. He grew up in nearby Paradise, the site of the 2018 Camp Fire, the most devastating blaze in California history. Alan's father ran The Pagoda, a *chop suey* restaurant in his hometown. The menu included chicken-fried steak, rib steak with french fries and vegetarian offerings suitable for Seventh-day Adventists. Alan worked there during summers to earn money to buy record albums.

Alan has loved the arts since he was a kid. His grandmother guided his hands with a brush over sheets of Chinese calligraphy paper in her kitchen, teaching him to write his Chinese name. In the late 1960s, he participated in the Asian American student movement and strikes at the College of San Mateo and San Francisco State University. After living in Santa Cruz, a hippie town that time forgot, he grew weary of its lack of multicultural sensibility. He became very curious about Seattle's strong Asian American literary roots after attending an Asian American writers conference at the University of Washington on a balmy summer day in 1978.

I met Alan in person in 1981, but I had been receiving mail from him for about a year. He was living on Capitol Hill. He sent hand-scrawled postcards with doodles and notes written on the back of discarded paper. His typewritten letters never included capital letters. I assumed that either the shift key on his typewriter was broken or that he was trying to make an artistic statement. He said he loved the *Examiner*. He offered insightful observations and plenty of suggestions for stories.

David Ishii, the bespectacled proprietor of a tiny bookstore in Pioneer Square specializing in antique publications and Asian American titles, had also mentioned Alan to me. "You should get to know him," David told me one day when I was delivering newspapers.

David's store was in the Grand Central Building on First Avenue South, beyond our main distribution hubs in the International District and Beacon Hill. David was an avid fan of our publication. I always made a point of dropping off a small stack of the latest edition. When David saw me from the window, he would pop up from his rolltop desk to meet me at the door. He wore a khaki-colored fishing cap pulled down close to his brow, a plaid flannel shirt and corduroy pants. He dressed the same way whether it was winter or summer. I wondered if he ever got hot.

David said, "I think Alan would be interested in writing for you." I told him that Alan was already in touch with me. David said, "Great. There you go. He's got really good connections."

David's store was a magnet for local Asian American artists, especially writers whose titles had been ignored by the big chains like D.B. Dalton, Borders, Waldenbooks and Tower Books. Alan had published a collection of poems, *Songs for Jadina,* which earned him a bit of renown among local Asian American literati. I bought a copy from David. I learned that Alan was friends with a cluster of rebel artists, including Frank Chin, Lawson Inada, Garrett Hongo and Shawn Wong.

When Alan finally visited the *Examiner* one day, he shuffled in, peering around somewhat sheepishly. He was a slightly round fellow with suspenders and a fuzzy, long-sleeved cotton shirt rolled up from the cuffs. He wore wire-rimmed glasses. He had a receding hairline, a barely visible goatee and a toothy grin. A canvas backpack hung over his shoulder. I thought he was a hippie. I pondered if he would go bald before me. As we spoke, he impressed me with his thorough knowledge of Asian American arts. Bringing him into the *Examiner* fold would be a real boon. "Hey, would you like to write for the paper?" I asked. He scratched his chin, then replied, "Sure, I can try. What did you have in mind?" He had lots of ideas. His flowing prose offered a lyrical contrast to the hard news and political commentary in the rest of the paper.

Alan elevated arts coverage into an *Examiner* bedrock, varied in its scope and viewpoints. He became an unpaid publicist and cheerleader for overlooked authors, visual artists, filmmakers, performing artists, musicians and others trying to carve out a life in the arts. I considered Alan our poor man's version of medieval arts patron Lorenzo de' Medici. Alan was masterful at coaxing reluctant volunteers into contributing reviews, dangling a free book or concert tickets as the incentive.

Alan worked in the produce department at the Asian specialty supermarket Uwajimaya. He stopped by the *Examiner* office during his breaks. He drifted naturally into the flow of office banter while picking through press releases stacked up in his mailbox. He said he often saw my father shopping at the store. Alan told me he was the only Chinese customer who ever put produce back into its original location after scouring through potential buys.

A native of Japan, Alan's wife Kazuko Nakane was an Asian American arts aficionado in her own right. She worked at the Merchants Parking Association office across the hall from the *Examiner*. She was bespectacled like Alan, only her lenses were twice as thick, giving her an owlish, bookish appearance. When she grinned, she looked like she was squinting. She had an easy smile and long hair with bangs. In contrast to Alan, Kazuko was thin and petite. She carried a backpack like Alan.

The achievement she found most gratifying was bringing into book form an oral history project on the Issei and Nisei in California's Pajaro Valley in 1985. This labor of love began as a class project at the University of California, Santa Cruz in 1978. I helped edit the manuscript, titled *Nothing Left in My Hands*. I asked Alan, "Why don't you help with editing? You're a terrific writer." He drolly remarked that it would be less unsettling to their relationship if he simply played cheerleader. Kazuko later worked at the Paper Cat, a small card and stationery store around the corner from David Ishii's bookstore.

In mid-December, Alan brought offerings of overripe Hachiya persimmons to the office. He knew that I loved to feast on them as a delectable treasure from my childhood. They came wrapped in a white foam tray, four to a pack. The skin on the fruit was shriveled, nearly broken and mottled with black spots. "Ripe enough for you, Ron?" he asked wryly. "I rescued them for you before they made their way into Uwajimaya's dumpster."

"Thanks, Alan," I said. "Perfect. Exactly how I like them. And they're free, best of all."

At the *Examiner*, I ate very little fruit. The persimmons from Alan helped supply a bit of nutritional balance to my daily French baguette and hot water.

CHAPTER 32

Tomo Shoji

Tomo Shoji, a Nisei resident of the International House Apartments, came by the *Examiner* office to test stories for a one-woman show about her life. Tomo was born in 1913 in the Ohio Hotel in the International District. But she grew up in the sawmill camps of rural Washington where her father worked as a laborer. Many of her memories came from that bygone era.

Tomo was quite the spectacle. When she stepped into the office—always unannounced—all heads turned her way. She was tiny, stooped and old, but hardly invisible. She stood in the center of the room, hand on one hip, head cocked to one side, wagging her finger, stamping her foot for effect. Her voice thundered. She was brusque, almost to the point of rudeness. But she was saved by her wit, humor and insight. She didn't care about appearances. She wanted to share her personal truths with the world. I wondered if she was Japanese American.

She flooded us with tales, like a prisoner who had just been unmuzzled after years of enforced silence. She spoke about growing up in the sawmill town of Onalaska, Washington; incarceration at Manzanar during World War II; her long and stormy marriage to Kazuo, a traditional Issei man; and how she finally came to resolve, late in life, many painful episodes, including the trauma of losing her baby.

Tomo had redefined herself as a feminist. She had two role models: her mother, an independent-spirited woman who came to the United States as a picture bride, and Waka Yamada, a prostitute in Seattle in the early 1900s who freed herself from bondage and returned to Japan to crusade for women's rights.

She made us roar with laughter. After she was done with us, she drifted across the street to the second floor of the Bush Hotel to visit Sue Taoka at InterIm and Theresa Fujiwara and Joyce Yoshikawa at Asian Counseling and Referral Service. She regaled them with the same stories.

Tomo was proud that at a very young age, she helped de-segregate a movie house in Longview, Washington. Her family moved there in 1926. "The Japanese and the blacks were put way back in the balcony, even when there were many empty seats closer to the front," she recalled. She and her sister complained to one of the vice presidents of the Long-Bell Lumber Company. They got the theater to change its policy. "I remember what my father had told me: 'You are an American citizen. You have the same rights as white Americans.'"

When Tomo was 14, a boy from Japan named Slim threatened to commit suicide after she spurned him. He had scrawled "I love Tomo" all over the walls of his room. He had written and sealed about half a dozen unsent letters to her.

"I always thought I would have a hard time catching a man because I'm such a blunt person," she explained. "But I thought to myself, 'Even if I never catch a man, at least for that short time in my life, someone loved me enough to consider committing suicide.' That made me feel special. Someone loved me that much."

Tomo also relished telling us about her high school prom. She really wanted to go, but she was poor and she didn't have a date. Nor did she know how to dance. "One day in class, I asked my teacher whether I could go to the prom. The teacher, Mrs. Bakke, said she would have to think about it. The next day, she said, 'You're going to go with me.' It turned out that I ended up helping pour the punch. But at least I got to go and see the couples dancing. When I was talking to my friends, they were all crying because they couldn't go to the prom, but I told them I got to go."

She asked me whether I had attended my high school prom. "Are you kidding, Tomo?" I said. "I didn't even know what a prom was. Besides, I was too shy. I couldn't talk to girls without stuttering and turning red." This prompted a hearty cackle from Tomo.

One of Tomo's most poignant stories was about the crib death of her three-month-old baby Kazuko in 1940. She held the cold, lifeless infant in her arms, waiting for a goodbye embrace from her husband. He left the house without providing her comfort. Later that day, Tomo, overcome by grief, burst into tears in the arms of a young man who came to offer his condolences. For years she had suppressed feelings of guilt about that moment. The guilt, she said, had remained sealed in her private "hellhole" until she began working on the script of her one-woman show.

At the *Examiner*, Tomo usually aimed her impromptu story-telling sessions at Ken Mochizuki and me. She apologized to Serena and Elaine Ito, our ad sales representative, for ignoring them. She said she tended to gravitate toward men. "Maybe that's because my husband has been in Keiro Nursing Home too long," she said with a straight face. "But don't worry," she added coquettishly as she turned to leave. "At my age, my interest stops with talk." We all roared in laughter.

Tomo couldn't remember names. She always referred to Alan Lau as "the vegetable man" after stumbling numerous times to extract his name from her cluttered memory banks. She came by the office to report on her regular visits to see him at Uwajimaya. I pictured Tomo chattering loudly with one hand poised on her hip for effect, Alan patiently restocking fresh fruit and leafy greens on the display stands, smiling and shaking his head, bemused.

In the 1950s, Tomo watched famed author and actress Cornelia Otis Skinner perform a spellbinding one-woman show. She never forgot that experience. Two decades later, after attending a writing workshop at Northwest Asian American Theatre (NWAAT), she decided to do her own one-woman show, with encouragement from Bea Kiyohara, artistic director of NWAAT. Tomo signed up for a drama class where she met actor Chris Wong. He agreed to help direct her.

In May 1987, at the age of 74, Tomo appeared on the stage at NWAAT in two performances of *Born Too Soon...It's Never Too Late!* The Asian Pacific Women's Caucus hosted a reception for her after the second performance. Tomo was embraced as a community celebrity and role model.

She did an encore performance at the Nippon Kan Theatre on August 14 to raise money for the Asian Counseling and Referral Service.

Tomo began to call me more frequently at home in the evening to talk privately instead of coming by the *Examiner*. The conversations lasted well into the night as she shared the latest gossip she collected during her neighborhood rounds.

She suspected that several individuals befriended her during production of her show in the hopes of plagiarizing her stories. "Why don't you just publish a book?" I suggested. "It's your stuff, and you're a really good storyteller." I told her I would help her edit the stories and get the book published.

Meanwhile, she was repackaging her stories for a second one-woman show centered on a newfound understanding of her five-decade-long relationship to her husband. Kaz never fulfilled her desire for romantic love, but he expressed his love in other ways. When she prepared one of his favorite dishes, *natto*, a Japanese dish of fermented soybeans, the expression of delight on his face—as he hungrily shoveled the *natto* and rice into his mouth—"made up for the hugs and kisses he never gave me," she said.

Ken helped Tomo refine her stage delivery for the second show. They met in the lobby of the International House Apartments. When she lost her train of thought, she stared up at the ceiling. Ken tried in vain to keep her focused. "What's up there, Tomo?" Ken barked at her. "See it in front of you!"

In October 1988, she performed her second show, *A Nisei Love Story*. It was a hit like the first. It mattered little that Tomo was getting more absent-minded. When she muffed a line—or lost her place—an audience member or two yelled out a few lines to prompt and steady her. Her forgetfulness became part of the show. From the stage, Tomo laughed along with everyone else.

One evening, I came to pick up Tomo after dinner to discuss her prospective book. We had scheduled a "cheap date" at the McDonald's on Madison Street on First Hill. I parked in the load zone in front of her apartment building. She waited just inside the lobby. As I walked over to open the door for her, I noticed that she had put on rouge and lipstick. She also wore shoes with a slight waffle heel, not her usual flats. "Hey, what's with the fancy getup?" I asked. "Are you trying to impress me?" She thundered: "Well, this is a date, isn't it?" I responded, "Don't get any ideas, Tomo. Remember—your husband is still in the nursing home. You might create a scandal in the community." She cackled.

When we got to McDonald's, she ordered an ice cream cone. I ordered a fruit pie, french fries and a Diet Coke. I listened to her tell her favorite stories again. I suggested some additional stories based on other anecdotes she had shared during our phone conversations. As I drove her back to her apartment, she beamed. She had a new ambition: to become an author.

The next day, Tomo gave me a pineapple in a brown paper bag at the office. I thanked her. After work, I brought the pineapple back to my apartment and placed it in my refrigerator. I didn't tell her that I didn't know how to slice it open or how to eat it.

Tomo continued to call me to talk about her book, sometimes several times a night, usually when she had a hard time sleeping. Her excitement grew. "Do you really think anyone would be interested?" she asked. I reassured her that she would have an audience. "At least you know I'll buy a few copies."

Tomo began to reflect more deeply about her relationship with Kaz. During one of her last visits to Keiro, she probed: "I wasn't a very good wife, was I? It wasn't a bad marriage, was it?" When he responded that their life together had been "fun," she was reassured. She asked him directly whether he loved her. He nodded yes. Not satisfied, she asked him to say the words in English. He did. Now she felt liberated. She had made peace.

Kaz passed away on November 11, 1988.

One evening, I fielded three calls from her. The last call was brief. "I know it's getting pretty late, but I forgot to tell you something. You can have a girlfriend."

I was taken aback. "What do you mean, Tomo?"

"I didn't realize it, but here I am—a selfish old woman—taking up all your free time with these phone calls," she said. "I really appreciate it. But you should go out and get a girlfriend if it makes you happy. Don't let me hog all your time. I'll be okay."

I reassured her that I appreciated our talks and that I was grateful she was willing to share her most intimate stories with me. "By the way, I *don't* have a girlfriend, Tomo," I said. "Is that what you were fishing to find out?" She was speechless for once. I had my answer. I could see her grinning at me over the phone.

The pineapple sat in my refrigerator for at least a month. It was still there when I received word that she had suffered a massive stroke in her apartment.

On January 21, 1989, just two months after her husband died, I visited Tomo at Providence Hospital. I went twice, once in the morning and again in the evening. She was in a deep coma. She was breathing on her own, her mouth agape. She looked eerily peaceful lying in the hospital bed. She had suffered massive hemorrhaging on the left side of her brain.

Her daughter Janice Matsuoka told me that the doctors didn't hold out much hope. I met Tomo's son Gordon, who owned Asian Express, a deli on Beacon Hill. I chatted with Tomo's sister Mollie Fujioka, who lived in Walnut Creek, California. I had met Mollie—12 years younger than Tomo—a year earlier at the Japanese American Citizens League national convention in Seattle. She had run unsuccessfully for national president.

That evening, I also met Tomo's other daughter, Nancy Shoji-Parent, who just arrived from New York. Tomo had told me that Nancy was the daughter who was most like her, a "free spirit" who had told Tomo, "Go for it, Mom!" She was visibly shaken by the sight of her mother lying helpless in a coma.

On Sunday, January 22, 1989, exactly two months short of her 76th birthday, Tomo passed away. Her service was held at St. Peter's Episcopal Parish in Seattle.

On February 21, I received a small package in the mail from her daughter Janice. Inside was a handwritten letter, a black-and-white photo of Tomo and the image of an ox. Janice thanked me for an article I wrote about Tomo for the *Examiner*. The story had been reprinted in the *Hokubei Mainichi* in San Francisco. Janice said the piece captured her "honestly" and "brought tears to my eyes because it's all so real to me yet." Janice said Tomo had "displayed the ox in her apartment to show the stubbornness & determination of her sign" from the Chinese zodiac. Janice wrote:

> *The many hours I spent at the hospital during the "vigil" gave me time to reflect about our relationship. I remember when I was in elementary school, I often wished my mom was more like the other traditional type mothers who baked cookies, etc. As I grew older, I appreciated her more for the person she was. But it wasn't until these past 3-4 years when I realized how fortunate I was to have a mother like her. She taught me things without my knowing—about independence, to find my own way of survival & always showing me examples of fairness & honesty.*
>
> *Thank you again for being such a "special" friend to mom—you seemed to understand her for what she was & accepted her as is & so she felt very free about sharing her thoughts with you.*

Nancy was a gifted storyteller like her mother. She sent me a story she wrote about her trauma as one child of five in Manzanar, watching the fiery arguments between her parents over whether to go to Japan or remain in America. Her father wanted to go. Her mother wanted to stay. These deeply seared memories, coupled with horrific images of Nazi concentration camps, drew her to a life in Israel, where she taught and raised her children.

After Tomo's death, I got to know Fran Matsuoka, Tomo's youngest sister. Fran and I began a long friendship which continued even after I joined the Wing Luke Museum. She was loquacious and funny just like Tomo. Fran worked as a page at the Beacon Hill library. She began to call me in the evening like Tomo once did, regaling me with her frank viewpoints.

One Sunday in April, we went to lunch. Fran revealed that she was a good friend of Ruth Woo. Fran said she used to play jacks with Ruth when they were in high school. "I never thought she would become the political powerhouse that she's become," Fran said. Ruth had called to enlist her help in finding a girlfriend for Gary Locke, now divorced from Diane Wong. Ruth was a behind-the-scenes political dynamo who helped push many young Asian American activists into seeking public office, including Gary. "Do you know anybody I can suggest?" Fran asked. I couldn't help her out.

During one especially long, rambling phone conversation in May, Fran told me that she thought Elaine Ito's father looked like a Japanese deity. She said Andy Shiga, owner of Shiga's Imports, did, too. "They both have round bodies and little round heads," she said. "They could be the Japanese god of good fortune." In July, she told me about an argument she had just had with her library manager. She had complained to him about a janitor who was doing "a half-assed job." Her manager retorted,

"I don't want to hear those things. I'm a Christian." Fran shot back: "Well, I'm 60 years old, and I'll say what I want."

I chuckled and thought to myself: *Tomo and Fran—cut from the same hardy material. Both independent of mind and spirit. Both eggs.*

After I joined the Wing Luke Museum, Fran found opportunities to pop into the museum when we were hard at work developing new exhibits. She often dropped off a large, fresh platter of homemade *inarizushi* to feed staff and volunteers.

I regret never completing the book with Tomo. It would have been a load of fun. Her typewritten story chapters, some of which I had begun editing by pencil, now languish in a file folder among other papers in my basement. I had lost not only a dear friend, but also the opportunity to collaborate on a publication that would have illuminated the sensibilities of a woman who lived beyond the conformity of her generation.

Tomo's daughter Nancy passed away on December 10, 2013. Fran died January 17, 2015, and Mollie Fujioka passed on June 18, 2015.

CHAPTER 33

Nobuko Awaya

BECAUSE I HADN'T TRAVELED MUCH outside Seattle, I wasn't very well informed about world affairs before the Internet, email and social media opened the floodgates. My regular news sources, *The Seattle Times* and *Seattle P.I.,* held to a rigidly domestic, Eurocentric outlook. There was little coverage of Asia beyond the convulsion of war in Vietnam. At the UW, my friends were mostly American-born, even though the number of international students was sizable. My Beacon Hill friends knew as little as I did.

In 1981, Nobuko Awaya, a young freelance journalist from Tokyo, Japan, traveled to Seattle to join her husband, Junji Shiba, who was attending graduate school at the UW. Nobuko had studied at Southern Methodist University in Dallas as one of a handful of Asian students on campus. There, she had felt horribly out of place.

Alan Lau brought her by the *Examiner* one day. She first met him and his wife Kazuko when he did a reading at a small bookstore on Yesler Way. I was immediately drawn to Nobuko's low-key, vibrant personality. Like me, she was a journalist, passionate about using the power of storytelling to awaken the social conscience of readers. She wanted to learn about Japanese Americans and to correct misconceptions about Japan. She discovered the *Examiner* as a perfect bridge to her work. She contributed pieces on Mayumi's brother, jazz pianist Deems Tsutakawa, the Tokyo chapter of the Japanese American Citizens League, and the 1945 Japanese atomic bomb survivors.

She was the first overseas Asian I met whose political and cultural perspective matched mine. She helped me fill voids in my knowledge. She kept apologizing about the quality of her English, although she really had no need to. Except for an accent and a few halting searches for the right word, she spoke nearly flawless English.

When she stopped by the office to chat, I interrogated her—tongue-in-cheek—about trivial matters, always prompting wild laughter from my staff. I asked whether Japan had Western fast food establishments such as McDonald's and Kentucky Fried Chicken. She responded that "Makudonarudo"—the Japanese translation of "McDonald's"—was indeed very popular, as were a number of other American fast-food chains. And by the way, she added, the hamburgers in Japan were equally devoid of nutritional value.

Nobuko was especially insightful about people. After interviewing George Tokuda, a Nisei, to learn about his family pharmacy and the *matsutake* mushroom-hunting culture of Japanese Americans, she returned with the observation that his mother must have taught him how to speak Japanese. "Why do you say that?" I asked. She said George "spoke Japanese like a woman," with soft inflections and a feminine tone. I had no way of knowing this; I did not speak Japanese and only knew George from our conversations in English. Many years later, his daughter Marilyn confirmed that her late father had, indeed, learned Japanese from her grandmother.

Nobuko was keenly attuned to the racism and insensitivity of white Americans.

On September 10, 1985, Sankai Juku, an avant-garde dance company from Japan, was performing in Pioneer Square. The *Examiner* had published a story on the group. The event included dancers hanging upside down from a building. Soon after it began, the rope holding one dancer, Yoshiyuku Takada, broke, sending him falling five stories to his death in front of a large group of aghast spectators. Nobuko was among the eyewitnesses.

Two days later, a candlelight ceremony was held for the deceased performer in nearby Occidental Park. As the media spoke about the existential symbolism of the dance performance and used overwrought metaphors about life and death to analyze the tragedy, Nobuko bristled at how racist and insensitive this was. She said that any attempts to tease out symbolism—to talk about the ghosts haunting the building and to use cute headlines like "Dying for the Spotlight" or to pontificate that "death onstage bears its own strange poetry"—cheapened the loss.

Nobuko moved back to Tokyo in 1986. In the summer of 1987, she visited me at the newspaper after spending time in Hong Kong and northern China. She had traveled to these places to write an article for a Japanese magazine on the shooting of a documentary titled *Man Behind the Sun*. Nobuko's friend T.F. Mou was the filmmaker. It recounted the disturbing story of Dr. Shiro Ishii, the director of a Japanese research program that had performed horrific germ warfare experiments on Chinese prisoners of war in Manchuria during World War II. Some 3,000 people died because of Ishii's work. The location where the atrocities took place was partially in ruins because Ishii bombed his own building and destroyed records before scurrying back to Japan as the war ended.

She believed it was wrong for the Japanese emperor to escape responsibility for these crimes. She condemned the U.S. government for enlisting Ishii to contribute to its chemical warfare research during the Korean War. This gruesome program was detailed in a famous book published in Japan in 1982. We both remarked on how quickly each generation forgets—and escapes responsibility for—its own unconscionable history.

Since returning to Tokyo, Nobuko has written seven books on gender and cross-cultural issues. She now teaches intercultural communications at a college in Japan.

In 2000, Nobuko inherited an ancient Edo home located two hours south of Tokyo in the tiny town of Ohito on the Izu peninsula. The structure had a lovingly preserved interior, thatched roof, gigantic beams, traditional hearth and ancestral altar, and shoji and wooden screen doors. She revived the home as a community gathering space, hosting workshops, art installations, concerts and performances.

In an interview for the *International Herald Tribune*, she explained: "I didn't want to keep the house, where my maternal ancestors had lived and where I was born, just as a museum. I wanted to restore its cultural vitality by actually using it."

Without knowing it, Nobuko and I were moving in parallel orbits. I had completed a campaign to reimagine the Wing Luke Museum, a process rooted in the same vision of a living museum bridging the past and present.

To ___Henry A. Monroe___
_____Chinese and Immigrant Inspector,_____
_____Seattle, Washington_____

(Chew) Quay Fong: Age: 36.
Height: 5ft. 5in
Occupation: Cannoryman
left ear pierced;pit outer
corner each eyebrow.

SIR: It being my intention to leave the United States on a temporary visit abroad, departing and returning through the Chinese port of entry of ___Seattle, Washington_____, I hereby apply, under the provisions of Rule 39 of the Chinese Regulations (Bureau Circular No. 25), for preinvestigation of my claimed status as an American citizen by birth, submitting herewith such documentary proofs (if any) as I possess, and agreeing to appear in your office personally, and to produce therein witnesses, for oral examination regarding the claim made by me.

This application is submitted in triplicate with my photograph attached to each copy, as required by said rule.

Respectfully,

Signature in Chinese 簽　唐　字　名　(Chew) Quay Fong
Signature in English 簽　番　字　名
Address 具禀人之住址 719 King St. Seattle, Wash.

相　簽　詢　委　亦　憑　國　九　而　來　遊　欲　委　管
三　名　問　員　親　據　出　歇　回　亦　外　暫　員　理
幅　禀　口　之　與　呈　世　依　茲　卽　邦　離　知　外
　　上　供　公　證　上　所　三　依　由　今　美　之　人
　　並　照　辦　人　查　有　十　例　該　由　國　我　入
　　附　例　房　到　驗　之　　　在　埠　華　出　現　口
　　　　　　　　　　　　美　　　　　　　　　　　

27380
Seattle

Port of ___SEATTLE___
___DEC 1 1913_____, 19___

Respectfully returned to
_____Henry A. Monroe,_____
_____Chinese and Immigrant Inspector,_____

With the information that I am ___✓___ prepared, on the basis of the evidence submitted with the original of this application, to approve said application.

Henry M. White
Officer in Charge.

11—2847

My paternal grandfather, Chew Quay Fong, is buried at Lakeview Cemetery in Seattle.

CHEW QUAY FONG
1945

My father came to Seattle in 1930 at age 14 from Hoisan, China. At left is an early photo. At right, we meet at my brother's deli at the Pike Place Market, 1988. Below, he poses at Tai Tung for *Reflections of Seattle's Chinese Americans*, 1990. *Dean Wong photos.*

(Left) My parents with my paternal grandmother after their wedding on June 2, 1937. (Below) My mother toiled for low wages in Seattle sewing factories to support our family here and relatives in China. She returned to her home village in 1988 to pay respects to her late father (center). Relatives greeted her as Muk-Lan, the woman warrior (bottom).

(Above) Me in a very early photo. *(Above right)* My siblings *(from left)* Tom, Linda, Harvey and me. *(Below)* We play on the swing set at our Beacon Hill home. I'm at the far right.

In 1958, our family moved to a new home on Beacon Hill. The living room TV was the focal point of family activities. *(Below, from left)* Tom, Harvey, my mother and father, me and Linda on our sofa.

Each May, my mother prepared *doong*, glutinous rice wrapped in bamboo leaves, to celebrate the Dragon Boat Festival. When we had ailments, she relied on traditional Chinese medicine to treat us. *Han Eckelberg photos.*

My Franklin High School teachers *(clockwise from top)*: Robert Maestas, Alice Allen, Barbara Nilson and Rick Nagel.

MR. DUANE MUNRO: Mathematics

MR. RICHARD NAGEL: Social Studies

MRS BARBARA NILSON: Language Arts

ASSASANATOR CONVICTED

Think - A - Newspaper

Washington— The assasanator of Dan Evans was convicted yesterday when they found the gun that shot Evans, in his room. It was found hiden under his pillow. The assasinator was James P. Agrit 50, of West Hill Lane, Seattle. The ass will get the electric chair.

CHURCHES

M...
a...
s...
ot...
o...
g...
c...
ha...
ma...
The...
the...
of...
Ken...
plac...

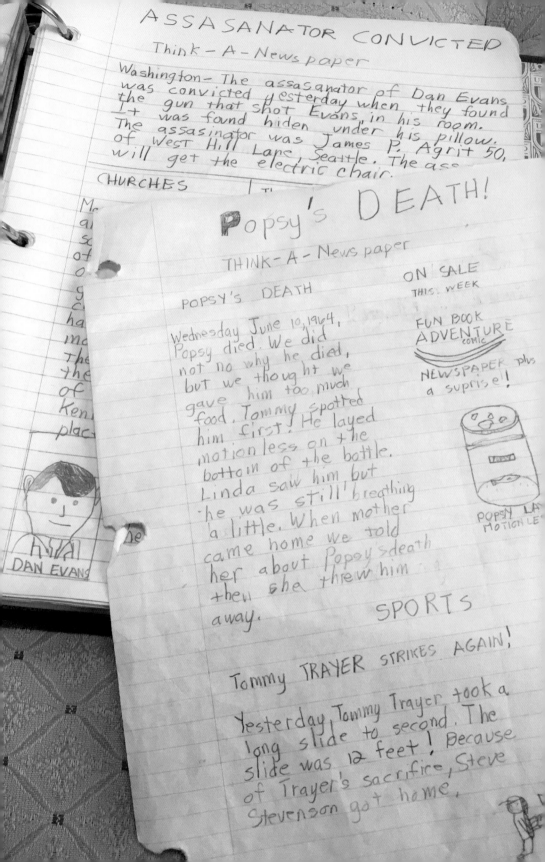

DAN EVANS

Popsy's DEATH!

THINK - A - Newspaper

POPSY'S DEATH

ON SALE
THIS WEEK

Wednesday June 10, 1964, Popsy died. We did not no why he died, but we thought we gave him too much food. Tommy spotted him first. He layed motionless on the bottom of the bottle. Linda saw him but he was still breathing a little. When mother came home we told her about Popsy's death then she threw him away.

FUN BOOK
ADVENTURE comic

NEWSPAPER plus
a suprise!

POPSY LA
MOTION LE

SPORTS

Tommy TRAYER STRIKES AGAIN!

Yesterday, Tommy Trayer took a long slide to second. The slide was 12 feet! Because of Trayer's sacrifice, Steve Stevenson got home.

My Give-A-Show projector provided hours of amusement. *Han Eckelberg photos.*
I amassed my tiny toy cars from buying Tomoe Ame rice candy. *Rick Wong photo.*

(Opposite page) At age 11, I began producing my own newspaper in my parents' basement.

(Left) Two views of the Hip Sing building at 418 Eighth Avenue South, 2005. *Karen Ducey photos. (Right)* Jimmy Mar at Yick Fung Company, 2006. *Karen Ducey photo.*

David Louie at Kwan On Wing Company, 1976. *Steve Suzuki photo.*

Filipino old-timers in Chinatown hang out at the Hi-Lite Café on the corner of Maynard Avenue South and South King Street, 1970s. *Courtesy Maxine Chan.*

(Above) Florence Chin Eng at Wa Sang Company, 1990. *Dean Wong photo.*

(Right) The Kitamura family operated the Kokusai Theater from the 1960s until 1983. *Courtesy Elaine Kitamura.*

(*Above*) Vintage Hong Kong Restaurant postcard.
(*Right*) My brother Tom busses dishes at the
restaurant, late 1960s.

(*Bottom right*) Owner Sam Yee at Luck Ngai Musical
Club, 1990. *Dean Wong photo.*

Top row: Roy and Jean Chu. Second row: Janine,
Tiu Ngut Chin Chu, Ngew Chu, Christopher and
Cindy. Ngew was one of three Hong Kong owners.
The family poses in front of Fay Chong mural in
restaurant, 1963. *Courtesy Janine Chu.*

(Above) Beacon Hill Library, ca. 1962. *Courtesy Seattle Public Library, [spl_shp_35084].*

(Above right) The certificate I received for reading books over the summer.

(Right) The venerable downtown establishment where I purchased many used books, 1968. *Courtesy Seattle Public Library, [spl_wl_str_00466].*

(Left) My boyhood friend Keith Wong and me at the University of Washington, 1973.

International Examiner staff, 1978. Back row *(from left)*: Melody Leo, Lorraine Sako, Michael Cervantes, Gary Iwamoto, Julia Laranang, Jeanette Aguilar, Debbie Murakami, Randy Okimoto, Georgene Kumasaka, Mark Mano, Gene Viernes, Tim Otani, Anne Mori. Front row: Karen Chinn, Julie King, Kathryn Chinn, Sue Chin, Vicki Woo, me, Jesse Reyes. *John Harada photo. Center photo Nobuko Awaya.*

Staff in mid-1980s. Back row *(from left)*: Esther Sugai, Carlos Smith, Greg Tuai, Alan Lau, me, John Harada, Julia Laranang, Steve Goon, unidentified, Greg Castilla. Front row: Sumi Hayashi, Margaret Kawasaki, Gary Iwamoto, Jesse Reyes. *Nobuko Awaya photo.*

The Alaska Cannery Workers Association

Recently, Asian and Native American workers have come together to combat the long history of discrimination in the Alaska salmon canneries.

(From left) Bob Sotelo, Gene Viernes and Andy Pascua, Red Salmon cannery, Naknek, Alaska, July 21, 1970. *Courtesy Steve Viernes.*

Silme Domingo in his Monte Carlo, 1970s. *University of Washington Libraries, Special Collections, CWFLU Local 7 Papers.*

(*Top*) Chris Mensalvas, Sr., addresses a crowd in Hing Hay Park, May 5, 1976. *Courtesy* International Examiner.

(*Center*) I participate in a 1977 demonstration in downtown Seattle, organized by the National Committee to Overturn the Bakke Decision. *From Discovering Washington by Ruth Pelz.*

(*Right*) Craig Shimabukuro, a fiery radical who moved from Los Angeles to Seattle in 1979. *Courtesy* International Examiner.

(*Above*) Glenn Chinn, head of Merchants Parking Association, at the International District Summer Festival, late 1970s. *Steve Suzuki photo.*

(*Left*) In 1979, my friend Julia Laranang found this old brochure. I urged her to make sure that the vintage lettering on the facade of the hotel would be retained after it was remodeled.

Mayumi Tsutakawa (*center*) and Neil Asaba (*far right*) at a sit-in protest, El Centro de la Raza, early 1970s. *Courtesy Wing Luke Museum.*

(Right) Uncle Bob Santos was the visionary behind creation of the International District Community Garden in 1975. He supervises young volunteers. *Courtesy International Examiner.*

(Left) Uncle Bob turns the spit at the annual pig roast in July, late 1970s. Pictured from left are neighborhood kids Debbie, Judy and Danny Louie, Kay Chinn and Johnny Chan. *Courtesy InterIm.*

(Below) ID residents Hui Juan and Chun Shiang Chen tend their garden plot with daughter Wu Yue-Mei Chen, 2018. *Thomas Barwick photo.*

Pioneer entrepreneur Goon Dip
built the Milwaukee Hotel in
1911. In 1977, housing activists
organized a 24-hour fire watch
to prevent low-income residents
from being evicted from the
deteriorating structure.
Left photo Tom Mar.

Bob Santos speaks at an open house for the newly remodeled Bush-Asia Center on
September 26, 1981. With him *(from left)* are King County Council member Ruby Chow,
U.S. Senator Henry M. Jackson, McDonald Sullivan and Ben Woo. *Dean Wong photo.*

(Above) The Higo Variety Store was established in 1907. Pictured are sisters Aya (left) and Masa Murakami. *Dean Wong photo.*

(Left) Higo exterior, 1997. *Lawrence Wong photo.*

(Below) The business is now Kobo at Higo. Owners Binko Chiong-Bisbee and John Bisbee. *ML Harris photo.*

When I worked at the *International Examiner*, my favorite lunch hangout was Ying Hei Restaurant. It was previously Little Three Grand Café. *Courtesy Seattle Public Library, [spl_wl_res_00010].*

Pictured above is Kam Lee, owner and cook. Below, the Lee family poses in front of the restaurant in 1984. *Courtesy Angela Lee.*

(Top) Pioneer labor contractor Chin Gee-Hee established the Quong Tuck Company in the late 1800s. He is pictured in front of his store in the East Kong Yick Building on South King Street. *Courtesy Wing Luke Museum.*

(Above) Chin Gee-Hee's grandnephew Danny Woo reopened the storefront as Quong Tuck Restaurant in 1977. *Dean Wong photo.*

(Right) Danny and his wife Wilma donated property to establish the International District Community Garden. Wilma is on the left with Sue Taoka in the garden, 1980s. *Courtesy Teresa Woo.*

Donnie Chin, pictured in 1978, founded International District Emergency Center (IDEC) in 1968. *Rey Sabado photo.*

IDEC provides emergency assistance to residents and businesses. Back row *(from left)*: firefighter Craig Hanada, Capt. Ron Hiraki, Lt. Preston Bhang and paramedics Jeff Jinka and Randy Foy. Front row: Donnie Chin and IDEC volunteers Lap Woo and Jia Yuan Zeng. *Dean Wong photo, 1990.*

Donnie's mother Myra Chin ran the Sun May Company at 672 South King Street. The cramped shop sold imported knick-knacks, collectibles and antiques. *Shannon Gee photo.*

At age 74, storyteller Tomo Shoji appeared onstage in a solo performance of her life story in 1987. She is pictured at top on her wedding day. *Courtesy Janice Matsuoka.*

Japanese journalist Nobuko Awaya converted her family's ancient Edo home outside of Tokyo into a community arts space. *Courtesy Nobuko Awaya.*

Asian Family Affair published its final issue in February 1985. From left are staff members YK Kuniyuki, Kathy Tagawa and Frankie Irigon. *Dean Wong photo.*

• HAPPY NEW YEAR!
• MEMORIES OF NEW YEAR'S IN CHINA
• NEW YEAR'S INJECTS MONEY INTO CHINA

Diony Corsilles established the *Bayanihan Tribune*, a Filipino American community newspaper, in 1975. He is pictured in that same year with his family. *Courtesy Michelle Corsilles.*

Ken Mochizuki tried his luck as a Hollywood actor before returning to Seattle to work at the *International Examiner. Courtesy Ken Mochizuki.*

Lori Matsukawa and I were among the founders of the Seattle chapter Asian American Journalists Association in 1985. *Courtesy King Broadcasting Company, 1998.*

(Below) The Quong Tuck Restaurant bar was the setting for a scene in Ken's movie *Beacon Hill Boys*. From left, Gregg Hashimoto, Ed Locke and Arnold Mukai.

Silme Domingo and Gene Viernes memorial, June 1981. *Dean Wong photo.*

(Above) In 1986, I participated in a march commemorating the 100th anniversary of the Chinese expulsion from Seattle. Maria Batayola holds a picket sign. I'm wearing a jacket my mother made in the sewing factory.

(Left) My friend Steve Goon and I lived in the Evergreen Apartments immediately behind him, mid-1980s. *Nobuko Awaya photo.*

(Right) Seattle Taiko Group founders constructed drums on the third floor of the Evergreen Apartments. From left are Michio Teshima (a tenant), Stan Shikuma and Bill Blauvelt, 1989. *Dean Wong photo.*

In January 1988, Đức Trần established the Viet Wah supermarket in a building that previously housed Connors Furniture and Appliance Store. It became the anchor of Little Saigon, centered at 12th Avenue South and South Jackson Street. *Dean Wong photo. Connors store photo courtesy Leeching Tran.*

(Above) Photographer Dean Wong with his soulmate Jan Ito.

(Right) Visual artist and poet-writer Alan Lau and his wife, art historian and writer Kazuko Nakane. They are at Rakushisha, a historic landmark in Kyoto, Japan, 2017. *John D. Pai photo.*

I helped many community couples tie the knot.
(Top left) Greg Tuai and Ben-Ling Wong, 1991.
(Top right) Debbie Louie and Pete Martone, 2012.
(Center) John Pai and Lorraine Sako, 1996. Melanie Sako served as maid of honor, Jim Sander was the best man.
(Bottom) Shannon Gee and Ian Devier, 2011.

Members of the Asian Pacific Women's Caucus were steadfast and reliable partners when I was editor of the *Examiner*. *(From left)* Martha Choe, Teresita Batayola, Joan Yoshitomi and Nancy Lim, late 1980s. *Courtesy Teresita Batayola.*

(Above) Maxine Chan, an authority on early Chinese American cuisine, at the ID summer festival, 2009. *Rick Wong photo.*

(Left) The Theatrical Ensemble of Asians later became Northwest Asian American Theatre. *(From left)* Larry Wong, Yoly Irigon, Stan Asis, Marilyn Tokuda, Maria Batayola and Henry Tonel, 1972. *Courtesy Wing Luke Museum.*

Say, would you be interested in working on an upcoming show on the young API's of today?

Accepting fatherhood...

Where's Rondo?

Um. Ya know, it's really easy. Just put a few pictures on the wall...

Giving his support...

(Above) Michelle Kumata birthday card illustration, 1995.

(Right) Loan Nguyễn and me with Cian and Kino.

Loan Nguyễn's family, 1977. Front row *(from left)*: Loan's dad, Huy, Duy, Tina and Thành. Back row: Loan, Oanh *(top)*, Loan's mom, Hoàng and Dũng. *Courtesy Duy Nguyễn.*

(Top) Chinese oral history volunteers (from left): Steve Chin, Greg Tuai, Jeni Fung, Joanne Lee, Bertha Tsuchiya, Fred Yee, Heidi Chang, me, Amy Wong, James Wong, Bettie Luke and Cal Fung, 1990. (Right) I interviewed World War II veteran David Woo for the oral history project, 1990. Dean Wong photos.

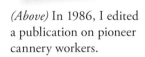

(Above) In 1986, I edited a publication on pioneer cannery workers.

(Right) I coordinated an exhibition for the state centennial. From left, Sally Yamasaki, David Takami, Ruby Macadangdang, me, Dean Wong and Kamol Sudthayakorn, 1989.

My father sketched this family tree, marking "paper" relatives in red.

(Center left) My uncle Lee Hong, at left, with classmates. He was killed in combat in Italy. The army photo was sent to Seattle with his belongings.

(Bottom) Lee Hong was reinterred in 1949 at Evergreen Washelli cemetery. A Cathay Post veteran hands the folded flag to my uncle Hung Hong.

(Above) My mother's English class. Instructor Jim Lourie *(in the back with mustache)* called her "The Boss." She was the oldest student. *(Below)* Her dictionary and class notebook.

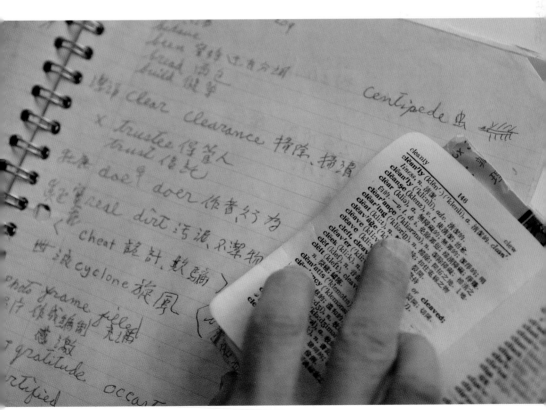

(Clockwise from top left) Dolores Sibonga, Velma Veloria, Arlene Oki, Vera Ing, Ben and Ruth Woo, and Cheryl Chow *(left)* and Martha Choe. *Top four photos courtesy* International Examiner. *Bottom left photo courtesy Teresa Yoneyama.*

My predecessors at the Wing Luke Museum: Peg Marshall *(top left, Steve Suzuki photo)* and Kit Freudenberg *(Dean Wong photo)*. *(Top right)* Me at the Seattle Art Museum in Volunteer Park. Bob Ohashi, museum board member and Beacon Hill pharmacist. *Dean Wong photo.*

Charlene Mano came aboard as education director shortly after I replaced Kit Freudenberg as museum head in 1991. *John D. Pai photo.*

(Above) Ruthann Kurose championed the redress movement as aide to U.S. Congressman Mike Lowry. (Right) She is pictured with Rod Kawakami, Cherry Kinoshita and Lowry. *Courtesy Ruthann Kurose.*

(Bottom right) Karen Seriguchi is recognized in 1983 for her redress work by Dr. Kelly Yamada of the Japanese American Citizens League. (Below) She gets a degree from the University of San Francisco at age 56. *Courtesy Karen Seriguchi.*

(Above left) Executive Order 9066 exhibit opening, 1992. Front row *(from left)*: Sally Yamasaki, Pat Norikane, Beth Takekawa. Second row: Cherry Kinoshita, Haru Ishikawa, Nobue Shimizu, Yuki Miyake, Shigeko Uno. Third row: Harry Fujita, Sharon Aburano, Sachi Iwami, Laurette Mitsuoka, Shigeto Ishikawa, Tets Kuramoto, Leslie Mano Matsuda, unidentified. Fourth row: Roger Shimizu, Ed Suguro, unidentified, Hideo Hoshide, Mas Odoi, Mary Akamine, Jerry (Eiichi) Yamashita, me, Norio Mitsuoka. Back row: Michelle Kumata, Debbie Louie, David Takami, Bob Shimabukuro. *Courtesy Wing Luke Museum.*

(Above right) Sally Yamasaki, Michelle Kumata and I share a laugh during exhibit planning.

Proudly celebrating completion of the *Executive Order 9066* exhibit *(from left)*: David Takami, Michelle Kumata, Bob Shimabukuro, Sally Yamasaki, Hannah Yamasaki, Jeff Hanada, Sumi Ikeda and Ed Suguro, 1992. *Dean Wong photo.*

20 Years After the Fall of Saigon project members *(from left)*: Mary Douglass, Jessica Phú Nguyễn, Ann-Marie D. Nguyễn, Hương Nguyễn, Theresa Duque, Loan Nguyễn, Thái Nhật Lĩnh, Nguyễn Công Khanh and Trần Quang Thành, 1995. *Dean Wong photo.*

If Tired Hands Could Talk (2001) featured untold stories of Seattle garment workers like my mother. Video was projected on fabric suspended from the ceiling. *John D. Pai photo.*

The recreated barrack from the *Executive Order 9066* exhibit was preserved as a permanent centerpiece in the Wing Luke Museum gallery. *John D. Pai photo.*

Tripat Singh speaks at the opening of *Sikh Community: Over 100 Years in the Pacific Northwest*. It was featured at the museum in 2005. *(From left)* Sukhminder Singh, Sital Singh, Gurdev Singh Mann, Avtar Singh Adampuri, Harvinder Singh, Swarnjit Kaur Neel, Gurdial Singh Neel and Savraj Singh. *Courtesy Wing Luke Museum.*

The museum partnered with the U.S. Forest Service on two Chinese heritage bus tours. This carefully preserved site in John Day, Oregon, reminds me of Jimmy Mar's Yick Fung Company store in Seattle. *Top photo Dorothy Ng. Bottom photo John D. Pai.*

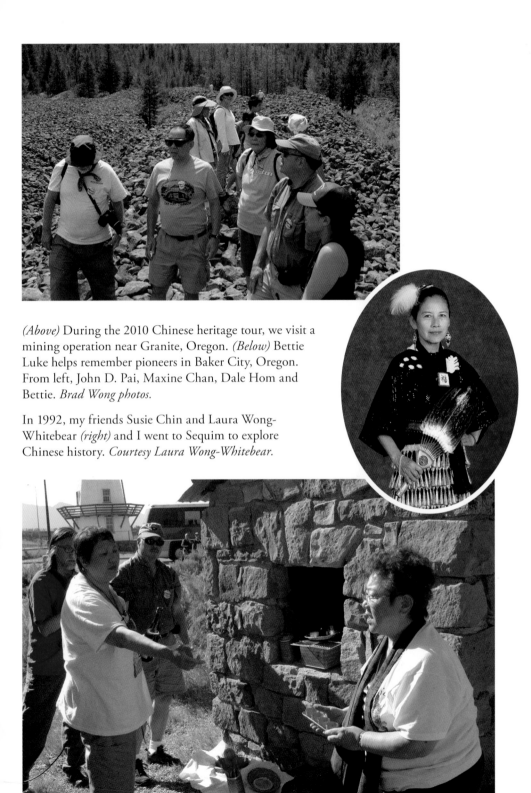

(Above) During the 2010 Chinese heritage tour, we visit a mining operation near Granite, Oregon. *(Below)* Bettie Luke helps remember pioneers in Baker City, Oregon. From left, John D. Pai, Maxine Chan, Dale Hom and Bettie. *Brad Wong photos.*

In 1992, my friends Susie Chin and Laura Wong-Whitebear *(right)* and I went to Sequim to explore Chinese history. *Courtesy Laura Wong-Whitebear.*

First Lady Hillary Rodham Clinton presents the 1995 National Award for Museum Service to me and museum board co-presidents Gloria Lung Wakayama *(far left)* and Helen Kay. *Courtesy Wing Luke Museum.*

The Museum of Chinese in the Americas featured the core exhibition *Where is Home? Chinese in the Americas,* curated by Adrienne Cooper and Fabiana Chiu-Rinaldi. Today, the institution is called Museum of Chinese in America. *Courtesy Fabiana Chiu-Rinaldi, 1995.*

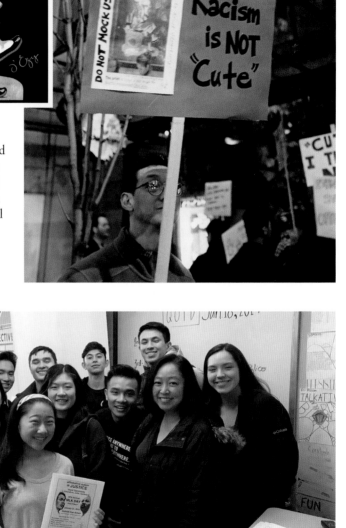

ObaChine, an upscale pan-Asian restaurant in downtown Seattle, displayed this stereotypic poster in its window. Angry protests led to closure of the business in 1999. *Courtesy* International Examiner.

UW instructor Connie So has mentored countless students, directing them to volunteer at the Wing Luke Museum and at other nonprofit groups. Front row *(from left)*: Amanda Quach, Phan Su, Katherine Kang, Leyi Lei, Daniel Doan, Connie So and Wen Eckelberg. Back row: James Doan, Johnny Do, Jaren Tilley and Han Eckelberg, 2019. *Julie Son photo.*

The East Kong Yick Building, constructed in 1910 by Chinese civic leaders as the cornerstone of a new Chinatown, became the home of the Wing Luke Museum in 2008. *Top photo courtesy Wing Luke Museum. Bottom photo John D. Pai, 1996.*

The East Kong Yick Building shortly before its remodel. *Top right photo Karen Ducey. Other photos John D. Pai.*

The Lee Family Association and the Luke Family Association *(below)* were on the east side of the East Kong Yick Building before it was remodeled. *John D. Pai photos, 1996.*

KeyBank Foundation executive Margot Copeland was an early supporter of the museum vision. She provided a significant grant and came out from Cleveland to celebrate our successes.

(Left) Wing Luke board member Paul Mar at a Bruce Lee exhibit opening. He is pictured with Marge Young *(center)* and Maxine Loo, 2015. *Courtesy Wing Luke Museum.*

(Below) Board members Victor Mizumori and Ellen Ferguson join me at the opening of the new museum, May 31, 2008. *John D. Pai photo.*

(Above) Carol Szeto in her souvenir shop, Kong Sun Company, 2008. She was forced to close after a steep rent increase. *Karen Ducey photo.*

(Right and below) Ed Echtle redesigned Debbie Louie's childhood home as a Canton Alley apartment exhibit and helped move Jimmy Mar's old store into the new museum. *Ed Echtle photos.*

(Right) Ruby Luke, one of Wing Luke's sisters, cheerfully escorts me into the new Wing Luke Museum, 2008. *Courtesy Wing Luke Museum.*

(Center) The historic curtain from the Nippon Kan Theatre was installed as the stage backdrop for the Tateuchi Story Theatre. *John D. Pai photo.*

(Bottom) As promised, the new core exhibit told the story of the horrific injustice against Japanese Americans during World War II. *Dorothy Ng photo.*

In 2008, my sister Linda and I brought our kids to Fow Seck, my father's village, to pay our respects to deceased relatives. We visited our ancestral home and a cemetery. *(Top left)* My son Kino makes an offering. *(Top right)* When our charter bus broke down, villagers helped us get going again. *(Bottom)* Our group poses with villagers in front of Fow Seck middle school.

Brian Lock introduces me to his father's old *chop suey* restaurant in Shelton, 2007. *Ed Echtle photo.*

After I began working at International Community Health Services (ICHS), I rediscovered a passion for running. *(Top, from left)* My sister Linda, my niece Noel, Christina Twu, Cherry Cayabyab and Heidi Park, 2014. *(Center)* In 2014, I finish my first half-marathon in Burlington, Washington. *(Bottom)* In 2015, I dedicate the Seafair Torchlight run to Donnie Chin, who was murdered three days before the event.

(Above) In 2007, Ed Echtle built this tiny retreat in my back yard from recycled materials. He also introduced me and my kids to wilderness hikes and camping.

(Below) On a trip to Dewey Lake near Mount Rainier, I sit in an alpine meadow surrounded by wildflowers. After discovering the wonders of nature, I began planning my own garden. *Ed Echtle photos.*

(Above) Steve Goon and his girlfriend Laura Bautista at the Château du Clos Lucé in Amboise, France, 2019.

(Left) My gardener neighbor Kim with grandchildren Renzo, Coco and Genevieve, 2012. *Bill Backus photo.*

My nephew Orion Burt and Josie Pratt get married at Rancho de Chimayó, Chimayó, New Mexico, 2019. *Courtesy Orion Burt.*

(From left) ICHS founders Susie Chin, Sister Heide Parreño and Bob Santos, 2014. *Courtesy ICHS.*

(Right) Seattle Waldorf School students Mika Kodama-Chew *(top)*, Kabir Sethi and Harper Hall paint a mural on plywood covering Fortuna Café 2.0, June 8, 2020. Many Chinatown businesses were damaged following the murder of George Floyd in Minneapolis. *Karen Ducey photo.*

Volunteers bring supplies to Chinatown residents during COVID-19 crisis, April 6, 2020. *(From left)* Stephanie Shek, Sally Lau, Chau Nguyen, Lt. Lora Alcantara, Sharon Tomiko Santos, Henry Liu, officer Mike Gore, Eliza Guan and Derek Lum. *Courtesy InterIm.*

CHAPTER 34

The Rise of Ethnic Community Press

S HORTLY AFTER I ARRIVED AT the University of Washington, I discovered the publication *Asian Family Affair* (*AFA*). Founded in February 1972, *AFA* billed itself as an independent voice of Asian American student activists searching for identity and political expression. It was Seattle's version of *Gidra*, the underground publication by Asian American students at UCLA.

Francisco "Frankie" Irigon was *AFA*'s editor. Al Sugiyama and his wife Kathy headed up the news staff. Al had led protests at Seattle Central Community College which resulted in the Asian American studies class I had taken there a year after the protests. Silme Domingo was in charge of newspaper distribution. He became editor in 1973 and 1974.

AFA was headquartered at the UW Ethnic Cultural Center. It later relocated to a space above a Japanese restaurant just outside the International District. It took its name from the title of a popular 1971 hit by the soul group Sly and the Family Stone. The newspaper reported on protests against the Kingdome, the Asian American student movement, drug problems, housing struggles and liberation movements abroad and in the United States.

I thought about volunteering, but balked. I had seen Frankie, Al, Silme and the *AFA* crowd at several community meetings and demonstrations. They wore black leather jackets and sported long sideburns. They loved the bullhorn and were born to mau-mau. Their combativeness drove me away. I chose to work at the *UW Daily* instead.

After the *Examiner* began to establish itself in the late 1970s, *AFA* contributors who wanted to practice "straight journalism" in the International District made their way to the *Examiner*. This led to whispered accusations that I was trying to siphon off *AFA* supporters. Frankie, Al and I tried to quash those rumors. *AFA* began to publish sporadically until 1985, when it folded.

It was after I met older journalists like Emiliano Francisco, publisher of the *Filipino American Herald,* that I began to see *AFA* and my own work in the context of a long tradition of ethnic publications that had guided and informed people of color for generations. In the African American community, the "race press" had long been a rich platform for writers, religious and business leaders, scholars, poets and civil rights advocates. It was no different for Asian Americans.

Mr. Francisco had put out his monthly newspaper continuously since 1933, an incredible feat of stamina. He told me that he published a weekly forerunner to the *Filipino American Herald* during the Depression. "Back then, I nearly lost my shirt," he said.

By the time I got to know him, Mr. Francisco must have been in his 80s. He didn't write stories anymore. He simply collected the mail and attended community functions. The paper was an odd grab-bag of press releases, advice columns, reprinted articles and muddy snapshots of community queen contestants and Filipino lodge officials. He said his wife handled the billing for ads and did the paste-up because "she's good at filling up all those cubby holes on the page."

I usually bumped into Mr. Francisco near the U.S. Post Office in Chinatown. He dressed in a suit, tie and topcoat, with a hat tilted jauntily over his brow. He took small careful steps, struggling to hold onto his armful of mail. When he spotted me, he stopped and barked, "How's the millionaire?" I smiled. "Ronnie, how did you get all those ads in the last issue? Maybe you can share some of them with me!" He said his goal was to cover all of his printing and typesetting costs and still have "some coffee money left over."

Mr. Francisco kept 20 copies of every back issue in his basement. But researchers depleted his supply of some editions. "My wife, she tells me, 'What happens when you die? There won't be any community newspaper.' Anyway, that's why I keep doing it."

He vied for the local Filipino American corner of the ethnic press market with Diony Corsilles, the boyish-looking editor of the *Bayanihan Tribune*, a biweekly publication which started in 1975. He had a small, cramped office at 524 South King Street, in the American Hotel.

I found it amusing that Diony and Mr. Francisco were the only two people besides Serena Louie who called me "Ronnie."

Diony's paying gig was putting together a monthly tabloid for the Seattle division of Todd Shipyards called *Todd News*. The *Bayanihan Tribune* was a side passion. Diony kept the tools of his trade—a typewriter, light table, layout sheets, X-Acto knife, wax machine and roller—in his home so he could work on paste-up into the early morning hours.

Young Filipino American activists favored Diony's newspaper over the *Filipino American Herald* because Diony was willing to run articles on progressive causes like the anti-Marcos movement. As with Mr. Francisco, Diony and I traded tips about which businesses to solicit for ads, commiserating about the curt refusal of the downtown department stores to support Asian American community newspapers.

One newspaper serving Japanese Americans was the *North American Post*. There had been several others, but they all vanished before I entered the profession. The *Post* was founded in 1902 and published daily until 1942. It resumed publication in 1946. It was located in a musty, old office on South Jackson Street and accessed by way of a steep flight of stairs from the street. As the Japanese-fluent population began to dwindle, the newspaper began publishing in both Japanese and English. Under the prodding of Tomio Moriguchi, an all-English newspaper called *Northwest Nikkei* tried to make a go of it in the 1990s. I served as an advisor. It lasted as a separate publication until 1996. Then it became the English section of the *North American Post*.

One of my journalism heroes was Eira Nagaoka, a short man in thick glasses, a polyester suit and muffler. For over 20 years, he produced the *JACL Reporter*, the monthly newsletter of the Seattle Chapter of the Japanese American Citizens League. Eira never went anywhere without a large reel-to-reel tape recorder slung over his shoulder. He functioned a bit like an unpaid court reporter, making sure that there was an accurate public record of decisions made at community gatherings.

The *JACL Reporter* was crammed with meeting notes, significant gossip and tidbits of news that hinted at issues beginning to develop. Eira didn't consider himself a journalist—hardly anyone would have used that term to describe him. But that's what he really was: a professional who disseminated vital and hard-to-find community news.

During the time I knew Eira—from the late 1970s to his death in 1983—he had already become a dinosaur, and he knew it. His manual typewriter gave way to self-correcting electric models, and the mimeograph machine that printed his newsletter had long since yielded to the offset press. But he held fast, undeterred, driven by his herculean commitment to service. Seeing what he did inspired me to stay at the *Examiner*.

One of the last times I saw Eira, he was in the deli section of Uwajimaya, located on South King Street at the time. Both of us were refueling between meetings. I told him, as I often did, how much I admired his steadfastness. He shrugged, as if to say, "Well, someone has to do it." Then he looked at me out of the side of his glasses, his lips pursed in a slight grin, and said, "You know, I can write about many things because I can also speak Japanese. The younger generation, they have a good education, but they can't communicate with the Issei."

By the early 1980s, I joined with the heads of local ethnic publications to create the Northwest Minority Media Association. The group included Andrew Cho, editor of the Northwest edition of the *Korea Times*; Fitzgerald Beaver, publisher of *The Facts*; Chris Bennett, founder of the *Seattle Medium*; and Assunta Ng, publisher of the newly-formed *Northwest Asian Weekly* and *Seattle Chinese Post*. *The Facts* and the *Seattle Medium*, both based in the Central Area, served African Americans.

Assunta was the newest kid on the block. After she left the UW, she taught social studies at Asa Mercer Junior High. My only contact with her was when she asked me to help her edit a student creative writing magazine. In 1981, she called to tell me she had decided on a career shift. She wanted to start a Chinese language newspaper. She asked for advice. I told her about the challenges of getting enough revenue to sustain the *Examiner*. "I think I have an advantage because I will be publishing in English and in Chinese," she said. "I can reach a very big audience."

On January 20, 1982, Assunta came out with the first edition of the *Seattle Chinese Post* (西華報), published in Chinese. On February 5, 1983, she printed the first issue of an English language companion, the *Northwest Asian Weekly*.

Assunta's newspapers targeted the same Asian American readers as the *Examiner*. But Assunta and I had different contributors. The *Examiner* had richer arts content, thanks to Alan Lau, and deeper coverage of Asian American community issues because of our relationships with social justice activists. The *Northwest Asian Weekly* had stronger breaking news coverage because of its more frequent publication schedule.

The *Examiner* had been established as a nonprofit corporation, enabling the newspaper to apply for grants and seek tax-deductible donations. Assunta's publications were for-profit enterprises, allowing Assunta the freedom to operate as a private business without having to answer to a board of directors.

Although Assunta and I were intense news competitors, we joined as allies in the fight to bring advertising dollars to our respective organizations.

In 1982, the Washington State Legislature established a lottery commission to generate revenue to support education and worthy state programs. But we were outraged that the state didn't commit advertising dollars to promote the lottery in our newspapers. We saw a lot of money going for television spots and huge ads in *The Seattle Times* and the *Seattle P-I*.

It was only after much haranguing that these exclusionary practices began to break down. Government agencies, mainstream businesses and private firms began to see the value of reaching niche audiences in communities of color, including populations that didn't speak English.

By then, *Asian Family Affair*, Emiliano Francisco, Diony Corsilles and Eira Nagaoka were long gone.

In 2017, Al Sugiyama died after a valiant two-year battle with cancer. After working at *AFA*, Al channeled his activism into establishing the Center for Career Alternatives, a nonprofit job-training program for underserved communities, and serving on the Seattle School Board as its first Asian American member.

Al's parents had worked in sewing, like my mother. His father was head tailor at Albert Ltd. in downtown Seattle; his mother was a tailor's helper. His father resigned abruptly after the firm wouldn't apologize for leaving them out of ads that exclusively featured the white tailors. His father's gesture of defiance—when Al was in college—fueled Al's commitment to social change.

I saw Al on his porch on my daily morning runs. His house was several blocks from mine. He was a runner, too. "But this is too damn early for me," he said one morning when I stopped to chat, shaking his head. I told him I long admired his early work at *AFA*. "Shoot, Ron, what I did ain't nothing compared to what you did at the *Examiner*," he said. "What you did was real journalism."

"No, Al," I interrupted. "What we both did was journalism. You were one of the pioneers."

CHAPTER 35

Kingstreet Media

M ANY *INTERNATIONAL EXAMINER* CONTRIBUTORS WERE passionate about film, radio, TV and photography. They bristled against the media typecasting of Asians as inscrutable villains, war spies, coolie houseboys and exotic China dolls. They wanted to master the skills that would allow them to portray themselves and their communities in a truthful and humane light.

In 1980, under the initiative of Dean Wong, Kingstreet Media, a multimedia collective, was formed as an offshoot of the *Examiner*. Other founders were writer Mark Mano, photographers Sumi Hayashi and John Harada, former actor Ken Mochizuki and graphic artist Jeff Hanada.

Dean served as the group's leader and spokesperson, largely because no one else wanted to take on that role. Dean had just returned to Seattle after two-and-half years in the Bay Area, working under the tutelage of Emmy award-winning filmmaker Loni Ding. In 1979, Loni produced *Beansprouts,* a half-hour children's series on Chinese Americans which aired on public television in 1979. Dean saw the potential for similar work back home in Seattle.

Dean modeled Kingstreet Media after two Asian American media arts collectives formed during the early 1970s—the Kearny Street Workshop in San Francisco's Chinatown and Visual Communications (VC) in Little Tokyo, Los Angeles.

In the summer of 1978, Mark had gone down to Los Angeles to take a TV class. He also volunteered for VC. On the way there, he visited Dean and they began talking about creating a community media group back in Seattle.

Ken Mochizuki returned home around the same time as Dean. Ken had tried to make it as a Hollywood actor. But he was able to score only a single substantive acting part in 1978, as a South Korean kid dodging the draft in an episode of the TV show *M*A*S*H*," a role for which he still gets residual earnings. Disillusioned, he came back to Seattle and began volunteering at the *Examiner* in 1981.

Dean came up with the name Kingstreet Media. He was partial to King Street because that's where he grew up. The name also alluded to an old TV repair shop on South King Street and Fifth Avenue South. Kingstreet Media wasn't on King Street though. It was housed in the Jackson Building, on Jackson Street, in the same office as the *Examiner*.

The *Examiner* provided the budding organization with a free meeting space, a mailing address and a place to store video equipment, tapes and paper files. Most Kingstreet Media members were also *Examiner* contributors, making the location especially convenient. I joined and attended most meetings, but I stayed in the background, respectful of Dean's leadership in a realm in which I had little expertise.

Kingstreet Media began organizing small workshops on photography, video and audio production. After William "Bill"

Satake Blauvelt and Dean Hayasaka, film students at The Evergreen State College, joined, the collective hatched more ambitious plans. Bill, born in Tokyo, had previously lived in Germany and New York. He came to Washington state in 1979 to pursue his education. He attended an early workshop where he met Dean Wong and Ken. Dean Hayasaka was a local. His father Phil served as the first director of the Seattle Human Rights Commission.

In 1981, Kingstreet Media organized its first big event, sponsoring the Seattle premiere of *Hito Hata: Raise the Banner*, a poignant telling of the Japanese American incarceration story through the eyes of an elderly bachelor laborer in Los Angeles's Little Tokyo. The film was produced by VC's Duane Kubo and Robert Nakamura. Veteran actors Mako and Pat Morita appeared in the film.

Kingstreet Media members spent countless hours promoting *Hito Hata*. It was the first Asian American feature film ever written and produced by Asian Americans. The screenings took place at the Toyo Cinema at 5608 Rainier Avenue South. Like the Kokusai Theater, the Toyo typically featured action flicks from Japan with English subtitles. Terry Nakano, who ran the 300 Restaurant with his mother, owned the Toyo Cinema. He spearheaded the Japanese Community Queen Pageant contest for many years.

The film premiere drew an overflow audience. Kubo came to Seattle for the event. Kingstreet Media hosted several other screenings that weekend. The proceeds allowed the collective to purchase a video camcorder from VC.

In 1984, Ken, Bill and Dean Hayasaka teamed up to produce Seattle's first Asian American dramatic film, *Beacon Hill Boys*. It was based on Ken Mochizuki's unpublished novel about 16-year-old Beacon Hill resident Dan Inagaki and his struggle to discover his identity during the destructive drug culture of the 1970s.

Ken had drafted the novel in Los Angeles. He continued writing when he returned to Seattle. I liked the draft he showed me. I offered some editing assistance and suggested that he tighten the prose. He continued to tweak it, sometimes staying very late at the *Examiner* office and sleeping on the small couch.

Ken submitted one chapter to an *Examiner* short story contest. It didn't make the final cut, but Bill and Dean Hayasaka decided to use his story as the basis for a film that would serve as their senior thesis.

The film, created on a paltry $10,000 budget, was shot at community locations, including the Imperial Lanes bowling alley at 2101 22nd Avenue South, just off Rainier Avenue, and at the South Beacon Hill home of Dean Wong's mother. Imperial Lanes, the home of Asian American bowling leagues for over 50 years, closed in 2015. Volunteers helped with every aspect of the production.

I lent my beat-up old car—a dark green 1974 Dodge Dart Swinger—for one scene. After the project was over, I asked Bill if he wanted to keep it. The car had frequent mechanical failures and leaked badly when it rained. It was too costly to fix. He shrugged. "Sure." Bill, a starving artist, also had no money for repairs. The vehicle sat unused near Bill's Capitol Hill apartment until the city towed it away.

Beacon Hill Boys was shown at the first ever Seattle Asian American Film Festival at the Nippon Kan Theatre during the first weekend in May 1985. Dean Wong and Dean Hayasaka were festival coordinators. May was chosen because it is Asian Pacific American Heritage Month.

After a one-year hiatus, the *Examiner* took the lead on organizing the Seattle Asian American Film Festival in 1987. By then, Dean Hayasaka had left for California to attend graduate school and pursue a career in the film industry. I hired Nellie Fujii Anderson as festival director. Bill, who had become the *Examiner's* regular film critic, was programming director. The festival was held at the University of Washington's Kane Hall.

Nellie had worked in TV news, marketing and sales at KIRO-TV in downtown Seattle. She had a keen interest in cinema, especially the work of Akira Kurosawa. Her parents had taken her as a child to the Toyo Cinema and Kokusai Theater to watch *chambara*, Japanese sword-fighting movies.

Nellie's bubbly personality masked a deep sorrow. Her younger brother Ernie died in a motorcycle accident in 1980. She left KIRO and rented a small room in the Jackson Building down the hall from the *Examiner* to start her own business. She kept the film festival going and pulled together a special program supplement in the *Examiner*.

Kingstreet Media went on to produce the documentary *Taiko: Nikkei Expression*, and short videos on well-known modern dance instructor Martha Nishitani and Chinese American kite-maker Lawrence "Larry" Chinn. Nishitani taught at her studio at 4205 University Way N.E. for nearly five decades. Chinn, a retired Boeing supervisor, was Greg Tuai's uncle.

The group organized demonstrations in downtown Seattle against the 1985 Michael Cimino film *Year of the Dragon*, an action thriller that stereotyped Chinese Americans in New York City's Chinatown. By then, Greg Tuai had become head of Kingstreet Media. He was so incensed that he refused to go see it. The demonstrations, part of a nationwide protest, took place on August 24. At a testy press conference in the ID, mainstream reporters were hard on Dean, Ken Mochizuki and protest organizers. They said they didn't understand how anyone could complain about a film they hadn't watched. One reporter dismissively stated that gangs and organized crime were real. The event left Kingstreet Media members feeling angry and disheartened.

Erin Morita, the daughter of actor Pat Morita, joined Kingstreet Media when she lived in Seattle. I met her father when he arrived to film a commercial for the Uwajimaya cooking school. Dean Wong picked him up in his Pontiac Firebird and brought him to the store. Dean watched in amazement as Morita downed cup after cup of real sake during the shooting, the alcohol barely fazing him. Morita had not yet achieved the fame that the film *The Karate Kid* would later bring him as a professional actor.

Over the years, *Beacon Hill Boys* has become a minor cult classic, reappearing at campus screenings and Asian American film festivals. The film is Kingstreet Media's enduring legacy.

Kingstreet Media also introduced other early independent classics to Seattle crowds, including Wayne Wang's *Chan is Missing* and *Dim Sum: A Little Bit of Heart*, Stephen Ning's *Freckled Rice*, Arthur Dong's *Sewing Woman*, and Philip Kan Gotanda's *The Wash*.

Alan Lau and Bill Blauvelt wrote about these films in the *Examiner*, and *Seattle Times* film critic John Hartl offered up supportive reviews.

After I left the *Examiner*, I lost touch with Kingstreet Media. When Dean Wong moved on to other career pursuits, the group became dormant. By the 1990s, the collective had disbanded. Few people remember its pioneering role.

In 2004, Ken's unpublished novel, *Beacon Hill Boys*, finally made its way into print as a Scholastic Press title. It was stripped of the drug scenes and expletive-filled dialogue. It was pruned to about 40 percent of its original size and positioned for the mass market. Ken believes that the manuscript was "disemboweled."

I was curious to read it again. By then, Ken had already made a name for himself as a children's author. His most famous title was *Baseball Saved Us,* published in 1993 by Lee & Low Books. On January 1, 2004, Ken gave me a copy of the uncorrected proof of *Beacon Hill Boys.* He signed it, "To Master Ron, Hope you find this story fine-cut and voluminous! Thanks, Fearless Leader!"

CHAPTER 36

Asian American Journalists Association

MY DISCRIMINATION CASE AGAINST THE *UW Daily* had quashed my earlier dream of a career as a crusading reporter in mainstream journalism.

But I stayed in touch with friends who made a life in the profession. Dean Paton was a freelancer at the *Christian Science Monitor*. Lynn Thompson joined *The Seattle Times*. Evelyn Iritani and Roger Ainsley were both hired by *The Los Angeles Times*. Tim Egan became a columnist for *The New York Times*. Joni Balter floated between a variety of local media outlets.

I began seeing Asian American bylines in print media. Japanese American and Chinese American females appeared as TV reporters and news anchors. I heard Asian American voices on radio as deejays, reporters and program hosts.

In 1981, the Asian American Journalists Association (AAJA) was formed to represent this new generation. It was founded by broadcast journalists Tritia Toyota and Frank Kwan, several *Los Angeles Times* reporters and Dwight Chuman of *Rafu Shimpo,* a Japanese American community newspaper.

At first, I ignored AAJA because its focus seemed to be locked on the concerns of Asian American mainstream journalists rather than ethnic community journalists like me. The issues that spurred the formation of AAJA—combating discrimination in the industry, professional development and fostering culturally sensitive media coverage—were not my highest priorities.

I wanted more resources for the ethnic press. I wanted mainstream journalists—Asian Americans included—to stop ripping off content from *Examiner* stories without attribution and to treat us with professional courtesy. I wanted robust career paths from the universities back into the community.

In 1985, Karen Seriguchi, a good friend who formerly worked for the JACL, returned to Seattle to start an AAJA chapter here. She had been hired as AAJA's first executive director. I agreed to help. I knew that she would champion the ethnic press.

She told me that Bill Sing, a reporter at *The Los Angeles Times*, was a leader in AAJA. Bill was a Seattle native. I saw Bill's dad at meetings of Cathay Post #186, a veterans' group affiliated with the American Legion. He was immensely proud of his son's career. Bill Sr.'s one disappointment was that his son was not married. His refrain was "Ron, tell him he's got to stop and smell the roses."

In establishing the Seattle chapter, Karen and Bill also corralled Lori Matsukawa, Frank Abe and Sharon Maeda. Lori was a prominent on-air news personality with a longstanding interest in community journalism. Frank was a news reporter at KIRO News Radio. Sharon was executive director of Pacifica Radio in Los Angeles. At one early meeting, Karen, Lori, Frank and I met at Dilettante café on Capitol Hill to strategize about how to move forward.

I first met Lori when she was a reporter at ABC affiliate KOMO-TV channel 4 covering the dramatic eruption of Mount St. Helens in 1980. She later anchored a morning news show with sports reporter Tony Ventrella. Dean Wong worked as a production assistant at the station, doing the thankless job of lugging the heavy camera, lights and cables around for the news crew. Dean stopped by the *Examiner* for lunch and to gripe about the physical perils of his low-rung job.

When the Seattle chapter of AAJA was formed, Lori was an evening news anchor at NBC affiliate KING-TV channel 5. I asked her how long she expected to last, given the industry's bias in favor of young faces. She told me that she was safe as long as Jean Enersen, a popular fixture at the station since 1972, stayed on. Enersen didn't leave until 2014.

The "coming out" meeting of the Seattle chapter of AAJA took place on July 13, 1985, in the basement of the Bush Hotel. There were 45 attendees, including Tritia, Karen and Bill. I told Bill that his father wanted me to set him up. His lips parted into a small smile. Karen appeared in a skirt and hosiery instead of the denim jeans she typically wore in Seattle. "What's up with the dressy clothes," I kidded her. She shrugged, pointing out that "discomforts" came with her new job.

As the event began, Lori nudged me to give welcoming remarks. I was nervous. I wasn't used to speaking in public. I strung together a few rambling sentences. Lori rescued me by saying that we would distribute a questionnaire to guide the development of local AAJA programs. Later, I prompted Ken Mochizuki and other *Examiner* contributors to join so that AAJA wouldn't ignore the community press.

Lori became chapter president and I agreed to be secretary-treasurer. I told Lori that AAJA could share the *Examiner*'s mailing address. Meanwhile, I set up a bank account at the

International District branch of SeaFirst Bank, where the *Examiner* already had an account.

In 1986, the Northwest Minority Media Association and the Seattle chapter of AAJA joined forces to establish a scholarship program for high school and college journalism students. Funds were donated by *The Seattle Times*, Gannett Foundation, KING-TV, KIRO-TV, *The Tacoma News Tribune*, the Medina Foundation and the *Seattle P-I*. In 1988, the National Association of Black Journalists became another sponsor.

On April 7, 1989, I attended the AAJA national conference in San Francisco. By then, Karen had left AAJA, moving to San Francisco to work as copy chief for *The San Francisco Bay Guardian*. Diane Wong, editor of *East/West*, took over as national executive director of AAJA. It was nice to see another friend from Seattle at the helm. Diane stayed until December 1991, when she left to pursue independent writing projects.

I flew down to the conference with Leslie Mano and Ken Mochizuki. Leslie and Ken were at *Northwest Nikkei*, a new Japanese American community newspaper in Seattle. I stayed at the Richmond, California apartment of Karen Seriguchi and her partner J.K. Yamamoto, English editor of the *Hokubei Mainichi*, a daily bilingual Japanese American newspaper. They graciously showed me around town.

Leslie and I returned on the same flight to Seattle. She peppered me with questions about how to tackle her job as editor of *Northwest Nikkei*. I thought about her swift transformation from a shy, apologetic young person into a confident journalist. I was flattered that she considered me to be her mentor.

The close link between the *Examiner*, Northwest Minority Media Association and the Seattle chapter of AAJA in the early years helped guarantee that the national AAJA would remain sensitive to the needs of ethnic community journalists.

I stayed with AAJA for several years after I left the *Examiner*, believing that I would someday return to a profession that had been my first love. Decades passed and the press—or what I once knew it to be—had been dethroned by social media and a plethora of bogus online news sources. Rumormongers, ideologues and spin doctors with no obligation to truthful or fair reporting had taken over. I became disillusioned.

Like Eira Nagoika, I had become a dinosaur. I lost my appetite for reentering the tough day-to-day practice of journalism. I admired my peers who stayed true to the profession's highest principles in this new climate. But I needed to find another way to pursue my passion for writing, storytelling and community.

CHAPTER 37

Murders of Silme Domingo and Gene Viernes

TWO HEARTBREAKING TRAGEDIES TOOK PLACE in the International District on my watch as editor of the *Examiner*: the murders of Silme Domingo and Gene Viernes in 1981 and the "Wah Mee (華美) massacre" in 1983. The Wah Mee incident was the deadliest mass murder in Washington state's history.

Because I knew the individuals at the center of these news stories, I had a head start on dozens of potential scoops. I chose not to pursue them. These events devastated me personally, and I didn't want to contribute to the sensationalism of mainstream media or exploit the trauma and grief. At the end of the day, long after the TV news cameras departed, I had to return to my community. I struggled to manage my grief, offer comfort to others, and tell a necessary story for the public as a journalist and news editor.

I had worked side by side with Silme and Gene in the same office. When Gene died, I lost my best friend. Gene's and Silme's friends were my buddies, too. I had worked at the

Hong Kong Restaurant with the gunman who fired the bullets that took the lives of the 13 victims at the Wah Mee Club. I knew many of the murder victims. I grew up on Beacon Hill with their children.

From the summer of 1981 through the end of 1983, I followed the endless police investigations, the court trials and the nonstop media coverage. The carefree magic of Chinatown and Beacon Hill vanished, along with my youthful innocence. I felt like Ralph in *The Lord of the Flies*, watching a troubling shadow descend over the world I knew.

Silme Domingo and Gene Viernes were murdered at the Local 37 union hall in Pioneer Square on the late afternoon of June 1, 1981. The gunmen were Pompeyo "Ben" Guloy and Jimmy Bulosan Ramil, members of Tulisan, a Filipino gang that controlled gambling in the Alaska canneries. Gene was shot twice in the back and died at the hall. Silme, shot four times in the abdomen, managed to crawl outside and summon help before he lost consciousness. He helped authorities identify the gunmen before he died.

David Della, a friend of Silme and Gene and an activist with the Union of Democratic Filipinos (KDP), arrived at the union hall shortly after the two were shot. He saw Silme's burgundy Monte Carlo parked outside. The police stopped David at the front door. They told him there had been a shooting. By then, Silme had been transported to the hospital. David walked in to see Gene's bloody body on the floor. He told the police, "I was late for a meeting with these guys. They were my friends."

In a daze, David went across the street to a pay phone to call KDP national leaders Leni Marin and Dale Borgeson. They informed others and the news spread quickly.

I was at my parents' house on College Street when I received

307

a grim call from Chris Mensalvas, Jr. He lived at the College Street Collective, a ranch-style house next door. Chris was a housemate of Gene, David and KDP comrades Alonzo Suson, Mike Kozu and Rick Furukawa. I knew each of them well. I had worked with Mike on the local steering committee of the National Committee to Overturn the Bakke Decision. David had done sketches for me at the *Examiner*, providing visual support for Gene's series on the history of the Alaska canneries. I saw Alonzo and Rick nearly every day at the ACWA office.

In a freaky coincidence, the house occupied by the College Street Collective was owned by a Chinese American couple who would be killed two years later at the Wah Mee Club in a second sensational murder case that shocked Seattle.

"Gene was shot dead," Chris told me as he wept. "Silme was shot, too. He's at the hospital." I was jolted. My throat tightened. "What?" I asked in horror and disbelief. He told me again. Catching my breath after a moment of silence, I asked what else he knew. "It happened at the union hall a little while ago." He had few other details.

I hurriedly turned on the TV. I saw a flurry of breaking news reports. It felt like my world had caved in. My head spun. I didn't know what to do next. Chris was just next door at the Collective, but all I could do was sit in my parents' living room and stare mutely at the wall in front of me. Questions ping-ponged through my brain.

With a chill, I recalled my last encounter with Gene. He had just come back into town from one of his frequent visits to Wapato to see family. I was riding with him in his green 1969 Volkswagen van. Near the Beacon Avenue Junction, the old engine sputtered and rattled. "You know, Ron Chew, when I went back home, everyone thought I was dead," he said, chuckling. "A guy named Rudy Nazario, who used to be the dispatcher, was murdered in an ambush in front of his apartment. It was probably a gang-related thing. But everyone in Wapato thought that it was me. I told folks, no, I'm still alive. Look, I'm here. I still got a lot of work to do."

Gene told me that he visited the Philippines in April as part of a union fact-finding trip and had spoken with members of the New People's Army, the armed wing of the Communist Party, and the KMU (*Kilusang Mayo Uno*), an alliance of labor unions. He also visited his father's family in central Luzon. He noted with glee the striking physical similarities between his father and the relatives. He said he was proud of his humble roots, but he also saw the impact of Western colonialism. He asked me if I had ever visited my father's village in China. I told him I hadn't. "If you ever have the chance, do it!" he said. "You understand things about yourself that you never realized."

He knew that union reform efforts were entering a dangerous phase. As the newly installed dispatcher, he angered people by refusing to accept bribes in exchange for jobs in Alaska. Although his tone was somber, he didn't appear afraid. He emphasized that the work had been consuming a lot of his time.

Within 24 hours after the shootings, Silme died at Harborview Medical Center. I couldn't believe Gene and Silme were gone forever. I staggered around for days in numb denial. *Why did this happen? Were there spies and killers still lurking around in the community? Were others targeted? Was I safe?*

Several folks at the *Examiner* asked me about Gene's book on the history of the Alaska canneries. *What were my plans?* I didn't know. The manuscript, photos and handwritten notes from Gene were in the basement of my parents' house. Rick and Mike told me there were other pictures and slides at the College Street Collective. Within a week of the murders, dozens of community members contributed over $1,000 in cash and checks in amounts ranging from $5 to $20 to help pay for the book's completion. But finishing the book was the last thing on my mind. I needed time to grieve. I donated the money to the Committee for Justice for Domingo and Viernes (CJDV).

I accompanied Bernardo Taclay, a Filipino elder who lived in the Downtowner Apartments, on a car trip to attend services for Gene in Wapato. It was my first time there. The memorial was held at the Filipino Community Hall, on the same block as the funeral home. I met Gene's sister Barbara, a warm, artistic soul who worked as a barber, and Gene's two younger brothers Stan and Steve. Stan had worked four summers at Wards Cove Packing Company with Gene and others from Wapato.

Taclay had worked in Alaska with Gene's father Felix. Gene had sought the support of Taclay and other old-timers during union-organizing efforts. When we arrived in Wapato, it became clear to me that the tight-knit farming community knew little about Gene's life in Seattle. They were respectfully quiet during the service but looked surprised and puzzled to hear him described as a revolutionary.

After I returned from Wapato, I shifted my attention back to my job as a journalist. It was hard. In the first issue of the *Examiner* after the murders, I wrote about Gene's evolution into an activist. I interviewed Taclay and Andy Pascua, a boyhood friend. I learned that Gene first worked in Alaska at age 14 at Wards Cove after his father paid a $50 bribe.

I asked Julia Laranang to craft a story about Silme for the same issue of the newspaper. She wrote about his role in starting the KDP and organizing the 1976 Filipino People's Far West Convention in Seattle. She described him as a loving husband to his wife Terri Mast, who worked alongside him in the KDP, and a devoted father to their two girls, Ligaya, age three, and Kalayaan, one year old.

Sue Chin wrote the first news stories on the evolving murder investigation. King County Superior Court Judge Lloyd Bever presided over the trial of Guloy and Ramil. Superior Court Judge Terrance Carroll heard the charges against Tony Dictado, the Tulisan gang leader and getaway driver. Sue covered the first trial; I reported on the second. On several occasions, I felt so sick to my stomach I just couldn't go.

King County senior deputy prosecutor Joanne Maida argued that Gene and Silme were murdered because Gene refused to dispatch Tulisan members up to Alaska, disrupting their lucrative gambling operations. She presented dozens of witnesses. In the end, the case against Ramil and Guloy rested on the final brief words of Silme. At the union hall, he told firefighters that he had been shot by the two men. He repeated their names on his hospital deathbed. A key piece of evidence in the trial against Dictado was the testimony of Robert San Pablo, a cannery foreman. He said that on May 31, the day before the shootings, Ramil told him at the Hong Kong Restaurant that Viernes was going to be killed the next day.

Guloy and Ramil were convicted of aggravated first-degree murder on September 24, 1981. Dictado was convicted of aggravated first-degree murder on March 12, 1982.

For me, the most heart-wrenching moment was listening to King County Medical Examiner Donald Rhea testify about how Gene died. Rhea said that Gene dove to the floor just as he was hit by bullets from the murder weapon, a MAC-10 .45 outfitted with a suppressor. Rhea deduced this from the fact that the entry wounds were in Gene's back and the exit wounds were in his chest. As Rhea spoke, I could picture Gene's response—a skilled wrestler's first instinct kicking into gear. But Gene's reaction couldn't match the speed and power of the .45-caliber weapon. I lowered my head and blinked back tears.

When I couldn't make it to the courthouse, I attended the meetings of the Committee for Justice for Domingo and Viernes at the Bush-Asia Center. The co-chairs were Silme's brother Nemesio and ID activist Elaine Ko. I had worked briefly with Elaine at the *UW Daily*; she supported my discrimination complaint. Silme's sister Cindy, who returned home from Oakland after the murders, served as national coordinator of CJDV. Elaine and Cindy became the twin faces of the community justice effort.

I learned that two labor rights attorneys—Mike Withey and Jim Douglass—were probing more deeply to get to the bottom of the case. Mysteries remained. They posited a second motive for the murders. After uncovering secret U.S. and Philippine intelligence agency documents, CJDV filed a wrongful death civil suit, fingering Philippine President Ferdinand Marcos and First Lady Imelda Marcos.

The suit alleged that Silme and Gene were murdered as part of a conspiracy to silence Marcos's opponents, paid for through a $15,000 "intelligence slush fund." Shortly before the murders, Silme and Gene had sponsored a labor convention resolution calling for an investigative team to travel to the Philippines to examine treatment of workers.

On November 20, 1989, the case went to trial in Seattle before U.S. District Judge Barbara Rothstein. Mike Withey had interviewed Marcos during a deposition for the civil suit in 1986 and 1987. Ferdinand and Imelda were living in a posh beachfront home in Honolulu after being driven from power. Two months before the trial, Marcos died. The videotapes were played in the courtroom. Not surprisingly, Marcos denied any connection to the intelligence efforts against U.S.-based opponents of his regime. When asked about the intelligence slush fund and the murders, he invoked the Fifth Amendment.

I attended much of the civil trial. After 18 days of testimony, I waited anxiously like everyone else for word of a decision from the six-member jury. By then, I had left the *Examiner* to work at Seattle Central Community College. Bob Shimabukuro was editor. David Takami was covering the trial.

On Friday, December 15, I received a call from Mike Kozu. "There's a verdict," he said simply. The jury met for only half an hour on the previous day before retiring. I hopped a bus to the federal courthouse and walked into the courtroom with David Della. We were among the first dozen people to arrive. There was a lot of anxious banter as we waited.

Earlier in the day, I had asked Cindy about her birthday party the previous evening. She had just turned 36. "Hey, we're the same age," I said. She wryly responded, "Now that I'm done celebrating, it's time for the jury to go ahead and make its decision." I remembered that Silme and Gene were only 29 when they were slain. I felt a pang of sorrow. They were so young.

When Terri came into the courtroom, I walked over and asked her how she was feeling. She shrugged. She said she was eager for the verdict. She added that she didn't feel properly dressed. "You can borrow my shirt," I said, pointing to the K-Mart flannel under my jacket. She laughed. She knew I rarely dressed up. She explained that her blouse looked alright, but that she should be wearing a skirt, not pants. "Just don't let them photograph you below the waist," I responded. She laughed again.

So much had changed in both our lives in the past decade-and-a-half. I thought of the staggering load that she had borne: the grief of the murders, the solo parenting of two young daughters, the stewardship of a troubled union and the prolonged fight for justice. I wondered where her strength came from. Before the murders, I had watched her summarily dismissed—even by Silme, Gene and others at the ACWA office—as "too emotional." This facile judgment was typical of the unchallenged sexism I witnessed, even among activists. So many people had underestimated Terri's resourcefulness, intelligence and leadership capacity.

Other family members and friends began to arrive. They occupied half the courtroom. The anticipation ended when the jurors—three men and three women—filed quietly out of the jury room at 3:33 p.m., each taking their assigned seat. The courtroom grew still. Reporters opened their notepads and readied their pens.

The verdict sheets were handed to Judge Rothstein, who looked them over, then carefully announced the jury's decision. Point by point, the jury had determined that Ferdinand and Imelda Marcos were guilty. *Were they part of the conspiracy?* "Ferdinand Marcos, yes; Imelda Marcos, yes." *Had their negligence resulted in the deaths of Silme and Gene?* "Ferdinand Marcos, yes; Imelda Marcos, yes."

Loud weeping broke out as the judge read the jury's damage awards: $12,794,000 to Silme's family and children, and $2,254,000 to Gene's family. The awards were far more than the plaintiffs had asked for.

As the jurors vanished back into the jury room and court was adjourned, the crowd began chants of jubilation that justice had prevailed. There were many sobbing embraces.

Nemesio Sr., Silme's father, looking very spent, walked up to me, shook my hand and said, "Now, I treat you to lunch." I responded, "You'll treat me to lunch—*and* dinner?" We laughed. As he and his wife Ade, the unyielding emotional pillar of the family, headed toward the elevator, he added, "Now I can sleep."

Outside, on the steps of the courthouse, Cindy, other members of the Domingo family, Terri and the attorneys for CJDV huddled in a semicircle in front of television news crews. Mike Withey, looking very tall and lawyerly, said that CJDV would again ask the King County Prosecutor, in light of the verdict, to pursue criminal charges against former Local 37 President Tony Baruso.

As jury members filed from the courthouse, the crowd of CJDV supporters broke into spontaneous applause. Two female jurors smiled as they walked away. On the steps, I spoke to one juror, Bob Bible, a balding young man with a sincere expression who worked as a head custodian in Port Angeles. He said the resolution—referring to the ILWU resolution to send an investigative team to the Philippines, sponsored by Silme and Gene after Gene's trip to the Philippines—was the evidence that sealed their verdict.

I walked back to the International District with Donnie Chin and Emma Catague. I had first met Emma in 1977, several years after she immigrated from the Philippines. At the time, she was a waitress at Eight Immortals Restaurant, owned by Wesley Tao. She had gone on to make her mark as a cannery union organizer, anti-martial law activist, executive director of the International District Housing Alliance and cofounder of the Asian Pacific Islander Women and Family Safety Center. As with Donnie, Emma and I had much shared history.

At the first intersection, I suddenly felt the chill of the early evening air. My teeth chattered. I pulled up my collar and zipped my jacket. Emma, Donnie and I didn't say much on the trip back. We were spent by the drama of the jury decision. Silence said more than words. A lump formed in my throat. Tears welled in my eyes. I took several long breaths and exhaled. At last, we could all begin to move on.

After the successful civil suit, one remaining piece rolled

into place. In 1991, the King County Prosecutor's Office brought charges against Baruso, a close Marcos ally long suspected of complicity in the murders. The murder weapon was his, but he claimed that it had been stolen from him. On March 8, he was convicted on one count of first-degree murder and sentenced to prison without the possibility of parole.

CHAPTER 38

Wah Mee Murders

TWO YEARS AFTER THE MURDERS of Silme and Gene, the Seattle community was rocked by the mass murder of 13 individuals at the Wah Mee Club, a closed-door gambling establishment in a basement storefront along Maynard Alley in the Louisa Hotel.

In the early morning of Saturday, February 19, 1983, three young men—Benjamin Ng, Kwan Fai "Willie" Mak and Wai-Chiu "Tony" Ng—entered the club. All three drew guns and ordered everyone to the lower level, where they were told to lie on their stomachs. The gunmen hog-tied their victims with nylon rope and shot each person in the head at close-range in a storm of 32 bullets from two weapons, a .22-caliber Ruger semi-automatic and a .22-caliber Colt revolver. Twelve people died at the scene. One victim, former restaurant owner John Loui, died at the hospital a short time later. The three robbers fled in a 1979 Pontiac Opel with thousands in cash.

The 14th victim was 61-year-old Wai Chin, a retired cook and a dealer at the club. Like the others, he had been tied up and shot. Miraculously, he survived. Earlier, Chin had pleaded with Tony Ng to loosen his bonds because he was an old man. Bleeding profusely, he wriggled free and was rescued after another club member, George Ong, arrived at 12:45 a.m. Police were called from the Tai Tung Restaurant across the alley. Two officers arrived and pried open the outer and inner doors to the club and discovered the carnage inside.

Chin was rushed to Harborview Medical Center. Despite wounds to his jaw and neck, Chin was able to talk to detectives. He fingered 20-year-old Benjamin Ng and 22-year-old Willie Mak. He said he didn't know the identity of the third robber. He told them that high-stakes gambling routinely took place inside the club and that Mak and Ng knew gamblers would be carrying large sums of money. Mak and Ng were arrested hours later. Ng was at his girlfriend's South Seattle house. Mak turned himself in.

The "Wah Mee Massacre" dominated local and national headlines. The crime was replayed in ghastly detail for two full years. Many local Chinese American families were caught up in an ever-widening dragnet of ghoulish media fascination, heightening their personal anguish. Stereotypes of a dark Chinatown past were rejuvenated. It was a horrific time.

On the morning of the murders, I received a phone call at my parents' house on Beacon Hill. My mother picked it up. "Someone wants to speak to you," she said, rousing me from sleep. I stumbled into the living room. It was Donnie Chin. "You better come down here right away," he said. "A bunch of people have been shot. It's pretty bad. It's in the alley, Maynard Alley. You know where that is, don't you?"

"Sure," I told Donnie. "But tell me what happened. Who's involved?"

He reiterated that "a bunch of people had been shot." In

an urgent voice, he ended the call by saying, "Look, I gotta go. You want to get down here as fast as you can."

My mother asked me who had called. I told her it was the medic in Chinatown, a Chin. I repeated that some people had been shot. She was alarmed. She urged me to be very careful. I reassured her, then dashed out of the house. Arriving in the ID, I saw a flock of reporters and curious passersby bunched together on the King Street side of Maynard Alley. The crime scene was cordoned off with yellow police tape. Television crews had set up cameras. They jockeyed to get closer. Emergency vehicles with flashing lights were nearby.

It was dark, cold and damp. The sky began to brighten. At 6:52 a.m., police and medical examiners began pulling blue and green plastic body bags out of the club and loading them into vans. Donnie helped. It was sickening. They finished at 8:10. Donnie stood with me for a moment, shaking his head. His jaw was taut. He sighed. A few reporters tried to interview us, but we walked briskly away. Donnie told me a few more details. He didn't offer up the names of victims, but he said ominously, "Ron, these are people you and I know."

When I stopped by the *Examiner* to begin to make calls, I noticed that the light on the answering machine was blinking. Nearly a dozen calls had come in from news organizations and television stations—both local and national—requesting interviews. I sat quietly in the office, trying to settle myself. I was in no mood to return calls. I was eager to phone a few friends to find out what they knew.

In the past, many local journalists had relied on me to provide names of sources and background information. I usually helped. Now, as I watched and listened to television and radio stories spill forward about the sensational murders which had taken place in the "mysterious" Chinatown community—a place I did not recognize from the media's portrayal—I balked. I was sure my words would be taken out of context.

The media swarmed to the Wing Luke Museum to use it as a backdrop for broadcasts. One day after the murders, Kit Freudenberg started work as its new executive director. Growing up in an all-white farming community outside Detroit, she was ill-prepared to deal with an aggressive urban press. We commiserated.

An unsettling sense of *déjà vu* came over me. A week earlier, I dreamed that Donnie Chin had called to tell me about some terrible shootings in Hing Hay Park. At least a dozen old Filipino men were gunned down. As with many vivid nightmares, I woke with a start, relieved to find myself in bed.

Many friends went to Chinatown the morning of the murders. They knew their father gambled after work, but they didn't know where. They asked around. The weekends were prime time for *mahjong* and *pai gow*, two popular high-stakes games. Families streamed into the King County Medical Examiner's office at Harborview Medical Center. The unlucky ones left stunned, their faces seized by grief.

When I learned that one suspected gunman was Benjamin Ng, I was floored. I remembered him as a quiet young man working as a dishwasher in the kitchen of the Hong Kong Restaurant. He was short and slight. He stood on top of a vegetable crate because he was barely tall enough to reach the spray hose for rinsing dirty dishes. He seemed ill-suited for his job. *How could someone like this be a cold-blooded killer?* Although he was born in Hong Kong, he and I were part of the same community.

My mother worked in the same sewing factory as Benjamin's mom, Willie Mak's sister and the widow of one of the victims. My mother returned home from work each day with grim reports of rising tensions, grief-torn outbreaks and awkward silences among the Chinese women workers pulled apart by this unspeakable crime.

Benjamin's sister was an employee at International Community Health Services. Benjamin's brother worked at the U.S. Post Office. I imagined the agony that the Ng family must have experienced, trapped inside the media circus while trying to come to terms with what had happened.

One victim, Henning Chin, was a locksmith and handyman carpenter who lived with his family in Canton Alley apartment #2. Donnie was in #5. Debbie Louie, one of the kids who hung out at the Emergency Center, lived with her mother, two brothers and sister in #6. When Debbie was just three, Henning figured out a way to disassemble the front door and rescue her after she inadvertently locked herself inside.

Another victim was Dewey Mar. He ran Chinese movies at the Kokusai Theater. Mr. Mar worked as manager of the Bataan Recreation Club, a Filipino gambling establishment just outside the ID. His widow worked with my mother at Farwest Garments. The family lived on Beacon Hill not far from us. I grew up with and attended school with Dewey's sons.

Two victims—Chong L. Chin and Wing "Bill" Wong—were members of the Cathay Post veterans group. They both worked as cooks: Chin at the Chopsticks Restaurant (竹筷) in Edmonds and Wong at the Sun Ya Restaurant in the ID. Chin was the father of Henry Chin, my mother's dentist. My mother worked with Henry's mother at Farwest Garments and Roffe. Henry's office was on South Jackson Street just around the corner from the Wing Luke Museum.

Two other victims—husband and wife Moo Min Mar and Jean Mar—ran the Kwungtung Country Restaurant in Redmond. They owned the house occupied by the College Street

Collective. Their home was next door. I often saw their daughter leaving the house in the morning.

Kam Lee, the owner of Ying Hei Restaurant, narrowly escaped the ghastly fate of the others. The restaurant supplied take-out food for Wah Mee Club patrons. At the last minute, Mr. Lee, a club regular himself, decided not to go there that night. He noticed his daughter Jeannie crossing the street to the Kong Yick Apartments and decided to follow her home instead.

Donnie Chin was inundated by reporters pounding on the door of his Canton Alley apartment. He steadfastly refused to open it. He called to ask, "Ron, is it crazy over there, too?" He invited me over for dinner. After I arrived, he led me up a short flight of stairs leading to his tidy kitchen and living space. In all the years we'd been friends, I had never been there before. He boiled a pot of rice and stir-fried broccoli, *bok toy* and small pieces of chicken over a hot wok. He was an excellent cook. We sat down to eat and talk. The food was delicious.

Donnie was grieving. He was also indignant. Henning had helped him install the stairwell and plumbing in IDEC. Henning's widow and younger daughter had been pursued by a *Seattle P-I* reporter who came to their apartment. When his widow refused to respond to questions, her silence was written up as "mysterious." According to the story, she had to be "persuaded not to shut the door." She was described as a "heavy-set woman" with "hardly any accent." The headline read: "Families: a shroud of silence."

"Damn, Ron!" Donnie boomed. "The media, they don't know when to quit and leave people alone. This is *messed up!*"

I, too, was appalled at the insensitivity of my press colleagues. I overheard several say that they were unsure they would return to Chinatown to dine. One reporter was afraid that his waiter might be a hoodlum. Another journalist who had been eating breakfast at Denny's Restaurant—famous as the site of the pre-robbery discussions—said he became frightened when he saw a group of Asian kids in dark jackets. I was grateful that the Asian American reporters I knew left me alone.

Early on, Benny Ng, a waiter at the Hong Kong Restaurant, was mistaken for suspect Benjamin Ng. Benny was startled to find reporters converging outside his Beacon Hill home. I felt very bad for him. Benny was a skinny, doe-eyed immigrant, a goofball with a mournful smile. The busboys had nicknamed him "Benny the Beanball." He entertained us by crooning "Smoke Gets in Your Eyes" or Elvis songs like "Don't Be Cruel" and "Jailhouse Rock." He had been part of a band in Hong Kong.

Donnie and I saw the murders in the context of a changing Chinatown. Our parents' generation was on its way out. Gambling spots like the Wah Mee Club—operating in private under a police tolerance policy—were a carryover of the bachelor society that flourished during the era of Chinese American exclusion.

In its heyday, the Wah Mee Club was a popular late-night speakeasy. It had bright hanging lanterns, a long, serpentine bar and gambling tables. It was *the* place to drink, gamble and dance. In the early 1970s, it came under new management and began offering bingo three days a week. When I walked past the weathered brown-and-green entrance with its four rows of heavy glass bricks, I never saw any signs of activity. I assumed it was another dead Chinatown space.

Donnie and I reminisced about specific residents and quaint shops we remembered from childhood. I thanked him for dinner and returned to the *Examiner* to work on the latest of what would turn out to be many Wah Mee stories.

Several weeks after the murders, the trial for Benjamin Ng began at King County Superior Court in downtown Seattle. The city was riveted by the dramatic words of Wai Chin, the frail old man who had survived. He had been placed under heavy guard. No one knew where. The press—including major national media outlets—occupied a full bench in the packed courtroom. *The Seattle Times* and the *Seattle P-I* printed lengthy trial reports with endless sidebars.

The *Seattle P-I* began tagging "THE CHINATOWN MASSACRE" to its front-page coverage. There was a torrent of wildly inaccurate and brazenly stereotypical articles about "Chinatown gambling dens," tong rivalries, potential "gang warfare" and "the veil of secrecy in Chinatown." The term "International District" was excised from the media vocabulary. Shopkeepers and restaurant owners told me that the number of non-Asian customers had dropped precipitously.

I worked with Sue Chin on stories for the *Examiner*. We used the phrase "Wah Mee murders" rather than "Wah Mee massacre." In a March 1 editorial, I pointed out that any Chinese person loitering around King Street who demonstrated at least a faltering command of English could become "a source." Rumor and gossip were reported as "the talk on the street." Anyone who declined comment was "a source that declined to be interviewed."

Family members of the victims, recoiling from the sensationalized coverage, refused to talk to members of the press except at the very end of the trial. I usually sat with them rather than my media colleagues. They knew me. I felt their distrust and anger.

The prosecutors—two young attorneys, William Downing and Robert Lasnik—rested their case on the testimony of Wai Chin and police investigators. There were few witnesses for the defense. It was unnerving to gaze at the slender young man I had once worked with at the Hong Kong Restaurant sitting at the defense table next to his tall, flamboyant attorney John Henry Browne. A year earlier, I had watched Browne unsuccessfully defend Tony Dictado for his role in the murders of Silme and Gene. Benjamin didn't testify. He didn't show much emotion, only occasionally leaning toward Browne to exchange a few words.

Shortly before the trial, I received a surprise call from Downing, who invited me to his office to chat. Downing had an easy manner and a quick laugh. After we shook hands, he introduced me to Lasnik, who seemed much more cerebral, peering at me through a pair of black-framed glasses. I was immediately drawn to their thoughtfulness and intelligence.

They told me they appreciated my article in the March 2 edition of the *Examiner*, titled "We Lost Thirteen." The piece described each victim. It put a name and face to some individuals for whom they had no other information. That piece, they told me, gave them the first insight into how profoundly the murders had impacted the Chinese community.

During the trial, I met regularly with the two of them—Downing more often than Lasnik—to receive updates in advance of the proceedings. In turn, I told them how the community was responding. They asked me for further background on a few victims. I explained Chinese cultural beliefs to them and helped them separate truth from stereotype. I shared what I learned from the prosecutors with the relatives of the victims.

On August 24, an all-white jury of eight men and four women deliberated over two hours before returning a guilty verdict against Ng on 13 counts of aggravated first-degree murder and one count of first-degree assault. The jury returned to sentence him to life in prison without the possibility of parole.

In early October, another jury convicted Willie Mak of the same charges as Ng. Mak, depicted as the ringleader, was sentenced to death. His death sentence was overturned on appeal, but his conviction was upheld.

Mak's trial was a bizarre sideshow. His attorneys, Donald Madsen and James Robinson, tried to promote the theory that the murders were committed as part of a rivalry between Chinese tongs fighting for control over gambling turf, drug dealing, diamond smuggling and prostitution. Without evidence, they played on stereotypes harkening back to the early days of tong warfare and more recent reports of underworld violence by the triads, secret societies linked to organized crime in the Chinatowns of San Francisco, Los Angeles and New York. They argued that Mak was simply a tool of larger, dark forces. Mak fingered Ruby Chow, then a King County Council member, in this sinister web.

Mak claimed that he had gone to the Wah Mee Club on the orders of Roy Chu, president of the Hop Sing Tong, to "rough up" the leader of the rival Bing Kung Tong. He said he brought Benjamin and Tony with him.

I was appalled to hear Uncle Roy's name pop up like this. He was the kindly cook at the Hong Kong Restaurant who fried extra chicken wings to assuage the bottomless stomachs of young busboys like me. I had seen him perform with the Luck Ngi Musical Club at the Chong Wa Benevolent Association hall. I played at his house on Beacon Hill with his three kids and worked with them at the Hong Kong. Was it possible that there was a hidden side to this man that I didn't know about? I was skeptical.

I later learned from his daughter Cindy that following Mak's sensational accusation—widely reported in the mainstream press—Uncle Roy was assaulted by several strangers at the China Gate Restaurant (龍門酒家). Feeling abandoned by his friends, Uncle Roy avoided Chinatown. He stepped down as the head of the Hop Sing Tong. Several months after the end of the trial, the Hong Kong Restaurant was sold.

I was startled when Mak's attorneys subpoenaed me as a potential witness. *What were they trying to get from me?* I was sure they didn't know either. They were floundering. Donnie and Bob Santos also received subpoenas. Uncle Bob did testify, but he offered nothing of relevance. Donnie and I were relieved that we weren't called. I was prepared to invoke my First Amendment protection as a journalist.

I thought back to the murders of Silme and Gene. The Committee for Justice for Domingo and Viernes tried to prove the existence of a high-level international conspiracy. Their case had substance. Mak's lawyers also tried to establish a conspiracy. But it was a legal strategy without basis, aimed at spawning doubt.

During Mak's trial, one of Dewey Mar's sons, Tommy, seated with other family members of the victims, was abruptly escorted out of the courtroom by three officers. Donnie Chin and I noticed the commotion. We left to find out what was going on. An armed officer, who stopped us in the hallway, said the court had received a report from Mak's attorney that Tommy was a "hitman" from one of the tongs. "This is ridiculous," I said. "Do you realize that he's the son of one of the victims? This is outrageous." The officer assured us that Tommy would be released promptly after he was questioned. "It's just a precaution," he said.

Donnie and I found Tommy in the Public Safety Building about 10 minutes later, bewildered and agitated. "What happened, Tommy?" I asked. He said the officers took turns interrogating him. They asked, "Did you ever threaten to kill anyone?" They took Polaroid snapshots of Tommy and finger-printed him. After some checking, they realized that Dewey Mar was his father. They were thoroughly embarrassed.

I told Downing and Lasnik about this incident. They told the judge. Tommy was still very shaken. He said, "Hey, I want them to give my photo back. I don't know what they're going to do with it." I told him it wouldn't do any good. "How do you know they're not going to keep a copy, Tommy?" At least, I said, they knew who he was, in the event that Mak tried to pull a similar stunt again.

At the end of Mak's trial, I chatted with Larry Chin, a son of Chong L. Chin, outside the courthouse. He flew into Seattle for both trials from his home in Hawaii. He told me that Ng had pointed him out to police during the pretrial hearings. "Later, when they realized who I was, one of the police apologized for what happened," he said. Larry shrugged. "You can't blame the police. They were only doing their job."

"I feel bad for the parents of Ng and Mak, too," Larry added. "After a certain age, what can they do to control their kids? They are probably taking a lot for what Ng and Mak did, but it's not their fault."

On October 19, 1983, following Mak's conviction, I wrote a rare opinion in the *Examiner*. "The story wasn't what the justice system did to Willie Mak," I said. "The story was what Willie Mak did to Chinatown. Willie Mak dragged Chinatown into court with him as an uncharged co-defendant. Willie Mak, seeking to disguise his testimony as confession, passed blame on a mythical Chinatown he fabricated out of half-truths and stereotypes that work best on those who know the least about Chinatown."

I noted that Mak's attorneys, reduced to calling defense witnesses who denied Mak's allegations, suggested that the witnesses had not been truthful and that a secret Chinatown knew more than it would tell.

"Willie Mak didn't succeed," I wrote. "And now we are left to build and revitalize the same community Willie Mak had calculated to destroy. It won't be easy."

The third suspect, Tony Ng, had fled to Canada. He was finally apprehended the following year in Calgary, Alberta. He was convicted in April 1985 on lesser charges of first-degree robbery and assault with a deadly weapon. I was relieved. I couldn't quite believe that this was nearly over.

During jury selection for Tony Ng, I discovered that an independent film company in California was coming to town to shoot a low-budget mystery film *The Border of Tong*. It was about a brutal mass murder in a gambling establishment in Seattle's Chinatown. Writer and producer Michael Chu planned to film in the alley behind the Wah Mee Club.

News of the film project spread. Donnie Chin and I were furious. I wrote a story for the April 3 edition of the *Examiner*. A Seattle Police Department representative told me, "We can't legally force them not to come up here and film; we just won't cooperate with them." Chu went ahead anyway, filming in Seattle and Vancouver, B.C. I was invited to the premiere at the Beverly Theater in Beverly Hills, California, on January 28, 1986. I didn't respond. The film was widely panned. It died an obscure death.

The grief lingered. There were many legal appeals and predictable news stories marking each anniversary. As mid-February approached, Donnie and I checked in with each other to find out which reporters and camera crews had begun showing up in the ID. I hadn't forgotten how the children of Dewey Mar and Henning Chin were callously pursued. I returned only calls from friends like Lori Matsukawa and a few others at *The Seattle Times*. I pleaded with them to avoid reopening old wounds.

Gradually, the media drifted on to newer crime stories with greater curb appeal.

In 1993, as the 10th anniversary of the murders approached, Dean Wong called me to ask for a quote for the *Examiner*. "This is a surprise, Dean," I said. "Don't tell me you've decided to jump on the media bandwagon, too." Dean explained defensively that *Examiner* editor Jeff Lin gave him the assignment. After we spoke, he decided to compose an elegy to Henning Chin. "I thought of all the men and women who died there," Dean wrote. "Faces I had seen all my life, walking up and down King Street. A generation of old-timers lost to a senseless crime."

On May 3, 1993, Wai Chin, the lone survivor, died of natural causes at the age of 71.

Prosecutors Lasnik and Downing would later go on to become judicial superstars. In 1998, Lasnik was appointed to the federal district court by President Clinton. In 2004, Downing became the first trial judge in the nation to rule against the Defense of Marriage Act, opening the way for gay marriage.

On December 24, 2013, a mysterious fire raged through the Louisa Hotel. The businesses in the building—including the Sea Garden Restaurant (一定好海鮮酒家), Mon Hei Bakery (萬禧餅家) and Liem's Pet Shop (林家鳥魚店)—were forced to shutter. The heavily damaged western half of the building was demolished. The infamous gambling place with the steel-reinforced doors at 507A Maynard Alley was finally gone. *Did the spirits decide that it was time to close the book on the murders?* Maybe. It had been 30 years. For me, the dark memories had already receded.

On June 17, 2019, I witnessed the grand re-opening of

the Louisa Hotel on an overcast day. Members of the Mak Fai Washington Kung Fu Club performed a lion dance, and monks from the Fa Sheng Temple chanted. By early afternoon, the sun pierced through the clouds.

I toured with Tanya Woo, whose family has owned the building since the 1960s. The apartments above had been refurbished. The historic Chinese bulletin board was back on the Seventh Avenue side of the building. Prohibition-era art deco murals from an old jazz club, discovered during the renovation, were salvaged. A Korean barbecue restaurant and ice cream shop prepared to move in.

The spirits had returned for this happy occasion. The nightmare was over.

CHAPTER 39

Living in the International District

FTER I LEFT THE UNIVERSITY of Washington, I moved back into my parents' house while I searched for another apartment. Gene Viernes said, "Why don't you take over my place? I'm moving." He was living in an old home at 1807 18th Avenue on Capitol Hill. The owners were Mr. and Mrs. Tobias, a kindly Filipino couple on Bainbridge Island. The house had been subdivided into three apartment units.

I took it on the spot. This was 1977. It was only $90 a month fully furnished. Gene left behind a random collection of dishes, silverware and pans. I was set. My buddy Steve Goon was renting one of the other units. "Ah, we meet again!" I exclaimed. "What a surprise!"

Steve and I lived three blocks from each other in the University District during college. We cemented our friendship over countless late-night meals at the brightly lit Herfy's on the corner of N.E. 50th Street and Brooklyn Avenue N.E. Steve ordered two or three hamburgers. I bought two orders of greasy french fries and a cherry pie dusted with powdered sugar. I shared a generous helping of fries with Steve. We sat for hours talking about the latest pop hits, the Lakers and Knicks, the Oakland A's and the New York Mets, Nixon's impeachment and the future of China under an aging Mao Tse-tung.

Even though it was nice renewing my friendship with Steve on Capitol Hill, I didn't stay in Gene's old place very long. My sister Linda bought a home near Holly Park, a public housing community in Southeast Seattle. I had not seen her in over 10 years. She had a tiny, detached dwelling on her property. She asked if I wanted to live there. She knew I didn't make a lot of money. "Pay whatever you like," she offered. "Stay as long as you want." I jumped at it.

One day, water pipes in my roof burst, flooding my place. Linda invited me to stay over. That evening, she cooked a tasty meal of rice with stir-fried greens and chicken. It reminded me of my childhood when she took care of my brothers and me. We talked for a long time. She revealed to me that her former husband had physically abused her. She hid at the downtown YMCA. She pulled her life back together. She volunteered at New Beginnings, a shelter for battered women. I wish I had known and could have helped. But her resilience didn't surprise me. She had a steady job as a checker at the Capitol Hill Safeway.

I told her I was still working in Chinatown. Its history drew me in. I told her I wanted to live there. In 1986, after a short search, I found a vacant unit in the Evergreen Apartments, a three-story, rust-red brick building on the southeast corner of Maynard Avenue South and South Jackson Street. It used to be the Tokiwa Hotel. Built in 1916, it was renovated in the early 1980s with a federal loan. It was the first market-rate housing in the International District.

My mother didn't understand my move. "Old people and

poor people live in Chinatown," she said, sneering. "It's not sanitary. The apartments are too small." She had escaped the poverty of China to land at last in the coziness of a modern home on Beacon Hill with a full-sized kitchen, three bedrooms and a garage.

I moved my few belongings—the kitchen items from Gene, a plywood dresser from Fred Meyer, a worn brown sofa, a file cabinet, an armful of clothes, two dozen favorite books and two textured poster prints (Van Gogh's *Starry Night* and Munch's *The Scream*)—into a one-bedroom apartment that I would call home for the next decade. Friends gave me four stackable Darigold milk crates and a wooden door, which I assembled into a makeshift desk and shelving for my books.

My father took me to Connors Furniture and Appliance Store at the northwest corner of 12th Avenue South and Jackson Street to buy a twin-sized, metal-framed bed. He got a good deal. He knew the Nisei owners, the Shiomis. It was one of the last outposts of the Japanese American businesses that once stretched up and down Jackson Street. By then, Connors had been overtaken by Sears, JCPenney and the Bon Marché. In January 1988, the store reopened as Viet Wah supermarket. Đức Trân, a refugee from Vietnam, stocked his shelves with a broad array of Vietnamese and Chinese foodstuffs and household goods.

On the street level of the Evergreen Apartments building were Asia Barbecue (亞洲燒臘), a popular lunch take-out place, and Kue Hing Company, a Chinese video store patronized by my mother. Kue Hing included an herbal section run by Vincent Chiu, an herbalist and family friend from Fow Seck. My mother went there to buy long strips of dried salted fish from a large glass canister.

After I moved in, three good friends became fellow tenants:

Ken Mochizuki; Jesse Reyes, a brash but precocious illustrator for the *Examiner*; and Michio Teshima, a quiet, bespectacled young community organizer with a wispy goatee. Michio came from Chicago, where he had worked as a cab driver. He attended The Evergreen State College in Olympia, then moved to Seattle to become director of the International District Housing Alliance.

I lived on the third floor in unit 301. Ken lived directly below me in 201. Jesse was in 206, and Michio was in 208. In time, Steve Goon moved to the Evergreen Apartments as well. He was in unit 308, across from the elevator. He became the apartment manager.

Ken and Michio were part of the Seattle Taiko Group, started by third-generation Sansei determined to reclaim an ancient Japanese drumming tradition as part of their cultural identity. Masaye Okano, another Seattle Taiko stalwart, was also an Evergreen Apartments tenant. At times, it felt like our building had morphed into an Asian American arts collective.

Among the other Seattle Taiko pioneers were *Examiner* staffers Jeff Hanada, Stan Shikuma, Michelle Kumata and Bill Blauvelt. They made their drums from whiskey barrels and cowhide purchased from MacPherson Leather Company at 507 12th Avenue South. MacPherson was in the space formerly occupied by the Seattle Glove Company. The drums were constructed in a vacant apartment on the third floor of the Evergreen Apartments.

The convenience of living in Chinatown came at a price. When buses or delivery vehicles rumbled up Jackson Street, the building shook and fine particles of mortar from my brick walls rained onto the carpet and the top of the electric baseboard heaters. I vacuumed nearly every day.

In the summer, my apartment became an oven. I didn't

want to open the windows. The alley below was filled with dumpsters and restaurant grease pans. I went outside to the front of my building for fresh air. Near the entrance was a tall, vertical bronze sculpture by George Tsutakawa, installed in the summer of 1978 as part of a city-funded streetscaping effort. Its circular base provided a comfortable place to sit, relax and people-watch. I lingered very late, waiting for my apartment to cool down.

The building was infested with mice. I went to Higo Variety Store across the street to get sticky mouse trap pads. The traps worked, but the mice returned. Once, Ken came upstairs to help chase down a mouse. It kept circling in a bizarre zigzag pattern; Ken dubbed it a "mutant mouse." We finally trapped it in my bathroom under an overturned water glass. Ken took it outside and released it into a grassy field up the street.

Despite these unpleasantries, I loved living in the ID. It was close to work. There were cheap Asian meal choices. I was close to my activist friends and surrounded by a history that nourished my soul.

I felt a powerful sense of belonging. I remembered a passage from a book I read in high school, Carson McCullers's *Member of the Wedding*. The main character Frankie laments, "The trouble with me is that for a long time I have been just an 'I' person. All people belong to a 'we'—except me."

At the center of the neighborhood's resurgence was the six-story Bush Hotel, across Maynard Avenue from my apartment. Constructed in 1915, the Bush Hotel was once a first-class establishment like the Milwaukee Hotel, attracting visitors who came by train in the early 1900s. After it was remodeled in the late 1970s, many Asian American social service agencies established offices on the bottom two floors. They were staffed by idealistic young activists eager to rediscover their roots and work with Uncle Bob Santos to improve the quality of life for ID residents.

When I delivered copies of the *Examiner*, I met longtime residents at the Bush Hotel, Publix Hotel, Panama Hotel, Alps Hotel, Republic Hotel, Eastern Hotel, Puget Sound Hotel, N.P. Hotel and International Apartments. These elderly Filipino and Chinese bachelors sat for hours on the worn couches in the hotel lobbies. They invited me to coffee and lunch at the Hi-Lite Café and Puget Sound Café. They told me about *chop suey* houses, grocery stores, cleaners, clothiers, barber shops, jazz clubs, pool halls, cab companies and photo studios before my time.

I also began to spend a lot of time with the elderly Chinatown shopkeepers. They knew my parents and my family history. They were fabulous eyewitnesses to the past.

One of the best was Florence Chin Eng, the proprietor at Wa Sang Company, a Chinese grocery store at 663 South King Street, near Maynard Alley.

Auntie Florence was a stoop-shouldered woman with a frosted perm, determined spirit, melodious voice and very accurate memory. She was a regular at the Chinese Baptist Church. She came to Seattle's Chinatown in 1923 at the age of 14. Five years later, she established Wa Sang with her father, who had partnered with Chin Gee-Hee in establishing the Quong Tuck Company. Because of Chinese exclusion laws, Florence was one of the few Chinese women allowed to immigrate to Seattle in the early years.

Florence raised her four younger siblings as well as her own four children. She watched over other kids in Chinatown, making sure they got home safely at night. Her customers spanned the gamut from the single bachelor men of the 1930s to the first wave of Vietnamese refugees who arrived in 1975.

I stopped by Wa Sang every week, ostensibly to buy ginger candy or a snack. But I really came to talk to Florence. Her sons Darrel and Donald greeted me and kept me occupied until their mother could break free from the cash register. Florence pulled off her white apron, and we went in the back. I sat on a wooden stool and listened. She told me about the campaign to establish the Chong Wa Benevolent Association, the "paper" business partnerships that Chinese immigrants established to get around the Chinese Exclusion Act, the Japanese American stores that once lined King Street and the vanished African American homes on Weller Street. She shared colorful stories about Goon Dip and Bertha Landes, the first female mayor of Seattle. I relished her stories about my grandfather and my late uncles Kin Hong, Hung Hong and Lee Hong.

Florence's younger brother Raymond Chinn—he spelled the Chin surname with two "n's" in contrast to his sister—also painted vivid pictures with his razor-sharp recall. He was a civic-minded Rotarian with an eternally youthful face and a twinkle in his eye. I didn't meet him until years after I began visiting Florence. He was busy tending to their family's four restaurants—two in Bremerton, one in downtown Seattle and the Lun Ting Restaurant in the University District.

Raymond was born in Maynard Alley in 1925. He told me about warm summer nights when he and other kids gathered over a bonfire and told ghost stories in an open field on Eighth Avenue South and South King Street. They played softball and touch football. The shops stayed open late, and apartment dwellers came down to sit and cool off, the men smoking long water pipes, the women fanning themselves.

Another loquacious King Street storyteller was Guay Lee. I usually found him at Wah Young Company, perched in a mezzanine alcove that served as his work space at the store. He was a short, stocky man with wire-rimmed glasses and a firm handshake. Like Sam Yee, he wore an awful-looking black toupee to mask a receding hairline. He dressed in a polyester suit, tie and vest.

Guay Lee came to the U.S. in his early teens and worked in the kitchen at Virginia Mason Hospital before joining Wah Young as bookkeeper. He outlasted the other employees and took over as manager. He meticulously compiled a large scrapbook filled with newspaper articles about his involvement in Chinatown events. He pointed to them with undisguised pleasure. He was proud of his many years as president of the Chong Wa Benevolent Association and the Lee Family Association.

When I visited Guay Lee, I also stopped at Yick Fung & Company nearby. The shop opened in 1910, the same year as Wah Young. The owners were Jimmy and Howard Mar, Donnie Chin's uncles. Uncle Jimmy, once dubbed the "unofficial mayor of Chinatown," sat in the back near a cast iron, potbelly stove, watching daytime soap operas on a fuzzy black-and-white TV with Howard and a few other old-timers.

Jimmy served as a funeral director for the Chinese community. He dressed nattily in a suit and tie for funeral services, consoling grieving family members, carefully explaining traditional Chinese funeral customs and chauffeuring mourners around in his gleaming dark Cadillac.

Howard managed the day-to-day business at the store. He wore a billed cap and a soiled white apron over his work clothes. He sported a week's worth of facial hair. He tottered down the sidewalks of King Street wheeling boxes of fresh produce and canned goods on a hand truck to nearby restaurants.

Jimmy told me that he kept the store open mostly so that his unmarried brother Howard "could have a place to hang out" and so that he himself could have a place to hang his hat. "But truthfully, Ron," he confessed, "I don't need this anymore. Everything is so expensive now that if you haven't made it as a business, it's really too late."

For years, Auntie Florence, Raymond, Guay Lee, Jimmy and Howard Mar filled my head with facts and lore about a home community I had just begun to know. They made me glad all over again that I chose to live in the International District. They were my teachers, nurturing me and guiding my work in documenting the past.

Florence worked at Wa Sang until she retired in 1998 at the age of 88. She died on February 12, 2001, at 91. Guay Lee passed away on October 14, 1998, at 84. Howard passed away on December 18, 2002, at 90. Jimmy Mar lived the longest, passing away on July 11, 2008, at 98. Raymond Chinn died on July 22, 2012, at 87.

CHAPTER 40

Ghosts in Chinatown

MY MOTHER BELIEVED IN GHOSTS. My father didn't. I was dubious. After I moved to the Evergreen Apartments, I became a believer.

That's not to say that I couldn't be spooked. In my early teens, my sister Linda purchased a small paperback book, *The Enigma of Reincarnation: We Have Lived Before*. The author was Brad Steiger, an authority on the occult and the paranormal. It features profiles of men and women who claim to have lived previous lives. The most famous case was that of a housewife in Pueblo, Colorado, who, under hypnosis, became Bridey Murphy, an Irishwoman from the 19th century. Linda and I took turns reading the book and scaring each other to death.

Still, reincarnation wasn't the same thing as a ghost, a disembodied presence drifting about in spaces inhabited by the living. I thought that when a person died, the body simply decayed and that was the end of it.

In June 1988, I drove to Pike Place Market to pick up my father from Pike Place Deli. The business was formerly Brehms

Deli, until my brother Tom and his friend Jack Fong bought and renamed it in 1986. Tom, who worked full-time at the U.S. Postal Service, ran the deli as a side enterprise until he sold it in 1991. My father, then retired, helped with bookkeeping. He had asked me to drop him off at Ocean City Restaurant in Chinatown for a wedding reception.

As we neared Chinatown, I asked my father to first show me where his father Quay Fong had lived. He directed me up King Street. He pointed to a weathered three-story brick apartment building on Eighth Avenue South. Quong Tuck Restaurant and King Café were on the street level. I realized for the first time that my late grandfather lived upstairs from two of my favorite eating spots.

After I dropped off my father and returned to my apartment, I began boiling rice for dinner. In the middle of this mundane chore, I suddenly recalled two times when I had been visited by spirits. They had remained odd mysteries.

The first ghostly encounter took place days after I moved in. I brought the last of my possessions, two large boxes of favorite books, into my living room. I stocked the refrigerator with fresh produce and meat, and filled my cupboards with my favorite dry goods: Folgers Instant Coffee, Cup O' Noodles, Chinese sugar wafers, tea bags, Nilla Wafers, Honey Maid Graham Crackers and Nabisco Premium Saltine Crackers.

At last, I felt settled in.

Just before I turned off the lights to go to bed, I sensed a presence hovering near me. I didn't see anything, but a tingling sensation traveled down my neck. Suddenly, there was a rush of very cold air in the middle of the room. It began to move. I followed it from my bedroom into the living room where it came to rest next to my sofa. I stood in the living room for the next five minutes, seeing nothing, but knowing that something or someone was in a corner of the room with me. Suddenly, the presence dissipated. The air returned to a normal temperature. After puzzling over this for a while, I went to bed.

The second encounter took place during a dinner at my apartment a year later. This time the same cold, invisible presence brushed me from behind while I was seated at the dining table with Ken and Jesse. The two were both a little tipsy, laughing and talking loudly over beers. Whatever the presence was, it was not discernable to either of them. I felt the same rush of cold air as before. It migrated over to the sofa, where it lingered for about five minutes before vanishing. Again, I was puzzled, but I didn't say anything about this to my guests. I remained distracted during the rest of the dinner.

Now, as I stood by the kitchen counter, waiting for my rice to cook, an explanation came to me. The conversation with my father in the car sparked an answer. *It had been my grandfather's spirit.* He had come to welcome me. That's why I had not panicked or felt fearful. *Ah Yeh,* a man I had never met, had found a way to reach me across the chasm of space and time. No wonder I felt so much at home despite the crumbling mortar, the rodents and the odious alley smells.

Just across the street, on the other side of Maynard Avenue, there was a stone memorial in Hing Hay Park, erected in honor of my late Uncle Lee Hong and nine other Chinese Americans from Seattle killed in World War II. Did Uncle Lee's ghost return during Memorial Day and Ching Ming? Maybe it did, and I hadn't been paying attention.

Were other spirits poking around in the neighborhood? This was a very old place. I likely had other deceased forebears—related both by blood and by village kinship. Maybe their souls inhabited these streets and buildings, occasionally crossing into the world of the living.

I had left the Hong Kong Restaurant in 1975. The restaurant, still marked by its bright neon sign, was one block south of my apartment. My father and *Ming-bok* no longer worked there. But I imagined one day in the distant future when I was long gone, I might join both of them and my grandfather and Uncle Lee for a quick flyover. My insistent curiosity and unbroken connection to this place would draw me back for a peek.

CHAPTER 41

Lily Yamada

A T THE EVERGREEN APARTMENTS, I met Lily Yamada, an older woman with a bun of white hair, a smooth, broad face, a warm smile and a very sweet personality. She lived on the same floor as I did, in apartment 306 at the far end of the hall near the elevator. She worked at a hair salon in Uwajimaya.

She never let anyone inside her apartment and cracked open the door only a few inches to talk. Her place was filled with stacks of newspapers and junk, piled nearly to the ceiling. She told me that she was going to have trouble getting her place cleaned up before the fire inspectors came through to examine units in our building. She had too much stuff.

She revealed to me that she was in Hiroshima when the U.S. dropped the atomic bomb. She was what Japanese refer to as a *hibakusha*, which translates as "bomb-affected person."

I pieced together her story from many long hallway conversations. Lily stood just outside her door, the elevator screeching in the background as other tenants came and went. She nodded and bowed politely as she relived vivid moments from her past.

When the U.S. bomber the Enola Gay dropped the atomic bomb on Hiroshima, Lily was 25. She was at home with her parents, both 66, her sister, 22, and brother, 16. They were at the epicenter of the explosion, a zone from which few Japanese emerged alive. Lily had just stepped out of the house. The force of the bomb sucked the windows of her house inward, shattering them to bits. After the explosion, "black rain" dropped from the sky. Lily's clean school uniform turned black.

Fires broke out everywhere. Lily saw victims hobble about aimlessly, calling for water. Their clothes were tattered. Their twisted faces and bodies were seared. Skin melted away, exposing raw bone and ghastly purple flesh. The lips of many were vaporized. People collapsed and died without a sound. Children's screams of pain filled the air. Lily soaked towels under broken water pipes, squeezing out the water above the mouths of victims.

Everywhere, anguished people lurched toward the river. "But the tide was out, so they couldn't get to the water," she told me. "Pretty soon, you see all these bodies lying out there. And the tide came in, and the water turned red and all these bodies swelling up all along the river."

Lily tried to assist her badly injured parents and sister. She went to the army hospital. The doctors were overwhelmed by the flood of arrivals.

Lily left the city before nightfall to find food through the black market to bring back for her family. "It was so quiet, you couldn't hear nothing," she said. "Not even the sound of the wind. There were no dogs, no birds, no mice. I was so scared. I was afraid I would step on those skeletons all around me. I ran and I hurdled over them. Good thing I had been running track so I could run fast."

Lily had been a star track athlete. She was stronger than most men. She believed that her exceptional physical conditioning contributed to her survival.

Her mother, father and sister all died within 20 months of the explosion. Lily and her brother spent a lifetime dealing with the chronic effects of radiation.

It took a year for Lily to recover from her injuries. She recalled injections of B vitamins and doctors pricking her to find blood vessels. "There was no blood," she told me. "The worst thing is what the future may bring. You never know if something inside might be wrong. The kidneys, the lungs, the heart, all those things you never know until it goes wrong."

From Lily's apartment, which faced Jackson Street, the playful screams of little children lining up for the school buses troubled her. She avoided Asia Barbecue downstairs. The smells of roast duck, chicken, sausage and barbecue pork hanging in the window sickened her.

Lily's brother Frank was in the U.S. during the war. He was fortunate to have escaped the bomb. But like thousands of other West Coast Japanese Americans, Frank was incarcerated by the U.S. government. He volunteered and became a bilingual interpreter for the U.S. military. "If I was in the U.S., I would have suffered either way," Lily reasoned.

Frank also lived for a time in the ID. When he asked her to prepare roast turkey for Thanksgiving, she told him she wanted to make another dish instead. She didn't tell him the real reason—that it would remind her of the children in Hiroshima. "It's just like someone put them in an oven and turned on the heat and cooked them," she lamented, shaking her head.

On Sunday, May 13, 1990, I bumped into Lily after a morning visit to my parents' house for Mother's Day. I had just given my mother a gift-wrapped box of macadamia nuts, almonds and cashews. After thanking me, my mother said, "Next year, please don't buy nuts for me. I like them, but I can't eat them. I don't have teeth." *Oops.* I had forgotten about my mother's full dentures.

I told Lily this story. She beamed. "That's nice of you," she said. "You only have one mother for your lifetime. That's all."

I suddenly remembered that Lily's mother had been killed by the Hiroshima bombing. *Oops again.*

On this Mother's Day, Lily was heading out to work. Lately, she said, her health had not been good. On her way to Uwajimaya, she had to stop three times in four blocks to catch her breath. She spoke about how stressful it was at work. The salon manager yelled at her and talked badly about customers behind their backs, which she didn't like.

Lily said that getting angry made her stomach bleed. She felt better after the blood passed out of her body. Doctors couldn't diagnose the cause. She was checked for colon cancer, but the test came back negative.

Worried about her health, Frank urged her to return to Japan to live with their younger brother. "But what can I do?" she told me. "If we are both retired, then there is nothing to do except stay home and fight all the time."

She was in a quandary. In Japan, the government took care of her medical costs. But there she didn't have Social Security. In the U.S., Medicare covered 80 percent of her health care. "If they find cancer," she said, "nothing I can do. I just die."

She railed against those who supported war. She said she sometimes thought it would have been better to have died in the Hiroshima bombing.

I was speechless. I listened quietly. After realizing the time, Lily apologized for imposing on me. She bowed and hurried toward the elevator. It was time for her to go to work.

I thought back to grade school. During the October 1962 Cuban Missile Crisis, I watched chilling public service announcements about underground survival shelters. I learned about drinking water from the toilet bowl tanks and eating dry rations from tins. I saw how people could build backyard bomb shelters.

But I never had to face the reality of an atomic bomb attack. Lily's story reminded me of the war experiences of my own parents. My Chinese name *Jick Ping* (植平) translates as "plant peace." I hoped I could remain faithful to the meaning of my name.

Several months after I moved out of the Evergreen Apartments, I went to pick up lunch at the deli department of Uwajimaya. I asked at the hair salon if Lily still worked there. I was told that she had left months earlier. I also discovered that Lily no longer lived at the Evergreen Apartments. Maybe she had returned to Japan. I never saw or heard from her again. I never had a chance to say goodbye.

CHAPTER 42

Friends and Dating

L IVING NEAR A LOT OF friends meant I was rarely alone. My ID apartment became the default gathering place for bachelor guys craving companionship, conversation and food on dateless evenings and weekends. If I answered the downstairs intercom buzzer, it was usually a male friend who needed a break from dining solo on Nalley's canned chili over white rice and Chinese take-out. In return, I got an earful of fresh, unfiltered community news.

Thanks to my mother, I was comfortable preparing a variety of dishes from scratch. When the bachelor guys came, I set the table with a large pot of rice, stir-fried greens, *chow mein*, and steamed pork. The drinkers brought their own beer, usually Budweiser. I had lots of Diet Coke and Coca-Cola in the fridge. Steve cooked an extra pot of white rice to ensure there was enough "volume." He gobbled bowl after bowl. He finished an entire pot himself. He called it "the food of the gods."

After dinner, the guys returned to their apartments or tried again to find a late evening date.

I was so consumed by my work at the *Examiner* that I had no interest in pursuing a romantic relationship. Even if I did, I wouldn't have known how to go about it. I had no cues from my parents, siblings, or close male friends. Beyond what I saw on popular TV programs like *The Dobie Gillis Show*—which depicted a dreamy teenager who fantasized about dates with all the pretty girls in school—I didn't know how this peculiar ritual played out. I stayed on the sidelines.

I also was wary of commitment. I didn't want to trade away my free-wheeling, workaholic lifestyle. Still, I went to occasional dinners, lunches, parties, movies, concerts, lectures and shows with female friends. We shared deep and long conversations about Asian American causes, identity, community, life, feminism and the world.

Steve loved the local dance clubs. His favorite was Celebrity in Pioneer Square. It drew huge weekend crowds. According to Steve, most patrons were much younger than him. "But I can share in their youthful exuberance," he said with a big grin. "Sometimes you go to these places—there's 90 guys to three women. The type of music doesn't matter as long as you can dance to it." He lifted weights in his apartment every day and went running every other day so that he could stay fit. "Me, get old?" he wise-cracked. "Hell, no! I'm going to be the Dick Clark of the International District." He was referring to the eternally youthful-looking host of *American Bandstand*, the program we watched every afternoon on ABC-TV.

Ken introduced me to the singles bar scene. One late summer afternoon at the office, he revealed where he went after work when he wasn't hanging around at home. He mentioned three popular bars in South Lake Union: Triples, Benjamin's and the Rusty Pelican. Nellie Fujii Anderson explained that these places were collectively known as the "Herpes Triangle."

I startled Ken by shutting off my computer and saying, "So take me there. I'm curious." He looked at me in disbelief. "Huh? Are you serious?" I said yes. He shrugged and turned off his computer. Then we hopped into his silver Mazda GLC hatchback and headed to Triples.

The place was packed. We were surrounded by a boisterous, roving crowd of tall white guys in open-collared linen shirts, chino shorts and canvas boat shoes trying to make eye contact with young women in heavy eye make-up, low-cut blouses, short skirts and high heels. "Check it out," Ken said to me, chuckling. "This is what goes on at these places. It's a meat market."

After we found a table. Ken ordered a Heineken beer. I looked at the menu and mused, "What's this Long Island Ice Tea? Why don't I try this?" Ken didn't dissuade me. After just one sip, I got drowsy. My head felt like a giant watermelon. I wanted to take a nap. It took forever to push my way through the swelling crowd to the restroom.

We didn't stay long. Ken wanted to take me to another bar to witness more of the singles scene. We never made it. I fell asleep in the back of his car and couldn't be roused. The evening was over. Ken drove us back to the Evergreen Apartments. Once I opened my door, I took off my shoes, flopped onto my bed and slept until morning.

Nellie initiated me into a different kind of cultural scene: the world of opera. She had season tickets to Wagner's *Ring* cycle at the Seattle Opera House. She asked if I wanted to join her. In the wake of her brother's death, she had preached to Ken and me, "You guys should savor every moment of living, not take anything for granted and open yourselves up to new experiences!" Sitting in a suit and tie in the balcony of the Opera House with Nellie for several hours, trying to appreciate a lavish dramatic production that I couldn't quite grasp, definitely qualified as a new experience. It mirrored the earlier Cantonese opera performances at the Chong Wa Benevolent Association. In both places, I understood very little of what was going on.

In 1987, I was invited to Nellie's 30th birthday party at her home on Hunter Boulevard in the Mount Baker neighborhood. The house was beautifully appointed, with richly colored Persian carpets, Japanese prints, porcelain vases and a pair of Chinese stone fu dogs. It was unlike any residence I had ever visited. As a surprise, Nellie's husband Cappy and a friend hired a male stripper. Donnie Chin and I were among the guests when a pudgy, G-string-clad entertainer pranced through the front door. Donnie, the macho protector of the ID, blushed, then fled back to IDEC. Nellie was mortified. I felt embarrassed, too. I thought to myself, "Hmm, I'll bet if Nellie was in charge, she would have gotten a much better deal."

Many of my social evenings were spent at a house on Beacon Hill shared by Sue Taoka and Arlyne Sevilla Day. It was a four-bedroom Dutch colonial near 15th Avenue South and South Spokane Street. Arlyne, recently divorced, had two young daughters. She worked as an executive assistant at the Commission on Asian American Affairs. Sue had just completed law school at the University of Puget Sound in Tacoma and worked part-time at InterIm, following in the path of Uncle Bob Santos.

Sue and Arlyne were both friends of Craig Shimabukuro. Arlyne worked with Craig at the Commission. Sue first met Craig in 1973 in Denver at a Japanese restaurant where she waited on tables. Craig and a "cadre" from the "Yellow Brotherhood" in Los Angeles were storming across the country on a clandestine mission to bring supplies to members of the American Indian Movement who occupied the town of Wounded

Knee in defiance of federal authorities. Craig and his friends stopped by the restaurant for a rice fix.

I came to Sue and Arlyne's house to participate in fierce after-dinner Scrabble matches in their living room. Arlyne and I were evenly matched competitors, each with a different strength. She was a wizard at concocting seven-letter words. I knew a plethora of obscure two- and three-letter words, the fruit of countless hours spent in my college years trying to solve crossword puzzles in the *Seattle P-I* and the *National Observer* at the UW Husky Student Union Building before classes.

Arlyne usually came out on top. Once, to "psych me out," she turned on the record player and played Pink Floyd's album *The Dark Side of the Moon* at high volume. The English rock band's loud music not only psyched me out, it "freaked me out," as Arlyne reminded me many times.

I finally defeated Arlyne in a ferocious head-to-head tournament. I gloated. The prize was that she had to treat me to a "fine-dining experience" at FX McRory's in Pioneer Square. It was my one and only time there. First, the waiter got my order wrong. Then he spilled water all over the single pair of dress slacks that I owned. After I got toweled off, he proceeded to spill wine on me during his return trip. The highly touted boxed beef special arrived after a long hiatus, too raw and bloody to eat. It turned out not to be a fine-dining experience, but Arlyne and I enjoyed many light moments nonetheless.

Even though I didn't date, my time outside work was filled with unforgettable conversations. I became a confidant, guiding friends through traumatic career changes, relationship crises and family issues. I fielded anxious late-night telephone calls. I met with friends in small coffee shops outside the International District. Friends knew I always kept private matters confidential. "How did you become so wise," Vicki Woo once asked me, after we had spent the past two hours psychoanalyzing her relationship with her mother. "I just try to be a good listener," I said. "That comes from my journalism training."

Some of my friends were befuddled by my seemingly monk-like life-style.

"Don't you ever get lonely?" Dean Wong asked one evening. We had just put to bed an edition of the newspaper which featured a number of his photos. The final layout sheets had been delivered to Consolidated Press. We were catching a quick meal at McDonald's on Madison. Dean ordered a cheeseburger. I had a plain hamburger with ketchup and a pickle, no mustard. We shared french fries. I felt tired but satisfied. The place was nearly empty. An up-tempo Muzak track played in the background.

"What do you mean?" I asked.

"Female companionship," he said. "I mean, you can't talk to the sheets of newsprint at night."

I laughed. "You're right about that. But I guess I'm pretty happy making the newspaper my life and reading my stack of books before bed. Look, I've got friends like you and others to hang out with. It's not that bad, really. You can't have everything. I enjoy the freedom. Maybe I'm just a loner by nature. What about you?"

He shrugged. He stared at me with his big, round eyes, several sighs punctuating a long, quiet stretch. Dean was like this. Sometimes, he just sat without talking for a very long time. No one I knew could top the length of his silences. If he shook his leg, I knew he was thinking. He shook his leg. He didn't say any more. But I knew that he was hoping to find a soulmate and hadn't been making much headway.

"You'll get there before I do, Dean," I said. "Trust me, you will."

We talked about Donnie Chin, another bachelor. Dean and Donnie spent hours together in Donnie's chilly Canton Alley apartment watching over the rowdy kids in Chinatown, trying to keep them occupied and out of trouble. "I guess I'm a little bit like Donnie," I said. "I'm not opposed to being with someone, but I'm pretty happy having the freedom to do what I like and not having to answer to anyone."

"Donnie's never going to get married," Dean complained. "He's married to his job, and he's too damn stubborn and set in his ways. Know what I mean?"

I nodded. Pauline Zeestraten, director of the Chinatown-International District Business Improvement District, asked Donnie about his hopes and dreams, knowing that he lived in danger's path. He told Pauline he wasn't going to get old. "Why don't you go to China and get yourself a wife," she teased, prodding him in a way that Dean and I couldn't. He kept very quiet and shook his head. That was Donnie.

My mother, growing more anxious that I might never marry or have kids, showed me several sky-blue aerograms from China. They contained small black-and-white photos of young, unmarried women who wanted to come to America. "They may be poor," my mother explained, "but they come from good families. With both of you working, you can save up some money quickly. Why not?" I shook my head no. The cultural gap was too vast.

My mother never pushed the point, knowing me well enough that to do so would backfire. Instead, she relied on old-fashioned guilt. "I'm getting old," she said. "I don't know how much longer I'll be on this Earth. It would be nice to know that all my sons are taken care of before I'm gone. It doesn't matter who you marry, as long as that person has a good heart. You choose."

I eventually did get married, but it wasn't until 1993, after I turned 40.

Dean got married on September 27, 2004—to Jan Ito, Elaine Ito's sister. He first met Jan at an *Examiner* office party in 1992. Dean sat quietly with Elaine and Jan on a bench in Kobe Park and showed them photographs he had taken of San Francisco's Chinatown. That's when he found his soulmate.

Donnie stayed single to the end.

CHAPTER 43

From Matchmaker to Ordained Minister

ALTHOUGH I REVELED IN MY bachelorhood for years, I embraced playing matchmaker to two couples: Greg Tuai and Ben-Ling Wong, and John Pai and Lorraine Sako. All four were dear friends of mine. Greg and Ben-Ling married in 1991. John and Lorraine tied the knot in 1996.

I knew that Greg had been seeking a committed relationship for a while, and I wanted to help. One day at the *Examiner*, Serena Louie, who made a habit of scouring the personal ads in the back of *The Seattle Weekly* for fun, spotted an ad from an Asian male looking for a progressive, community-minded woman with a passion for the outdoors. "I wonder if this is anyone we know," Serena mused.

"Let me see that," I said.

After looking over the ad, I asserted, "I bet you it's Greg Tuai. The guy fits Greg's description perfectly. I mean, how many Asian guys do you know who like the outdoors?"

Serena shook her head. "No way! Do you think?"

"Let me call him and find out." Serena was aghast. I dialed

Greg's number before she could talk me out of it. He picked up right away. "What's up, Ron?" he asked. He was accustomed to my frequent calls about computer issues. I asked him point-blank whether he had placed the ad. He paused, a little embarrassed. "Yeah, it's me," he said. "Ah, how did you guess?"

"Come on, Greg. How many Asian guys do you know who are interested in outdoor activities? You're one of the few in Seattle." I told him that I knew a woman with very similar interests who was single and looking for a partner, and that I would be happy to make an introduction.

Ben-Ling Wong had worked at the Seattle Public Library since 1975. I first met her in 1977 after I learned about a letter she wrote to KZAM-FM, a progressive rock-jazz radio station. She had accused it of "blatant neglect" in hiring people of color. Her letter was co-signed by 100 others. I wrote a story about Ben-Ling's complaint in the September 1977 edition of the *Examiner*. When I later worked at the Coalition for Quality Integrated Education, she helped me assemble a list of library resources on school desegregation.

Ben-Ling and I became close friends after I was hired by the Seattle Public Library as publications assistant in the fall of 1979. I worked on the fifth floor; she was on the second floor. She was an American-born Chinese like me. She chose to be called Ben-Ling, her Chinese name, in junior high school because she thought "Gloria," her legal name, sounded awful, like the name of a Southern belle. We discovered that our mothers worked alongside each other at Farwest Garments.

Ben-Ling loved kayaking and snowshoeing. At the time, she didn't know how to swim. But she learned after she met Greg. I never did learn myself. My mother believed that capricious spirits lurked in the sea. Chairman Mao tried to banish this old idea by swimming in the Yangtze River in a propagandistic show of virility in 1956. But old ways persist. Activist Doug Chin quipped, "If you line up 10 Chinese in a row and you push them into the water, I guarantee that at least nine will drown."

I agreed to host a dinner—featuring my homestyle *chicken chow mein*—for Greg and Ben-Ling at my apartment.

The chicken dinner never took place. I came down with the flu and couldn't shake free of its grip. Ben-Ling also got sick. Greg, tired of waiting, finally decided after several weeks to take the initiative. He got her phone number from me and called. They hit it off right away, as I suspected they would.

On February 3, 1987, weeks after they met, I called Ben-Ling. She said they had gone out together to see a weekend performance of *Miss Minidoka 1943*, a musical by Gary Iwamoto, the first show at the newly-opened Theatre Off Jackson. She said the play was great fun. What did she think of Greg? "Oh, we're just friends," she said. But, in the same breath, she asked, "When are you going to fix dinner for us?"

On May 2, 1990, Greg told me that he and Ben-Ling had decided to get married. "Well, it's about time," I said. After spending a month together in New Zealand, they realized they wanted to share the rest of their lives together. Ben-Ling's mother's response? A matter-of-fact "When?" Greg's parents made their delight more apparent. "My dad was grinning from ear to ear," Greg told me. I joked, "That's one less kid for him to worry about trying to marry off."

On July 20, 1991—after a four-and-a-half-year courtship—Greg and Ben-Ling tied the knot at the Center for Urban Horticulture at the University of Washington in a wedding ceremony performed by Greg's father, a Superior Court judge. Maxine Chan prepared food for the dessert reception and decorated special mini-cakes from Pacific Dessert Company for each guest. Greg and Ben-Ling rode off in a horse-drawn carriage for an evening at the Inn at the Market overlooking Elliott Bay.

My second successful foray into matchmaking involved John Pai, a transplant from Manhattan's Washington Heights, and my friend Lorraine Sako. I met John in 1990, a year after he moved to Seattle. He volunteered for the Chinese oral history project I had just launched. He worked at Oppenheimer Camera Products just outside the International District. I was immediately drawn to his quiet, soulful nature.

He later worked as a videographer and photographer on several projects at the Wing Luke Museum. After his first marriage fell apart, I told him about Lorraine. My intuition told me that the two of them were made for each other. I was right. After they decided to get married, John approached me, "Lorraine and I are so grateful to you for introducing us. Now you have to marry us." I hesitated. "I can't do that, John," I objected. "I'm not qualified." He said coolly, "Don't worry, Ron. I've got that figured out." He explained that he knew an organization in North Seattle that would give me the proper credentials for a fee, which he offered to pay.

On July 25, 1996, John drove me to the International Assembly of Spiritual Healers and Earth Stewards Congregations—SHES, for short—in Seattle's Crown Hill neighborhood, some 11 miles north and a world away from the ID. I sat down at a small table with a woman in a floral dress. She led me through a brief ritual, then rang a bell. That was it. I was an ordained minister. I received a *Minister's Handbook* with legal and ethical guidelines and sample wedding scripts.

On November 17, 1996, I administered the wedding vows for John and Lorraine in a cozy meeting room in a historic brick building at the corner of Boren Street and Denny Way.

Word spread that I was an ordained minister who performed wedding ceremonies. Over the years, I've helped more than a dozen other couples—mostly very close friends—get hitched, helping craft written vows and making suggestions for the ceremony. Instead of accepting a fee, I ask couples to donate to a nonprofit community group for my service.

As an ordained minister, I formed a member congregation which I named the International District Fellowship. My congregation has never met. *Why not?* I don't preach and I don't like extra meetings.

CHAPTER 44

Asian Pacific Women's Caucus

I N THE EARLY 1970S, MY friendships with a trio at the University of Washington Women's Commission—Cassandra, Leslie Cossitt and Jane Segawa—brought me to the doorstep of the women's movement. They knew about my discrimination complaint against the *UW Daily*. Outraged, they wrote letters on my behalf. They welcomed me into their office. They gave me emotional support.

The Women's Commission office was on the second floor of the Husky Student Union Building (HUB). Their tiny room was always teeming. Jane remarked, "People pop in and out of the Commission like Pop Tarts!" The Commission hosted campus programs, helped students lodge discrimination complaints and provided other services. I was one of the few men to pass through its doors. I was invited in as a journalist friend from the *UW Daily*. Jane said, "This is a cigarette label: 'Caution: Men are hazardous to your health.' We make an exception for you, Ron."

Cassandra, a friend who firmly eschewed using a surname,

had worked at *UW Daily* shortly before me. She knew well how the culture there prevented students of color from rising through the ranks. Leslie was a work-study student at the UW under Cassandra. She started out pursuing a communications degree but switched to women's studies.

Jane was a soft-spoken but assertive Japanese American from Lihue, Hawaii. She had a radiant smile, hearty laugh and sweet nature. She spoke pidgin. She was very different from the mainland Japanese Americans I knew. She called them *kotonks*. She left home after her parents tried to force her into an arranged marriage. She first attended Eastern Washington State College before she came to the UW. She took classes in Asian American studies to try to understand how her mother, a war bride, had shaped her attitudes and behavior.

During lunch hour, I went by the Women's Commission to see if Jane was free for lunch. We ate downstairs at the HUB cafeteria. On nice days, we took our food outside near the front entrance to a sunny spot on the lawn, away from the roving crowd of leafleters and political proselytizers.

Jane and I wrote each other long, rambling letters. In one dated December 2, 1974, she said she couldn't sleep. "Tonite, Anne, myself and 2 of our friends are going to 'The Messiah' at the Seattle Opera House. It's a dressy-up thing and I haven't got a thing to wear…. Thought I'd wrap my new bedspread around me and go…. Do you listen to KIXI? They play really mellow music and it's soothing to the soul for a wound up person like me at the end of the day! I'm listening to it now…. It's almost 4—better sign off or else I'll be spaced out again…. Good nite Ron…see ya in lab?"

The gang at the commission—especially Cassandra— helped me get exclusive interviews with visiting feminist activists and authors. In 1975, I met Rita Mae Brown, who had two years earlier penned a remarkable first novel, *Rubyfruit Jungle*. I met and wrote about Yvonne Wanrow, a Colville Indian convicted by an all-white jury in Spokane of murdering a man who tried to sexually molest her 11-year-old son. Wanrow appealed her prison sentence to the State Supreme Court.

I also wrote about Joan Little, a 20-year-old African American woman in North Carolina facing the death penalty after stabbing to death a white jail guard who tried to rape her. The Women's Commission was raising money to support Little through the Southern Poverty Law Center. I wrote many articles on Title IX, a new law which mandated that all federally-funded programs—including athletics—be provided on an equal basis to men and women.

On International Women's Day in 1975, I interviewed Jocelyn Gan, a Berkeley student organizer. She had participated in strikes against the Jung Sai shop, a large Chinatown factory run by Esprit de Corps, a San Francisco clothing company. The militant strike for union representation failed after nearly a year of protests, arrests and court injunctions.

I took several classes in women's studies, curious to discover more about pioneers in the early fight for gender equity. I wrote a term paper on Sylvia Pankhurst, an English socialist and suffragette in the early 1900s. After learning about Alexandra Kollantai, a Bolshevik revolutionary, I found a U.S. Communist Party bookstore in downtown Seattle where I bought Kollantai's translated works—*Women Workers Struggle for Their Rights* and *Communism and the Family*.

During the spring of 1975, my final quarter at the UW, I had one last lunch with Jane on the lawn in front of the HUB. By then, she had already left the Women's Commission, overwhelmed by schoolwork. She was preparing to graduate and return home to Hawaii. I felt sad. We had grown very fond of each other. We listened to the cheeping of birds in the trees and watched the sun disappear behind ashen clouds. Folksinger Jim Page was singing and strumming his guitar behind us.

Jane nodded her head in the direction of a small group of passing students. She cupped her hand beside her mouth and whispered mischievously, "There go some more *kotonks*!" I retorted, "How do you know they're not Chinese?" We laughed a lot that day. There was a brisk chill. The air was misty, as if it would soon rain. I shared a piece of my Tootsie Roll with her. We were quiet for a long spell.

"There's no sun here," she said finally. "I have to return home before my skin turns pale like the *kotonks*." I smiled and nodded. I didn't want her to go, but I gave her an awkward and long embrace as we parted.

I had one last get-together with Leslie. We ate at the HUB cafeteria, then walked across Red Square as dusk approached. The sun's rays reflected off the wide expanse of red bricks, creating a shimmering surface of light. We sat on the concrete steps near the *Broken Obelisk*, a tall, rust-colored metal sculpture that many students detested. I laid on my back, enjoying the warmth of the bricks underneath me. We joked and reminisced about the Commission. I stared up at the sky, looking across the horizon. I remembered when I used to watch the clouds drift across the sky at my parents' house. I sighed deeply. It was a long time ago.

After I left the UW, I drifted away from Cassandra, Leslie and Jane. I never saw Cassandra or Jane again. Jane and I exchanged letters for the next year, but the cards and letters ceased as our lives moved apart. I kept in touch off and on with Leslie. We reconnected 13 years later at Seattle Central Community College.

Returning to the Asian American community, I met many

outspoken Asian American women leaders who had been shaped by both the global and the domestic movement toward gender equality in the 1960s and 70s. I knew some of them before I went to college. Our interests reconverged.

These friends became my abiding touchstones to the women's movement. They—and other like-minded activists that I met through them—established the Asian Pacific Women's Caucus (APWC).

APWC began in 1977 following a statewide women's conference July 8 to 10 in the central Washington city of Ellensburg. A contingent of Asian American women from Seattle—budding activists—made the trek there: Maria Batayola, Dolores Sibonga, Arlene Oki, Maxine Chan, Diane Wong, April West, Rita Fujiki (now Rita Brogan), Yuri Takahashi, Ticiang Diangson and Sally Kazama.

Conference participants fought for passage of the Equal Rights Amendment (ERA), which was ratified by both the U.S. Senate and the House of Representatives. The ERA needed approval from three-fourths of all 50 states to be enacted as part of the U.S. Constitution. Those efforts failed—only 35 states ratified the amendment.

The Asian American attendees, intent on challenging the twin oppression of sexism and racism, returned to Seattle to form APWC. They sported brown and white t-shirts and buttons proclaiming "Lotus Blossom Doesn't Live Here Anymore," a take-off on a popular film which portrayed the struggle of a widowed white woman named Alice who is determined to forge a new life of independence for herself as a singer.

Mayumi Tsutakawa attended the Ellensburg conference as a *Seattle Times* reporter. She joined the caucus in a second wave, as did Maria's sister Teresita Batayola, Nancy Lim, Joan Yoshitomi, Diane Narasaki, Martha Choe and Akemi Matsumoto, all of whom became close community allies in later years.

As editor of the *Examiner*, I relied on caucus members for news leads and story suggestions. APWC also prepared a regular column, "Lotus Blossom," for the editorial page.

In the late 1970s and early 1980s, the caucus spoke out against budget cuts affecting communities of color, supported the appointment of Asian Pacific Islanders to high government posts, fought proposed decreases in funding to the Washington State Commission on Asian American Affairs and lambasted mischaracterizations of Asian Americans. They joined political campaigns, expanding the number of female and minority elected officials. They were skillful coalition builders, working across racial, economic and political divides.

I miss the APWC pioneers who have passed away: Yuri Takahashi, Nancy Lim, Ticiang Diangson and Sally Kazama.

Yuri died of stomach cancer in 1987 at age 43, leaving behind her husband Jim Canfield and an eight-year-old daughter, Maya. She was an affirmative action specialist at King County and supported a nuclear-free and independent Pacific.

Ticiang and Sally both passed away in 2015. Ticiang was 74 and Sally was 93. Ticiang, an environmental justice activist, was half-Polish and half-Filipina. I knew her as "Pat" when she first barnstormed into Seattle with her free, inquisitive spirit. She had a distinctive, loud laugh, which rose from the bottom of her gut and ended in a heaving cackle. Sally was a founding board member of International Community Health Services and Seattle Keiro Nursing Home. She lived next door to the house I live in today on Beacon Hill.

In December 1979, Ticiang called me, livid that Sears was selling racist "Iwo Jima Battle Set" plastic toy soldiers. The U.S. Army figures were dark green, but the Japanese ones were mustard green and had slanted eyes, buck teeth and crazed expressions. She and Maria Batayola met with the Sears public affairs director to demand that the toys be taken off store shelves and withdrawn from catalogs. The Seattle chapter of the Japanese American Citizens League and Bob Santos joined the effort. The toys were pulled. The *Examiner* featured a cover story.

I grew close to Maxine, Maria and Nancy during my years at the *Examiner*. Our personalities jived. We had much in common as Asian Americans navigating between our personal dreams and the expectations of our immigrant parents.

Maxine attended Cleveland High School with my brother Harvey. Everyone called her "Max." To some of us, she was "Mad Max." She shattered the stereotype of the docile, quiet Asian American female. She laced every other sentence with four-letter words. I cringed when she unleashed her torrent in front of total strangers. In a *Seattle Times* series on *Ordinary People*, Max told writer Carey Quan Gelernter that she yearned for a life of "hedonistic decadence" and that her fantasy was holding court at her own version of an 18th century salon."

Max loved cooking and exploring the history of dishes prepared by early Chinese American settlers. She dined at lowbrow dives as well as sophisticated establishments. She worked in her parent's *chop suey* restaurants, first at Ding How Restaurant in Burien, then at Chinese Garden in Lacey. The owner of Ying Hei, Kam Lee, got his start as a cook at Ding How. Max once headed up Uwajimaya's deli department. She also catered community events, usually for free and with gusto.

In the late 1980s, Max and Nellie teamed up to assemble an "*International Examiner* Best Recipes" booklet. Jeff Hanada designed the cover. Greg Tuai contributed a smoked salmon fettuccine dish and four dessert recipes, including an amaretto cheesecake which he pointed out to me "had lots of cream cheese and sour cream." He knew how I felt about dairy. Author

Ruthanne Lum McCunn gave us a recipe called "Pie-Biter's Chinese-American tarts." Seattle City Council member Paul Kraabel offered a recipe for stuffed spareribs. Maxine contributed the classic Chinese sponge cake, Chinese sausage over rice, pork with shrimp paste, Buddha's Feast and scallion-poached chicken.

Max once invited me to lunch at Ho Ho Seafood Restaurant when she was especially hungry. She ordered a set menu for a party of six to eight people. "Are you sure, Max?" I asked. "It's just the two of us." She fluttered her lashes, laughed coyly, then responded, "Shit, R.C., why not? You only live once." She polished off a massive portion. While we ate, I winced, thinking about the bill.

Max became an activist when she was 16 and still in high school. She worked for the International District Youth Council, which operated a weekly food bank in the N.P. Hotel. Her community involvement continued for over four decades—at InterIm, ACRS, Merchants Parking Association and ICHS. When Max was at InterIm, she ran a nutrition program which provided vouchers for low-income seniors to use at local restaurants. She helped start a food buying co-op in 1978.

I occasionally tapped her to write for the *Examiner*. After I stepped down as editor for a brief spell, she even served as my replacement for two issues in 1979—the January/February and March editions—before realizing that the demands of the job did not match her skills and her unstructured lifestyle.

After the Wah Mee murders, the Seattle Police Department hired Maxine as a community liaison. Gambling had restarted behind closed doors, and the police were terrified that another horrible crime might happen again under their watch. I told Max that she was crazy for taking the job. She was trapped in a no-win situation, trying to represent the police department *and* a community which thoroughly distrusted authorities, especially the police.

One day, she came by my place on the third floor of the Evergreen Apartments. She hemmed and hawed before explaining the point of her visit. "Fuck, I hate to ask you this, R.C., but I have to," she began. I waited. "The police want to monitor some gambling that's taking place in a storefront on the other side of your alley. How would you feel about letting them set up a video camera from the back window of your apartment so they can see who's coming through the alley?"

I snapped, "Are you serious, Max? I can't believe you're asking me this!"

She stammered. "Okay. Sorry I asked. Not my idea, okay? It's part of my job."

It turned out the police didn't need me. On the morning of January 14, 1992, federal marshals seized the Milwaukee Hotel and two other sites in the International District after a nine-month undercover operation. Eight people were arrested, 40 others received citations, and money, gambling chips and *pai gow* tiles were seized.

I met APWC's Maria Batayola at the UW. She was a political science major like Steve Goon. Maria's second major—and personal passion—was drama. I was drawn to her vibrant energy and creative spirit. We became very close friends. She and Marilyn Tokuda helped found TEA (Theatrical Ensemble of Asians), which evolved into the Northwest Asian American Theatre (NWAAT).

I also got to know Maria's older sister Teresita after she joined APWC. Maria, Teresita and Nancy Lim were almost inseparable. Teresita and Nancy were best friends; they both wore Big Mac bib overalls from JCPenney. I joined the trio at B&O Espresso or Pacific Dessert Company, where they would indulge in chocolate torte or cheesecake and strong coffee. I was predictably unadventurous, ordering peppermint tea and the blandest pastry on the menu. I enjoyed their irreverent gossip and wacky humor. We sat for hours. I was the quiet one, the listener, fishing for story ideas.

Maria and Teresita immigrated with their family from Pasay City, just south of Manila, in 1969. They grew up in Seattle's Central District. Maria found her spiritual home in the intersection between the arts, ID activism and the women's movement. I attended her NWAAT performances, marveling at her ability to transform herself into a panoply of characters. We had leisurely post-performance debriefings at one of our favorite hang-outs, Quong Tuck Restaurant.

Maria complained that she never got to play a romantic lead. She was often cast as a frail, old woman. "I don't mind doing this, Ron," she told me, "but it would be nice to be someone else for a change."

Growing up, Maria was thin and sickly like me. I told her about my migraine headaches, which continued in spurts through my first two years at the UW, and my childhood visits to Dr. Kaplan. Maria suffered from fainting spells and had at one point been diagnosed as epileptic.

She amused me with updates on her futile search for an Asian American male partner. "Got any new leads for me?" she prodded. I shrugged, then rattled off a few prospects, each of whom was an unlikely match because he was either spoken for or didn't rank as a golden pick. "Hey, at least you can always hang out with me at Q.T.," I offered. "This workaholic ain't going nowhere."

I relied on Maria to write last-minute articles for the *Examiner*. She didn't mind if I completely rewrote articles, which I often did. She only cared that the final version was credible and useful to the community. As an editor who often dealt with fussy writers, I appreciated her flexibility.

In late 1984, Maria asked me to write a story for the *Examiner* to support installation of a granite headstone at Carlos Bulosan's gravesite at Mount Pleasant Cemetery on Queen Anne Hill in Seattle. Bulosan, author of the seminal *America Is in the Heart*, died a pauper in 1956. He had lived in the Eastern Hotel. It was only with great difficulty that Maria and Stan Asis, a fellow actor who produced Bulosan's folktales as a UW student, were able to locate the spot where he was buried. Over $1,000 was quickly raised for the headstone.

Nancy Lim was a second-generation Chinese American like me. When I first met her, she wore a white, frilly peasant blouse, dark shorts and black canvas kung-fu shoes. She had tidy bangs and big front teeth. She crossed her arms thoughtfully. She reminded me of my sister—low-key, but steely. She hailed from California, the second of six children. She grew up under the rule of a strong mother who owned a Chinese American restaurant in Riverside, California. Her father died when she was only six. Her stepfather, whom she described to me as a "wife beater," had also passed away.

Nancy was another fellow migraine sufferer. She worked at the Fremont Clinic. Her dream was to become a credentialed medical professional specializing in women's health—and to have a baby. As her biological clock ticked down, she became fixated on having a child. But like Maria, she wasn't having much luck. "Where are all the Asian men?" she pleaded. "Help me out here, Ron!" She lived in an apartment on Capitol Hill, hardly the nerve center of the Asian American dating scene. I told her that all the Asian males I knew were on Beacon Hill.

"The only Asian guys I see are at the magazine section of the Fred Meyer store on Broadway," she lamented. "But it doesn't seem like they're interested in talking to anyone. Probably they're not interested in hooking up with a feminist like me anyway."

"I don't know," I countered. "I suppose it depends on what kind of magazines they're interested in." She laughed. I confessed to patronizing the store, but I didn't reveal to her that *Car and Driver* and *U.S. News & World Report* were what drew me there. I loved squeezing in as much reading time as I could before a clerk would remind me that the store was not a free library. I admonished her, "You shouldn't be so hard on yourself. You're bright. You're attractive. I think you put too much pressure on yourself. I'm sure you'll find someone."

Nancy was admitted to Yale University, where she pursued a nursing degree. After graduating she returned home to California, settling in Berkeley. We stayed in touch through letters. In one, she asked if the Capitol Hill Fred Meyer store—her "reliable lookout for Asian men"—had closed. She wrote that our mutual friend Teresita Batayola had also moved away from Capitol Hill and would have to help her "search out a new spot for sighting Asian men." She wryly remarked that she was "just hanging out, becoming old and lazy as all good Chinese women shouldn't."

She finally found a male partner, Michael Barnes—not Asian as she had fervently sought—but someone with whom she could have a child. The child wasn't a girl, as Nancy first hoped. But she was ecstatic to become a mother. Maximilian Theodore Chen was born on April 19, 1992, in Oakland. Chen was Nancy's real surname. Lim was her father's "paper name."

In the meantime, Teresita married Dionnie Dionisio, a Filipino activist and postal worker, in 1988. Their baby girl Gabriela arrived on July 14, just three months after Maximilian.

Unexpected complications from childbirth and medical errors at the hospital permanently damaged Nancy's health. Max, at 9 pounds, 2 ounces, had been too big for Nancy to deliver vaginally. She had a C-section. But then she had to undergo a second major abdominal surgery and a temporary colostomy, which resulted in severe bleeding. She wrote me a letter from her hospital bed: "I have Max, the world's sweetest little boy. Ron, I remember your enjoyment of your nephew. I was so wanting a girl, but now I cannot imagine having a daughter. Max is a wonderful part of my life—I couldn't have asked for better." She wrote to me while she was still under morphine.

After I became executive director of the Wing Luke Museum, Nancy learned from National Public Radio about an exhibition I helped create on the incarceration of Japanese Americans during World War II. She came to visit, wheeling "big-headed" baby Max in a stroller. She was glowing with maternal pride, but she didn't look well. I was happy for her but it worried me that she had not returned to full health.

It wasn't long after she returned to Oakland that I learned she had died. The news crushed my heart. I felt a billowing sorrow that I couldn't shake for months. It was like losing a sister.

Nancy's sister Virginia and Michael buried her ashes in a Chinese cloisonné urn at Sunset View Cemetery north of Berkeley. The headstone reads "Nancy Lim, Max's Mom Forever." The quote came from a letter Nancy sent to a friend when Max was a little over six months old: "I love this boy enormously—can't imagine how empty my life was without him. I realize that nothing else was filling this big hole in my heart before…And just think, I get to be Max's mom forever."

Nancy's Chinese name—陳綺娜—was engraved on her headstone. The first character is the Chen surname, not Lim. Like other Chinese Americans who return to the earth, she cast aside her fake name in a final act of reclaiming identity.

Chapter 45

Time for a Career Change

FOR YEARS, THE *INTERNATIONAL EXAMINER* was my sole passion. But the relentless day-to-day challenges—budget shortfalls, unforgiving deadlines, volunteer turnover and petty community strife—wore me down. At the end of 1979, I decided to step down as editor for a year. I contributed articles, but I cut my time way back. Sue Chin reluctantly agreed to take my place at the helm in 1980. Dean Wong followed Sue as editor in early 1981, also grudgingly.

I returned as full-time editor in October 1981. Refreshed, I stayed on for seven more years before I ended my journalism career. In total, I spent 13 years at the newspaper.

During my final stint at the *Examiner*, I yearned to do more in-depth writing, but I had no time. I began to think about working elsewhere or turning to freelancing. My choices in Seattle were limited. I didn't want to work for *The Seattle Times* or the *Seattle P-I*, even if I could. Nor did I want to start another publication.

In the mid-1980s, a neatly dressed young Asian American

man came by the *Examiner* with the intriguing proposition of starting an Asian American magazine. He was bursting with energy, charming and articulate. He said he wanted my help. The only pan-Asian American magazine I knew of was *Bridge*, a low-budget publication issued by the Basement Workshop in New York City.

He introduced himself as Martin Pang and vigorously shook my hand. He explained that he worked for his family's business, Mary Pang Food Products. He asked me if I had heard of it. "Sure," I said. "It's down the street." Pang said that he was a faithful *Examiner* reader and admired my work. He laid out his grand vision. "How would you like to work with me on making this happen?" he asked. He said he would bankroll the effort. But it was clear that he didn't know anything about publishing. Despite his smooth pitch, something didn't feel right. I told him I would get back to him. He left his business card. I never called, even though he left several phone messages.

I was stunned when his name re-emerged years later as the person who set an arson fire at the family warehouse in 1995 to collect an insurance payout. This tragedy took the lives of four firefighters. I was relieved that I had not followed up with him.

In 1987, I received a call from David Lattimer, one of the publishers of *Rice*, a new Asian American magazine in San Francisco. He asked if I might want to contribute. In that same year, another Asian American magazine also surfaced: *AsiAm*, a glossy, full-color magazine based in Los Angeles which targeted the growing upscale yuppie market. Its embrace of materialism and sexist photographs of skimpily clad Asian models did not appeal to me.

Lattimer asked if I wanted to be a "man about town" correspondent in Seattle, focusing on the local club, restaurant and gallery scene. He offered 10 cents a word. If I helped recruit other Northwest writers, I would be paid an additional stipend.

I told him that I was a news writer, not a critic. I asked him what writing style was expected of *Rice* contributors. He said it was up to me. "But," he added, "if you're the kind of guy who likes to spit and chew, then that's all right, too."

I was in the office with Serena, Elaine and Ken. I asked them what "spit and chew" meant. I said I didn't understand this "*lo-fan*-ese term." *Lo fan* (佬番) is a Chinese euphemism for "white person." They laughed. They didn't have a clue either. We had spent too many years on Beacon Hill. I then called David Takami and Nellie Fujii Anderson. They had a general idea, but even they weren't sure. In the end, I decided not to take Lattimer up on his offer.

By 1988, I was ready to leave the *Examiner* once and for all. I hadn't lined up another writing gig, but I had accomplished most of my personal goals.

On July 15, 1988, I gathered my staff in the office—Serena Louie, Ken Mochizuki, Ann Fujii, Leslie Mano, David Takami, Pam Horino, Greg Tuai and Dean Wong. I was exhausted, having just completed a huge edition with a special supplement from InterIm and an ID Summer Festival program. I told them I would step down as editor after the end of September or October. I thanked them for putting up with my quirks and for their long hours of low-paid and unpaid service. I confessed that this was the hardest transition I ever had to make.

The room was hushed. The mood was somber. Pam and Serena cried. Ken, my sole paid writer, was speechless.

The next day, I received a card addressed to "Former Anteater." It was signed by staff and volunteers. Maxine, addressing me as "R.C. Cola," a nickname she sometimes used, wrote: "Sorry to see you go, but there will be more lunches at Ying Hei in your memory." Ken scrawled, "Hey, Chief, Thanks for the EGGciting and EGGtraordinary tenure here. You were an EGGcellent teacher. P.S. It was very fine cut!"

Alan Lau's thank you card expressed appreciation for "the fact that you dug my story about *No-No Boy* out of the trash bin and were patient enough to let a poet try his hand at prose." He said he always regretted that the stories I wrote for the paper were "few and far between." He offered to help with the transition during his "spare time away from produce."

Andy de los Angeles, former managing editor of *Northwest Indian News*, also sent a nice note, praising me as "an inspiration to the journalism community." He shared with me that "passing the torch on in this business can be very difficult" and "breaking 'old habits' and work 'addictions' was equally hard." He added that it was rewarding for him to see writers, photographers and broadcasters who worked at his newspaper travel "farther down the journalism trail" than he could ever go. "I know they are taking a piece of me with them wherever they go," he wrote. "I know that they know this because the feelings in their eyes and hearts are special."

After I left, Ken and Pam took over as co-editors, but the arrangement proved challenging. Bob Shimabukuro followed them as solo editor.

I thought briefly about starting a nonprofit Asian American news service similar to Pacific News Service (PNS). When I was at the *UW Daily,* the editors printed PNS's thoughtful alternative viewpoints on the Vietnam War. Shortly after I left the *Examiner,* I stopped by my parents' house for dinner. My father asked about my next career move. He listened attentively to my idea, then offered, "It sounds interesting, but how are you going to support yourself?"

After returning to my apartment, I mulled over what he had said. He was right.

By November, I found a half-time job as multicultural program coordinator at Seattle Central Community College (SCCC). This was a safe step. My boss would be Leslie Cossitt, my old friend from the UW Women's Commission.

I reconnected with her when she worked as a ticket seller at The Fifth Avenue Theatre in downtown Seattle. By then, the cavernous Chinese-inspired movie theater with the ornate dragon dome inside was in its death throes. It began showing classic films from the 1950s. One day, Leslie snuck me in for free. When I arrived, she sat in a small free-standing ticket box just outside the theater. She wore an ornate costume with a Mandarin collar, the hot sun on her face. The movie was *The Ten Commandments*, the 1956 epic starring Charlton Heston. Busloads of seniors made up most of the sparse audience. I was the youngest person there.

Leslie had sent me a copy of the job announcement for the SCCC position. But before I applied, Leslie cautioned, "Are you sure you want to work at the College? You seem way over-qualified." I explained that I enjoyed working with students: "And this part-time job pays way more than my full-time gig at the *Examiner*. It's also got medical and dental benefits, too. You can't beat that."

At SCCC, I helped student clubs organize activities and navigate the college system. I shared duties with Tina Young, a New York City transplant who moved to Seattle several years after marrying Wilson Chin, the son of Ark and Winnie Chin. The two met in 1980 in Taiwan. Tina had a fine arts degree in printmaking and painting. She later headed the college's new art gallery. She was one of the sharpest minds at SCCC.

I got to know Frank Fujii, Ann Fujii's father, at SCCC. He taught graphic arts. Frank's wife, Michiko, had recently passed away and he was still grieving. He coaxed me into joining him for leisurely, early lunches at the nearby Jack in the Box and donut breaks at the college's bakery across the street. He challenged me: "Break the mold, Ron. Don't be one of those stereotypical hard-working Asians who just slaves away all day. Life is short. Let's go eat." Frank knew my father well; he and his family were regulars at the Hong Kong Restaurant. Frank saw my mother at SCCC after she began attending English as a Second Language (ESL) classes. He made the mistake of saying to her, "*Nee ho mah?*" (你好嗎). She rattled on to him in Chinese, and he didn't understand a word.

Through Frank, I met Rachel Hidaka. She had developed the college's ESL program. She was head of Basic Education. She was smart and tough, adored by her staff. She was a tireless voice for immigrants and refugees. Like my colleague Tina, she rose above the useless office politics. I recognized her from afar in her red lipstick, neatly trimmed bob, stylish suit and bright scarf, clacking down the main hallway in high heels. Sally Yamasaki was a part-time instructor under Rachel.

I knew Rachel's husband Tom. He had a small shop, Jackson Furniture Company, on the corner of Maynard Avenue South and South Jackson Street. I went there for odds and ends—light bulbs, batteries, adapters, Fuller Paints and key replacements. The interior hadn't been refreshed since the 1950s, just like the Higo Variety Store. Tom was a gentle man with wire-rimmed glasses, long sideburns and a toothy grin. A loyal *Examiner* advertiser, he was always ready to sign petitions on behalf of ID causes. He sat at the back of the store watching a soap opera on his portable TV if he wasn't hunched over a spinning wheel, grinding and polishing a duplicate key for a waiting customer. He had told me that his wife was at the college. Now I had finally met her.

In 1990, I went to work at the Washington State Commission on Asian American Affairs (CAAA) under Executive Director Patricia Lee, a former attorney. She had been hired by Democratic Governor Booth Gardner in 1989. I worked full-time in a clerical support role. The job was boring, but at least I was engaged in Asian American issues again. I stayed at the Commission for one year.

Three *Examiner* volunteers followed me to CAAA to work in staff positions under Patricia: Sally Yamasaki, Ken Mochizuki and Brian Lock. The chair of the CAAA advisory committee was Cynthia Rekdal, another former *Examiner* contributor. It felt like a homecoming.

One day, Sally and I drove down to the State Office of Financial Management in Olympia for a meeting. I remarked to her about the surprising number of people we had passed in the hallway contentedly munching on donuts and sipping coffee from white Styrofoam cups. The men wore white shirts, perma-press slacks and slip-on loafers. They had big round bellies and waddled like ducks. They looked like they were holding on for retirement. I said to Sally, "Is that what's in store for me in a few years? God, I hope not!"

As CAAA neared the end of its fiscal year, we rushed to spend the remainder of our budgeted funds. Concerned we might lose a few hard-fought-for dollars, Patricia instructed Sally and me to buy stamps. We walked to the post office in the ID and came back toting several huge envelopes full of stamps, which we stashed in our white metal credenza. We probably had enough stamps to last into the next century.

I mentored two idealistic UW interns, Debbie Louie and Selena Dong. They both had family roots in Chinatown. Selena's grandfather owned property in the extinct Chinatown near Second Avenue and South Washington Street. Debbie, a street-tough kid with an acerbic tongue, grew up in Canton

Alley across from Donnie Chin. Her mother was a seamstress and single mom of four who worked at Seattle Quilt Manufacturing Company and Roffe with my mother.

The CAAA office was on the ground floor of the Prefontaine Building, a triangular beaux arts structure at the intersection of Third Avenue and Yesler Way. Street people ambled in and out of the building, so we kept the front office door locked. I was comforted knowing that lunch in Chinatown was just a five-minute walk away. Selena loved to eat. I took her to Green Village Restaurant for spicy Chinese fried noodles. She gorged like a famished beggar, pausing only to wipe pearls of sweat from her brow.

Across the street from CAAA was Tashiro Hardware Company. Frank Tashiro, a Japanese American veteran blacksmith, was the owner. He made cutlery, saws, chisels and other tools. I used to deliver the *Examiner* to Frank's shop and linger to discuss the latest community news.

The positions at SCCC and CAAA provided a measure of job security, but I felt profoundly unchallenged. Restless, I restarted the private journal I had kept while I was at the UW.

On the side, I received a grant to develop the first traveling exhibition on the history of Asian Americans in Washington state. A staff member at the Washington State Centennial Commission approached me. Frantic, she said that State Representative Gary Locke had secured money for a project, but there wasn't anyone qualified to do it. The Centennial Celebration was just a year away.

I agreed to tackle it. I enlisted the help of Dean Wong, David Takami, Sally Yamasaki, Michelle Kumata and Ruby Macadangdang. When it was completed in 1989, the display, titled *Shared Dreams: A History of Asians and Pacific Islanders in Washington State,* became a big hit. For four years, Exhibit

Touring Services, based at The Evergreen State College, circulated the exhibit to area colleges and libraries.

During the development of *Shared Dreams*, I realized what I had been missing most since I left the *Examiner*. It was the opportunity to work collaboratively with a creative team. I also missed the thrill of chasing a deadline. My spirit withered inside the straitjacket of the community college and the state system. I belonged back at a community nonprofit. There I could breathe. There I could use my leadership and organizing instincts to make things happen. I had to find a way to return.

CHAPTER 46

Marriage and Parenthood

I N 1990, AFTER I LEFT the Commission on Asian American Affairs, I was asked by Patricia Lee to train my successor. Her name was Loan Nguyễn. She lived in South Tacoma. She was a stranger to Seattle. She and her large family—which included one grandparent, father and mother, four brothers, two sisters and other relatives—were part of the first large wave of refugees who poured into the United States after the military takeover of Saigon by North Vietnamese troops on April 30, 1975. That event ended the Vietnam War.

After I finished orienting Loan to the job—and flippantly telling her not to "stuff the file cabinets with useless paperwork"—we continued to meet socially over lunch and dinner. It was nice to spend time with someone outside my usual circle.

We had fulfilling conversations about life, cultural identity, language and political activism. The Seattle community—with its more expansive and outspoken Asian American network— appealed to Loan. She felt isolated growing up in the white neighborhoods of Tacoma. Through Loan, I met other refugees of her parents' generation, including those who worshipped at Chùa Việt Nam, a Vietnamese temple on South King Street. I attended Saturday services with her family and stayed for the vegan meal. The monk, realizing that I raised money for the Wing Luke Museum, implored me to help him get an audience with Paul Allen or Bill Gates. He was trying to complete a remodel of the temple.

Loan also introduced me to business owners in the budding Little Saigon area, centered at 12th Avenue and South Jackson. Asian Plaza was built in 1984 and Jackson Square in 1986. Signage at these mini-malls appeared in Vietnamese, Chinese and English. There were *phở* houses, jewelry stores, hair salons, travel agencies and stores selling herbs, videos and magazines. I stepped inside more jewelry shops than I had ever visited in my entire life.

Loan described to me how her family, fleeing conflict, first arrived in Camp Pendleton, California, a U.S. Army base shelter. Then-Governor Dan Evans authorized the immediate transfer of 500 refugees to Camp Murray, the National Guard facility near Fort Lewis. Loan's family stayed there for three months. They were sponsored out by Tacoma Baptist Church and Skyline Presbyterian Church. By the summer of 1977, Loan's family bought their first home in north Tacoma.

Loan's parents—Mr. Nguyễn Văn Chung and Mrs. Nguyễn Thị Phượng—both worked in the laundry department at Western State Hospital. Her father later opened C & H Auto, a used car dealership and auto repair shop in Tacoma. Her parents spoke broken English, but we were able to communicate. They had the same problem as my mother had in trying to be understood by those unaccustomed to the heavy accent of a non-native English speaker.

As I listened to Loan speak to her parents in Vietnamese,

I heard similarities between Vietnamese and Chinese. Many words were the same, but they were spoken with slightly different tones. I could decipher the meaning of printed words in Vietnamese newspapers and signs because the Vietnamese language—unlike Chinese—relied on Latin-based script. I could sound out words and guess their Chinese equivalents.

Loan's mother was a terrific cook. She prepared home-cooked Vietnamese dishes like *phở, bún riêu, bánh cuốn, bún bò Huế, bánh xèo* and *bánh chưng*. I enjoyed the mix of cooked ingredients with raw, fresh greens and garnishes. I began to make my own stir-fried dishes with a dash of fish sauce (*nước mắm*), sometimes using it in place of Chinese oyster sauce (蠔油). When Loan and I visited shops in Little Saigon, I snacked on *bánh mì* sandwiches, *bánh tiêu* (fried bread sprinkled with sesame seeds), and *chả lụa* (pork loaf wrapped in banana leaves).

After dating for several years, Loan and I decided to get married. I asked Ron Mamiya, a fellow Franklin High graduate and a Seattle Municipal Court judge, to officiate. He had been a leader in the JACL's National Council on Redress. In 1978, his law office on Jackson Street hosted planning meetings for the first Day of Remembrance, a caravan from Seattle to Puyallup calling for reparations for Japanese Americans incarcerated during World War II. Ron's family donated a stone *usu*, used to make *mochi*, to the Wing Luke Museum's *Executive Order 9066* exhibit, the first project I spearheaded as director.

"How much do you charge?" I asked. He shook his head. "Please don't mention payment. I'd be thrilled to do it." I thanked him, then added, "Now that I've gotten that out of the way, I'm in the middle of a membership drive at the Museum…." He stopped me, laughing. "No need to explain, Ron. Happy to do that, too."

On August 30, 1993, Ron performed a brief marriage ceremony at the Wing Luke Museum. The witnesses were Bob Shimabukuro, his wife Alice Ito, and Maxine Chan. Ron finished by signing the marriage certificate and filling out a museum membership form.

Loan and I had a traditional wedding banquet at the Four Seas Restaurant with over 400 guests. Most were relatives and friends of our parents. The ceremony was conducted in three languages. Steve Goon was my best man. In the Chinese wedding invitation, the surname Nguyễn appears as 阮, the same Chinese character as Steve's surname Goon. I joked that Steve and Loan were probably related.

We settled into very busy lives. Loan continued at the Commission on Asian American Affairs under a new director, former cannery union activist David Della, who previously served as aide to Mayor Norm Rice during his first term. The Commission moved from the Prefontaine Building to an office on South Jackson Street. I became absorbed with raising money and developing community-based exhibitions at the Museum.

Loan moved from her parent's Tacoma home into my modest place at the Evergreen Apartments. Our first son Cian (明心) was born on May 21, 1995. He lived his first year in Chinatown. Our small apartment—near the filthy dumpster-lined alley, constant noise and ambient cigarette smoke —wasn't the best environment to raise a child. Loan and I relocated to an apartment on Beacon Hill.

With the arrival of our second child Kino (啟心) on December 8, 1997, we bought an old house which had served as the parsonage for the Blaine Memorial United Methodist Church. It was the home that Washington State Legislator Sharon Tomiko Santos grew up in. Sharon's father had been pastor of the church. We hired contractors to remodel the house while we lived in the Beacon Hill apartment.

I had never imagined that I would become a parent. Neither had Loan. But it happened. I found joy in the mundane ritual of diaper changing, bathing, bottle-feeding and rocking the little ones to sleep with made-up stories and Chinese folk rhymes. In my early 40s, I was a more patient caregiver than I would have been if I were younger. I adapted to the interrupted sleep cycles. But for several years, I was saddled with tendinitis in my elbow. I wisely decided to stop acceding to the irresistible plea, "Papa, pick me up!"

Strangers are especially kindhearted to a man with an infant. When I took Cian to the toy department in the basement of The Bon Marché to explore the Thomas the Tank Engine table display, he soiled his diaper. It was a big, smelly mess. I forgot to bring the diaper bag. But within minutes, I was rescued by five women who converged with disposable diapers and wet wipes.

It was exhausting to work full-time, participate in community activities and tend to two young kids. Our parents— her father and mother in Tacoma, and my father and mother on Beacon Hill—helped out. Although Loan's parents were 40 minutes away by car, they became the default babysitters. They were much younger than my parents. Mr. and Mrs. Nguyễn both adored children. They raised Cian like their own child. They chased him around the house, spoon-feeding him porridge Mrs. Nguyễn lovingly prepared every morning. Loan and I called it "the mush." It was made of chicken broth, rice and yellow squash. Sometimes Mrs. Nguyễn added prawns, pork and other veggies. In a pinch, I dined on Cian's leftovers. It was hearty and delicious.

As Cian got older, we enrolled him in nearby childcare programs, including Megumi Preschool and the José Martí Child Development Center at El Centro de la Raza. The Megumi caregivers spoke Japanese; the staff at El Centro spoke Spanish. Cian clung to one caregiver named Marta at El Centro. He called her "Hola Marta," not realizing that *"hola"* meant "hello" in Spanish, the greeting the kids were instructed to give at the beginning of class.

After Kino was born, Loan left the Commission, staying home to care for him during his first few years of life.

CHAPTER 47

Documenting Community Stories

S HORTLY BEFORE I LEFT THE Commission on Asian American Affairs, I launched the Chinese Oral History Project. I had dreamed of doing something like this for years. When I was a young teen, my ears perked up when the waiters and kitchen employees at the Hong Kong Restaurant began talking about their earlier lives. I rarely asked questions, but I listened attentively. I wished that I could sit with them and record their words.

In college, I resolved to one day initiate an oral history project. At the *UW Daily*, I had dutifully written dozens of news stories following the traditional inverted pyramid style. As much as I liked this, I also found it constraining. I chased deadlines. I couldn't follow my natural curiosity to probe deeper into the experiences of individuals. I began asking for assignments to write feature profiles.

In 1975, I wrote a piece about Bill Wong, a young waiter who dreamed of moving to Vancouver to start a hairstyling salon. I worked with him at the restaurant. Others simply called him "Wong" to distinguish him from an older waiter with the same English first name. He was a good-looking man with a receding hairline, a square jaw and a strong disposition. Wong styled the hair of several bar waitresses. He practiced English by reading the *Wall Street Journal*. He taught himself French by playing a set of language learning albums on a used record player in his Chinatown apartment.

As the years rolled by, Wong remained trapped at the restaurant. His hairline continued to recede, making it difficult to keep a greased-down comb-over in place. One day, after getting in a fight with a kitchen employee, he came into the restaurant to say goodbye. He wore shiny new, pointy dress shoes and a stylish sports coat. He dramatically dumped his black work shoes into the garbage can behind the front counter. He said he was heading to Vancouver. I never saw or heard from him again.

I enjoyed interviewing Bill Wong and documenting his story. Friends at the *UW Daily* complimented me on the article. I heard that Bill Wong loved the piece. I felt privileged that he would welcome an American-born Chinese like me into his private world.

In July 1987, I visited the Sun May Company to see Donnie Chin. His mom was at the front counter, busy with a customer. Donnie told me that his dad, one of the Chinatown old-timers who helped found the Chinatown Chamber of Commerce, had suffered another stroke and died at a Ballard nursing home.

I offered my condolences to Donnie and his mom. He and I continued to talk. We discussed the outrageous price of funeral arrangements, the tide of old shops starting to close and rising crime in Chinatown. We could foresee a time before long when our parents' generation would be gone. The thought of the stories dying with them didn't feel good.

It seemed like the ideal time to begin recording the China-town community's stories. But before I had a chance to start, I was pulled into the Alaskero Oral History Project. This was the brainchild of photographer John Stamets, a former *Seattle Sun* staffer who had reported on the murders of Silme Domingo and Gene Viernes. Fascinated by the aging Filipino immigrant men who created the cannery union in their younger days, John successfully applied for a grant from the Washington Commission for the Humanities to tape-record interviews and photograph the surviving Alaskeros.

It had been several years since the murders. The last of the old-timers who inspired Gene and Silme's reform efforts were passing away. The crumbling Pioneer Square union hall had been abandoned. Local 37 had merged with the Inlandboat-men's Union, moving to a new location.

With the help of the union, interviews were conducted with 25 pioneers. John shot a series of memorable black-and-white portrait images. An exhibition opened at the Wing Luke Museum and traveled to local colleges and libraries. I came aboard—in the midst of a big squabble between John and several volunteers—to help produce a tabloid publication to accompany the exhibition. UW instructor Peter Bacho, whose father Vincent was profiled, wrote the history. Jesse Reyes designed the publication. Jesse's father, Antonio Paragas "Tony" Reyes, a cannery foreman, had passed away in 1982 before Jesse had a chance to interview him.

I had a blast working with Peter and Jesse. I had known both for a long time. Jesse grew up in South Seattle's White Center neighborhood. He participated in the Summer Youth Employment Program at IDEC under Donnie Chin. He was a comic book collector like me, and did graphics for the *Examiner*. Peter had written several pieces for the paper, including an eloquent tribute to Chris Mensalvas, Sr., president of Local 37 during its radical heyday in the 1950s. Mensalvas died on April 11, 1978, from a fire in his room in the Downtowner Apartments.

Peter taught Asian American studies at the University of Washington. He was funny and wildly irreverent. I visited him at his tiny office in Padelford Hall. He pecked away on a manual typewriter, endlessly polishing his short stories. "I try to work on the rhythm of the words," he told me. "It doesn't matter what you're trying to say if the words don't sing and move in harmony." Peter called me in the middle of the night to rail against the stodgy leadership in the Asian American studies department, then pivoted to a wry discussion of the latest rivalries in the World Wrestling Federation (WWF). We agreed that the villain-good guy storylines in the WWF might benefit from his creative debauchery.

Peter invited Jesse and me to the Manila Café in Chinatown to share greasy Filipino food and hear him read the latest passages from what would become his 1991 novel *Cebu*. After lunch, we passed by the very folks he was writing about—the *manongs*—resting on benches in Hing Hay Park just around the corner from the café. They were smartly dressed in sport coats, creased slacks and fedoras, just as Peter described.

On January 24, 1987, I met Peter, Jesse and Steve Chin, Susie Chin's younger brother and a talented illustrator, at a small bar in Pioneer Square. We celebrated the news that Peter had received a contract for publication of *Cebu*. Peter showed us the plot outline and the first chapter. He told us he'd be getting a $6,000 advance, which he would use to pay off overdue Christmas bills. Half-jokingly, he told us that the lure of money kept him going; he still had two more chapters to complete. He asked Jesse to design the book cover. Jesse was elated.

Peter's mother Remy, a slight, silver-haired woman, was a regular at the International Drop-In Center. I saw her there mingling with other Filipino seniors. She called out: "Ron, I have to show you something!" She pulled from her purse the latest news clipping on Peter's literary accolades. She was a very proud mother.

The Alaskero Project introduced me to Velma Veloria, a former KDP activist. She moved to Seattle from New York shortly after the murders of Silme and Gene. We met at the Ayutthaya Thai Restaurant, a quaint place near First Hill Physical Therapy, where she worked. Over lunch, she and I reviewed all the interview transcripts to cull the best quotes to pair with John Stamets's photos for the tabloid. Our opinions easily jibed, and we became good friends.

After finishing the Alaskero Project and the *Shared Dreams* exhibit in 1989, I finally kicked off my own oral history project. On May 7, 1990, I sent a letter to 15 Chinese American leaders and friends, inviting them to a planning meeting at the Bush-Asia Center. I pointed out that "no one had ever done any substantive oral history projects or photo exhibitions on the Seattle Chinese community," in stark contrast to Japanese Americans and Filipino Americans.

Separately, I met with Kit Freudenberg to see whether the Wing Luke Museum would feature the oral histories in an exhibition and with Pat Soden, longtime director of the University of Washington Press, to see if he would publish a book. Both said yes.

My first challenge was deciding who to feature, what to ask and how to convince people to cooperate. I devised a survey to gather prospective subjects and bolster the legitimacy of our requests for interviews. Gloria Lung Wakayama's mother, Bertha Tsuchiya, quietly explained to me the secret "paper" identities of many local families. Some individuals didn't want to speak openly about their past. We provided reassurance that we wouldn't publish anything without their consent.

Rita Wang, Chinese Information and Service Center (CISC) director, offered to translate. James Wong, an elder in the Wong Family Association and a CISC employee, was an early subject. Former colleagues at the *Examiner*—Kathryn Chinn, Karen Chinn, Greg Tuai, Serena Louie, Dean Wong, Marci Wing, JoAnne Lee and John Pai—served as interviewers. Dean and John took photographs.

Fred Yee, director of Kin On Nursing Home (健安療養院), the first bilingual Chinese nursing home in Seattle, came to the planning meeting, along with his wife Amy Wong. They helped create Chinese Information Center in 1972, which later became CISC. Kin On had just taken in its first residents. "The timing is perfect," Fred said excitedly. "We should interview some of them."

Fred had a high-spirited laugh and an unbounded zeal for helping those in need. He loathed pretense, rivaling me for dowdy, mismatched attire. Amy was just as down-to-earth. She came from Hong Kong in 1971. Her uncle was Sam Yee, owner of the Hong Kong Restaurant. When I was there, she served as greeter and cashier. Her father was a cook. It warmed my heart when she told me, "Your dad was the only waiter who took time to talk to me. He brought me a glass of 7Up and welcomed me."

We scheduled an interview with Fred's father, George K. Yee. Fred barely knew him. Like Amy, Fred grew up in Hong Kong, immigrating to Seattle in August 1969 at the age of 18 after his mother passed away. His father, who was 61, first took him to Denny's on Fourth Avenue South and to Pay 'n Save on Rainier Avenue South to show Fred "how American people eat and shop." Fred spent his first three weeks at a small, dismal room in the Frye Apartments, waiting for a dorm room at Seattle University. His father stayed with him, but much of that time was spent in awkward silence. Through the oral history project, Fred learned more about his father's work as a partner in the Wah Young Company.

At the suggestion of Ben Woo, I interviewed his 80-year-old mother-in-law Dorothy Chun in 1991. Dorothy was the mother of Ben's first wife. She collected payments at the senior meal program in the basement of the Bush Hotel. She broke into a radiant smile, grabbed me by both my hands and pulled me to a side table to share bits of her past. She ran the Shangri-la Café in downtown Seattle in the 1940s. Dorothy's late husband was a descendent of Chun Ching Hock (陳程學), the first Chinese settler in Seattle. Dorothy's father, a Chinese merchant, had financed the Sunning Railroad (新寧鐵路), which was built in Hoisan in the early 1900s by Chin Gee-Hee.

Ruth Jung Chinn, a powerhouse elder, brought credibility to the project by endorsing my effort from the start. She cheerfully agreed to an interview. She was born in 1914 in Los Angeles in a house her father bought from Supreme Court Justice Earl Warren. She moved to Seattle in 1935, joining Ruby Chow and five other women in a daringly successful effort in 1948 to infiltrate the all-male board of the Chong Wa Benevolent Association. My mother took an English class from Ruth there.

In 1960, Ruth and her husband Robert started United Savings & Loan as the first Asian American-owned savings and loan institution in the U.S. According to my mother, Ruth's husband, an insurance salesman, had tried unsuccessfully to pry my father away from the Hong Kong Restaurant to help with this effort. Ruth also established the Jade Guild, a Chinese

American women's service organization, in 1966. The group still meets today.

I conducted many early interviews to set the pace. Fierce curiosity drove me. I felt like a starving kid at the Kokusai Theater, madly grabbing for popcorn spilling from a broken machine. The more interviews I completed, the more I wanted to do. When the oral history project ended 12 years later, we had amassed the stories of 102 community elders. I had interviewed 65 individuals myself. It was a rich, intoxicating course on the history of Chinese Americans in Seattle.

My eyes became red and sore from many unbroken hours of transcribing interviews in front of the computer screen. I went back and forth over sections of interviews because of the poor sound quality of early tapes. Some subjects mumbled and spoke in broken sentences. I conducted follow-up interviews to check details. I knew I might not have a second chance.

We interviewed members of the Cathay Post, the Chinese American veterans group formed after World War II. Among them were Jimmy Mar (a charter member and the first Chinese American drafted from Seattle in 1941), James Locke (Gary Locke's dad), Dan Mar, Chong Wing Mar, Cal Fung and Bill Chin. I learned about the Post's scholarship program to support needy students, blood drives, a moon festival, holiday parties for Chinatown kids and the annual Memorial Day commemoration in Hing Hay Park.

Donnie pulled out a striking black-and-white photo from a huge stash of documents in his Canton Alley apartment. It was a close-up of a Chinese American man in uniform firing a machine gun. "If you really want to find out more about the Cathay Post, go find him," Donnie said. "This guy's name is David Woo. They call him 'Gobby.' He knows everything. I'm not sure if he's still alive though."

I asked my father if he knew David. "Of course," he said. "We're shirt-tail relatives." That was news to me. David's father was Woo Gen, one of the pioneers who testified for my grandfather Quay Fong Chew when he petitioned for entry to the U.S. in 1911. My father explained that my grandfather's older sister had married Gobby's father.

My father told me that Gobby lived alone on South Forest Street, not far from us. He gave me a phone number, and I set up an appointment. David turned out to be gregarious and warm, with a sharp wit and clear memory. He explained to me that he started the Cathay Post in 1945 to help returning World War II vets petition for their wives in China to join them in the U.S. He figured that the vets, after serving this country in war, deserved the opportunity to start families here.

Gobby was a gunner pilot during a U.S. bombing mission over Germany. He was shot down and survived 27 months of confinement in German prison camps. He was in the infamous Stalag 17, an Austrian camp immortalized in a classic film starring William Holden. He knew Donald Bevan, a fellow prisoner who wrote the script. They kept in touch through letters.

I spent many afternoons perched on a sofa at Gobby's house, lost in his stories. I taped interviews with him in 1990 and 1991. His body was weak after many years of kidney dialysis. I timed my visits for the days when he came back from his treatments at the Veterans Hospital.

During one visit, he pulled open a dresser drawer, extracting some old Chinese lottery tickets and two ancient Chinese wooden combs from his mother. "Give these to the Wing Luke Museum," he said. "They have historical significance."

He asked me to help him find a shop to repair his old, black Underwood manual typewriter. It was a keepsake from Stalag 17. He used it to type up "underground news" to keep up the morale of fellow prisoners. I searched for a place that would fix it. Few people used typewriters anymore. I finally located a shop on Capitol Hill. I left it there for several months. Meanwhile, David had passed away. When I went to retrieve David's typewriter, the business had closed. I never got it back.

David told me about his older sister May, the first Chinese woman to graduate from the University of Washington. Born in 1896, she earned a bachelor's degree in education in 1921. Unable to find a job, she settled in Canton, China, and taught there for 30 years. "Here's her address in China," David said. "Why don't you write to her? Her memory is even better than mine." I was stunned. "She's still alive?" I asked. David nodded.

I carried on a four-year correspondence with May. She asked me to address her as "Grandaunt May." David wrote to her every month. She threw away most of his letters, but kept two from 1975 which detailed his capture by Germans, his survival in prison camps and a 300-mile forced march out of Vienna, Austria, culminating in his rescue by American soldiers. She told me that Chin Gee-Hee's granddaughter, Margaret Chin, was the first Chinese woman to attend the UW, but that she never graduated.

Through May's letters, brief though they usually were, I learned about the early 1900s. In addition to May and Gobby, I interviewed two other colorful Woo siblings in their final years: Henry, who had moved to Los Angeles, and Helen Woo Locke, who was living in San Francisco.

May wanted to make it to age 100. But she died on January 11, 1995, at 99. At the end of the project, I donated May's letters to me—along with the tapes, transcripts and photographs for all the interviews—to the Museum's collection.

CHAPTER 48

My Family's Hidden Past

During the Chinese Oral History Project, I sat down to talk with my mother and father. My mind overflowed with questions. Approaching 40, I still didn't know much about either of them, and I knew even less about my grandparents and other relatives.

I bought a mini-cassette tape recorder from Radio Shack. I taped my mother in my parents' living room after dinner. My mother told me about a world I could barely imagine. She grew up without plumbing, refrigeration, electricity or telephones. She relied on chamber pots, kerosene lamps and candles. There were no paved roads or cars. She walked to get places. She spoke in loving terms about her rags-to-riches father and less kindly about an ill-tempered mother who died of an unexplained ailment after the Japanese invaded Ai Gong Village.

My mother told me that her family prospered after my grandfather returned to China from Canada. With money saved, he became a clothier. But his business was ransacked and destroyed by Japanese invaders. After the Communist Revolution in 1949, the new government seized his two large houses. During the tumult, he fled to Hong Kong and lived on the streets. He was discovered by a friend who helped him find a place to live, a house near the woods. That house burned down, and he narrowly escaped death. He finally found refuge on a sampan after being taken in by an elderly woman.

The Cultural Revolution of the 1960s brought more turmoil. Mao's Red Guards tortured and humiliated one of my mother's brothers, forcing him to kneel on broken glass in the streets. She lost touch with both brothers. After she became a garment worker, my mother sent money to support her father and the children of her two missing brothers.

I pleaded for early family photos. She didn't have any of her mother or her brothers, but she kept a tiny snapshot of her father. She said he resembled Chiang Kai-shek, his face lean, his head bald. But when she went to look for the photo, she couldn't find it. We were both very disappointed. Years later, after my mother passed away, I found an envelope among her possessions, scribbled with the Chinese characters 我父—*my father*. Inside was the lost picture.

My father's interviews were very different from those of my mother. His responses were terse, to-the-point. This was his nature. I interviewed him at the Wing Luke Museum and at home. Instead of using a tape recorder, I scribbled notes on a pad while he talked.

My father spoke about his father and his brothers. He didn't mention his mother or his two sisters, who never left China. I assumed that they became strangers after he resettled in America. My mother berated him for not sending more letters to his mother. I learned very little about his early years in China. He focused on his career as a laundryman, then as a waiter.

Finally, he explained to me the covert tangle of family

immigration, pulling from a hiding place in the basement his faded family coaching papers, written in Chinese, nestled in an envelope. The envelope was wedged between several stacks of dusty, cobweb-covered *Life* and *Look* magazines from the late 1960s and early 1970s.

He showed me his identification certificate. He called it "*ji mei*" (紙尾) or the "paper stub." His *ji mei* was his proof of citizenship. He carried it with him everywhere. It shielded him if he were ever stopped and questioned by an authority.

From another folder in the basement, my father pulled the original copy of my grandfather's *ji mei*, issued on May 16, 1911, by the Department of Commerce and Labor's Immigration Service. In the photograph, my grandfather is wearing a Chinese-style collar, his face placidly facing forward, a tiny smile creasing his lips. My grandfather's document was in a small gray envelope. His name—Quay Fong—and the Number 14308 were written on the cover. My father handed the document to me and said, "You keep it."

I asked my father about his younger brother, Lee Hong Chew. He was a mystery. I was born in 1953, eight years after his early death in World War II. Stacked on two basement shelves in our Beacon Hill home were his school papers, books, letters, yearbooks, slide rule, math compass and camera gear. There was a Purple Heart and a folded American flag with 48 stars and 13 stripes. I didn't understand why my father kept these things, especially since he hardly said a word about Uncle Lee. These items gathered a thick layer of dust.

It was because of the oral history project that I summoned the nerve to ask my father about his younger brother. He didn't say much and his face filled with a sadness I had never seen before. My father relayed a few facts and directed me back to my Uncle Lee's papers in the basement. That was it. I never asked him more than a handful of questions about his brother after that.

I found out more from Cathay Post veterans who were my Uncle Lee's high school buddies. I spoke to Thomas Lew, Cal Fung, Ray Lew, Raymond Chinn, Bill Sing and Bill Chin. They described his low-key manner and intelligence, his love of photography, his outings to the downtown YMCA to play pool and his swimming trips at Lake Washington.

Kim Chinn, another old classmate, told me that Uncle Lee's nickname was Alpha. He had an unruly cowlick just like Alfalfa, the round-eyed character from the old *Little Rascals* television program. At last, I found out where I had gotten my middle name. I had wondered: How did I become the first letter of the Greek alphabet?

Uncle Lee was part of the famed 87th Infantry Battalion, dispatched to Italy to spearhead the Allied offensive to capture key mountain peaks in Italy and to end German aggression during World War II. He was gunned down at the head of his battalion on February 20, 1945. He was only 23. Bill Chin told me that Uncle Lee single-handedly attacked a German machine gun nest. He was nominated for a Silver Star.

His body was transported back to Seattle in 1949 and buried at Evergreen Washelli Memorial Park. American Legion honor guards remembered him with a military burial and a 13-gun salute.

In 1989, Raymond Chinn told me that Uncle Lee had attended Broadway High School a few years ahead of him. "I remember him well," Ray said. "He was a pretty good athlete and swimmer. He helped me in gym class." They were both members of the school's Chinese club. Uncle Lee was also in the school patrol.

In that same year, I showed Cal my late uncle's 1941 yearbook from Broadway High School. I pointed to a long message Cal had written to him. Cal smiled, trying to remember. "Just a great guy—like a saint," Cal said. "He was a lot like you. He was kind of soft-spoken, not real forward. He wasn't shy, but he didn't talk that much unless you asked him questions."

I showed Cal—and his wife Jeni, seated by his side—several old black-and-white photos of Uncle Lee. In one picture, Uncle Lee was stepping down from the side of a boat. Another young Chinese American man stood behind him. "That's Tommy Lew," Cal and Jeni said together. Cal said Tommy was a retired Boeing engineer. Cal gave me his phone number.

I saw Tommy—or Thomas—at a Cathay Post banquet in Chinatown on August 20, 2017. He was 94, a lanky, spry man with bushy eyebrows and a cheerful manner. He was honored by the Cathay Post for "being a member in good standing for 70 years." I sat at the same table with him, Cal, Jeni and Bill Chin. All were in their 90s, still going strong.

Thomas told more stories. "There used to be a boathouse at Seward Park. Lee and I would rent a canoe and go canoeing across the water to Mercer Island. Back then, there were no houses on the beach in Mercer Island." They practiced archery in the streets and went target-shooting in the Renton Highlands with a .22-caliber rifle purchased from Sears.

My mother told me that Uncle Lee's death had deeply saddened my father because the two were so close. His death devastated my grandmother in China. For years, family members didn't tell her that he had been killed. When I told Ray, he said that this made sense. "Why add to her suffering?" Ray said. "Let her go on believing her son is alive, and the two will eventually meet in the same place after death."

In a letter to my father, Uncle Lee stated that he would soon be going into combat and instructed my father to "take care of the insurance" as soon as possible. The letter was signed "Your loving brother, Lee." Another letter from the Veteran's Administration certified that Lee Hong Chew had applied for $10,000 of insurance, payable on death. I also found a letter to a woman in Seattle, someone named "Lulu," whom I presumed to be his girlfriend. These discoveries broke my heart.

Under the leadership of Gobby Woo, the Cathay Post erected a memorial in 1950 to honor Uncle Lee and nine other Chinese Americans from Seattle who lost their lives in World War II. The upright red granite slab, originally sited in a playground across from the Chong Wa Benevolent Association, was moved to Hing Hay Park in the early 1990s for greater public visibility. The memorial stands between two clumps of bamboo.

As my two sons entered their early teens, I began to tell them more about Uncle Lee when we visited his gravesite at the military section of Evergreen Washelli cemetery during Ching Ming and when we paid respects to him in Hing Hay Park on Memorial Day. "Did you know that all of you wouldn't be here today except for your Granduncle Lee?" I said.

I explained that the Chinese American soldiers in World War II paved the way for the U.S. Congress to repeal the Chinese Exclusion Act. The sacrifice of their Granduncle Lee not only contributed to the war effort, but also allowed my mother and my aunts to immigrate. As the Chew clan began to reunify in the U.S. after World War II, my two brothers, my sister and I were born in Seattle, as were a number of my cousins.

During one of my last interview sessions with my father— it was on a Sunday in the fall of 1990—my father revealed to me a family secret that illuminated the complexity of my parents' relationship.

I had asked my father to lunch at Ocean City Restaurant. Neither of us was especially hungry. We ordered single plates of *ha gow* and *siu mai*, nibbling as we talked inside the noisy front area. My father worked at the restaurant as a *maître d'* briefly after he retired from the Hong Kong Restaurant.

I looked over notes from an earlier interview with him. I still had questions. "If you went back to China to marry mom in 1937 and she didn't come to this country until 1950, doesn't that mean you were separated for over 10 years?" I said.

My father nodded. "Remember, the laws were very different back then," he said solemnly. "It was not easy to get your wife over. I tried."

"That's a long time to wait to start a family," I said. "All of us—me, Linda, Tom and Harvey—weren't born until the 1950s."

My father hesitated. He told me to put down my pen. "You had a brother who died in China," he said.

"What?" I blurted out. I was bewildered. My jaw froze. I couldn't speak.

After another pause, my father explained that in 1938, the year after he married my mother, she gave birth to a baby boy in the village. He was named Sen Jeung (善彰). My father spent time with his healthy first child in Fow Seck before returning to America. About a year later, my mother wrote to tell him that Sen Jeung had died. No one knew the exact cause of death. The village lacked quality medical care. "Your brother would be pretty old now if he was alive," my father added.

After I left this interview with my father, I thought about asking my mother what happened to Sen Jeung. But I caught myself. The timing was bad. Earlier that year—on April 6, 1990, at 2:45 in the morning—my sister Linda had given birth to her son Orion at University Hospital. He was my parents' first grandchild. He brought jubilance to the family. I didn't want to spoil the long overdue reunion between my sister and

407

my parents. She had been estranged from the family for over a decade. I held my tongue.

My mother never mentioned a child in China. To lose Sen Jeung—while my father was away—must have been crushing. *Had she told my father to keep quiet?* My mother, like other Chinese of her generation, held strong superstitions about death. If I spoke about death or illness, she roundly scolded me, as if by bringing up the topic, I might launch a curse on someone.

My mother rarely spoke about my cousin Won May—the second daughter of my father's brother Hung Hong. She died in Seattle in 1983 at age 34. In several family photos, her image was clipped out because my mother felt it would be bad luck for us to see her in the photograph.

In 1991, a year after I launched the Chinese Oral History Project, I pried open another door to my family's past. The immigration records of Chinese who came to the U.S. under the Chinese Exclusion Act had been made public. More than 60,000 files—the paperwork for Chinese who immigrated through Port Townsend and Seattle between 1882 and 1943—were transferred from the Immigration and Naturalization Service building on Airport Way to the National Archives for the Pacific Northwest region at Sand Point Way N.E.

I called Sue Karren, assistant director for the regional National Archives, to see if she could locate the file for my grandfather Quay Fong. Sue had negotiated transfer of the records. "Let me see what I can do," she told me. "We're still in the process of indexing most of the files. We'll need to look through the arrival volumes to find a case number. Then we can get to his file. All these files are cross-referenced."

About a week later, Sue phoned to tell me that she found my grandfather's file, along with the linked files of my father, my uncles and my mother. Thrilled, I set an appointment. The

National Archives was in a squat one-story, gray utilitarian warehouse behind an imposing stretch of barbed wire fencing, along a fir-tree-lined street about five minutes northeast of the University of Washington.

Sue greeted me with a handshake, warm smile and quick observation, "Wow, you really look like your grandfather!" I was baffled. "How do you know that?" She handed me my grandfather's folder. "His picture is right in here." I flipped open the folder and saw a clear back-and-white photograph of a young Chinese man with a Chinese collar, high forehead, prominent nose, thin brows and placid expression. I stared at the picture, entranced.

My grandfather's file included the transcript from his April 25, 1911 interrogation when he first arrived, as well as paperwork relating to all his trips to China. The file had a reference sheet with numbers for other "cases" connected to my grandfather, including my uncles Hung Hong, Kin Hong, Lee Hong, my father, my mother and two "paper" uncles.

I asked Sue for copies of all the case files. I showed them to my father. He confirmed which uncles were blood relatives and which were not. He cautioned me not to rely on the veracity of responses in the interrogations. He reminded me of the memorized coaching papers.

Several weeks later, my father gave me a faded 3"x2½" black-and-white photo of my grandfather. He wore a pinstripe suit, white shirt and dark tie. My grandfather's demeanor hadn't changed. He just looked older. He had settled into middle age. "Keep this," my father told me. "I'll see if I can find any other photos." He never did.

My mother scolded me for investigating this paper trail. She didn't want the government to come after any of us should word leak out that *Ah Yeh* had come to America illegally. She said that my grandfather, like most Chinese immigrants, had bought false papers—*mai ga gee* (買假紙)—to establish native residency, allowing my father and others to come over as "paper sons." She also mentioned a black market (黑市) payment that helped my father surmount a discrepancy in testimony. She refused to explain further.

We were in the living room. She scooted closer. Her hand gestures were animated. Her eyes were wide. She looked fearful. Her voice lowered to a whisper and her eyes darted about as if the *luk yee* might be lying in wait on our back step, ready to batter down the door and handcuff us.

I don't think this anxiety ever left her. I began to understand the ferocious secrecy with which she guarded aspects of our family history. Some answers went with her to the grave. For this loss, I feel a deep sadness.

CHAPTER 49

My Mother's English Lessons

AFTER SHE RETIRED FROM SEWING, my mother became fiercely determined to learn English so that she could communicate with Linda, Tom, Harvey and me. We had each lost our ability to speak to her in Chinese. An awkward wall had risen between her and us. She wanted to reclaim her authority. She wanted our respect. She also wanted to be understood when she shopped at department stores and places outside Chinatown.

In 1985, for Mother's Day, I gave her *The New Golden Dictionary*, a children's publication by Bertha Morris Parker. It contained 1,712 words illustrated with full-color pictures. Simple sentences provided examples of how words were used. She used it to learn basic words on her own.

She wanted more. Two years later, approaching the age of 70, she began English conversation classes at Seattle Central Community College. From a color snapshot, I saw that she was the oldest of the 21 students.

It wasn't easy for her to get there. She walked five long

blocks downhill to Rainier Avenue South to catch a bus that dropped her off near the entrance of Seattle Central's brick building on Broadway Avenue. She started out early because she was slow and unsteady on her feet.

My mother didn't miss a single day of school. Heavy rain, snow and frigid cold didn't deter her. Once, she trudged through over a foot of snow, arriving only to find out that school was closed. She returned home fuming. She called to tell me that her day had been ruined.

Each night, she sat at the dining table under a dangling overhead light, wading through her class workbook, practicing her lessons. I came over after work to help with pronunciation and writing. She filled several spiral notebooks with sentences written by hand in careful cursive lettering. In the margins, she scrawled two sets of Chinese characters: one to mimic the English sounds and the other to provide meaning.

She patiently slogged through her lessons with the aid of a 1968 edition English-Chinese dictionary and a big hand-held magnifying glass. She treated her well-worn dictionary with care, covering it in a book jacket fashioned from a discarded Wah Young Company calendar. Her hands—contorted by years of work at the sewing machine, arthritis and advancing age—balked at the task of moving the pencil. Her knuckles bulged as she wrote.

After homework time, she made a full Chinese meal: rice, stir-fried greens, steamed pork and other side dishes. My father, who parked himself in the basement in his cracked leather wingback chair, came up to dine at the kitchen table while my mother and I returned to the living room with our bowls to eat and watch TV. There was plenty of extra food for my older brother's two young kids, who were dropped off for childcare while my brother went off to work a late shift at the post office.

Working with my mother on these lessons gave me a chance to retrieve my Chinese language skills. As she practiced her English, I learned Chinese. When she looked up the English words, I examined the Chinese characters.

Soon, my mother was teaching me how to make the strokes that formed the foundation of written Chinese. I wrote my Chinese name and the names of my siblings. She told me what our names meant. I wrote her name and my father's name and the names of their villages. With practice, I learned many other characters. I eased into a new world of understanding. A curtain lifted.

My mother struggled with pronunciation. For one homework assignment, I asked: "How many syllables are there in the word "post office?" She counted off the syllables with her fingers while saying the word aloud: *"Pose-off-fah-see. Thlee gah sill-ah-bow."* Four syllables.

No, I told her. There are three. I sounded out the word correctly to her. She tried to emulate my sounds. She couldn't.

Pointing to the next word, I asked, "How many syllables in "sandwich?"

"Som-mon-gee," she responded. *"Thlom gah sill-ah-bow."* Three syllables.

"No, leng gah sill-ah-bow," I corrected. Two syllables. She laughed.

"How many syllables in 'house'? Easy one."

"How-see," she said. *"Leng gah sill-ah-bow."* Two syllables.

"No, no," I said. "Only one syllable." By this time, we both couldn't stop laughing. I was holding my sides. We had to take a break.

My mother struggled to distinguish between words that sounded like homonyms to her but weren't. When she spotted the word "tank"—as in "tank of gas"—she asked whether that was also the word in "thank you." She was puzzled because she pronounced "tank" and "thank" the same way. Over and over, she tried to say the word "thank" correctly, but each time it came out as "tank."

My mother complained to me about criticisms from her teacher on an assignment to write a letter to a friend. My mother wrote: "On Wednesday, I went to West Seattle and bought material for a blouse." With a red pen, the teacher changed "material" to "materials." The instructor didn't know that my mother, a veteran sewing woman, *did* mean "material," as in fabric. The word had been used correctly.

In the same letter, my mother wrote that she had "washed the kitchen." The teacher changed "washed" to "cleaned." I saw why the teacher made the change, but I also understood why my mother used "washed." My mother cleaned the kitchen by using a rag, water, soap and bucket—scrubbing and rinsing. She "washed" the kitchen. That was how she cleaned.

At the bottom, my mother signed the letter, "Gam Har Chew." Above the name, the teacher added the words "Your Friend." My mother grumbled that the addition was unnecessary. Again, she was right. *Of course her friend would know my mother was her friend.*

During the spring quarter of 1988, my mother was introduced to idioms and American slang. It wasn't something I was especially adept at, as my friend Karen Seriguchi often reminded me. When I told Karen about this lesson, she cackled loudly, "Kind of like the blind leading the blind." But I wasn't alone. Idiom deficiency was a common Chinese American handicap. My friend Keith Wong often told the story of how his Franklin woodshop instructor directed him to "put some elbow grease" into sanding a tabletop book rack; he looked around, clueless: "Where can I find that?"

My mother tried to learn phrases such as "bring home the bacon," "spill the beans," "broke," "go Dutch," "on the blink," "buddy-buddy," "hit it off," and "hang in there." At first, she interpreted the phrases literally and jumbled them. "Spill the beans" became "Bring home the beans." Her confusion was understandable. For example, if "hit it off" means you are friends with someone, why would you want to hit that person? And what is the "it" that is being hit? I couldn't explain. She turned some of her newfound vocabulary against me. She composed the following: "If I hang in there, my sons will get married."

One day, my mother called me and read two essays she had written. The teacher, she explained, had told the class to "write about one of the worst days in your life and one of the best days in your life." My mother needed help fixing the grammar. She directed me over the phone in Chinese, "Take a pen and write down these stories while I recite them."

The first essay read: "I remember about 30 years ago I took a citizenship. After that, I took the driver license. The policeman passed me. That is the best day of my life because inside the gentleman congratulation to me."

I helped her rework the sentences. It then read: "I remember about 30 years ago, I took a citizenship test. I passed the first time. I was happy because I wanted to bring my relatives from China to America. That is the best day of my life because, inside the court, the gentleman congratulated me. After that, I took a driver's license test. The policeman passed me. This day was one of my best days, too."

My mother's second essay needed very little correction or elaboration: "I remember long time ago, the worst day of my life was when my mother died."

On Sunday, June 26, 1988, when I stopped by to visit, she showed me her report card. She asked if she had failed. She received a U. In the past, she had always gotten an S. I looked at the back of the report card; U stood for unsatisfactory. She was right.

My mother said she figured that the U was not good. She said the letter "u" was at the beginning of words like "uncomfortable" or "unhappy."

My mother knew the bad mark was coming. She said the teacher was mean—he used maps with tiny print that older students like her couldn't see and didn't allow enough time to respond to questions. The teacher spent too much time on "*die-lek-shun*" (the closest she could come to pronouncing the word "direction") and the concepts of "*boh-dah on*" (border on) and "*fah light, seh-coon low*" (far right, second row). All the students had trouble understanding, she said, not just her.

On December 10, 1988, when I came over for a Sunday English lesson, my mother groused that her instructor was trying to move her from her 8 to 10 a.m. class to a 10 a.m. to noon slot. She resisted. She said it would interfere with the rest of her day. If she couldn't stay in the earlier class, she huffed, she would drop out and study on her own.

She launched into a tirade. *The instructor didn't like her because she was old. That wasn't fair.* Just the other day, she said, she bumped into a former classmate—a white-haired Vietnamese woman—in Chinatown. My mother asked her why she wasn't in class. The woman explained that she had missed two days and was asked to withdraw. In contrast, my mother said, the younger students were permitted to miss up to 10 days of instruction.

My mother complained that old people were treated like slaves in early America. Just as the *hock gwee* (黑鬼) or black ghosts couldn't go to the nice schools with the *bok gwee* (白鬼) or white ghosts, seniors couldn't attend classes with younger students. Slavery ended, she said, when *"Abe-lah-hom Lin-coon"* issued the Emancipation Proclamation. She couldn't quite pronounce "Proclamation," but I understood what she meant. *How did she know this history?* It was from her citizenship test. She remembered.

It was the first time I ever heard her compare the oppression of one group to another. I felt proud.

After disgorging her bottled-up fury, we settled down to her weekend homework assignment. My mother told me that on Monday, she would confront her instructor. I thought, "Good for her!" Of late, she had been lamenting her age. *Nah lo ghien ga mo yung* (老人家冇用) was a common refrain. (Translation: Old people are considered useless.) Her comments revealed to me that her feisty, fighting spirit remained intact.

On January 5, 1989, my mother's time at Seattle Central ended abruptly. She was hit by a black pick-up truck on 21st Avenue South and South College Street on her way to catch the bus to school.

My brother Tom called to tell me. My sister rushed to join Tom, my father and me at Harborview Medical Center. We gathered in the waiting area, full of apprehension. Finally, the doctors let us in. My heart broke when I saw her bloody face, heard her moaning in pain and saw her body lying battered on the hospital bed. Linda cried, held her hand and told her that she loved her. I rubbed my mother's shoulder and tried to reassure her. She was weak, but clear-headed. Fortunately, she had not suffered any broken bones or trauma to her vital organs.

However, a scan revealed that she had a slow-growing tumor in her brain. Now we knew why she was having such difficulty walking. After talking it over with us, she chose not to operate, even though over time she would lose her ability to walk. She decided that surgery was too risky.

Five days after the accident, back at home, my mother finally sat up on her own. The swelling around her left eye had gone down, but she remained in a lot of pain, primarily on her right side. Dizzy, she couldn't walk without assistance. Tom stayed with her. He bought a Stratolounger from Sears for the living room and brought over extra pillows. He asked a friend to install handrails in the bathroom.

I went to Seattle Central to tell her instructor, Jim Lourie, why she had been missing. My mother pronounced his name *"Lough-lee."* He revealed to me her nickname—"The Boss." He explained that she organized the class party at the end of the quarter. The other students weren't eager to chip in money, but my mother insisted. She gathered the cash, bought paper plates and food, and made a batch of shrimp chips.

During her recuperation, my mother brewed herbal teas with dried ingredients from the jars in the kitchen cupboards. She used Tiger Balm and Wood Lock Medicated Oil and applied a poultice to her wounds. She continued to pore over her English workbooks.

Her limp became more pronounced after the accident. Her body listed to one side. She never returned to Seattle Central. She drove everywhere instead of walking, even though her eyesight and driving skills had eroded.

At home, she watched televangelists Jimmy Swaggart and Jim and Tammy Faye Bakker on cable TV. She was enthralled by the outrageously emotive sermons, the healing miracles and the music. She also tuned in to reruns of her favorite television series, *I Love Lucy*, laughing heartily at the silly slapstick comedy. At the same time, she listened intently for new English words. She jotted them in a spiral-bound notebook, saving them for our next English lesson together.

During one visit, we watched the *Kung Fu* TV series starring David Carradine. She didn't understand the dialogue, but she noticed Carradine's slow speech and trademark squint. "What's wrong with that white guy," she asked me in Chinese. "Why does he talk so funny? How come his eyes are like that?" I told her that he was trying to impersonate a Chinese person.

Despite spending her last decade of life trying, my mother never mastered English pronunciation or grammar. Non-Chinese still couldn't understand her. It was simply too hard to move to another country at the age of 34, spend the next 30 years cocooned in Chinatown culture and in front of sewing machines in a factory, and emerge with the proper foundation for mastering a second language so different from her native tongue. In her final years, her hard-won English vocabulary slipped away. She reverted to speaking only Chinese.

I was inspired by her effort. She never gave up. During her journey, she taught me how to read and write Chinese. We built a bridge together. She taught me that everyone can become better, whatever their age or circumstances. Anything worth doing is worth doing with all your heart. The payoff is in the quest.

CHAPTER 50

Electoral Politics

I N 1971, WHEN I WAS a senior at Franklin High School, 18-year-olds gained the right to vote in Washington state. But I didn't register to vote until several years after I began college. My parents didn't vote. None of their friends did either, despite the glowing, historic 1962 election win of Wing Luke. He was the first person of color elected to the Seattle City Council and the first Asian American elected to public office in the Pacific Northwest. No one implored me to step up to my civic responsibility.

Electoral politics wasn't my thing. Entering journalism right after the Watergate scandal, I had an outsized distrust of the motives and integrity of those seeking office. I didn't think that journalists should get ensnared in the machinations of an inherently corrupt political system or become an ally of those willing to forgo principles to attain power.

That didn't mean the *Examiner* didn't cover local races, especially the contests for Seattle Mayor, Seattle City Council, King County Executive and King County Council. Our readers deserved to learn about the policy stances of those poised to make key decisions affecting the International District and Asian American lives.

But the newspaper didn't do endorsements. I didn't either. As a nonprofit, the *Examiner* was legally barred from directly or indirectly participating in political campaigns.

During the fall election season, I welcomed ads from candidates of all stripes, and from proponents and opponents of ballot measures. This was good money. Allies of the *Examiner* steered ads our way to help the paper financially and to target potential voters.

Sam Smith, a perennial candidate for the Seattle City Council, gave me a prudent piece of advice when he came to the *Examiner* to buy an ad for his campaign for mayor in 1981. Smith was the first African American on the Council. I immediately recognized who he was by his round face, close-cropped hair, thin mustache and cat-like smile. After agreeing on the size of an ad, he pulled a thick wad of cash from his wallet. I stopped him. I said we could invoice his campaign later. "Young man, always get the money up front," he said, pressing the bills firmly into my hand. "You won't find me *or* the money if I lose."

By the 1970s, Asian American activists lined up behind the Democrats. The Democratic Party had a more progressive agenda than the Republican Party, embracing affirmative action, low-income housing and bilingual social service programs. These activists included Ben and Ruth Woo, Dolores Sibonga, Phil and Lois Hayasaka, Arlene Oki, Ruthann Kurose, Vera Ing and Joan Yoshitomi.

The titular head of the political activists was Ruth Woo, a tiny woman barely five feet tall who served as their guru. She had been a Republican early in her career. By the time I met her, "Auntie Ruth" had gravitated over to the Democrats. But she refused to formally align with it, pointing out that it was a Democratic President—Franklin D. Roosevelt—who authorized the incarceration of Japanese Americans during World War II. In the late 1950s, she was a receptionist for Seattle Mayor Gordon Clinton. In the 1960s, she played a similar role for Governor Dan Evans, a progressive Republican. She guided the successful campaigns of Dolores Sibonga, Gary Locke, Kip Tokuda, Sharon Tomiko Santos and Ron Sims.

A handful of more conservative business leaders like Tomio Moriguchi, Wesley Tao and Ted Choi worked for Republican candidates. In 1976, Tao supported the U.S. presidential re-election effort of Gerald Ford by hosting the state campaign at his Chinatown insurance office.

Ben and Ruth held many political fundraisers at their Mount Baker home, but they respected my independence. Ruth forcefully intervened when a guest tried to strong-arm me into an endorsement. "Hey, leave him alone!" she barked. "He's a newspaper editor. Why don't you buy an ad?"

Every year, without prompting, Auntie Ruth sponsored a table at the *Examiner* and Wing Luke Museum banquets through her business, the Puget Sound License Agency. But Ruth rarely attended, even after promising to show up. "If you ever honor me, I'm not going to come," she warned, sternly peering up at me through her big round glasses. "If you recognize me from the podium, I'm not going to stand up. You would make me very mad. Don't you dare do it!" With the many charitable events she supported, I wondered how she stayed afloat. I'm convinced that she set up her business so she would have a piggy bank to draw from for community causes.

During my stint at the Coalition for Quality Integrated Education, I met Arlene Oki, a fiercely loyal Democrat. She had worked as a registered nurse at the now defunct Doctors Hospital. She championed Robert Kennedy's 1968 Presidential bid and was heartbroken when that effort was brought to a shocking end by an assassin's bullets in Los Angeles.

Arlene fought passionately for under-resourced public schools in Southeast Seattle, packed with students of color and immigrants. Arlene gently pressed me to report on the campaigns of Asian Americans. But she didn't badger me for endorsements. Like Ruth and Ben Woo, she respected my independence. After I became *Examiner* editor, she wrote articles under the pseudonym Takako.

Bob Santos ran for elected office unsuccessfully three times—twice for Washington State Senate in the 1970s and once for King County Council in 1984. In his bids for the State Senate, he first ran as a Republican, then as a Democrat. They were narrow defeats.

In 1984, some young activists who canvassed for him asked me to join the campaign. I explained that I had to stay neutral because of my job at the *Examiner*. I didn't tell them that if Uncle Bob had asked me directly for an endorsement—which he never did—I would have agreed. I couldn't say no to him.

Uncle Bob, taking his election losses in stride, wryly pointed to missteps like hiring Ted Bundy as public affairs director during his first campaign. Bundy was later nabbed as a suspect in a string of unsolved murders. He eventually confessed to 30 murders and was executed in Florida. Bundy's name emerged in the news when I was at the *UW Daily*. Mary Parker, a friend at the paper, told me Bundy had asked her out on a date. Trusting her instincts, she turned him down. Mary had long brown hair, parted in the middle, like Bundy's other female victims. I shuddered when she told me.

Uncle Bob's final try for public office was fought against

two strong adversaries: Ron Sims and Cheryl Chow. All three were vying for the King County Council vacancy left by the retirement of Cheryl's mother Ruby Chow, Uncle Bob's long-time community nemesis.

Sims won. His victory propelled him into a long political career ending in a cabinet post under President Obama. I met Ron four years earlier when he tried unsuccessfully to unseat Ruby Chow in 1981. He had gained the backing of many Chinese American leaders, an unusual feat for an African American candidate. Ruby's contentious style had turned off many of her Chinatown constituents.

During the 1984 King County Council contest, I bumped into Cheryl Chow handing out fliers at A Piece of Cake (西點餅店), a popular Hong Kong-style bakery at 514 South King Street. She was well-known as a teacher, administrator, basketball coach and advisor to the Seattle Chinese Girls Drill Team.

She didn't recognize me. I was wearing a suit and tie for a funeral service. She began to hand me a leaflet, then did a double-take when she saw my face. "Oops, I didn't know it was you, Ron. I guess you're supporting Bob Santos. But in case you're interested, I've got some campaign materials."

I responded, "No worries, Cheryl. Nobody recognizes me when I'm dressed up. And by the way, I'm not endorsing anyone. I'll take one of your fliers."

An amiable chat ensued. I told her that my mother had just seen her picture in the newspaper: "She kept saying that she was jealous of how smooth and youthful your face is." Cheryl drolly patted both cheeks with her fingers. We both chuckled. She said, "If you're interested, I'd love to sit down with you and talk more about my campaign." She ended by emphasizing that she did not necessarily agree with her mother's stance on many issues.

She didn't elaborate. I realized then that it must be challenging to live in the omnipresent shadow of her mother, a polarizing politician with strident views. *What did Cheryl herself believe?* I thought about Greg Tuai. He loved his dad, but Liem was a conservative city council member who publicly endorsed the construction of the Kingdome. He was vilified by young Asian American activists.

Vera Ing was the first local candidate I ever agreed to help. In 1984, she ran a spirited campaign to become the first Asian American woman to serve in the Washington State Legislature.

I had worked with Vera in 1980 on the first major Asian American art exhibition at the Wing Luke Museum, *Made in America*. The show featured the works of luminaries like George Tsutakawa, Andrew Chinn, Josel Namkung and Val Laigo, as well as lesser known artists.

I knew that Vera's father had owned Don Ting Café (洞天), which later became Eight Immortals, then Sea Garden Restaurant. Vera grew up in Canton Alley before moving to the Central Area and then to Mount Baker, where she and her husband Joey, a Hawaii-born architect, raised their kids. Their home, overlooking Lake Washington, was the site of many lively political fundraisers.

Vera decided to run against John L. O'Brien, a crusty incumbent who had represented the 37th District since 1939, a year before Vera was born. O'Brien had long roots in the Rainier Valley, but Vera said he had grown out of touch with his increasingly diverse district. Vera had volunteered on the past campaigns of City Council members Norm Rice and Dolores Sibonga.

I agreed to write a front-page article on Vera's campaign for the *Examiner*, publicizing her kick-off at the House of Hong Restaurant on February 22. She thanked me. "But I need you to help me directly with my campaign," she said. "You're really knowledgeable about all the local issues because you cover them in the *Examiner*."

Before I could respond, she added, "I know you probably consider me a prima donna—that's what a lot of people in the community think. But I'm dead serious. I know I can do a great job."

I countered, "Have I ever called you a prima donna? No! But I do think of you as a socialite. You like to schmooze. I don't. You know how to dress. I don't."

By this time, we were both laughing. "Vera, you know how I feel about political campaigns. I'd rather cover them than get directly involved." Still, she didn't take no for an answer. I found myself coming over to her house to help with practice interviews. She dressed in her favorite bright red "campaign" outfit from Value Village. She hadn't thought through many issues. She rambled. I scolded her, "Vera, what are you trying to say? Don't beat around the bush. Clarity!"

Halfway into the sessions—as other campaign volunteers and I struggled to keep her focused—she pivoted, "Anybody hungry yet? Let me fix something to eat." Without waiting for a response, she scurried into the kitchen, and the practice session, barely underway, was over.

In the end, Vera fell short in her bid. But I had some fun times at her house and was well fed. Concerned about my "ragged appearance," she gave me a blue Calvin Klein ski jacket she bought on sale at Frederick & Nelson. I wore that jacket and a chocolate brown jacket my mother had sewn for me on the sly at Roffe. The Calvin Klein jacket gave way to excessive wear—the lining began to shred—and it went to Goodwill. My mother's jacket, while not very stylish—Vera derisively called it "a Metro bus driver's jacket"—lasted. I still wear it.

The year after her election defeat, she opened the Prima Vera Gallery Café at 112 Fifth Avenue North. She darted about, fussing over patrons, making sure each one felt welcome. She was in her element. She wouldn't have been if she had been elected. I helped her design fliers for events such as the visit of author Ruthanne Lum McCunn, who had just released *Sole Survivor*, a sea survival tale. I also invited Vera to write a column for the *Examiner*.

Several years after Vera's campaign, Velma Veloria came knocking. She told me that three-term Seattle City Council member Dolores Sibonga was considering running for mayor. Velma had been inspired by Dolores's humble origins and her fierce support for affirmative action. "I really need you to get involved," Velma pleaded.

Velma was persistent and her enthusiasm, infectious. Dolores's story mirrored my own. Dolores had waited on tables and bussed dishes at the Estigoy Café, operated by her parents in a small storefront in Manilatown at 504 Sixth Avenue South. It was a half-block from the Hong Kong Restaurant. She studied journalism at the University of Washington. In the late 1960s, Dolores and her husband Marty published the *Filipino Forum*, a monthly community newspaper promoting "united minority action."

On March 21, 1989, I joined over a dozen other friends of Dolores at a breakfast meeting. She wanted our frank assessment of her chances. Just before the meeting, Eva, Dolores's trusted aide, scanned the faces of the people seated at the long table and quipped, "This looks like the Last Supper."

Ruth Woo, the savvy political veteran, stressed fundraising and quickly finding a campaign manager. The two white males felt that Dolores needed to reach out beyond her base in communities of color. Someone suggested paying for a voter poll, but the idea was rejected as expensive and unnecessary.

I encouraged her to run. I said she was perceived as independent and not controlled by special interests. Moreover, the Asian American community embraced her as one of their own. I thought her biggest challenge was getting enough volunteers.

Dolores ended the listening session without revealing whether she would run. But I left confident that she would. She was clearly buoyed by all the words of encouragement.

Before long, Dolores officially announced her candidacy, and I was busy helping Velma edit campaign materials and posting yard signs around my neighborhood. Dolores's aide, Art Ceniza, asked me if I wanted to be media director for the campaign. I declined.

When a *Seattle P-I* editorial attacked Dolores for playing politics in calling for the Police Department to redeploy officers from the motorcycle squad to the patrol unit, I defended her. In a September 5, 1989, letter to the editor, I wrote that, as an ID resident, I was distressed to see how crime and drug-dealing had accelerated to the point where people felt fearful to walk the streets at night.

Dolores didn't survive the primary. In the general election, City Council member Norm Rice easily defeated former City Attorney Doug Jewett to become Seattle's first African American Mayor.

After Dolores's campaign, Velma thought about running for office herself. In 1990, she was hired as a legislative assistant to State Representative Art Wang. Inspired by progressive Democrats like Wang, Velma wrote in her diary on January 18, 1992, "I'm going to run for office to declare this country as my home." She announced her candidacy for a vacancy in the 11th Legislative District shortly thereafter.

Dolores donated the remaining $200 from her mayoral campaign fund to Velma's effort. Ruth Woo helped raise money and polish Velma's speaking skills. I told Velma she could bounce ideas off of me any time she wanted another perspective. She often did, especially during fatigued late-night phone calls where it was clear that all she wanted was reassurance that everything would turn out okay.

When Velma became stressed, she called and asked, "What are you doing right now? I need to get away. Let's go shopping!" I was not a shopper, but I went. It allowed me a few moments to refresh as well.

She picked me up, and we were off to Value Village. She moseyed through the clothing racks, eying bargains. "What do you think?" she asked, stepping out of the dressing room. I nodded noncommittally. She giggled, then returned the item to the counter. Once, she tried on a bright red blazer nearly identical to the one Vera wore during her campaign; it may, in fact, have been the very same blazer. After half an hour of exploring, carefree as a child, Velma dropped me back at work. She vowed that one day she would open her own thrift store and call it "Velma's Junk." I warned, "Don't. You'll end up buying all the stuff for yourself."

On November 3, 1992, Velma became the first Filipina American to be elected to a state legislature in the continental United States. It was wonderful to be on the winning side.

Although I had agreed to help Vera, Dolores and Velma, I didn't want to volunteer for any more campaigns.

In 1990, I heard through the grapevine that Martha Choe was considering the Seattle City Council. As with Uncle Bob, if she had buttonholed me, I would have found it very hard to refuse. She didn't. I cheered from the sidelines. She was elected to two four-year terms as the first Korean American member of the City Council.

I continued to attend Asian American campaign events and donate to candidates. But that was as engaged as I wanted to be.

In 1992, Patty Murray was elected as the first female senator to represent Washington state. A staff member reached out to me to see whether I might want to move to Washington, D.C., to serve as her press secretary. Flattered, I mulled over the offer but knew right away that it wouldn't be a good fit. By then, I was already at the Wing Luke Museum.

I suggested Patricia Akiyama, a former *Examiner* contributor and board member of the Wing Luke from 1987 to 1988. After two years as press secretary, she became Murray's chief of staff from 1995 to 1999. She was effective in both positions. Some people thrive in politics. I wasn't one of them.

CHAPTER 51

Joining the Wing Luke Museum

W HEN WING LUKE WAS ELECTED to the Seattle City
Council in 1962, I was just eight. I was in second
grade at Beacon Hill Elementary School. I have
a vague memory of my parents expressing awe at his victory.
Luke immigrated with his family to the United States when he
was five. He graduated from Roosevelt High School and the
University of Washington. His family's laundry was just down
the street from Campus Hand Laundry.

Wing swiftly became a rising progressive star in the Democratic Party. He fought for passage of the city's open housing ordinance, preservation of the Pike Place Market, Native
American fishing rights and cultural diversity. Sadly, on his
return from a fishing trip, his plane crashed in the Cascade
Mountains. He died on May 16, 1965, at the age of 40. In
1966, Wing's friends, including Ben Woo, established the
Wing Luke Memorial Museum.

In the fall of 1990, around the time I completed the Chinese Oral History Project, I learned that Museum Director Kit

Freudenberg was leaving. Her husband had taken a position in Idaho. Worried that my project might no longer be featured at the museum, I approached her. She surprised me by saying, "Why don't you go for my job?"

I brushed aside her suggestion. It wasn't that I wasn't interested. I loved museums. I savored my visits to the free Memory Lane Museum at the Goodwill store and the Seattle Art Museum at Volunteer Park. During my early years at the *Examiner*, my office was next door to the Wing Luke Museum; I often explored the gallery displays and objects in the collection. I just didn't think I was qualified.

When I was very young, I peeled off to explore the free museum at Goodwill when my parents took us with them. On display were hundreds of salvaged antiques, collectibles and knick-knacks. They were crammed inside a dozen large display cases, constructed with old windows from Seattle buildings. I moved among the cases—my nose pressed to glass—entranced, inspecting old typewriters, model houses, baseball mitts, vacuum cleaners, suitcases, pennants, faded black-and-white photos, kitchen tins, model trucks, baskets and toy robots. My mother had to shout loudly and repeatedly to get me to rejoin her.

I also visited Volunteer Park on Capitol Hill in the summer for family picnics on the big public lawn. My sister, brothers and I mounted the stone camels in front of the Seattle Art Museum and entered the building with its imposing stone art-deco facade. I pored over the never-changing collection of ancient Greek and Roman vases just down a flight of stairs. I was hypnotized by the etchings of mystical warriors, gods and animals.

On September 8, 1972, I discovered the Pioneer Square Wax Museum. On display were life-like characters out of Washington state's past: Henry Yesler, Governor Isaac Stevens, Asa Mercer and Doc Maynard. There were also figures of Presidents Nixon, Kennedy and Eisenhower, Napoleon, General George Marshall, Robert Goddard and the Apollo 11 astronauts. I stayed all day, until the museum closed.

A year later, I returned to the wax museum. Two tableaux caught my eye. The first was of Seattle pioneer Arthur Denny erecting a log cabin. The second was of Abraham Lincoln the moment before his assassination in Ford's Theatre. Before I exited, I read a news article on a bulletin board revealing that the "wax figures" were made of vinyl plastic for durability.

"False advertising!" I proclaimed. I caught myself. How smart would it have been to market the place as a vinyl plastic museum?

After Kit broached the topic of applying for her position, Wing Luke Museum board member Bettie Luke—Wing Luke's younger sister—called me, also suggesting that I consider the job. I had immeasurable respect for Bettie. She boarded a small plane during the search for Wing's missing plane and later issued press releases on behalf of the family. She sat in on early planning meetings for the museum, working with Ben Woo and watercolor artist Fay Chong to develop an annual art auction. She was on the board for over two decades.

She remembered my father from the Hong Kong Restaurant. Bettie's father, president of the Ho Nam Association and the Hip Sing Tong, brought her entire family to the restaurant. Bettie and her siblings wandered over to gaze at the fish in the aquarium while the men engaged in raucous drinking contests.

I first met Bettie when I was at the Coalition for Quality Integrated Education. Bettie worked at Project REACH (Respecting Ethnic and Cultural Heritage), developing multicultural curriculum materials for the public schools. In 1978, she asked me to help gather support letters for an African American woman who had been physically assaulted and called "nigger" by a secretary who worked for Seattle School District Attorney Gary Little. Bettie told me that Superintendent David Moberly had closed the case. "She needs support from other ethnic groups—to show Moberly that we as fellow people of color do not stand for this kind of brush-off," Bettie wrote me in a March 28 letter.

In 1986, I helped Bettie with a February 8 march from Hing Hay Park to the waterfront to commemorate the 100-year anniversary of the anti-Chinese riots in Seattle. In 1886, white mobs forced all 350 Chinese residents from Chinatown to the waterfront, attempting to drive them from the city. President Grover Cleveland declared martial law and ordered federal troops to put down the uprising. I covered the march, which attracted 150 participants, for the *Examiner*. At the waterfront, demonstrators released black balloons with red bows, symbolizing the release of bitter feelings and hope for the future.

I agreed to meet with Bettie to talk about the museum job. "We need to re-establish credibility in the community," she told me over dinner in Chinatown. "The focus on Asian folk art doesn't connect to Asian American audiences. You can bring some new ideas and energy through your connections. It doesn't matter that you don't have a museum background."

Still feeling ambivalent about this career shift—and doubtful I would be hired—I submitted my resume. Dolores Sibonga and Tina Young, my co-worker at Seattle Central Community College, wrote support letters. A few weeks later, I came in for an interview at the law offices of Gloria Lung Wakayama on the 32nd floor of the First Interstate Building, a towering steel-framed structure at 999 Third Avenue. Gloria, a lifelong Seattleite, was board president. She was recruited to the board in the mid-1980s by Helen Eng Kay, a long-time board member, after attending law school at the University of Santa Clara.

As I waited in the reception area, I peered through a small telescope at the gorgeous view across Puget Sound. Gloria used the telescope to check on her young daughter at the daycare center down the street. Soon, Gloria came out and led me into a small meeting room. Several other Wing Luke board members sat behind a long table in rolling leather chairs. I was candid about my lack of museum experience. I said that if I were hired, I would shift the focus away from Asian folk art toward local Asian American history and Asian American art. I said I believed the success of the museum rested on creating programs with greater resonance with locals. Several board members expressed skepticism that I could find the funds to execute this new vision.

One week after the interview, Gloria surprised me with a job offer. I agreed to start on January 1, 1991.

It wasn't until I took over that I realized the museum's finances were more precarious than anyone—including the board of trustees—realized. On paper, the museum had a $130,000 budget. In reality, the budget was much smaller. There was $50,000 of debt. The museum had no assets beyond its eclectic collection of Asian folk art, textiles and historical memorabilia from Chinatown.

On most days, the museum gallery had just four or five visitors. Sometimes, not a single person came in. A few school tours kept the gallery from remaining lifeless. Several loyal volunteers answered phones and handled purchases in the small gift shop. A few other volunteers conducted tours and catalogued objects for the collection. Most were white retirees who had worked as educators and traveled to Asia. Outside the doors of the museum—in the neighborhood where it mattered most—people were indifferent to the institution.

Demoralized, I called Gloria at home on a Saturday evening several weeks after I started. I told her I had changed my mind. "I didn't realize that things were this bad, Gloria," I said. "Everything is a mess. I don't know where to begin. I've thought things over and I've decided to leave. I'm sorry I have to do this."

"Oh, no!" Gloria exclaimed. "We were really looking forward to the changes that you had talked about, especially the shift toward the community." She implored me to stay. "We don't have a lot of choices at this point," she said. "If you can't turn it around, I'm not sure what else we can do. We may simply have to close."

I agreed to persevere a while longer. I told her not to expect miracles. We both discussed how we might infuse new vigor into the institution and find some quick dollars.

By the end of February 1991, irked by the internal disarray and the scale of the financial challenge, I again considered resigning. I had just hired Charlene Mano as our new education director. She was a third-generation Japanese American whose family, like mine, had deep Seattle roots. I loved Charlene's gentle, collaborative manner. She had done illustrations for me at the *Examiner*. She was the third Mano sibling to work for me. Mark and Leslie had been freelance writers. After I became involved with the Seattle Chapter of the Asian American Journalists Association, Lori Matsukawa and I hired Charlene to manage the expanding journalism scholarship program for minority students in 1988.

After several frank conversations, Charlene and I both decided to stick it out. If we both left, the museum's demise was likely. We didn't want that to happen.

I also didn't want to disappoint Alan Lau and Mayumi Tsutakawa. I had promised to bring young and emerging Asian American artists into the fold. For a brief time, Alan and two other artists—Lucia Enriquez and Irene H. Kuniyuki—joined the board.

Four others stayed on through the shaky transition: Lisa Ely, volunteer manager of the gift shop; Vernel Nicholas, the comptroller; Leslie Katsman, who staffed the museum on the weekends and managed the rental of the museum's "Asia on Wheels" curriculum kits; and Bob Luke, Bettie's brother, who faithfully donated the services of his alarm company to secure our facility.

Leslie, who worked at the museum from 1989 to 1999, did a little bit of everything. If a docent didn't show up for a scheduled tour, she stepped in at the last minute. If an overhead light went out in the gallery, she fearlessly mounted a rickety eight-foot wooden step ladder, ignoring the bold lettering, "DANGER, do not step above this level."

Under Kit, Olivia Taguinod had worked a few hours a week while taking classes at Seattle Central Community College. With her tousle of "big hair" and hip attire, Olivia offered a sparkling contrast to me with my receding hairline and bland wardrobe. I liked her wit, resourcefulness and gung-ho attitude. I promoted her to outreach coordinator. I felt she could help Charlene and me remake the institution.

I hired Debbie Louie as membership coordinator. She had just been laid off from a clerical position at a downtown law firm. I first got to know her as a student intern in 1990 at the Commission on Asian American Affairs. I felt that she, too, could help bring the Wing Luke back to its community roots.

Donnie Chin came by regularly to see whether I had changed my mind about staying. "Yep, I'm still here, Donnie," I told him each time. He smiled and said, "Good." Then he returned with a batch of new fire extinguishers, taking away the expired ones.

Six Wing Luke board members bravely stayed on through this crisis.

I called board chair Gloria daily to check in. Gloria's grandmother, Fannie Eng Lung, was the first Chinese woman born in Port Townsend. Gloria interviewed her for the Chinese Oral History Project in 1991 when Fannie was 95. Gloria's mother Bertha Tsuchiya was a silver-haired pharmacist in Chinatown who filled prescriptions for my mother.

Gloria's uncle, Hing Chinn, ran the China Garage, a repair shop that was remodeled into the museum's current facility. Hing visited to gaze wistfully at a black-and-white photo of a Chinese American baseball team he belonged to in the 1940s, on display in the gallery. He laughed about how he struggled to fix the cars of Filipinos who went to the Alaska canneries during the summer. These customers often returned to find their vehicles still not working.

Other board members included Helen Kay, a native of Newport, Washington, who operated a pharmacy with her husband Richard on Beacon Hill; Peter Moy, a plain-spoken consensus builder with family roots in Portland's Chinatown; Heng-Pin "Ping" Kiang, an uncommonly tall Chinese American with a booming voice but soft demeanor who worked as a partner in the law firm Perkins Coie; Beth Willis, a no-nonsense planner with a dry wit, employed at a large architectural firm downtown; Jim Linardos, an executive at Union Bank with a huge mane of brown hair who easily adapted to my vision and decided to stay on during the transition; and Bob Ohashi, the kindly Beacon Hill pharmacist who had indulged my comic book and candy habits during my childhood.

Another 10 board members either resigned in short order or stayed permanently missing in action. Joining as treasurer was Frank Kiuchi, a Beacon Hill native, accountant and political activist who returned from the East Coast in 1981 to help the Committee for Justice for Domingo and Viernes.

I decided to forgo my paycheck for several months and took a voluntary pay cut. At the first of many emergency meetings, the remaining board members pulled out checkbooks and wrote out donations to help keep creditors at bay.

I turned to Bob Santos. By then, Uncle Bob had left Inter-Im. He was now executive director of the Seattle Chinatown-International District Preservation and Development Authority (SCIDpda), the agency that purchased Hing Chinn's old garage and converted it into the museum on the street level and the Northwest Asian American Theatre in the basement. We both paid rent to the SCIDpda. Uncle Bob was our landlord.

I told Uncle Bob the Museum might have to close.

He didn't hesitate. "Shit, I knew things were bad, but I didn't know things were that bad, Ron!" he said. "Here's what I can do. I'll suspend payment of your rent for the next six months. You keep me posted on your fundraising efforts." I was stunned. "Are you sure?" I asked. He nodded. "Hey, you asked me for help, didn't you, guy?" He chuckled, then smacked me impishly on the shoulder. Lowering his voice to a conspiratorial whisper, he said, "But don't spread this around, okay? I'll do this for you guys, but I don't think I can do it for the Theatre as well. I'm sure they'll be asking me if they find out."

Uncle Bob's gesture lifted my spirits. I had time to plan.

Board member Bob Ohashi offered a quick fundraising fix. I hadn't seen him in two decades, but he looked the same as he did in the old days at Owen's Pharmacy, except for a few flecks of gray in his thick hair and mustache. Bob, an avid art collector, suggested a two-week collector's sale in the exhibition gallery. He knew many artists. He said that he and Nina Ventura, another Wing Luke board member, could gather the art.

The May 30 opening party at the museum attracted over 300 visitors eager to snatch up works by local artists like Kenneth Callahan, George Tsutakawa, Lois Graham, Paul Horiuchi, Alden Mason, Norie Sato and Frank Fujii. After the art collector's sale ended on June 16, a portion of all proceeds—over $13,000—went directly to the museum, providing a badly needed injection of funds.

"You helped keep me engaged when I was just a kid," I told Bob after the sale." Now, you keep me in business as an adult." He quietly beamed.

As the immediate crisis eased—thanks to the art sale and a successful annual art auction that same year—Charlene and I schemed about developing an exhibition that would give the Asian American community a reason to embrace the museum. The following year would mark the 50th anniversary of the incarceration of Japanese Americans. That occasion, we decided, might give us the best hope of rescuing and reinventing the institution.

CHAPTER 52

Two Champions of Japanese American Redress

I FIRST LEARNED IN-DEPTH ABOUT the Japanese American incarceration in the Asian American sociology class I took from Cynthia Chan-Toyoji at Seattle Central Community College. The World War II internment—now affirmed as one of the most egregious violations of the Constitution in U.S. history—was also discussed in my 11th grade social studies class, but little stayed with me.

Cynthia devoted several weeks to the topic. She explained that after Japan's attack on Pearl Harbor on December 7, 1941, Japanese Americans on the West Coast found themselves under assault by political demagogues labeling them traitors and "unassimilable" aliens. This culminated in the signing of Executive Order 9066, which authorized the mass incarceration of over 120,000 individuals.

Growing up on Beacon Hill—and going to school with many third-generation Sansei—I never once heard any of them utter a single word about what had happened to their parents and grandparents. After I heard Cynthia talk, I realized that

I didn't know my own friends. But my parents had their own shuttered past. My friends didn't really know me either.

Most Japanese Americans from Seattle were first sent to the Puyallup fairgrounds—euphemistically renamed "Camp Harmony"—where they were detained for several months in converted horse stalls. From there, they were shipped by train to a desert prison camp in Minidoka, Idaho, where they remained for the duration of World War II. I had only known Puyallup as the site of the annual Western Washington State Fair, about 30 miles south of Seattle.

In the decade between 1978 and 1988—paralleling my tenure at the *Examiner*—Sansei, inspired by the civil rights movement, discovered this chapter of their history. They expressed their outrage in opinion pieces in the *Asian Family Affair* and the *Examiner*.

These young activists, many of whom studied law, came together in the fight to overturn the conviction of Gordon Hirabayashi, a former University of Washington student imprisoned for violating military curfew orders. They participated in the larger fight for monetary redress for all camp survivors. The "radical" Seattle chapter of the Japanese American Citizens League (JACL), a national civil rights organization founded in 1929, was at the forefront of the movement for reparations. Redress was, in the words of Bob Shimabukuro, "born in Seattle," a phrase he adopted as the title of a book he wrote chronicling this effort.

The campaign culminated with the signing of the Civil Liberties Act of 1988 by President Ronald Reagan. In 1989, President George H.W. Bush signed a bill authorizing payment of $20,000 to every surviving World War II internee. By 1993, a total of 82,219 redress payments had been distributed.

My close friendships with Karen Seriguchi and Ruthann

Kurose, two resolute champions of redress, allowed me to watch the movement unfold up close. Karen was the Pacific Northwest regional director of the JACL. Ruthann served as aide to U.S. Representative Mike Lowry, a Democrat from Washington's 7th Congressional District. Karen was my regular dinner companion in the ID. Ruthann was my jogging partner.

Each put in 60-hour work weeks fighting for the cause. Karen needed little sleep. Ruthann injected her body with coffee and chocolate. Without their obsessive devotion—years of community meetings, strategy sessions, letter-writing drives, phone calls and pestering of legislators—redress would have remained a pipe dream, abandoned at the outer margins of political discourse as extremist folly.

Karen was born in Fukuoka, Japan. She was raised in Michigan, but moved to Berkeley, California, for college. In the 1970s, she joined the Asian American Theater Company in San Francisco. There, she worked with theater founders Frank Chin and Frank Abe. The "two Franks" believed that JACL leaders during World War II betrayed the community by advising passive cooperation with government authorities. Karen relocated to Seattle after Chin convinced her that the nucleus of any redress effort would be here.

Hired by the American Friends Service Committee, Karen developed programs in Seattle, Tacoma and Spokane to raise awareness of the incarceration. She moved on to work for the JACL for the paltry annual salary of $5,280.

Karen worked down the street from me in a chilly office in the T&C Building at 667 South Jackson Street. She had a wavy perm, big glasses, a youthful appearance and a restrained manner. We enjoyed many quick take-out meals at her office. Occasionally, we drove to a quiet café on Capitol Hill or the University District to spend an hour or two away from the claustrophobic grip of the neighborhood. I shared what was happening at the *Examiner* and she talked about the JACL and redress. We delighted in dissecting the idiosyncrasies and distinctive facial mannerisms of Asian American activists we both knew. We laughed so hard that we could hardly breathe.

We both amassed huge piles of paperback mysteries. Hers had broken spines and dog-eared pages. Mine looked new. She gravitated toward cerebral authors like P.D. James, Ruth Rendell, Janwillem van de Wetering and Ross Macdonald. I sampled a few of Macdonald's books, but I preferred Ed McBain police procedurals and Cornell Woolrich pulp noir. I collected nearly 50 of McBain's 87th Precinct series. In 1992, I waited for nearly an hour at a bookstore in downtown Seattle just so I could meet McBain and have him sign his new novel, *Mary, Mary*. Karen chastised me for my low-brow taste. I found her authors to be challenging reads.

We mocked each other's quirks. Karen periodically took a pair of scissors to her hair and cut a few snippets from the wavy locks on her forehead. I wondered if this was a nervous habit. She recoiled from loud noises, covering both ears with her hands. That's why she didn't want to have kids. She didn't believe in God or an afterlife. "The way I see it," she said, "you work and when you're done, you die and that's it. And you read some good books and have some good, hearty meals in between."

Karen was thin but inhaled enormous quantities of food, much like Steve Goon. She became cranky and got headaches when she became hungry. "You know, I'm not really as skinny as you think," she told me. "I just look skinny from the outside. I'm a bottomless pit. You're the one who's skinny."

True. She gave me an old pair of green khaki pants. "Here, try them on," she urged. To my surprise, they fit. "See what I mean!" she said. According to the tag, the waist size was 27". They were snug but comfortable, and on my *Examiner* salary, I welcomed serviceable castoffs from friends.

In 1980, Congress established the Commission on Wartime Relocation and Internment of Civilians to re-examine Executive Order 9066. Karen worked closely with Nisei leader Cherry Kinoshita to organize hearings at Seattle Central Community College and in Tacoma and Spokane.

During the 20 days of hearings, 750 witnesses testified, including former Japanese American internees, government officials and historians. In 1982, the Commission concluded in a report that the incarceration was unjustified and racially motivated. This set the stage for monetary redress and a Presidential apology.

I saw Karen emerge after lengthy planning meetings at the T&C Building with Cherry and others like Shigeko Uno, Chuck Kato, Tomio Moriguchi, Sam Shoji, Shosuke Sasaki and Henry Miyatake. Karen looked beat. "They drive me nuts," she growled. I responded, "Well, then let's go eat." She perked up and we immediately left in search of food. I admired Karen's patience in working with myriad strong personalities.

The Nisei were notoriously stingy with praise, but they treasured Karen. Chuck Kato once remarked, "I think that Karen was "*the* most important person. Every time I had to speak, she would prepare everything for me in advance. I don't know what I would have done without her."

While Karen organized the community hearings, Ruthann Kurose drove the legislative effort. I spent late evenings with Ruthann, jogging and exercising off all the food I had eaten earlier with Karen. That's how I managed to stay skinny.

I first met Ruthann at the Alaska Cannery Workers Association office in the early 1970s. She was a political science major at the UW. She was also an activist. Ruthann and her brother Guy were friends of Silme Domingo, Sabino Cabildo and Eddie Daba. They gossiped while I worked. I also saw them hanging out together at the *Asian Family Affair*. Ruthann was a member of the news staff.

Ruthann had shoulder-length hair, high cheekbones, red lips and a bright demeanor. She wore a sweater and rubber-soled slip-ons, no socks. She reasoned that sweaters didn't require ironing, and the shoes were suited for walking, which she did often as part of riding the bus around town.

Guy was stockier. He wore a long double-breasted overcoat, bell bottoms and platform shoes—adopting the brash street persona of an Asian American *Superfly*. He had a fearsome reputation as a black-belt karate master. He carried a set of nunchaku sticks, whipping them out to dazzle others.

Sabino, a Vietnam War veteran, was a fiery radical who helped establish the International Drop-In Center for Filipino seniors.

Eddie, a postal worker like my brother Tom, had a slow, shuffling gait and a droll sense of humor. He reminded me of Charlie Chaplin. Eddie, who also worked as a house painter, starred in *The Romance of Magno Rubio*, a 1983 NWAAT adaptation of Carlos Bulosan's classic short story. Tom, Eddie and Steve Goon all graduated from Franklin High in the same class.

Ruthann's mother Aki Kurose was an acclaimed Seattle public school teacher. Ruthann inherited her mother's tenacious spirit. Aki was sponsored out of Minidoka by Guy Gebhardt, an antiwar activist and Quaker in Wichita, Kansas. Returning to Seattle, Ruthann's mother met Floyd Schmoe, another Quaker activist, and began a lifelong crusade for social justice. As a member of Seattle Women Act for Peace, Aki helped bring "*hibakusha* maidens"—survivors of the Hiroshima and Naga-saki bombings—to Seattle for medical treatment.

Ruthann told me that she didn't fully appreciate her mother when she was younger. Aki, an early and steadfast critic of the Vietnam War, took Ruthann and her siblings to the King County Courthouse to participate in rallies and to hold up protest signs. Ruthann was embarrassed to be there.

In 1978, Ruthann became active in Mike Lowry's congressional campaign because of her opposition to incumbent Jack Cunningham, a Republican conservative who introduced legislation to abrogate Native American treaty fishing rights. Lowry vowed to defend those rights and to support redress for Japanese Americans. After Lowry's victory, Mike hired Ruthann. She became the first Asian American to work as an aide to a U.S. Congressional Representative from Washington state.

Ruthann and another Lowry staff member Kathy Halley organized support for the first redress bill, introduced on November 28, 1979. Although it failed, Ruthann and Kathy doggedly continued to organize and push redress until the U.S. Congress finally passed reparations in 1988.

Ruthann worked out of Lowry's district office on Rainier Avenue South, near the old Chubby & Tubby. To keep her diabetes at bay, Ruthann took up running. She sometimes binged on a full box of glazed donuts from Borrachini's Bakery. She dryly called it "carb loading." She then called me to join her on a run, frantic to get her system back into balance to avoid insulin injections. She picked me up in her taupe-colored Volvo with a sunroof and we headed over to Myrtle Edwards Park or Greenlake for a long, slow run. On late summer nights, we navigated around swarms of gnats and water sprinklers.

Ruthann talked about Lowry's promise to the Japanese American community. She made sure he stayed true to his word. I filled her in on my visits to my mother's house and my attempts to tutor her in English. She admired my mother's persistence. Her mother was the same.

During one run, she stopped to pick flowers that caught her eye. She made sure no one was looking. "These are nice," she said, laughing mischievously. "I know I'm not supposed to do this, but I can't help myself. I get distracted. I'm not good at following rules."

Ruthann told me that Nisei Congressional Representatives like Norm Mineta (D-CA) and Bob Matsui (D-CA) were hesitant to sign on to Lowry's bill, fearing backlash and accusations of self-interest. She was especially critical of Matsui, who wouldn't even meet with her to discuss the issue. Lowry, a white man who grew up in Eastern Washington, was different. He was a table-pounding defender of civil liberties who learned from his father and uncle about the incarceration.

Ruthann had another running partner in D.C. It was Phil Tajitsu Nash, a community journalist, attorney and unyielding proponent of reparations. Phil's and Ruthann's grandmothers were best friends. Phil's and Ruthann's mothers were also best friends. After work, Phil and Ruthann plotted redress strategy as they ran along the Mall from the Capitol Building to the Washington Monument. At her apartment a block-and-a-half away, they printed fliers and sent faxes to line up support from members of the House Judiciary Committee and the Congressional Black Caucus. After 11 p.m., Ruthann made a flurry of calls back to Seattle, taking advantage of cheap long-distance rates. In the dead of night, she returned to the Congressional offices to slip fliers under each door, positioning herself for morning calls.

By the early 1980s, as the redress education efforts picked up momentum and political support widened in Congress, the

Nisei elected officials—Mineta, Matsui and Senators Daniel Inouye and Spark Matsunaga—grew more comfortable about going public with the call for reparations.

On March 5, 1984, the Seattle City Council authorized $5,000 payments to three former city employees who lost their jobs due to the incarceration. On April 25, the Seattle School Board issued a formal apology and $5,000 redress payments to 27 Japanese American women forced to resign *en masse* during World War II. Cherry and Seattle JACL members were behind these campaigns.

On October 9, 1990, U.S. Attorney General Dick Thornburgh issued an apology and doled out the first $20,000 redress payments to nine elderly Japanese American camp survivors in a moving Washington, D.C., ceremony.

After Karen left the JACL, she moved to Los Angeles in 1983 to work for the *Pacific Citizen*, the national publication of the JACL. In 1985, she was hired as the first national director of the Asian American Journalists Association, a post she held until 1987.

In 1984, Ruthann left Lowry's office to join the city of Seattle as international trade and tourism coordinator. Dolores Sibonga, chair of the Seattle City Council finance committee, pushed for the position as part of the city's economic development plan. After Ruthann married Nathan Rothman and had kids, she shifted her focus. Daughter Mika was born on May 30, 1988, and son Mori was born on November 21, 1989. She settled into parenthood and family life on Mercer Island.

When I hear references to the incarceration of Japanese Americans during World War II or the redress movement, I think fondly—and with admiration—of Karen and Ruthann. I remember their central roles in working with the Nisei to win the hard-fought redress campaign.

After I went to work at ICHS, I made a point of inviting Mike Lowry, a champion of universal health care, to attend our annual fundraising gala. I thanked him for his work on behalf of redress. He grabbed my arm and pointed across the room to Ruthann. "No, no, no, Ron! That's the person who you want to thank."

At community events, Cherry Kinoshita said the same thing about Karen's contribution.

The history books credit Presidents Reagan, George H.W. Bush, Lowry, Mineta, Inouye and other elected officials for helping right the historic injustice.

The names of Karen and Ruthann don't even appear as footnotes. But I know better.

CHAPTER 53

Executive Order 9066 Exhibition

FTER OUR SPUTTERING START AT the Wing Luke Museum, Charlene and I dug in. I tried to figure out how to execute the grand Asian American dream I had spoken to the board about when I was first hired.

We canceled several scheduled exhibits of overseas Asian art. We made some people very angry, including a local curator promoting a show of Persian miniatures.

Charlene and I realized that the following year would be the 50th anniversary of the signing of Executive Order 9066. An exhibition could give Japanese American families a chance to share their most closely held, painful stories and allow the broader public—including schools—to link current civil liberties controversies with a compelling historical example. We could recruit new volunteers and tap new funding sources.

Before Kit Freudenberg left, she tried to launch an exhibit on the World War II incarceration, but the National Endowment for the Humanities rejected the grant request. We moved the project out of the realm of traditional humanities pursuits.

Charlene and I named the project *Executive Order 9066: 50 Years Before and 50 Years After.* This larger scope allowed us to include the very early stories of laborers in the sawmills, canneries and farms, in addition to the post-war resettlement and the redress movement.

Ken Mochizuki warned me that it would be tough to get Japanese Americans to cooperate because they believed that "a nail that sticks up gets hammered."

Collaborative leadership, therefore, was essential. We formed separate working committees to take on research, publicity, artifact selection, design and fundraising. The steering committee was composed of Bob Shimabukuro, Sally Yamasaki, David Takami and Michelle Kumata. Charlene and I provided oversight and leadership when difficult decisions had to be made.

Sally's father Frank and her husband Dan Benson designed and constructed a 3'x4' diorama of Camp Harmony. Sally's mother Sadie gathered historical photos.

I joined Frank and Sadie at their Lake Forest Park home during a spirited *mochi*-making ceremony in their garage shortly after one Christmas. Alternating teams of volunteers took turns pounding the *mochi* in a hollowed tree stump with wooden mallets. Frank led the rhythmic chant: "I've been working on the railroad."

I sat quietly with Frank as he recounted a childhood memory. He and a group of friends went to the Crystal Pool, a public swimming pool, on Second Avenue and Lenora Street in downtown Seattle. He was abruptly turned away because of his race. He was devastated. "When you're prepared for racism, you know how to handle it," he said. "When you're not, it really hurts." His eyes grew damp, and he began to sob. I didn't know how to comfort him.

Two Nisei, Ike Ikeda and Harry Fujita, shared their intimate knowledge as former prisoners at Minidoka. I knew Ike as the genial but feisty former director of the nonprofit Atlantic Street Center. In 1971, when I was a student at Franklin, I first noticed Ike's name in a *Seattle P-I* news article. He had helped set up a meeting between the school superintendent and Asian protesters complaining about the lack of bilingual staff at my school. I clipped the article and saved it. I didn't meet him until many years later.

Harry Fujita was an adroit performer for Northwest Asian American Theatre. Harry usually played a Nisei character. He appeared in Kingstreet Media's film *Beacon Hill Boys*. Harry agreed to head up research, patiently organizing many boxes of documents and private papers.

One Saturday, Charlene was startled to see her father, recently retired, come into the museum gallery, pick up a hammer and begin constructing a display wall. "What are you doing here?" she asked. Mr. Mano had heard about the need for volunteers from the Seattle Buddhist Church. He was joined by Paul Aburano, another Nisei who was handy with tools and low-cost design solutions. Charlene's mother joined later as a volunteer docent.

At one juncture, the exhibition plans nearly came apart over the question of how to treat the story of the "No-No Boys" and the draft resisters, the young Nisei men who chose to go to prison rather than volunteer to serve in the U.S. Army. Some of the Nisei veterans who fought overseas as part of the highly decorated 442nd Regimental Combat Team didn't want to include the dissidents' viewpoint. Charlene and the steering committee walked a very fine line to ensure that both sides were fairly represented without angering or alienating anyone.

As the scope of the exhibition expanded, the steering committee grew nervous about being able to deliver a professional product. A lot was on the line.

"Do you think we can really pull this off?" Sally Yamasaki asked at one meeting.

"Don't worry about it," I said casually. "It'll be easy. What's a museum exhibit, anyway? You just take some pictures and stuff and you stick them up on the walls with some words. What's the big deal?"

Sally and the others bellowed with laughter. My remark lightened a stress-filled moment. I thought then—and I still do now—that museum professionals would do well to remind themselves that what they do is neither so arcane or so sacrosanct that ordinary people can't be lead participants.

We found simple ways to release tension. We had impromptu jumping contests at the office doorway, competing to see who could place their yellow sticky Post-It note at the highest spot. We engaged in fierce arm-wrestling challenges. Sally was especially proud when she bested Jeff Hanada, a design team leader.

One day, Sally and Michelle vanished to the Westlake Center. The reason? To try on underwire bras at the new Victoria's Secret lingerie store.

Former internees donated tables and dressers made by hand from scrap wood and provided photographs taken on the sly at Minidoka.

Several told us about a rock-polishing craze in camp, coming forth with polished agate and soft stone rocks they had rubbed against the concrete floors of their shower rooms and buffed with army blankets. The rocks served as a metaphor for the irrepressible creativity and resilience of the internees.

The exhibition included stunning photographs of businesses, church activities, celebrations at the Nippon Kan Theatre and intimate family moments. Many came from large-format negatives supplied by the Takano Studio, run by Sally's aunt, Yuki Miyake, and Yuki's late husband, Henry, from 1920 until incarceration.

The centerpiece of the exhibit was the re-creation of a barrack from Minidoka, built out of shiplap and black tar paper. Bob Shimabukuro, a Hawaii transplant who admitted that he knew very little about the incarceration when he was growing up, worked with Paul Aburano on the fabrication. Bob became ardently committed to redress after moving to Portland, Oregon, in 1979. The barrack was filled with clothing and objects of the era and old tables and dressers made by camp residents.

Great care was taken to capture the right feel for the exhibition. Sally and Dan, David Takami, and Michelle drove to Minidoka, Idaho. They stayed overnight at an old, nearly abandoned roadside motel. When they finally made it to the site, they stared in noiseless awe at the desolate landscape. They heard the rush of the wind and imagined the barbed wire fences and the rows and rows of barracks that had once imprisoned more than 9,000 Japanese American men, women and children. They came back with a fuller grasp of what their parents and relatives had endured.

We had plenty of fundraising assistance. No one wanted us to fail, least of all Tomio Moriguchi. Back in 1970, as president of the JACL, he helped organize *Pride and Shame*, the first local exhibition on the incarceration. It was shown at the Museum of History and Industry (MOHAI), despite the reluctance of the director, who expected a tame display about Japanese American culture.

"I know how tough it is, Ron," Tomio said, scratching his chin, then grinning. "I admire your work on this project. Let me talk to some people."

We got grants from the Motoda Foundation and the Kawabe Memorial Fund. The Seattle and Lake Washington chapters of the JACL solicited their members, bringing forth a flood of checks ranging from $25 to $500. All the Japanese American churches contributed.

In total, the *9066* project brought in an astounding $150,000, more than the entire annual budget of the Wing Luke Museum.

Lack of sound-proofing between the museum and the Northwest Asian American Theatre (NWAAT) directly below us guaranteed scheduling nightmares. When NWAAT rehearsed or staged a performance, we had to stop work and wait in silence until they were done. Charlene and Kathy Hsieh, managing director of NWAAT, tactfully found ways to compromise. Bob went home to nap before returning to do construction in the late evening when noise wouldn't be an issue.

Weeks before the opening, Sally, Bob and Michelle worked nonstop late into the night and early morning. The anticipatory jitters, gleeful passion and sense of purpose were palpable.

A few days before the much-heralded media preview, I arrived very early. As I turned my key in the lock and swung open the door, I didn't hear the alarm. I thought that someone had forgotten to set it the night before. But as I walked through the unlit gallery, I saw two bodies huddled under blankets. It was Sally and Michelle. They were fast asleep inside the Minidoka barrack re-creation. After working late, they decided to get a taste of what the Issei and Nisei had gone through.

At the crowded February 18, 1992, community preview, I said, "Many people shared their stories and their family heirlooms to breathe life into this project. It's the community's exhibit. When you come back, remember each time the spirit of the Issei and Nisei pioneers whose sacrifices, courage and achievements are the heart and soul of what's presented. Many are no longer here, but they helped create this exhibit."

The following day, a crowd wrapped around the block outside the museum entrance waiting to enter. The exhibition was wildly successful, attracting over 10,000 visitors during a six-month run. We extended it for three more months.

The *Executive Order 9066* exhibit—the grand experiment on which I had gambled my survival as a leader—prevented the museum from closing.

Every day I came to work, I never knew whether I would interrupt a visitor wiping away tears with the back of a sleeve or sitting motionless on a bench, staring intently at a corner of the barrack display.

Olivia and Debbie worked overtime to keep up with all the school tours and public programs. After one especially grueling day, they went clubbing in Pioneer Square. Before they left, Olivia gathered Debbie's long hair up in a bun with a pair of decorative chopsticks from the museum store. At 2 a.m., they both returned to the museum to sleep. Bob's recreated barrack again bridged past and present.

In an article in the *Examiner*, Bob Shimabukuro wrote that he couldn't decide whether I was "a genius by accident or by design." On some days, he said, he felt that I had started a "runaway train down a steep hill and was watching to see where it landed." On other days, he "had an eerie feeling that everything was happening according to a master plan" I had devised. "This was high-stakes poker," he wrote. "There was no way this community was going to see him lose the bet."

After *Executive Order 9066* ended its run, a traveling version went to libraries, museums and community centers under the auspices of Exhibit Touring Services, which managed distribution of three other exhibitions I had worked on: *Shared*

Dreams, Alaskeros and *Reflections of Seattle's Chinese Americans*.

Meanwhile, a smaller re-creation of a barrack from Camp Harmony was built in the Wing Luke gallery as part of a new long-term exhibition on Asian American history. In 2011, Bob Shimabukuro constructed another Camp Harmony barrack at the Puyallup Fair.

At several *9066* planning committee meetings, I promised the Nisei that the new museum we hoped to build in the not-too-distant future would include their collective stories. I never forgot that promise, even as many of them passed away in the intervening years. That vow guided me during the next decade-and-a-half that it took to finally achieve that goal.

CHAPTER 54

A String of Community Exhibitions

A FTER THE *EXECUTIVE ORDER 9066* experiment, the museum could now unapologetically plan and fundraise for other community-based exhibitions. Museum colleagues no longer scoffed that my unconventional approach, which relied heavily on activists and nonscholars, would result in subpar exhibitions lacking intellectual rigor, integrity and aesthetic merit.

Over the next decade and a half, the Wing Luke Museum developed a string of ambitious exhibits on Vietnamese Americans, Sikh Americans, Filipino American artists, Korean Americans, war veterans, media stereotypes, photography, recent immigrants, adoptees, music, AIDS, racism and domestic violence. Each display drew new partners and volunteers into an ever-widening museum family.

At speaking engagements, I began touting "the community-response exhibition model." I said that museums should use their clout as respected arbiters of history and social movements to help lift up our society, much as African American churches

459

did during the civil rights movement. I urged museums to be as engaged in building a more just future as they were in reclaiming and commemorating the past.

One of the first of the museum's many awards came from the Association of King County Historical Organizations (AKCHO) for the *Executive 9066* exhibition. Through AKCHO, I reconnected with Mrs. Nilson, my journalism teacher at Franklin High. She left the school in 1982 and was working for the Maple Valley Historical Society. I was thrilled to see her but I had one faltering moment. I didn't know whether to address her as "Barb" Nilson—now that I was much older and she was a museum colleague—or "Mrs. Nilson." I chose the latter.

The second major exhibition after *Executive Order 9066* was *One Song, Many Voices*. It replaced *East Meets Northwest*, the museum's outdated permanent exhibition on the history of Asian Pacific Americans in the state. The new display borrowed heavily from *Shared Dreams*, the traveling exhibit I created for the Washington State Centennial Commission in 1989. *One Song* consisted of over 100 photos and dozens of artifacts, maps, timelines and individual stories. It opened on April 30, 1993, kicking off Asian Pacific Heritage Month.

In March 1994, the museum hosted *Reflections of Seattle's Chinese Americans: The First 100 Years*. It was a display of the best images and stories from my cherished Chinese Oral History Project. Sadly, some subjects—David "Gobby" Woo, Fred Yee's father George, Jeni Fung's brother Henry Kay Lock, famous Hollywood actor Keye Luke (a Franklin High graduate), Henry Chin and Hong Y. Chin—had already died. I was grateful we interviewed them when we did.

Later in the year, the museum and the University of Washington Press co-published a book of the oral histories. A modest run of 2,200 books sold out in a few years. A second edition of

Reflections, containing 31 additional interviews and portraits, was published in 2003.

My friend Mizu Sugimura, who worked at the Barnes & Noble store in Federal Way, invited me to speak on March 21, 1996. I met her in the late 1970s when she was Jane Aoyama. She was a fellow Beacon Hiller. Inspired by my discrimination complaint against the UW, she sought out the *Examiner* and contributed several articles. Like me, she stumbled around in an ADHD haze in her youth.

We renewed our friendship in 1984, after we bumped into each other at the opening of *Star Trek III: The Search for Spock* at the Lewis and Clark Theatre in Tukwila. She stood in the lobby, dressed in a Starfleet costume. I didn't know she was a Trekkie. She had married and moved out of Seattle. She changed her first name to Mizu—the Japanese word for "water." She believed that like water flowing out to sea, she would find her own way forward.

Only a handful of people showed up at Barnes & Noble. But I was flattered to be invited to appear in a major local bookstore as a bona fide author. Mizu rolled out the red carpet and even produced a large poster with a color photograph of me that first appeared in *The Seattle Times*. I was taken aback when she asked me to autograph a book for her.

Paul Mitchell, diversity marketing coordinator at The Bon Marché, showcased the *Reflections* exhibition at the downtown flagship store in February 1995 for Chinese New Year. The book was sold alongside the exhibit. The display was on the main floor for the entire month. Colorful banners adorned store pillars. The Bon built crates to transport the exhibit panels to other stores across the region over the next several years.

In 1994, the museum produced two other noteworthy exhibitions. The first was on the multi-ethnic history of the

International District. Based on oral histories, it was spear-headed by Susan Kunimatsu, coordinator of the International Special Review District board. She took on the project as she was leaving her job. Working with the museum led to her transition into becoming a jewelry artist.

The second exhibition, *They Painted from Their Hearts*, featured 18 pioneer Asian American artists whose works spanned from 1900 to 1960. It was curated by Mayumi Tsutakawa. The artists included Social Realist painters, members of the Chinese Art Club and abstractionist painters. Only six were still alive. Mayumi's 84-year-old father George came to the opening, shuffling with the aid of a cane. He turned to Mayumi, saying simply, "You did good." Greg Tuai's uncle Larry Chinn, an original member of the Chinese Art Club founded in 1936, died several months before the opening. I learned that Florence Chin Eng's late husband, "Howard" Shek Sheong Eng, was another founding member.

They Painted from Their Hearts was warmly embraced by young Asian American artists who had waited impatiently outside the doors of mainstream galleries and museums for opportunities. Two years later, Mayumi returned to curate *Beyond the Rock Garden: Craft Forms for a New World*. It featured both Asian Pacific American and Canadian craft artists. Alan Lau developed the show's themes and wrote the text.

In 1995, the museum received the National Award for Museum Service from the Institute of Museum and Library Services (IMLS). The award is the highest recognition in the field. The IMLS pointed to *Executive Order 9066* and other community-curated exhibitions as a new museum exhibition model.

Wing Luke co-presidents Gloria Lung Wakayama and Helen Eng Kay accompanied me to Washington, D.C., to receive the award at a ceremony in the White House on October

5. First Lady Hillary Clinton asked about our work. I was impressed by her genuine curiosity and her graciousness as a host.

The First Lady then invited us to the White House lawn to watch President Clinton congratulate the National Medal of Arts winners. They included comedian Bob Hope, poet Gwendolyn Brooks, artist Roy Lichtenstein and two personal heroes of mine, Ruby Dee and Ossie Davis, civil rights activists and theater stars. Gloria, Helen and I sat on chairs assembled under a big tent. It was a very breezy day, and the President's hair flapped vigorously with each gust. In contrast, the First Lady's hair barely moved. I wondered what hair product she used.

Gloria, Helen and I returned to Seattle feeling affirmed and reinvigorated. But with the eyes of the nation now trained our way, I knew we needed to expand beyond our traditional base in the longer-established Chinese, Japanese and Filipino American communities. The Asian American population had exploded in size and ethnic diversity, beyond the cloistered pockets of central Seattle. We had a lot of work to do.

In 1995, my wife Loan helped me launch an intergenerational exhibition that aimed to ease rifts between a rising Americanized generation and older leaders who held fiercely to the unrealistic dream of returning to Vietnam and ousting the Communists. The project was simply called *Twenty Years After the Fall of Saigon: The Vietnamese American Story.*

Khanh Nguyễn, a refugee center manager who graduated from Saigon University with a degree in public administration, led that effort, teaming up with his daughter Ann-Marie and Tâm Nguyễn, owner of the popular Saigon Bistro. Khanh and Tâm were the brains behind the Little Saigon business district. The two men also nursed the dream of a memorial park. In 1998, the city welcomed Little Saigon as part of the ID.

Loan conducted several interviews in Vietnamese with elders. Many spoke for the first time about the grief of losing their country and having to start anew. Loan's family members lent personal items for the exhibit. I began to understand the sadness that my mother felt as a newcomer who grudgingly exchanged her home for another that could never replace it.

In 1997, the museum began organizing a Korean American exhibit. Airyang Pahk, a community planner and Wing Luke board member, agreed to tackle this complex project. Airyang was recommended to me by Martha Choe, who had been elected to the Seattle City Council. "She's very sharp," Martha told me. "She shares the same vision you have about connecting the arts and historic preservation to community empowerment."

Airyang (now Julia A. Park) was a perfect bridge between the traditional Korean-speaking elders who controlled both the Korean Association and the Korean American Grocers Association, and the younger 1.5 generation (those who immigrated to the U.S. before or during their teens). Airyang worked with Ick-whan Lee, founder of the Korean American Historical Society, and the Tacoma-based Korean American Artists Association of Washington State. She performed a graceful balancing act. *Golden Roots, Korean Americans in Washington State* opened on September 25, 1998.

In that same year, Tom Ikeda, a former general manager at Microsoft, talked to me about a digital archive of Japanese American oral histories he had been assembling. The project was called Densho, which means "to pass on to the next generation." He proposed setting up computer stations on the museum display floor to gauge visitor interest.

When Tom first started Densho in 1996, he came to me for advice. I clearly remember the fire of determination in his eyes. I knew Densho was in good hands. The computer stations were installed in January 1999. This partnership allowed the museum to continue sharing the story of the World War II incarceration.

A year earlier, Hollywood legend Sylvester Stallone visited the museum. He was in Seattle to film *Get Carter*, an action thriller. A car chase scene was filmed on Seventh Avenue South, directly in front of the Wing Luke. During a break, Stallone sauntered through the front door and asked, "Yo, what's Wing Luke?" He listened and nodded politely as I led him around the gallery for a brief tour. I was flabbergasted at how short he was. Associate Director Beth Takekawa darted into the back of the museum to grab a poster for him to autograph. Other staff members looked on.

I marveled, thinking about how far the museum had come. We hadn't simply risen from the brink of bankruptcy and received a White House award. Now even Rocky knew about us.

Even as the museum grew, it never lost touch with its roots. The kids whose parents worked in the restaurants and shops came by. The boys bounced basketballs against the red painted brick wall under the museum's recessed entryway. On the weekends, a group of young girls played card games like Go Fish with staff members Jeannette Roden and Nancy Ng.

Donnie Chin was nearby if there was trouble. Once, the girls came running inside the museum, exclaiming, "There's a bad man outside!" Jeannette and Nancy peered outside the large glass front door and saw a man across the street exposing himself. They shouted at him from the doorway, then immediately dialed Donnie.

The museum's exhibits attracted the notice of the Museum of History and Industry (MOHAI), the Seattle Art Museum and the University of Washington's Burke Museum of Natural History and Culture. Their lead staff regularly trekked over to dissect our design and content decisions. They were trying to lift their institutions out of the doldrums of a static museum past. We shared tips and learned from one another.

In 1997, I advised both MOHAI and the Burke on new permanent exhibits.

MOHAI's Sheryl Steiffel told me that Director Michael Herschensohn wanted to do a makeover centered on five iconic objects from its collection. One was a salmon butcher machine, commonly referred to as an "Iron Chink." It was invented to replace Chinese laborers. But it presented a dilemma because of its racially charged name.

"I know that machine well," I told Sheryl. Gene Viernes had written about it in the *Examiner*. There had been a brass-plated sign from one of those machines at the ACWA office, pilfered from the New England Fish Company. It read "1927 The Iron Chink, Model (G), Patented—Aug. 8, 1905." There was red paint around the edges and mottled spots of green oxidation. It was used as evidence in the ACWA discrimination cases.

I helped Sheryl pull together a focus group to deal with the issue. Richard Rabinowitz, president of the American History Workshop, was brought in from New York as exhibition advisor. The MOHAI exhibition, *Salmon Stakes: People, Environment and Technology*, opened in February 1998, featuring stories from of Asian laborers alongside the Iron Chink. They followed the focus group's recommendation and used the historically accurate term along with signage explaining why.

Meanwhile, at the Burke Museum, Erin Younger, exhibition manager, was planning *Pacific Voices*, an exhibition on the history and culture of Pacific Rim people. She also asked me to serve as an advisor. I didn't hesitate to say yes. Years earlier, as assistant director of grants at the Washington Commission for the Humanities, she had provided funding to launch the Chinese Oral History Project.

In 2001, I happily returned to exhibition development at the Wing Luke for the first time in years. UW student activists were protesting the sale of garments made by sweatshop factories in Asia. I thought it was time to tell the stories of the forgotten workers in our own backyard, including my mother.

In Pioneer Square, the painted names of former sewing enterprises were still visible on the faces of old buildings. The Seattle Quilt building, where my mother labored, had been converted into high-ceilinged apartments. From 1994 to 1996, my friends Binko and John Bisbee, who later took over Higo Variety Store, lived in an apartment on the fifth floor.

I called UW Asian American Studies faculty member Connie So to recruit student volunteers. Connie understood the issue well. Her mother Big Yin Woo-So was a garment worker from Beacon Hill like my mother. She worked at Roffe, Black Bear Manufacturing Company and Olympic Sportswear.

Ben-Ling Wong also agreed to help. She worked one summer at Farwest Garments with her mother. Ben-Ling summoned her colleagues at the downtown Seattle Public Library to scour its holdings for relevant newspaper and magazine articles. Surprisingly, they came back with little. They couldn't locate a single published interview with a garment worker.

I told my mother I wanted to interview her again. She pushed me away, saying she had nothing more of value to contribute. She pointed out that she was no longer working. She gave me the names of friends. "Go talk to them first," she said.

We talked to them. We also interviewed Diane Wong's mother, Loan's mother, Loan's best friend, Ray Ishii's mother and Steve Goon, whose late mother was a tailor. Two museum staff members, Melanie Apostol and Van Diep, spoke movingly about their mothers.

Shannon Gee, a young videographer, filmed these interviews, sometimes teaming up with John Pai. She was a 1988 Franklin High graduate who earned her master's degree in cinema studies from New York University.

I returned to my mother. She grudgingly agreed to talk. Shannon videotaped my mother in her Stratolounger, across from her Singer sewing machine. John snapped photos. In a bright red sweater, my mother blinked back tears as she described the fatigue and hardships. Her spirits lifted as soon as she finished. The hurt flew away. In an aside, she told me she was impressed with John's gentle manner and warmth. "Is he married?" she asked. "Tell him I can introduce him to a nice young woman from China." I translated her words to him. It was my mother's way of saying thank you.

The project yielded 35 interviews. We titled the exhibition *If Tired Hands Could Talk: Stories of Asian Pacific American Garment Workers*. At the time, I had been reading James Baldwin's novel *If Beale Street Could Talk*.

Manuel Cawaling, associate artistic director of the Northwest Asian American Theatre, designed the exhibit. The gallery was converted into a factory floor with sewing machines, a cutting table, piles of fabric and bins. Videotaped interviews were projected onto a translucent curtain swaying from the ceiling. John added audio from the Filson factory. A group interview with seven former workers, including Big Yin Woo-So, appeared on a small TV. Quotes were attached like sales tag labels to the ski jackets and gloves of the women who made them.

In 2002, *Tired Hands* was recognized by the Western Museums Association as the best exhibition in the region. The *Tired Hands* exhibit marked the first time in the 100-year history of Seattle garment manufacturing that immigrant women, the backbone of that industry, had ever been publicly acknowledged, let alone featured in a museum.

I still consider my work on that project one of the most gratifying periods in my professional career. It took me deep inside my mother's life. Her experience—and that of her co-workers—was added to the historical record. She will be remembered.

On April 8, 2005, the museum opened its last major exhibition under my watch as director. Titled *Sikh Community: Over 100 Years in the Pacific Northwest*, this display arose out of a four-and-a-half year program partnership between Wing Luke staffers and the South Asian American community following the September 11, 2001, tragedy. The opening program was so crowded that disappointed visitors were turned away.

Charlene and Sikh Coalition co-founder Jasmit Singh, two consummate bridge-builders, led the effort. They drew connections between the bigotry against Japanese Americans during World War II and the recent targeting of South Asians. The two worked with a multiracial coalition on a candlelight vigil in Hing Hay Park to remember two hate crime victims, Chinese American Vincent Chin and Sikh American S. Balbir Singh Sodhl, murdered nearly 20 years apart.

In 2005, I visited the Gurudwara Sahib Seattle, a major Sikh temple in Renton, with others from the museum. Before entering, we took off our shoes and covered our heads with fabric in a show of respect. Sitting on the carpeted floor, we listened to prayers and music. It reminded me of being at the Chùa Việt Nam with Loan and her parents. I felt an exquisite sense of harmony and calm. John Lennon's song *Imagine* echoed through my brain. The service was followed by a delicious vegetarian meal and rich conversation.

I prayed that the new museum would be suffused with the same spirit of cooperation and tolerance that I felt that evening.

CHAPTER 55

Exploring Chinese American
Heritage Sites

A S A NATIVE OF SEATTLE, I was thoroughly a creature of the city. I thought I was exactly where I needed to be to find and study my heritage. I assumed that all Chinese American history was rooted in urban Chinatowns. I later found out how wrong I was.

As a child, I never left the city. I never walked through a pasture, saw a barn or tractor or watched a cow being milked. The only time I saw a live horse was during the Seafair Festival when members of the Seattle Mounted Patrol paraded through downtown. I stared as the horses click-clacked down Fourth Avenue, pooping as they pranced along, their excrement hurriedly scraped from the pavement by trailing workers with square shovels.

Seattle historian Doug Chin first kindled my interest in rural history. In 1973, Doug and his twin brother Art wrote *Up Hill: The Settlement and Diffusion of Chinese in Seattle, Washington*. It explained that Chinese immigrants farmed, fished and mined before settling in the city. I also discovered Lorraine

Hildebrand's *Straw Hats, Sandals and Steel: The Chinese in Washington State*. That book, published in 1977, documented the Chinese presence before the anti-Chinese uprisings in 1885 and 1886.

In 1989, Dale Hom came by the Commission on Asian American Affairs. Although he grew up on Beacon Hill, he worked as a district ranger at the Okanogan National Forest. Dale was passionate about promoting cultural diversity in government. He wanted to entice Asian Americans into careers in forestry and land management. Dale told me that recent archaeological excavations yielded objects abandoned by early Chinese miners, railroad workers and farmers as well as by other minority pioneers. He grumbled that collectors were scavenging these finds. At small-town museums, he spied Florida Water Bottles and small thin bottles with corks that he had seen in his grandmother's house. They were mislabeled as "Chinese opium."

Our conversations made me think about the unsung settlers who had shaped the land in places now isolated from streams of Chinese American habitation.

After I joined the Wing Luke Museum. Dale and I met again. He had moved to the Sawtooth National Forest in central Idaho. He coaxed me into collaborating on two Chinese heritage conferences. Olivia Taguinod organized both. The first was held at Lake Chelan in 1992; the second was in Port Townsend in 1993. Funding was provided through a U.S. Forest Service initiative called "Windows of the Past." The Port Townsend conference coincided with the 50th anniversary of the repeal of the Chinese Exclusion Act. Jimmy Mar and Raymond Chinn were speakers, along with San Francisco filmmaker Loni Ding.

Publicity about the heritage conferences reached the

Colville Indian Reservation in north-central Washington. I received a letter from the chair of the tribal council, who invited me to come and interview several Native American elders with Chinese surnames. When I called, he explained that in the late 1800s, Chinese laborers fled onto the reservation for safety after being attacked by racist white miners. Some Chinese married Native American women. Their offspring had rich stories to tell. "You shouldn't wait," he urged. "These folks are getting on in years."

I called Laura Wong-Whitebear. She said she would gladly accompany me to the reservation. She knew her way around. Growing up, Laura spent summers on the reservation, attending tribal council meetings with her mom. Laura's mother had property there, harvesting timber and selling it until she passed away in 1968. But before Laura and I had a chance to go, I received a tearful phone call from a staff member of the tribal council informing me that the chair had been killed in an accident involving a drunk driver. Our expedition was shelved.

Instead, Laura, Susie Chin and I journeyed to the small town of Sequim and Dungeness Spit on March 27, 1992, to do our own Chinese heritage tour. We heard that Chinese laborers worked in that obscure Clallam County region in the late 1800s and early 1900s as potato growers and houseboys. Laura drove us in a burgundy Chrysler she called her "pow-wow van."

We visited local author and historian Harriet Fish, quite elderly at the time, in her home. Fish told us that when she was a girl, there was only one Chinese resident left. He worked as a servant. Everyone else had died or moved away. I flinched when she used the word "Chinamen." She didn't know the term was offensive. I didn't correct her. We were guests at her house.

I was reminded of two earlier incidents when the use of the term "Chinaman" deeply offended me. A booklet on Chinese historical sites, distributed during the Chinese heritage conference at Lake Chelan, referred to "Chinamen" without quotation marks. I pointed this out to Dale. But when he informed the author, a veteran researcher, she reacted very defensively. On another occasion in the early 1970s, my UW English writing professor used the word "Chinaman" twice. We were in his Padelford Hall office, discussing my class paper. "Please don't use that word," I finally said, my anger rising. "It's racist." He was taken aback, explaining that he didn't know the term was unacceptable.

After our visit with Harriet Fish, Laura, Susie and I drove to Diamond Point, former site of a federal quarantine station where Chinese immigrants were "disinfected" and processed when they first arrived. All that was left was a surgeon's home—placed on the National Register of Historical Places in 1989—and the scattered remains of a former dock near the water. The three of us paused for a long time to marvel at the scenic beauty of the Dungeness Spit, a narrow strip of land stretching across the Strait of Juan de Fuca into the distant horizon.

Several years after the Chinese heritage conferences, Dale Hom cooked up a new idea. "Ron, why don't we do something a little more interactive this time?" he said. "How about renting a chartered bus and bringing community members out to some historical sites." My face instantly brightened. "Sign me up right now, Dale!"

After working out the tricky logistics, the Wing Luke Museum and the U.S. Forest Service collaborated on a five-day bus tour to Chinese American sites in Oregon and Idaho in 1994. The route, adjusted at the last minute because of forest fires, included stops in Pendleton, John Day, Baker City, Sumpter and Granite in Oregon; and Boise and Idaho City in Idaho.

The tour organizers were Olivia and Alina Hua, another

young museum staffer. As before, Olivia put in many long nights. She took breaks at Louie's Broiler, a 24-hour grill just around the corner from the museum on King Street. She dined on the cheap, ordering a baked potato with toppings of sour cream, bacon bits, cheese and green onions for just 29 cents.

Dean Wong and John Pai videotaped the tour, hoping to revive Kingstreet Media. Annie Xuan Clark joined the film crew as a new Kingstreet member. John trailed the tour bus in his own equipment van, a GMC 3500 Vandura that he dubbed "White Buffalo." Carey Quan Gelernter, who wrote a feature about me in *The Seattle Times*, and Alan Lau also came along to document the trip.

Carey had become a good friend. She arrived from California to start a job at *The Seattle Times* just days after the Mount St. Helens volcanic eruption, steering through a thick cloud of falling volcanic ash in her white VW Rabbit. She and her husband Jerry Large arrived at *The Times* during the height of the paper's efforts to diversify. Paula Bock, Lily Eng, Florangela Davila, Ferdinand De Leon, Alex Tizon and Barry Wong, who all became friends and associates of mine, were part of this talented wave.

Tour participants included Clifton Goon, Cassie Chinn and her mother, Seattle elder Bing Lum and his wife, musician-composer Byron Auyong and his mother, Wing Luke board member Helen Kay, Los Angeles residents Josie Woo and her daughter Serena, and Maxine Chan.

We discovered that our personal histories were deeply interwoven. Clifton was the grandson of Goon Dip. Clifton's eldest son was my best friend Steve Goon. Bing Lum had worked in one of the Goon Dip canneries in Bellingham as a young boy. Josie Woo, a former Seattleite, was married to Henry Woo, the son of Woo Gen, a partner in Wa Chong Company. Woo Gen had helped my grandfather enter this country in 1911. Serena and I were shirt-tail relatives. Helen Kay's grandfather Bob Wah took over the practice of the famous herbal doctor "Doc Hay" at Kam Wah Chung Company, which we were slated to visit in John Day. John Pai had worked at Louie's Cuisine of China in Ballard alongside Alina's mother.

Before the trip, Maxine and I found out that we were distantly related on our paternal side. It was a shocker. We were such opposites. She was loud and flamboyant. I was reserved and cerebral. Max was born in Hong Kong. I was born in Seattle. She was a Cantonese speaker. I was Hoisanese. I said, "But, shit, we're cousins!" She began to address me as her cousin, pronouncing the word "*ah-cah-sun.*"

After Max informed her father Robert, he visited me at the museum, bringing huge slabs of fresh roasted pork wrapped in butcher paper. Her mother came by during a shopping trip to Chinatown. She told me in Chinese that she worried incessantly about Maxine. "Please help Maxine find a nice Chinese boyfriend," she begged. "She's getting old and I don't want her to be alone." I reassured her that I would see what I could do.

During our journey, the tour group members evolved into a tight-knit family, moving beyond our superficial connections. We found ourselves reacting in the same way to the different sites we explored. Along the way, we established a collective identity in the vanished settlements, stony cliffs, silent river banks and verdant forests of the Pacific Northwest.

One of our first stops was Pendleton, a town along the Umatilla River in eastern Oregon. We learned that there had once been a bustling Chinese community of former railroad workers there. We bought tickets for the popular Pendleton Underground Tour. It was billed as an authentic tour of "The Real West." We were appalled. A guide led us through a series of connected passageways and rooms filled with bordellos, "secret Chinese opium dens" and "Chinese jails." Our history had been mangled and sensationalized for profit. We complained, but the tour managers weren't moved. The displays stayed as they were.

The Pendleton tour reminded me of the persistent myth of secret tunnels under Seattle's Chinatown. When asked, I said, "No, there's no such thing," then referred further inquiry to the Seattle Underground Tour in Pioneer Square. There, early storefronts and roads were entombed when the city rebuilt on top of the ruins after the Great Fire of 1889.

We were relieved to arrive in John Day, a small town in eastern Oregon that was home to more than 500 Chinese residents in the late 1880s. Still standing was the Kam Wah Chung Company (金華中藥店), a stone building with a canted wood roof. Built as a trading post in the 1860s, it was run by Ing "Doc" Hay, the famed Chinese herbal doctor, and Lung On, proprietor of the store. The building was abandoned in 1952 and deeded to the city of John Day in 1975.

The thoughtfully preserved interior reminded me of Yick Fung & Company. It was filled with old furniture, clothing, herbs, bottles, crates, account books, letters and store merchandise from the late 1880s and early 1900s. Many of the herbs and tonics were the same ones in my parents' Beacon Hill home. The faded red Chinese couplets that adorned the walls were the same ones in use today.

Helen Kay—her surname at birth was Eng (伍), the same as Doc Hay—remembered the store from the summers she spent there as a child. She sat on a swing in a nearby park while I asked her questions. Her parents had operated a restaurant in Newport, Washington. They dropped her and her brother off to stay with their grandfather, who cared for the aging Doc

Hay after apprenticing with him and taking over his practice. Helen recalled her grandfather leading Doc Hay, who had become blind, around in the courtyard by a rope outside the store.

Just north of nearby Granite, Oregon, we visited an early Chinese settlement established by the Ah Hee Placer Mining Company. Near a stretch of Granite Creek, we walked up a steep path alongside gigantic walls constructed of hand-stacked rocks. These were the tailings left by a mining operation. We carefully navigated over the steep and treacherous rock piles, holding the hands of older tour members to make sure they didn't trip. We shook our heads in wonder. How did the Chinese manage to muscle these huge boulders into place by hand?

After Granite, we visited the Sumpter Valley Dredge, site of an enormous apparatus built near the Powder River. The dredge featured a massive boom with 72 one-ton buckets that scooped up loose rock and filtered it for gold through an elaborate sluicing process. The dredge had fallen into disuse after 1954. Miles and miles of tailings lined the banks of the river. The site was a state heritage area. Marveling at the scale of the gold-digging operation and the harshness of the gouged landscape, I suddenly felt like the main character in the 1957 sci-fi movie *The Incredible Shrinking Man*.

Thirty miles east of Sumpter, we arrived in Baker City. It once had a bustling Chinatown with half a dozen stores and a population of 400. The residents included mine workers, laundrymen, vegetable growers, cooks, servants and fishermen. As we stood in a parched sagebrush-covered field near a highway, a local resident told our group about abandoned Chinese gravesites nearby. Some had been paved over during road construction. Maxine and I looked at each other, shaking our heads. We thought about the indignity perpetrated on the nameless pioneers after their deaths.

The trip changed me. I felt rejuvenated. History, which I once thought of as something to be wearily extracted from dusty tomes, danced in front of me, like a still orchestra suddenly brought to life with a conductor's baton. A flood of latent memories—harkening back to childhood when I played freely in the woods near my home—was stirred by this plunge into rural history. I left hoping to visit other heritage sites someday.

In July 2010, liberated from my demanding role at the Wing Luke Museum, I participated in a second Chinese bus tour. Expenses were again underwritten through a cooperative agreement between the Wing Luke Museum and the U.S. Forest Service. Dale had become forest supervisor at the Olympic National Forest. Now a parent, I brought my two young sons with me. Nearly 40 others joined the group.

Handling logistics were Dorothy Ng from the museum and Aleta Eng from the U.S. Forest Service. Dorothy grew up in Seattle's Rainier Valley and graduated from Franklin High School in 1999. Her mother and grandmother worked at Roffe. Aleta, who had been mentored by Dale, was the granddaughter of Florence Chin Eng, the remarkable storyteller of Chinatown. Like me, Dale felt relaxed, having passed his responsibilities on to the next generation. His wife Rebecca, a master storyteller from Olympia, told stories during fatiguing stretches on the highway. John Pai and Maxine Chan returned for this second trip. Maxine Loo, whose family owned the Quong Wah poultry shop on South King Street, and former *Seattle P-I* reporter Brad Wong joined, too.

Fred Yee and his wife Clara were also new to the heritage tour. Fred's bilingual skills were helpful in deciphering Chinese writing on unidentified artifacts. During the seven-day journey, we revisited some of the same Asian historic settlements in Oregon and Idaho included in the previous tour. This time, we skipped Pendleton and included other sites in Nevada.

Baker City had changed. As we stepped off the tour bus, we saw in the distance a new stone pathway, memorial marker and small shrine. It was hot and very windy. We gathered at the shrine to perform a ceremonial tribute organized by Bettie Luke. She led us through the lighting of incense and the burning of joss paper in a metal box. Bettie first politely asked me if she could enlist the help of my sons Cian and Kino. "Sure, Bettie," I responded. "Just pretend you're the parent. Tell them exactly what they should do." She laughed. Kino handed a stick of incense to each person and a piece of joss paper to light. Cian held the metal box and closed the lid after each participant placed their burning joss paper inside.

As we concluded, a red-tailed hawk swooped down through the bright blue sky, circling just above our heads before soaring off into the distance. "Look at that," Maxine said to me. "The restless spirits have been set free." The bird provided a magical conclusion to the poignant ceremony.

Arriving at the Sumpter Valley Dredge, we went to a small visitor center where my kids panned for gold. Cian and Kino each extracted a little gold dust from the water. They placed the sparkling gold particles in a tiny bottle as a souvenir.

After visiting the Idaho Historical Museum in Boise, which housed artifacts from a once-thriving Chinatown, we went on to Tuscarora, a ghost town in Elko County, Nevada. We stopped in a barren field under the hot sun and listened to Forest Service archaeologist Fred Frampton talk about the 2,000 Chinese immigrants who worked as placer miners and dug irrigation ditches. We spotted scattered bottles and other objects on the ground. We paid respects to these unknown Chinese laborers at a nearby burial site.

We drove on to Winnemucca, pulling off the highway after

our tour bus overheated. It was over 90 degrees outside. Luckily, we were near an air-conditioned McDonald's. My kids and the younger tour participants gleefully darted inside. After the driver got the bus started again, we continued along Interstate 95 to Carson City, where we stopped at the Nevada State Museum to examine historical artifacts brought to us by an Asian American staffer.

We continued on to Virginia City, wearily checking into our hotel. That evening, we were treated to a one-woman show at the Piper Opera House presented by University of Nevada historian Sue Fawn Chung. She adopted the costume and persona of Loy Lily Lee Ford, a Chinese woman born in California in 1882.

At our final dinner, participants offered personal thoughts about our journey. The room swelled with emotion. When it was my turn, I said I had been strengthened by a newfound appreciation for the pioneer struggle and the land. I said I would cherish this second heritage tour because Cian and Kino had come with me. I turned to my kids and said, "You'll always have a history here. No one can take that away from you."

In a last gesture, tour coordinators Dorothy and Aleta surprised Dale with the gift of a cowboy hat. Dale was speechless. It was a lovely moment. Although he treasured the present, he didn't wear it often. It was a half-inch too big. No one could ever accuse Dale of being big-headed.

I thought back to the Washington pre-college test I took before graduating from Franklin High School. It had predicted for me a possible career in forestry. While that wasn't the path I chose, it was uncanny how I arrived in the same space as Dale Hom.

CHAPTER 56

Lessons in Philanthropy

I N 1980, DURING MY ONE-YEAR hiatus from the *Examiner*, I worked for a nonprofit foundation called the McKenzie River Gathering (MRG). It was my first time in grant-making. The experience took me far outside my work passions and social comfort zone. In the end, it did me a lot of good. It introduced me to philanthropy. It cultivated skills that prepared me to fundraise for the Wing Luke Museum.

MRG was established in 1976 by 30 white social change activists who met on the banks of the McKenzie River in Oregon. Leslie and Jack Gray, an idealistic couple who inherited $500,000, wanted to figure out how to distribute the money to preserve the natural environment of the Pacific Northwest and address problems of social inequity.

The group set up community boards or "caucuses" in Eugene and Portland to allocate those funds to small, progressive nonprofits. I was hired to staff a caucus in Seattle to extend MRG's reach into Washington state. We awarded grants ranging from several hundred dollars to $5,000 to support projects in three categories: community organizing, human rights, and energy and environment. For the first time in my life, I got to hand out money, not plead for it. It was satisfying.

My office was on the 12th floor of the Smith Tower, a grand and hallowed space filled with rich marble and big windows. I was next door to the National Lawyers Guild and the Unemployment Representation Clinic. Gary Iwamoto, who just graduated from law school, worked as a staff attorney for the clinic. The building had a bank of old brass elevators run by uniformed elevator operators. This made for very long waits getting to and from my office. Several operators were not very skillful at lining up the elevator cage to the level of the floor. I got dizzy watching them struggle. I read an article listing the most stressful professions, leading to short life expectancies. Journalists and elevator operators were near the top.

I inherited a Seattle caucus without any people of color. I quickly invited Craig Shimabukuro, Art Ceniza and two other activist friends—Ron Dickens and Jeanette Aguilar—to join. I met Ron at the UW. He was a chatty African American who ended all his sentences with the phrase "You dig?" He jokingly referred to me as his twin because of our common first names. He wore plaid flannel shirts and a dark knit cap—even in the midst of summer—and drove a beat-up Volkswagen bus that shook loudly and died in traffic.

Jeanette worked at El Centro de la Raza. I met her when she was a receptionist at the Country Doctor Clinic. She grumbled to me about the sexism at El Centro and white hippie racism at the Clinic. She was from El Paso, Texas. Like Uncle Bob, her father was a boxer. She made a point of calling herself Mexican American. She said "Chicano" was a watered-down term. She found it amusing that she was always mistaken for Filipina in Seattle. She kidded Roberto Maestas that he was probably a

Spaniard because of his pale complexion. From Jeanette, I easily learned more conversational Spanish than I had from all my Spanish classes. She taught me how to make *menudo, mole* and handmade flour tortillas.

I felt ill at ease when I dealt with MRG donors, especially those in Portland and Eugene. I had a testy disagreement with a young white woman who gave a big hug to everyone after the end of meetings. I didn't reciprocate. "What's wrong?" she asked. I told her I didn't hug strangers. "But we're not strangers," she protested. She wanted to talk about it. I didn't. She suggested that my inability to touch her was a sign of emotional inhibition. I was offended, but I held my tongue. I told Art Ceniza about the incident. He chuckled sympathetically.

At a dinner meeting at a Portland donor's home, the hosts served unrecognizable vegetarian fare. There was a load of cheese. I didn't see anything I wanted to eat. I asked if I could help. The woman in the kitchen said, "Sure, why don't you bring this pot of soup out to the dining room? Careful, it's hot." When I asked where I should put it, she responded, "Oh, just put it on the trivet." I felt stupid. *What was a "trivet?"* I walked around aimlessly until someone else arrived. He pulled out a metal accordion-like tray on the side of the dining table. I looked up the word in the dictionary after I got back home.

During my time at MRG, I helped organize several "inherited wealth conferences." These were support groups held in secret among young activists trying to figure out what to do with their money. They felt guilty being born into financial and social privilege. When George Pillsbury, an heir to the Pillsbury Company fortune and a prominent ambassador for this alternative fund movement, came into town, my job was to drive him to one of these private gatherings.

George—who had been derisively dubbed the "Pillsbury

dough boy" by the media—was a handsome, clean-cut young man with a sparkling smile and a big mustache. His long brown hair was parted neatly in the middle. He wore a casual sports jacket, shirt with a wide collar, and slacks. He recently appeared with Leslie Gray on the popular national TV talk show *Donahue* to explain the new philanthropy.

After George came to my office, we headed out for the evening's meeting. After consulting the Texaco gas station road map in my glove compartment, we got into my decrepit Dodge Dart Swinger. I drove north to Laurelhurst, a quiet, upscale Seattle neighborhood. I got lost. George took the wheel, adroitly steering us to a large driveway outside a primly landscaped home set back behind a large gate. I was unable to open the gate without George's help. The only fence I had ever opened before was the padlocked chain link fence surrounding my parent's home, installed after my sister and I moved away. My parents' security fence had a row of barbed wire on top. This fence was nice to look at.

I spent the evening awkwardly trying to build rapport with attendees who were more interested in sharing stories about boarding school with one another than in talking to me. I was politely ignored. Even though my stomach was growling, the meat-free dishes and vegan ice cream didn't appeal to me. I nibbled on a few crackers.

George made a short, impassioned pitch for attendees to support social change causes like MRG. At the end of the night, I collected a few completed pledge forms. The yield was modest.

I lasted at MRG for about a year. I returned to the *Examiner* in August 1981 for a second round as editor, happy to be back in an ethnically diverse environment. Nevertheless, the MRG experience helped me understand the subtle interplay between the emotions of givers and receivers. I had taken my first baby steps into the world of philanthropy.

In 2000, Terry Collings, executive director of the Seattle Public Library Foundation, asked me to join the Libraries for All campaign to help raise money for a new downtown library and 22 neighborhood branches. Terry had done his homework. He knew the Beacon Hill branch sheltered me when I was growing up. He also knew that I was starting an ambitious effort to remodel an old hotel in the International District into the Wing Luke Museum's permanent home.

"Ron, our City Librarian Deborah Jacobs and I would love to have you be part of this library campaign because of your local roots," he said to me over lunch. "But I think you could benefit too because you'll get a chance to work alongside other people who know fundraising and are donors themselves. They could help your museum campaign, too."

I also met with Deborah over lunch in Chinatown. She was appointed to her position in November 1997. She impressed me with her big dreams, searing passion and relentless drive.

I joined the Seattle Public Library Foundation board.

My world expanded. The board was loaded with prominent philanthropists. They included Anne Farrell, a gracious and quietly effective consensus-builder who built the Seattle Foundation into a powerhouse; Charles Riley, executive vice president of U.S. Bank, a warm, upbeat man who exploded my stereotype of the aloof banker; David Skinner, an independent filmmaker and arts supporter with spunk and fire; Gil Anderson, former CEO of Redmond-based Physio-Control, Inc., who had a puckish sense of humor; Matt Medlin, a partner at international financial services firm KPMG, who often joined me at hole-in-the wall Chinese restaurants for lunch; David Williams, president of Harris Private Bank, who later joined the Wing Luke Museum board; and Lalie Scandiuzzi, a compassionate soul who invented Moonjar, a brilliantly simple tool for teaching financial literacy and social responsibility to children.

I also met Faye Allen, an avid bookworm. She convinced her son, Microsoft co-founder Paul Allen, to give a $20 million lead gift to the library campaign. I was flattered that she invited Loan and me for tea and pastries at her waterfront estate on Mercer Island. Her home was one big library, with rows and rows of bookshelves. I browsed the titles. I felt like I was back at Shorey's. She also had on display the original manuscript for *Dracula*. She laughed about discarding Paul's childhood pulp science fiction titles, only to find out that Paul had to spend considerable sums re-acquiring those same publications.

Loan asked Faye about her life goals. Faye looked at the two of us and said, "I'd love to see Paul settle down with someone. That would make me happy." Loan persisted, "Do you know if he's seeing anyone?" Faye shook her head: "If he is, he hasn't told me yet." As she spoke about Paul, I heard the voice of a doting mother.

Faye invited us to join her and Paul on his private jet to see a Portland Trailblazers game. Paul owned the NBA basketball team. "Which game do you want to see?" she asked. I chose Michael Jordan's last contest against the Trailblazers. It was his 1997 retirement season. Loan and I sat in the front row. Air Jordan, even in the twilight of his career, managed to score 20 points. The game was interrupted by several loud antiwar protesters, who were quickly led away by security guards. Faye turned to me and opined, "I don't know why they need to be arrested. They're not hurting anybody." This gave me the first clear sense of her political beliefs.

During the library campaign, I reconnected with Suzanne

Hittman, a former Seattle School Board member who spear-headed passage of the city-wide mandatory desegregation plan in 1977. I met Suzanne, a southeast Seattle resident, during my time at the Coalition for Quality Integrated Education. She worked closely with community advocates like Arlene Oki to pass the "Seattle Plan" so that the school district wouldn't lose control of the schools to a federal court.

Suzanne joined the library foundation board shortly before I did. We became buddies. At meetings, she turned to me and complained that I was too skinny: "You need to eat more." I made a face and retorted, "Right, *mom*!" Soon she began to say, "You need to eat more, *son*." I kept in touch with my second "mom" since the library campaign, joining her for lunch at her condo on First Hill to gossip about community politics and discuss our mutual disdain for political incompetents.

As I prepared for the Wing Luke Museum campaign, I also tried to learn as much as I could about other Asian American campaigns in Seattle that preceded ours. I knew of three—Keiro, the Japanese nursing home; Kin On, the Chinese nursing home; and International District Village Square, a complex consisting of senior housing and social services.

Tomio Moriguchi, president of the Seattle JACL, and Tosh Okamoto, commander of the Nisei Veterans Committee, headed up the Keiro effort. Tomio I knew well. We served on some of the same boards. I was touched by his humility, which belied his influence and power. When I stopped by Uwajimaya to get a take-out lunch from the deli, I saw him in the check-out area wheeling shopping carts back to their proper places and bagging purchases for customers. During the closing hours of the ID Summer Festival, he picked up garbage off the street with his hands and climbed up to the top of an open dumpster, jumping up and down to tamp down an overflow of trash.

The Keiro nursing home opened in a remodeled 63-bed facility in 1976. A second campaign allowed Keiro to relocate into a new 150-bed facility in 1987. Buoyed by these successes, money was raised to build Nikkei Manor, an assisted-living facility in the International District.

These efforts inspired a nursing home drive in the Chinese community. The project was dubbed Kin On. "Kin" (健) means healthy; "On" is peaceful (安). In 1987, Keiro's old facility reopened as Kin On Nursing Home after a gutsy $500,000 campaign. A decade later, a $3.5 million drive allowed Kin On to move into a newly-constructed 100-bed facility. The campaigns were spearheaded by Ben Woo, board president, and Ark Chin, fundraising chair.

I knew a bit about the Kin On campaign. I served on the publicity committee under Jeni Fung, an elder from the Lock clan in Olympia. For years, she faithfully served on the board, produced the newsletter and recruited volunteers. Her dominant concern—echoed by other board members—was steering clear of divisive community politics, which meant keeping Ruby Chow at a distance.

Ark was a partner in a prominent engineering firm in Seattle and served on the UW Board of Regents. His fussy, long-winded elocution—in both English and Chinese—and his snappy plaid sports jackets and bright bow ties concealed his modest origins. He immigrated to the U.S. at the age of 10 and grew up in Aberdeen, Washington, working in the Canton Café, his father's *chop suey* restaurant. When I told him I was planning to raise over $23 million, he arched his bushy white eyebrows in surprise. "Really?" he said, more as a statement than a question. "You are going to have to be very persistent. That's an awful lot of money."

Ben, Ark and Tomio reminded me that a pan-Asian American museum on the scale that I envisioned would be exceedingly difficult because there was no precedent, either in the region or anywhere else in the nation. "Where are your big gifts going to come from?" they asked.

I told them that I believed Seattle, with its progressive history, would be an ideal proving ground for a multi-pronged Asian American fundraising drive; and that I would reach out to both Asian and non-Asian donors. I said the library's campaign had expanded my vision of what was possible.

I visited Annie Xuan Clark to find out more about ID Village Square, which opened in April 1998 following a four-year campaign. I wanted to find out how Annie had raised $3.5 million in private donations.

"I don't know if I can help you," she began, laughing. "I think you know most of the same donors that we tapped. You'll just have to find a hell of a lot more donors and ask each of them for lots more money. My hat's off to you if you can do it."

Annie, a graduate of The Evergreen State College, was only 24 when Sue Taoka, director of the Seattle Chinatown-International District Preservation and Development Authority (SCIDpda), hired her. It was a big leap of faith. Annie, who previously worked for Bob Santos as his administrative assistant, had no prior capital campaign experience.

Uncle Bob had long harbored the dream of developing an empty parcel of land at Eighth Avenue South and Dearborn Street into a community center for three organizations he helped found: Denise Louie Early Childhood Education Center, Asian Counseling and Referral Service, and International Community Health Services. After SCIDpda acquired the property from King County Metro, it fell to Sue and others to put flesh and bones on Uncle Bob's dream. As I talked to Annie, I got a real picture of how much heavy lifting might be required to reach our museum goal. "It was a *l-o-n-g* four years," she told me.

These conversations made me think hard about how much blood, sweat and tears might be extracted for a new museum. I wasn't deterred. But if I was going to do it, there was no point in stalling. Time would be my worst adversary.

CHAPTER 57

On the National Stage

THROUGH COLLEGE, I STAYED SAFELY inside the bubble of Seattle. I never ventured outside Washington state, except to eat in Vancouver, B.C.'s Chinatown. I never flew on an airplane. I didn't have luggage. I didn't own a suit or tie. I never hailed a taxi. I never stayed overnight in a nice hotel. I didn't even know what room service was.

In 1972, at the ripe age of 19, I took my first big trip. "Geez, it's about time we went somewhere, don't you think?" my sister Linda said to me. We boarded a Greyhound bus for a one-week adventure in San Francisco's Chinatown. My parents called it *Ai Fow* (大埠) or "Big Port City." She and I stayed in a cheap, run-down hotel on the edge of Chinatown.

I gawked at everything. *So many Chinese-speaking people in one place!* We walked up and down Grant Avenue, Stockton Street and Kearny Street. We explored alleys lined with elaborate fire escapes and balconies. We bought thick, juicy strips of homemade beef jerky (牛肉乾) from a street vendor. We strolled through shops crammed with books and magazines,

491

paintings, scrolls, Buddha statues, clothing, fabric, souvenirs, toys, kites, herbs, candies and martial arts supplies. I took a dozen black-and-white photos of street scenes with a new Kodak Instamatic camera, my only mementos of that journey.

I went on my second trip in the late summer of 1976, a year after college. Steve Goon and I drove to Sacramento in his beige 1965 Dodge Dart. We stayed a few days with his aunt and uncle, Gladys and Harry Choi. Steve's car featured a Slant-6 engine, touted as dependable and trouble-free. But the car's aging heater was stuck in the "on" position, making for a sweat-dripping ride as we passed through the Siskiyou Mountains. On our drive back, we heard on the car radio the big news that Chairman Mao had passed away, opening wild speculation about China's future.

These were my only two out-of-state forays during my early 20s. Clearly, a sophisticated and well-rounded globetrotter I was not. "Beacon Hill bumpkin" was probably a more fitting description.

Later, as *International Examiner* editor, I was invited to speak at a journalism conference in Los Angeles. I stayed at the New Otani Hotel in Little Tokyo. When I opened the door to my room, I was dazzled by what I saw: tailored window drapes, a huge bed plumped up with soft bed linens and lush blankets, framed wall art and a stylish leather club chair. The sparkling bathroom counter was lined with mini-bottles of shampoo, bars of soap and skin lotion. A small refrigerator was stocked with beverages and small packets of cookies and nuts. I thought the snacks were free; I greedily ate them all. When I returned to my room after each day's sessions, the refrigerator was replenished. Finally, on the last day of my trip, during checkout, I was presented with a bill of nearly $50. Embarrassed, I learned the meaning of "incidental" hotel charges.

I decided to upscale my wardrobe so I wouldn't look so glaringly underdressed in formal settings. I bought a brown corduroy sport coat and two patterned silk ties from Sears. I found them in the *see-lop fong* bargain basement. With the help of illustrations in John T. Molloy's *Dress for Success*, I figured out how to tie the Windsor, half-Windsor, and four-in-hand knots.

Serena exclaimed, "Hey dare, Ronnie! Kind of *dressy-wessy* today. Must be going out to look for money." Ken peered up from his computer, squinting to see what kind of dimpled knot I tied. "Hmm. Looks kind of bulky—like some kind of cancerous growth. Must be a Windsor. No? I take that back. It's not quite that bulky. It must be a half-Windsor. It can't be the other one with the single loop because it looks fairly symmetrical. Final answer is 'half-Windsor.' Did I get it right?" At community events, Ken and I secretly scoured all the ties in the room, trying to guess how each was knotted.

Greg Tuai was a step ahead of me. He learned how to tie a bow tie from a magazine. Greg helped Maxine Chan cater private parties, weddings and other events. Maxine started Foreign Affairs Catering, which specialized in Asian nouveau cuisine. Those who worked for her—part-timers like Greg from the community—had to wear black-and-white dress attire.

The Wing Luke Museum propelled me onto a national stage. I was asked to speak on many panels, participate in workshops and join boards. At first, I turned away opportunities. I didn't feel ready. But I knew I needed to make these forays outside Seattle not only to represent my institution, but to cultivate funders and supporters outside my home base.

It took some time for me to feel at ease in large mainstream settings. In April 1994, at my first American Association of Museums (AAM) conference, held in Seattle, I went to the breakfast for museum directors. The banquet room was nearly devoid of any people of color except the wait staff. I didn't see anyone I knew. I felt like a Martian on Earthling soil. My plate was loaded with butter-drenched items which I couldn't digest and a grapefruit half which I didn't know how to eat properly. I left everything untouched.

With practice, I developed the confidence to deliver a lecture to an audience of unfamiliar, attentive faces, though the memory of a flubbed speech in high school haunted me. My mother told me what she did as a schoolgirl: "Drink a little water before you talk. It helps you relax, keep your throat moist and focus on what you have to do."

I began to travel frequently. I flew to Washington, D.C., to serve as a grant panelist for three federal agencies: the National Endowment for the Humanities (NEH), the Institute of Museum and Library Services, and the National Endowment for the Arts. I participated in long grant review sessions at the Old Post Office, a colossal Romanesque structure with a clock tower on Pennsylvania Avenue. (In 2016, the building was remodeled into a garish Trump International Hotel.)

Teresa Fang, my assistant at the Wing Luke Museum, scheduled my flights and booked hotels. She bought a Casio Cassiopeia, an early handheld personal computer, to consolidate all my contacts. On my flights back to Seattle, I used the tiny keyboard on my palm pilot to peck out board reports.

I gained insight into federal policy trends. I positioned the Wing Luke Museum for national grants.

I served as a reviewer for the Museum Loan Network in Boston, which provided support for long-term exchanges of cultural objects between institutions. Lori Gross, the founding director, recruited me. There, I served alongside Stephen Weil, a noted Smithsonian Institution scholar who chaired meetings.

I saw how he patiently and cleverly crafted consensus. From listening to his witty asides, I learned how museums had morphed from "cabinets of curiosity" into educational institutions serving nobler public purposes.

Claudine Brown, program director of the arts and culture program at the Nathan Cummings Foundation in New York City, guided me into national conversations. Claudine had previously worked at the Smithsonian. She left following the demoralizing failure of an effort to secure congressional funding to build a national African American museum on the National Mall in Washington, D.C. Claudine was luminously wise, calm and centered. She became my mentor, reassuring me during moments of personal doubt. She shared advice about museums—and parenting—over dinner in cozy New York restaurants. In later years, she returned to the Smithsonian to direct its work in educating children.

Marjorie Schwarzer, chair of the museum studies program at JFK University in Berkeley, became my West Coast sounding board. She wrote articles for *Museum News*, the magazine of the American Association of Museums. We met at a conference in Anchorage, Alaska. She described me as "honest and funny, two qualities often lacking in the museum world."

Marjorie invited me to speak to her museum studies class in 2003. We convened at the newly renovated YWCA building in San Francisco's Chinatown, home of the Chinese Historical Society of America. I reconnected with Melissa Szeto, a docent at the Wing Luke Museum from 1994 to 1997. She had just completed an impressive fundraising campaign for the Chinatown museum.

In October 2001, I presented a workshop at the Oral History Association conference in St. Louis. By then, I gained a national reputation as an authority on oral history. I evangelized about oral histories as a tool for interactive exhibitions and social justice.

In April 2005, the New Mexico Association of Museums invited me to deliver the keynote speech at its annual conference in Santa Fe. Now a single parent, I told Fran Levine, director of the Palace of the Governors, that I couldn't come because of my two young kids. "Don't worry," she reassured me. "Bring them. We'll pay." Mimi Roberts, director of traveling exhibits at the Museum of New Mexico, offered up her son Jacob for childcare. Cian and Kino explored the city's adobe buildings and visited the Santa Fe Indian Market on the plaza of the Palace of the Governors; I lectured about the keys to institutional transformation.

A high moment was serving on the National Council on the Humanities, the advisory body to the NEH. President Bill Clinton appointed me in December 2000. I was among 10 recess appointments he rushed to put in place before he left office. A museum colleague, Dr. Nina M. Archabal, director of the Minnesota Historical Society, was also named.

This was a highly charged political time. A battle raged between progressive supporters of the NEH and conservative critics who felt that the agency had tilted too far to the left. The NEH Chairman was William Ferris, a folklorist and leading authority on Southern culture. Even as he welcomed us, he expressed frustration that President Clinton had waited so long to appoint us. In the end, all of us served only a year.

We were doomed by the NEH's decision to allow legendary playwright Arthur Miller, that year's Jefferson lecturer, to go ahead with a prepared speech on March 26, 2001. Miller skewered U.S. political leaders as "actors," including George W. Bush and Republican leader Dick Armey. He spared no one. He compared Bill Clinton to Brer Rabbit, ravishing "people's vegetable gardens" before escaping down a hole. Ferris had reviewed Miller's speech and did not ask him to tone it down. We affirmed his decision.

In today's political arena—in which brazen insult and character assassination are commonplace—Miller's speech is laughably tame. But Miller's lecture prompted Supreme Court Justice Sandra Day O'Connor to walk out in disgust. It earned the disdain of conservative columnist William F. Buckley, who chastised the NEH for giving Miller a political platform. Soon the NEH came under fierce attack from Republicans. I got my first taste of how the partisan political divide plays out in Washington, D.C.

Ferris gathered his staff and NEH Council members to discuss how to respond to the controversy. All of us who spoke up felt that Miller's literary stature as author of *Death of a Salesman* and *The Crucible* earned him the right to say whatever he wanted at this late stage in his life. I offered a few suggestions as a former journalist about how we might communicate our defense of Miller. But there was no follow-up; the clock soon ran out. On June 1, President George W. Bush appointed Indiana University professor Bruce Cole to replace Ferris as the NEH chairman. My peers and I were ousted, replaced by more conservative scholars.

CHAPTER 58

Discovering Sister Institutions

A S I TRIED TO IMAGINE the new Wing Luke Museum, I was drawn to two like-minded community museums—the Museum of the Chinese in the Americas (MoCA) in New York City's Chinatown and the Japanese American National Museum (JANM) in Los Angeles's Little Tokyo. They, too, were in neighborhoods facing decay, gentrification and the loss of historical and cultural memory.

The executive directors at JANM and MoCA were relative newcomers to the museum profession. Irene Hirano joined JANM in 1988. Fay Chew Matsuda joined MoCA in 1989. We sought out one another at conferences. We commiserated about the challenges of living hand-to-mouth and trying to make our voices heard inside a profession mired in stodgy Eurocentric academic traditions.

Irene was a brilliant strategic thinker and titan fundraiser. I marveled at her ability to adroitly hopscotch into leadership roles at national foundations and at the American Association of Museums (AAM). Irene visited the Wing Luke and saw the

Executive Order 9066 exhibition. I visited JANM shortly after it opened in 1992. It was located in an ornate Buddhist temple. Irene and curator Akemi Kikumura walked me through the historic rooms, and I listened to their big vision of linking the temple to a massive new building across the plaza. They told me that our exhibition inspired the design of JANM's traveling display about Japanese Americans in Hawaii. Irene said they hoped the project, when completed, would allow JANM to pivot toward national partnerships. They were trying to develop programs for the third-generation Sansei who had grown up in a post-war multiracial society.

In 1996, I joined Irene at the 150th anniversary celebration of the Smithsonian Institution, participating in wide-ranging discussions with leaders about the future of museums.

Fay had a burning commitment to telling the vanishing story of New York Chinatown pioneers, many of them seniors. Fay had heard a lot about our museum, but she had never been to the West Coast. "You really should come visit," I urged. "I'm sorry I can't," she said. She revealed that she couldn't overcome her fear of air travel. This was the first time I had ever heard of this debilitating condition.

In 1994, three MoCA staffers—Jack Tchen, the bookish cofounder, Fabiana Chiu, deputy director of programs, and Cynthia Lee came to Seattle for the AAM conference. I walked them through the Wing Luke Museum. I told them I was embarrassed that our facility was only 7,200 square feet. But they said it looked huge. I then took them up the street to the East Kong Yick Building and described my vision of remaking it into a pan-Asian American museum.

Shortly after the MoCA gang visited me, I had the chance to reciprocate. MoCA was in an old school building on Mulberry Street. Walking up to the second floor, I was warmly greeted by Fay and Cynthia. Fay was in the middle of talking to a rowdy group of elementary school kids. I was surprised to see that the entire museum was scrunched inside four adjoining 500-square-foot classrooms, two of which served as galleries. Every available inch had been pressed into service, including the hallway. I could see why they thought the Wing Luke was spacious.

After Fay finished with the students, she led me through MoCA's main exhibition, *Where is Home? Chinese in the Americas*, which pondered questions of identity and remembrance. A translucent lantern illuminated the display. I saw old Chinese business signs, clothing from laborers, immigration papers and items from a hand laundry. The text was in English, Chinese and Spanish. Fay's bubbly hospitality made me feel welcome.

After my tour, Fay, Cynthia and Fabiana took me to *dim sum* at 20 Mott Street, a restaurant nearby. Jack joined us. His essay on "The Dialogic Museum" gave me a more precise vocabulary for what I had been trying to do at the Wing Luke. We walked through a glass door, went up a flight of stairs and sat down for a long conversation, thrilled that we had so much in common.

After listening to me describe my plan for the new Wing Luke, Fay insisted that I visit the Lower East Side Tenement Museum and talk to founder and historian Ruth Abram. She said Ruth had mastered the art of staging re-creations in old hotel apartments.

In December 2006, during a three-day trip to meet with several national foundations, I finally called Ruth. "I'd love to meet," she declared. "But you must take a tour of the museum first. Then we can sit down and talk about your project."

The Lower East Side Tenement Museum was located at 97 Orchard Street, in a desolate area next to Chinatown. I passed scores of graffiti-scarred brick buildings and piles of rubble and trash. The few people I saw on the street were panhandlers and skeletal drug addicts with vacant stares.

The museum was a beacon of hope for neighborhood revitalization to come. I waited with two dozen other visitors in a building that served as the museum visitor center, ticket office and museum shop. I was impressed with the young man who served as leader of my tour group. He was well prepared, knowledgeable and enthusiastic. He engaged us in conversation rather than lecturing as he led us through several restored apartments.

When I sat down with Ruth in her office, I told her that I was inspired by her achievement and that my dream was to remake the East Kong Yick Building into a West Coast Asian American version of the Lower East Side Tenement Museum.

Ruth cheered me on: "It's a big idea, but it's very impressive. I'm sure it will be a huge challenge, but if you can rally your constituents, I think you can succeed. It doesn't sound like you have any major opposition."

Ruth talked about her own obstacles. Leaders on the Lower East Side wanted her museum to focus exclusively on Jewish immigrants. Sheldon Silver, the powerful speaker of the New York Assembly, blocked state funding. Preservationists felt that there "was no redeeming architectural value" in the building they were trying to salvage, that there were "thousands of buildings like it" and that "no one important" had lived there. Finally, she told me, the foundations "couldn't imagine that we had no important collection."

Ruth had just delivered the keynote speech at the annual meeting of the National Trust for Historic Preservation. She was finishing a $15 million capital campaign for an endowment and restoration of additional historic apartments. In 1998, her museum had become an "Affiliated Area" of the National Park Service, opening the door to general operating dollars from the U.S. Department of Interior. She was trying to work out a strategic partnership with the National Trust.

"The fundraising never ends, Ron," she told me. "It's what you have to do."

Several capacity-building grants from national funders like the Ford Foundation allowed me to meet peers at other small and mid-sized cultural organizations in communities of color across the country. Beth Takekawa, Cassie Chinn and several Wing Luke board members joined me on these visits.

The Mexican Fine Arts Center Museum in Chicago (now the National Museum of Mexican Art) was the most assertive cohort in the Ford program. Carlos Tortolero, the high-powered president and founder, and Juana Guzman, the quietly efficient vice president, described how they mau-maued their way into procuring Chicago Park District funds to fuel the institution's meteoric growth.

During a break in a meeting, Carlos reflected: "You know, Ron, I don't think my parents have a clue what I do for a living. I can't explain it to them." I nodded: "It's the same with me, Carlos. I don't even try. But they know that whatever I'm doing, it's good. I make a little bit of money and it keeps me off the streets." My mother boasted to friends that I was the head of a museum or *bok mat gwan* (博物館). But she didn't know what my job entailed. She just knew I was the boss.

I met Rick Lowe, an African American artist and community organizer in Houston. He helped salvage a block-and-a-half of derelict row houses in the impoverished Third Ward, transforming them into vibrant art studios and attractive living spaces for single mothers.

I also met Judy Baca, a Chicana from East Los Angeles. In

the 1970s, she mobilized young people to create the Great Wall of Los Angeles, one of the largest murals in the world.

In the late 1990s, I toured the Massachusetts Museum of Contemporary Art (MASS MoCA), a sprawling complex of former factory buildings in the small town of North Adams. The town hit bottom after the Sprague Electric Company closed in 1985. Visionary leaders from the nearby Williams College Museum of Art were revamping the site into creative gallery spaces. MASS MoCA was a lofty experiment in using art as a tool for economic revitalization. It was still a fledgling enterprise when I visited. Only a few buildings had been restored. It looked like a ghost town where all the inhabitants had departed *en masse*, leaving furnishings and heavy equipment behind.

On the long bus trip to North Adams, I developed an awful migraine. I was barely able to keep myself from throwing up as the bus negotiated sharp turns and bobbed over uneven roads. I was relieved when we arrived and I could stand outside and breathe. But one of the first things I saw added to my vertigo: an art installation of upside-down sugar maples hanging from containers in a courtyard.

MASS MoCA was audacious and uplifting, as were the other projects I had visited across the country. I felt I wasn't alone. I felt the sky open. I returned to Seattle eager to get things rolling.

CHAPTER 59

UW Ethnic Studies and ObaChine Controversies

I N ADDITION TO MY EVOLVING national role in the museum profession, I was asked to speak out on issues as a community leader. During the summer of 1997, I received an urgent call from Connie So. The UW Ethnic Studies Student Association (ESSA) was protesting recent hiring and firing decisions. Student activists feared losing So. After a meeting of the UW Board of Regents, students angrily refused to leave the President's office. Police blocked the steps of the administration building to prevent others from joining the protestors.

"We need help getting the students out of there," Connie told me over the phone. "But they won't listen to anyone except you because they respect you." She said they knew about my discrimination fight against the *UW Daily*. Connie also called Ruth Woo, who, in turn, called Governor Gary Locke for assurances that the police wouldn't try to forcibly oust the protesters. I sped up to the UW, parking in the garage under the Suzzallo Library. At the entrance to the administration building, several police officers sternly barred my way.

"I'm here to negotiate with the students," I explained. They let me in. I went upstairs to the President's office where I was met by UW President Richard McCormick. He had a stoic expression on his face. He was flanked by a row of police officers with batons. After I explained who I was, McCormick nodded. I proceeded into the office.

Several occupiers told me that they really wanted to leave. One woman pleaded that she had to pick up her child from the daycare center or pay a hefty late fee. Another student wondered aloud if an arrest would go on his permanent record and prevent him from getting future employment. I told the whole group that those who wanted to leave should be allowed to; those who wished to stay could stay. No one should be coerced to do anything against their will, I said. My suggestion was met with resistance by several militant students who wanted to make a strong and unified political statement.

I noticed one male student edging over to an open window. After throwing down a long string, he hoisted it back up. Tied to the end was a bag of Doritos, probably supplied by an ally who had gone to the Husky Student Union Building for provisions. *What happened to the protesters of yesteryear who braved hunger and the brutal assault of police dogs and fire hoses to stand up for their beliefs?*

After talking to one leader about the foolishness of getting arrested and not having any media there to record the event, everyone agreed to go out with me as a group—as a statement of solidarity. I reassured them that they wouldn't be prosecuted. I had been sent in to negotiate their peaceful departure.

In the end, the UW renewed So's contract. In 2002, she became a senior lecturer and supervisor of the Asian American Studies Department's Community Practicum and Internship. She continues to teach at the UW to this day.

The year after the ESSA protests, I found myself embroiled in a much more visible hullabaloo that drew national coverage.

In early 1998, I spoke out publicly against the owners of ObaChine, an upscale Asian fusion restaurant established by celebrity chef Wolfgang Puck and his wife, designer Barbara Lazaroff. The restaurant opened in a bustling part of downtown Seattle at Sixth Avenue and Pine Street. Just inside the entrance, on prominent display behind the reservation desk, was a poster of a Chinese man with stereotypical exaggerated slanted eyes, coolie attire and "exotic" features. It was a turn-of-the-century advertisement for a colonial French tea company.

Two members of my staff—Byron Auyong and John Pai—told me about it. After I saw the image, I immediately understood and shared their fury. It was an "Oriental" version of "Sambo." I told the restaurant manager the poster was demeaning and racist. I asked that it be taken down right away. Using a phone at the front counter, I called their corporate headquarters to register my disgust.

Later, I called Ferdinand De Leon, a Filipino American reporter at *The Seattle Times*. His article elevated the story from a relatively obscure student protest to a much larger controversy involving a museum director.

I met with a group of angry UW students who confronted the restaurant manager about the poster. The student picketers drew into their ranks several older activists, including Doug Chin, former board president of the *International Examiner*, and Paul Bock, a retired University of Connecticut professor who two years earlier moved to Seattle to join his daughter, Paula, a reporter at *The Seattle Times*. I worried that there would be violence if the police arrived and clashed with the students. I decided to keep speaking out. But I stayed away from the pickets.

The *Examiner* ran two pages of letters on the ObaChine controversy. I was startled to see one from former Wing Luke board member Ping Kiang, now vice president and general counsel for Nextel International, Inc., a multinational corporation. I hadn't seen or spoken to him in years. He complained twice to the restaurant and vowed not to return as long as the image stayed up. Writer Frank Chin contributed a piece titled "From a Bastard Out of Los Angeles." He declared that Seattle was not a "rabidly racist city" like Los Angeles and didn't tolerate "racist pornography."

As the controversy escalated, Lazaroff came from Los Angeles to defend her decision. She invited me to meet her at the restaurant on March 5, 1998. I arrived to find a mob of local and national television crews, including ABC News, blocking the front door with microphones and a flurry of questions.

Lazaroff met with me in private inside the restaurant. She was not happy. Her demeanor was stern and aloof. Her heavy eye make-up and bright lipstick reminded me of Morticia from *The Addams Family* TV program. She boasted about her interior decorating skills, adding that she adored the "exoticism" of the Orient. She said she wanted to add an air of mystery and intrigue to ObaChine and seemed perplexed as to why I—or anyone else—would be upset about the poster, one of many she had collected.

I interrupted her monologue to tell her that the poster drew directly from racist colonial attitudes toward Asia, in an era in which Chinese people were cast as mysterious subhumans. The racism of that time, I continued, gave rise to the Chinese Exclusion Act, which barred Chinese laborers like my grandfather from legally coming to America and bringing their wives here.

We left the restaurant in a testy stalemate.

Other Asian American organizations joined the boycott.

Paul Bock painted his face with yellow pigment and kept up a one-man picket in front of the restaurant. I received updates about the diminishing number of customers from Dick, the Japanese American parking valet. I knew him from the Hong Kong Restaurant, where he was employed in a similar job.

A year and a half later, on May 31, 1999, the restaurant shut down. Frank Guidara, president and chief executive officer of the Wolfgang Puck Food Company, cited the lack of business as well as the protests. I like to think that those of us who spoke out had a significant hand in its closure.

Several people phoned to tell me it was hypocritical for the director of a museum to tread on the right of a private business to promote itself. Museums, they argued, should not support censorship of any kind. Others thought that a stereotypical image from the past was "not that big a deal." A white Wing Luke Museum docent even told me he thought the "little man" on the poster was rather "cute." I received several blatantly racist hate calls at the museum and at home. In each case, I hung up as soon as I understood the purpose of the call.

I agreed to a live interview over the phone broadcast by a local radio station. I didn't realize, until we went on air, that this was a right-wing "hate" radio program. It was hosted by an angry white male who kept interrupting me and accusing me of stupid political correctness. During one of his rants, I simply hung up.

On a return flight from a foundation meeting in New York City, I picked up a copy of *USA Today* on an empty airplane seat. I was surprised to find a prominent article on the ObaChine controversy, framed as a conflict between a famous business owner and a museum director. No one bothered to interview me. I was relieved that my picture didn't accompany the article.

My museum colleagues remained eerily quiet. I didn't expect them all to agree with my viewpoint, but I thought they would at least call me. Their silence baffled me. A white donor to the Wing Luke Museum wrote a letter threatening to rescind his donations to our collection. He said I was trampling on the free speech rights of others. He believed that museum personnel forfeit their right to offer an opinion.

This controversy was stressful, but I didn't regret speaking out. I had never seen my father, an immigrant waiter, cower in the face of insults. Why should I? These words of Martin Luther King, Jr., came to mind: "The ultimate measure of a man is not where he stands in moments of comfort, but where he stands in times of challenge and controversy."

CHAPTER 60

Getting My College Degree

I WAS OFTEN ASKED ABOUT my college degree. This question surfaced when I served as a scholarly advisor for grant projects. I never lied, but I dodged the question. I said I studied editorial journalism at the University of Washington from 1971 to 1975. Pressed, I admitted, "I'm still a few credits short of my degree." I said I left to work at the *International Examiner,* believing that this experience was more valuable than classroom study.

When the White House nominated me to serve on the NEH Council, I was asked for background information for a press advisory. "I hope you're not shocked by this, but I don't have a college degree," I told the person from the NEH. "If you need to withdraw my name from consideration, just let me know." I was reassured that not having a degree was a minor point and that I was chosen because of my expertise as a humanities scholar.

Bettie Luke asked me about my degree. She knew I had had a discrimination fight against the UW, but she didn't know the details. I rarely mentioned it, even to friends and colleagues. I didn't want to reopen emotional wounds. Bettie tried to pry more out of me by saying, "Hey, Ron. I want to donate the first $100 for a 'Send-Ron-Back-to-School Fund.'" I smiled, then turned away. I didn't tell her that I had no interest in returning to school.

Bettie's niece, Cynthia Denning (now Cynthia del Rosario), nominated me for a UW distinguished alumni award. She worked briefly at the Wing Luke Museum under Charlene Mano. She wanted me to be recognized for my work at the *Examiner* and the museum. I told Cynthia that while I was flattered, others were far more deserving. When she persisted, I finally said, "Cynthia, I can't accept it. I'm not an alumnus. I don't have a degree." Her jaw dropped. She cupped both hands to her cheeks. I revealed to her my battle with the *UW Daily*. "That's *so* not right!" she exclaimed. I told her that I considered my time at the *UW Daily* water under the bridge. I urged her to drop my nomination.

Cynthia didn't heed my words. Working behind the scenes with Elena Guevara, advisor at the UW Office of Minority Affairs and Diversity, the two dug through old paper files at the communications school. Jerry Baldasty, chair of the school, decided to give me my diploma and asked me to come to the UW campus.

When I entered the lobby of the communications building, I saw that the huge antique printing press was still there, bolted to the floor above an etching of words from the First Amendment. In a quiet, low-key ceremony in Jerry's office, I signed an application for my degree and a graduate diploma card. With me were Loan, Cian and Kino, Elena, Cynthia and Bob Shimabukuro (who wanted to write a piece for the *Examiner*). I was moved by Jerry's kind words. He apologized for my being denied the opportunity to earn my degree 27 years earlier. My eyes brimmed with tears.

After the ceremony, I walked across the narrow hall to the *UW Daily* office, accompanied by those who witnessed the event in Jerry's office. I carried a sleepy four-year-old Kino in my arms. Cian wore my barn jacket, draped over his skinny frame. I hardly recognized the newspaper office. The manual typewriters had been replaced by iMacs strung together with cable. I didn't hear the incessant clack-clack-clack of typewriters, the ping of warning bells and ripping noise of carriage returns. I felt weirdly out of place. A few student journalists peered at us, wondering who we were. They were young and scruffy like I once was.

"That's the news editor's desk," I pointed out to the others in my group. "That's where I wanted to be." There was graffiti and writing all over the walls. "That wasn't there before either," I added. Loan urged me to leave my mark before leaving.

I pondered this suggestion for a moment, smiled and said, "You know, I think I will. Where should I do it?" On one of the few blank spaces on the wall, I scrawled, "I have returned to the place where my writing began 30 years ago."

This turned out to be a poignant week. Properly credentialed, I was given a "distinguished alumnus" award by the UW Multicultural Alumni Partnership on November 2, 2002, during UW Homecoming Weekend.

In late 2004, I was surprised to receive three major honors: the Ford Foundation's Leadership for a Changing World Award, the Western Museums Association's annual Director's Chair Award, and induction into the new Hall of Fame at the UW School of Communications. The Ford Foundation award came with a $115,000 prize, which I directed toward museum operations. The WMA award was presented in Tacoma at the group's annual meeting. The Hall of Fame Award was bestowed at the UW. Other award winners included *NW Asian Weekly* publisher Assunta Ng, former Mayor Norm Rice, Washington State Attorney General Christine Gregoire (soon to be elected Governor), KOMO-TV weather anchor Steve Pool, editorial cartoonist David Horsey, and *Seattle P-I* investigative reporter Eric Nalder.

My head was spinning. I used the news stories about my awards to promote the Wing Luke capital campaign.

During the summer of 2004, Roberto Maestas excitedly called to tell me about his own award. He was selected as King Neptune for the coming year's Seafair Festival. Every year since 1950, Seafair recognizes two individuals as King Neptune, King of the Sea, and Queen Alcyone, Queen of the Calm Seas. Jeannie Nordstrom was Queen Alcyone. Maestas was the first Latino selected as King Neptune.

"How's my favorite successful Franklin High School student doing?" he began. "I hear so much about what you've been doing at the Wing Luke Museum these days. I would be honored if you could come to witness my coronation as King Neptune." I laughed to myself. I had been a shy, lackluster student. Now I was a famous museum director. Roberto had been a mainstream high school teacher. Now he was a prominent revolutionary preparing to be crowned King Neptune for the city of Seattle.

The coronation was on Roberto's home turf, El Centro de la Raza. As I looked on, I was transported back to my childhood by the musty smell of the building, the echoing hallways, the oak classroom doors, the high ceilings and banks of large windows. At the end, I stood up to congratulate my old Spanish teacher. I spoke for the first time about my humiliating childhood memory of being told that my mother couldn't enter the school unless she spoke English. I said it was ironic that a place that once condoned intolerance was now a home for the Latino community.

In June 2006, I returned to the UW to deliver the keynote speech to the graduating class of communications students. Kino, a second-grader at Beacon Hill Elementary School, asked to be excused from school to watch me deliver the speech. He may just have wanted a reason to skip school, but I felt blessed to see him sitting near the front nevertheless. I implored the students to follow their passion, to follow their hearts as I had done. Several parents came up to me after the speech to tell me they appreciated my remarks. This touched me. I realized—with Kino at my side—that I was a parent, too.

In July 2007, Uncle Bob took his turn at serving as King Neptune for the Seafair Festival. Mona Lee Locke, Gary Locke's wife, was Queen Alcyone. Uncle Bob gave me an honorary appointment as "The Smithsonian Connection," providing a burst of free publicity for the Wing Luke campaign. This was Uncle Bob, the cagey organizer, making a backdoor move to help the cause.

CHAPTER 61

The Dream of a New Museum

EVER SINCE THE SUCCESS OF the *Executive Order 9066* exhibition, I had dreamt about a new home for the Wing Luke Museum. At conferences, other museum directors advised, "Ron, every director has to lead one capital campaign in their lifetime. That would be your legacy. Then you can retire."

In 1996, as I entered my fifth year at the museum, I wondered if I had given all I could. I felt restless. I yearned to return to journalism. On the side, I wrote for *Museum News*, AAM's magazine. Ironically, one of my articles, "In Praise of the Small Museum," argued that it was often "not a bad choice" for small neighborhood-based institutions to stay the same size. Several museum directors I interviewed pointed out that bigger museums might have more money, but they had to grapple with bureaucracy and isolation from the community.

Despite the story, I knew that the right choice for the Wing Luke was to take advantage of our momentum, spread our wings and soar.

On August 12, 1997, I wrote a 14-page vision statement for a new Wing Luke Museum. The dream facility included a music teahouse, courtyard garden, library/resource center, auditorium/theater, meeting rooms, kitchen, museum shop, collections area, media center and offices. Core exhibitions would explore science and technology, politics, war veterans, entrepreneurship, women, language, food, herbal medicine, Bruce Lee, sports and Asian folk art.

I proposed the installation of a barrack from Minidoka, a refugee camp from Southeast Asia and the Yick Fung & Company store. I later suggested adding the Killing Fields Museum, a project founded in West Seattle by Dara Duong, a survivor of the Khmer Rouge holocaust.

The vision statement lit a fire. Velma Veloria and Vietnamese American leaders urged me to move quickly to secure artifacts from overseas refugee camps slated to close. On October 17, 1997, I wrote a letter to Philippine President Fidel Ramos, requesting permission to send a small delegation—including Velma and local refugee Kristie Nguyễn—to gather objects and conduct interviews in the Philippine Refugee Processing Center in Morong, Bataan, and in the camp at Palawan. I never got a response.

First, we had to tackle a larger question: Where would the new museum's home be? We couldn't squeeze anything more inside our current walls. We had to find a new location.

In 1996, we briefly considered moving into the cavernous Union Station. Our potential development partners were the Washington State Historical Society, the Burke Museum and the Jimi Hendrix Museum Project. Negotiations didn't go very far. The instigator of the idea, David Nicandri, director of the historical society, alienated my board leaders Gloria Wakayama and Helen Kay by his arrogant tone. His organization, heavily dependent on state support, lacked the capacity to move forward. The Burke Museum was still years away from expansion (the new Burke didn't open until October 2019). The Jimi Hendrix Museum, spearheaded by Jody Allen, sister of Microsoft co-founder Paul Allen, pivoted toward a solo location near Seattle Center. It was rebranded as the Experience Music Project (and is now the Museum of Pop Culture).

We looked elsewhere. In 1997 and 1998, architect Ken Kubota surveyed options in the International District. There were only a few vacant properties, and most were not for sale.

I talked to Barry Mar, whose family owned the quarter-block directly across the street from the museum. Seventh Avenue Service, an auto repair shop run by Pat Abe and former owner Ted Imanaka, had been there since 1946. But as we explored that site, we promptly realized it was too small.

Raymond Chinn said he knew Jim Polack, who owned the vacant Acme Poultry Company site at 1029 South Jackson Street. Raymond inquired. The site was large enough, but the prospect of cleaning up a former chicken processing plant was daunting. Talks never advanced. In 2018, another developer purchased it for $11.3 million with plans for a seven-story apartment building.

In 1999, Tom Im, a neighborhood planner at InterIm, approached me with the novel thought of constructing our new museum on top of the Metro bus tunnel lid, which spanned the property along Fifth Avenue South between Weller and South King Streets. He argued that plenty of daily foot traffic could be channeled toward our front door and that we could avoid the costs of property acquisition.

In that same year, Gloria and I met with Tomio Moriguchi to discuss taking over the Uwajimaya location as he prepared to open a new, expanded store one block south.

We even considered buying property on the Eastside, possibly in Bellevue, and building a new structure. But after further thought, we agreed that it would be a betrayal of our identity and mission to abandon our International District roots.

In the end, we trained our sights on a pair of four-story hotels along South King Street. They were known as the Kong Yick buildings. The Chinese-speaking elders called them *Gung Yick Lau* (公益樓). As I explored the history of how they came to be—and what they still meant—it dawned on me that our new home might be right under our noses.

CHAPTER 62

The Kong Yick Buildings

I N 1909, THREE LEADING CHINESE American pioneers—
Goon Dip, Chun Ching Hock and Chin Gee Hee—devised grand plans to build two hotels along King Street
between Seventh and Eighth Avenues South as the cornerstone
of a new community. The old Chinatown near Second Avenue
South and Washington Street had been declining for years.

To finance this bold undertaking, the Kong Yick Investment Company was established on June 6, 1910. Capital stock
of $55,000 was divided into 1,100 shares of $50 each. Nearly
200 names appeared on the roster of the original investors. The
big shareholders included Wa Chong Company, Quong Tuck,
Gom Hong Company (錦香行) and Goon Dip's business.

The new side-by-side buildings, separated by Canton Alley,
were designed by Thompson and Thompson, a local firm. The
structures were built of red brick and concrete and featured
projecting wrought-iron balconies with double doors. The east
building, at 715-725 South King Street, was known as the
Freeman Hotel. It contained 155 single rooms and nine store-

fronts. The west building, at 701-711 South King Street, was called the Kong Yick Apartments. It held 158 single rooms and nine storefronts.

Wa Chong, Quong Tuck, Gom Hong and Yick Fung became anchor tenants on the street level. In a 1910 *Seattle Times* interview, Jimmy Mar's father, founder of Yick Fung & Company. explained, "Seattle Chinese have outgrown the idea of close, cramped, dark quarters. In a few months Seattle's Chinatown will be a model for other cities to imitate."

When I joined the Wing Luke Museum, the upstairs apartments in the Freeman Hotel had been boarded up for years. The businesses below them were failing. The modest rents weren't enough to pay for the costs of remodeling the aging structures.

In June 1994, following an 18-month investigation by Seattle police, federal authorities raided two family associations and the Kong Yick office. The investment company, charged with harboring illegal gambling operations, agreed to pay a $325,000 fine. Demoralized, its officers explored selling the buildings.

Concerned about the loss of these fabled structures, Shannon Gee, John Pai and Grace Lee Park began filming the stories of past and present occupants. I served as the interviewer. In 1998, they completed a one-hour documentary *Finding Home in Chinatown: The Kong Yick Buildings*. I became intrigued by the idea of converting the buildings into the Wing Luke Museum's new home.

Jimmy Mar pointed me to Richard Lew Kay, Kong Yick treasurer. Jimmy said Richard owned a significant block of shares as the grandson of Goon Dip. Richard was married to Wing Luke Museum board member Helen Eng Kay. I also spoke with another Goon Dip descendent—Steve Goon's dad Clifton. Both Richard and Clifton were receptive to my vision.

Richard was a retired pharmacist, like Clifton. He watched TV in the back of the Yick Fung store with Jimmy, Howard and a handful of Chinatown regulars. He was cordial, but hard to pin down. He said, "Hi" and "How's it going?" Occasionally, his lips parted into a faint grin. Or, he'd shrug. That was it. Clifton was just as brief, but I knew where he stood. He growled, "Sell the building!"

Richard said the shareholders were waiting to find a buyer committed to preserving the legacy of the structures. That was the museum's desire, too, so his reticence puzzled me. One offer of $1.5 million for each building had been rejected because the potential buyer wanted to tear down both structures and start anew.

The current Kong Yick tenants included Wah Young Company, King Café, Gom Hong Company, ABC Garden (大排檔世界) the Kay Ying Senior Club (耆英會), the Yee Family Association (余風采堂), Ho Nam Association (南河公所) (also known as the Luke Family Association), the Lee Family Association (李氏公所), the Soo Yuen Association (遡源堂) and the Luck Ngai Musical Club. My own association—Lung Kong Tin Yee Association (龍岡親義公所), a confederation of Chews, Lews, Jangs and Quans—was located up a tall flight of steps on the second floor of the west building.

The upper floor of the east building included an ornate room with wood-paneled walls and a coffered-tin ceiling. It was last occupied by Gee How Oak Tin Family Association (舍路至孝篤親公所), the largest Chinese family association in Washington state. Those with the surnames of Chin (陳), Woo (胡) or Yuen (袁) were members. The room held a long wooden table draped with an elaborately embroidered Chinese tapestry. A portrait of Sun Yat-sen and framed watercolor landscape paintings hung on the walls.

All the Chinese family associations faced dwindling participation and membership. Their history was rooted in a clanship loyalty that meant little to American-born Chinese and those who immigrated after the 1960s. The Locke Family Association headquarters, next door to my old stomping grounds, the Alaska Cannery Workers Association, was abandoned following a fire in the 1990s. The Dong Association (曾家公所), in the basement of the Bing Kung Tong at 708 South King Street, disbanded after a fire on April 13, 1977.

Fred Yee took me to see the Yee Family Association on the upper floor of the east building. There was a prominent balcony, a meeting hall and several apartments. "Young people don't think about coming down here," said James Yee, the association's senior advisor, his voice tinged with sadness. "Their way of life is very different. They don't speak Chinese. This meeting area is too rundown. People smoke. In the old days, this was the place for bachelors to gamble. What do you think, Ron? Maybe we should set up some activities like pinball machines."

I didn't respond, but I was thinking that pinball machines had already been supplanted by video games.

My own family association faced the same survival challenges. I attended annual Chinese New Year banquets, but only because my parents brought me. Every year, I noticed fewer people. After retirement, my cousin Sen Poy Chew served as president because no one else wanted that role. His wife headed up the women's auxiliary.

I asked Donnie Chin what he thought of the museum taking over the Kong Yick buildings. The International District Emergency Center was in the west building. His eyes lit up. "Do it!" he exhorted. "Ron, that history is going to get lost before we're even gone. The buildings will probably collapse, too." Donnie was forever donating rescued objects and documents from abandoned apartments and alley dumpsters to the museum's collection.

In July 1999, Donnie called me at the museum, urgency in his voice. The Gom Hong Company at 709 South King Street was closing. Fay Eng, the owner, dispirited over the failure of his business, was disassembling the last contents of the store. Fay's grandfather started Gom Hong in the old Chinatown. My mother shopped at Fay's store for canned goods, produce and seafood. He stocked big cases of beef tendon and pig organs. But she saw very few customers there.

"How fast can you get down here?" Donnie asked. I dropped everything and ran over. Donnie and Mr. Eng's daughter Mandy watched helplessly while he heaved merchandise into large garbage bins near the front of the store.

I reintroduced myself to Fay as director of the Wing Luke Museum. He nodded, a dour look on his face. I asked him about several abandoned steamer trunks tucked away in a corner of the mezzanine. He was going to throw them away. He said bitterly, "They're useless (冇用)." I asked him in Chinese, "Have you looked inside?" He scoffed. "Why? There's nothing of value in them." I made up a story: "Back in the old days, the Chinese sewed gold coins inside their suitcases. Why don't you let me check? The gold coins could be worth a lot." He hesitated. His daughter said, "He's right, Dad. Why don't you let him check?" He relented.

Donnie, Mandy and I scurried up to the mezzanine. Donnie lit the way with a flashlight. Abandoned in a corner were several bundles of old, silver-colored menus from the defunct King Fur Café (瓊花樓). The restaurant was at 709 ½ South King Street. Donnie broke apart one of the suitcase locks with a tool. We found musty letters, envelopes, photos and papers dating back as far as 1910. They illuminated an incredible trail between Seattle, Port Gamble, Port Townsend, Oakland, Hong Kong and China. No gold pieces, but it was a treasure trove nonetheless. We hauled everything back to the museum.

This experience strengthened my resolve to help save the Kong Yick buildings. Still, I needed reassurance from the long-time tenants. I wasn't sure how they would react.

I talked to Tsee Watt Mark, founder of the Kay Ying Senior Club. Its 700 members played *mahjong* and went on group outings. Mr. Mark, a bright, effusive man with a wide, oval face, knew my father and my uncles. He once operated University Hand Laundry at 4222 University Way N.E., a half-block from my family's Campus Laundry. "I know you're doing a good thing," he reassured me. He patted me on the hand. "We can find another place. You need to do this. Otherwise the building will fall apart anyway."

I visited Steven Luke, president of the Ho Nam Association, on the Eighth Avenue side of the East Kong Yick Building. Steven, who immigrated to Seattle in 1949, had worked in Kiang Nam Restaurant (江南樓) on the upper floor. He was married to my cousin Won Ping Chew, Sen Poy's sister. Steven also welcomed the museum expansion. He took me down a wobbly flight of wooden steps to the association. It looked nearly abandoned. I saw an old sofa, a few chairs, a TV, a *mahjong* table, an altar and a small kitchen. "This is it," he said, spreading both arms to indicate how tiny the space was. "This is our clubhouse." With declining participation, he didn't see much of a future.

Steven changed the subject. He asked me to consider running for Seattle City Council. "Hey, I saw you on a program on Channel 9," he said. "I thought you had some good things to say. You speak real good English. Some of us in Chinatown were thinking that it would be great to have someone we trust that can represent us. We haven't had anyone like that since Wing Luke."

I pushed aside his suggestion. I said my place was at the museum. Besides, I was the busy parent of two young children. I reminded him that I spoke good English because I was born in America. "Maybe you can consider it after your kids are grown up," he offered. I told him I would leave elected office to others with a stronger taste for politics. "If you change your mind, let me know," he said. "We can help get the family associations and the people in Chinatown to vote for you, just like we did for Wing Luke before."

John Pai kept egging me forward. He was inspired by the rich connections to the past. During the filming of *Finding Home in Chinatow*n, he climbed an old fire escape with Donnie Chin to get inside the abandoned rooms and hallways strewn with the carcasses of dead pigeons. "Ron," John said, "It would be terrible if the buildings got sold to a developer and they got torn down and turned into a parking lot. You should just do it. People would be behind you. I'd do whatever I can to help."

John's words sank in. One night, I dreamt that the East Kong Yick Building had become a museum. There were visitors wandering through brightly-lit galleries and restored spaces. I went into work that morning happy and filled with purpose.

Still, I harbored many doubts. The stakes were high. Remodeling would be very costly. The project would displace cherished businesses and associations. Did I have the appetite to throw myself into fundraising full-time? Did I want to remain in the public limelight? I wouldn't be able to retreat back to writing, my heart's passion.

But an unexpected natural disaster pushed me off the fence.

On February 28, 2001, at 10:45 a.m., the Nisqually earthquake struck, creating widespread destruction from Olympia to Everett. The 6.8 magnitude quake injured nearly 400 people and caused massive damage to buildings, roads and bridges. The International District took a big hit because of its unreinforced concrete and masonry buildings.

I was in a small room above the main gallery of the museum. I ducked under a table. Associate Director Beth Takekawa tried to crouch under a counter in an adjoining office, only to find the space crammed full of boxes. Finance Director Ray Ishii raced down to the gallery to see if the barrack from the *Executive Order 9066* exhibit had collapsed. Docents were leading three school tours. We directed everyone to evacuate to an open space across the street. I called from my cell phone to find out if Cian and Kino were safe, but the lines were jammed. Traffic lights went out. Confused people filled the streets, sirens wailing in the distance. One person was injured from falling bricks in front of the Suey Sing Association (萃勝堂) on South Weller Street.

After things settled down at the museum, I ran over to Yick Fung to look for Jimmy Mar, manager of the Kong Yick buildings. Several years earlier, Jimmy told me that he would donate his business to us so it could be converted into a historical display. He met me at the front door. He told me that both Kong Yick buildings looked okay. Jimmy said all the residents had been safely evacuated. I breathed a sigh of relief. "The only thing that happened in my store was that a potted plant fell down," he said, laughing. "We're lucky."

The Wing Luke Museum wasn't so lucky. Falling bricks from the facade of the Milwaukee Hotel had punctured our roof. Directly below was the mezzanine, packed with thousands of artifacts in our collection.

The next day, just as heavy rain arrived, volunteers came to help us move these objects to dry, secure locations in the gallery. The volunteers included several sons of Lee Hong "Smiley" Young, an old-timer at the Luck Ngai Musical Club who had recently passed away. Smiley was featured in *Finding Home in Chinatown*. The sons, grateful to find information for their father's eulogy, helped us bail water from the collection area. I recalled that my mother used to buy raw glutinous rice dumplings from Smiley's mother, the old lady who lived behind Four Seas Restaurant.

Marpac Construction, a firm started by Dan Mar, a Cathay Post veteran, dispatched a full crew over to the museum to repair our roof that same day. They did this despite being besieged by many other emergency requests.

Our annual fundraising auction—vital to the museum's survival—was just weeks away. The Union Station hall where the event was scheduled to be held closed because of earthquake damage. But Ruth Jung Chinn, owner of the Asian Resource Center several blocks east of the museum, came to the rescue. She offered her facility, built as a gymnasium in 1994 to memorialize her late husband Robert Chinn. We hosted our most successful auction ever.

The catastrophe reminded me of the vulnerability of aging structures in the ID. The museum had survived this earthquake, but would we make it through the next big one? It was evident that we had loyal supporters right behind us. If we were going to start a campaign, the time was right.

Twenty months after the earthquake, Jimmy's brother Howard passed away, on December 18, 2002. Shortly before Christmas, I visited Jimmy at the Yick Fung store to offer my condolences. I was sad I would not see Uncle Howie's beaming face anymore. Several years earlier, the Mar Society (馬家公所) held its last New Year's banquet in the back of the store. *How much longer would Jimmy keep the lights on in his shop?*

The museum began formal talks with the Kong Yick Investment Company's board. We offered to buy just the East Kong Yick Building. It was too challenging to redevelop both structures.

I lobbied the key Kong Yick decision-makers in earnest: Richard Lew Kay, Jimmy Mar, Howard Dong, Wilma Woo and her kids Teresa and Curtis, and Steve Goon and his father Clifton. I strategized with minor shareholders Gloria, Cassie and Shannon, already in the museum fold.

Gloria represented the museum in negotiations. The investment company hired its own attorney. Each party sought an independent appraisal of the value of the East Kong Yick Building. Our appraisal came back at $2 million, theirs at $2.7 million. We offered $2 million.

The Kong Yick officers held a special meeting at their office at 508 Seventh Avenue South to consider sale of the East Kong Yick Building for $2 million. Jimmy Mar, Clifton Goon, Richard Lew Kay, Howard Dong, Rosemary Kay, Bernie Kay and Shannon Gee showed up. An awkward silence was broken when one person piped up: "Can you imagine how exciting it will be when we transform that corner of the street into a new museum?" Others nodded. The vote went quickly. It was unanimous.

On July 17, 2003, the purchase was completed. The building was ours for $2 million. There was no turning back.

CHAPTER 63

Preparing for a Big Campaign

FTER THE SUCCESS OF THE *Executive Order 9066* exhibition, the museum struggled to find enough room to accommodate the swelling number of staff and volunteers, new exhibitions, public programs and artifacts donated to our collection.

In one grant application, Beth Takekawa summarized our quandary: "We have been described as a family with five children living in a one-bedroom apartment."

Greg Tuai, the multitalented Renaissance man who guided the *Examiner* into the computer era, tried to help. He built a long wood-veneer counter and overhead shelving throughout our front offices, allowing us to get rid of individual desks and clear the floor of a mountain of cardboard storage boxes. He remodeled an exhibit display area into a tiny meeting room.

He and two other volunteers, Todd Fedorenko and Cliff Louie, constructed a small work loft and extra shelves in the back of the museum. In 1995, we acquired off-site storage in the SoDo district. We began assembling exhibitions outside in the front entryway. "We can't keep living like this," I groused to Greg. "We've got to start looking for a new home." He grimaced and said, "Go to it! Better you than me. I don't fundraise." I frowned. "That's what you and everyone else tells me."

The spirits inside the museum also beckoned us to move. Jeannette Roden, who worked on Sundays, noticed that small chunks of the ceiling above the front counter began falling. The old cash register took on a life of its own. At 4 p.m. closing time, when Jeannette and another staff member turned the register's key to the off position, the digital display refused to shut down. They joked that the cash register was haunted.

I knew that a capital campaign would not succeed unless I devoted my time almost exclusively to fundraising. Luckily, by this time, I had assembled a very resourceful executive team.

Second in leadership was Beth. She started as a *9066* exhibit volunteer. In 1997, I hired her as associate director. She took over day-to-day management. I didn't know it, but Beth's grand-aunt was Tomo Shoji, the colorful Nisei storyteller who visited me at the *Examiner*. Beth left a cushy job at the Seattle Housing Authority to take a position that didn't offer medical or dental benefits or even her own separate desk. On her first day, she found a vase of flowers in her work area along with a mysterious sheet of paper listing a "parking lot" of assorted tasks. Someone explained that it was her job description.

Under Beth's leadership, an organizational plan was adopted by the Wing Luke board on June 2, 1999. The document reshaped board and staff roles, sketching out the beginnings of a plan for a capital project.

Charlene Mano continued to provide a steady, guiding hand for the expansion of public programs and community partnerships.

Cassie Chinn blossomed into a prodigious exhibition developer. I first hired her in 1995 to inventory a cache of materials donated by Bettie Luke. Cassie's father, Charles Chinn, was a music teacher when I was a student at Franklin High. He led the concert stage band and orchestra. He was one of the few Chinese American administrators at the school. Cassie displayed a steely determination and wisdom beyond her years. In 2006, she authored a handbook on the museum's exhibition process, codifying the values underpinning the museum's community advisory committee model.

Ruth Vincent, a Vancouver, B.C., native with a background in cultural anthropology, came in 1991 to head up collections. She brought expertise in the care of objects along with a passion for textiles and a flair for designing visually pleasing exhibitions on a dime. After she left in 2000, Bob Fisher, who began in 1995 as a front desk volunteer, replaced her. He brought a strong interest in Asian and Asian American history.

Mayumi Tsutakawa became director of external relations from 1998 to 2002, strengthening our grants department. She had been caring for her ailing father George, who died in 1997. She left the museum to become grants director of the Washington State Arts Commission before we started the capital campaign.

Mary Ann Harper (now Mary Ann Goto) took over from Mayumi from 2002 until 2007. Mary Ann came from Hawaii to attend Seattle University in 1985. She had been doing development work at Habitat for Humanity before she joined us.

Tommer Peterson, a graphic designer and master calligrapher, managed grants from 2005 to 2006. As a child in Seattle's Wallingford neighborhood, Tommer's curiosity in Asian script was aroused during visits to the Fuji 10 Cent Store, which sold books of wooden matches emblazoned with Chinese zodiac signs. Under a fellowship, he later studied classical calligraphy in Kyoto and became a regular contributor to the Wing Luke annual art auction.

Ray Ishii, a Wing Luke board member and certified public accountant, stepped off the board in 2000 to become finance director. He stayed until 2005. I served on the ID Summer Festival planning committee with Ray's father Bill, who had an accounting firm in the building next to the museum. Ray's uncle was David Ishii, the bookseller in Pioneer Square.

I was thrilled Diane Narasaki came to work for me as the museum's first full-time development director. She prepared key grant applications that positioned the museum for the national stage. I met her in the 1980s when she volunteered for Gordon Hirabayashi's legal defense team. I also knew her as a dogged organizer at the American Friends Service Committee and an outspoken co-chair, along with Ticiang Diangson, of the Asian Pacific Women's Caucus.

When Diane left to join Asian Counseling and Referral Service as its executive director, Diane Wah, a first cousin of long-time board member Helen Kay, took over as development director. Diane Wah had been on the Wing Luke board. Her excellent writing skills—and unabashed passion for the cause—helped us continue to expand our base of support.

Having a well-grounded, mostly homegrown team allowed me to map out a framework for the fundraising campaign without having to divert my attention to the latest program iterations or daily operational issues.

I also had an exceptional board of directors. Joining Gloria and Helen on the executive committee were Victor Mizumori, Paul Mar and Ellen Ferguson.

Victor was International District branch manager of Key Bank. Ray Ishii suggested him. "I think we really need someone else who understands finances," he told me. "We'll be entering a phase where a lot of money is going to be flowing in and out of our books. Victor is very diplomatic. Me—I can be like a bull in a china shop. Victor, on the other hand, can help balance out my personality."

True to Ray's description, Victor had a gift for boiling down complex financial reports into easy-to-understand summaries. His rigid banker's attire—I rarely saw him outside his navy-blue suit, crisp white shirt, cufflinks and conservative ties—belied his easy laugh and affable demeanor.

During one Wing Luke auction, Victor and his wife Stacy bought a Crayola drawing I had sketched at home. It was inspired by the Little Golden Book Classics I read at night to Cian and Kino. On a whim, Mary Ann included it in the silent auction. "I owe you lunch," I told Victor and Stacy after they made the buy. I joked that my sketch represented a unique "broken-crayon" technique. Victor and Stacy never collected their meal.

Paul joined the board in 1999 after working with architect Ken Kubota to survey potential museum sites. His quiet tact and unerring problem-solving skills were a great boon to the campaign.

Paul spent his first two years of life in the back of his parents' business on Maynard Avenue South, the Excel Barbershop, next to the Hong Kong Café. As a UW college freshman, Paul worked with Wing Luke in the Chinese Community Service Organization, a group of American-born Chinese trying to loosen the grip of the conservative old men who controlled Chong Wa Benevolent Association. In the mid-1970s, Paul helped two property owners, Wai Eng and Gan Sun Lew, secure bank loans to establish restaurants in the ID. He also counseled the group that established the Seattle Chinatown-International District Preservation and Development Authority

(SCIDpda) in 1975 as a community-controlled public agency to remodel and manage historic buildings.

Ellen joined our board after touring the *Executive Order 9066* exhibition with a group of donors from A Territory Resource, now the Social Justice Fund. During dinner at Ho Ho Seafood Restaurant, Ellen—dressed in her usual sweater vest, brown khakis and penny loafers—sat pinned between Diane Narasaki and me. Ellen was a veteran staffer at the Burke Museum. She was active in the Western Museums Association (WMA), which prided itself on its early, strong commitment to diversity. Under the persistent coaxing of Ellen and Wanda Chin, an exhibit designer at the University of Alaska Museum, I agreed to join the WMA board. Ellen's father Hugh Ferguson was a respected philanthropist who contributed generously to the Burke Museum.

I discovered that Ellen was technophobic. She didn't know how to use a computer. She didn't use email. She didn't own a cell phone. When all the obsolete IBM Selectric typewriters were removed from the Burke, she bought her own for work. We communicated by office phone, fax machine or in person. We faxed her announcements of board meetings. It wasn't until 2007, after I left the museum, that she crawled out of her cave, got a computer and connected to the Internet. Later, we became Facebook friends.

Mimi Gan and Katherine Cheng joined the board as the campaign got underway. Mimi was a reporter and producer for KING-TV's *Evening Magazine*. Katherine served as an intern and a docent at the museum while an undergraduate at UW. She later served as public liaison officer for Governor Gary Locke before joining Starbucks Coffee Company as a program manager. Earlier, she was in the same class of White House interns as Monica Lewinsky during the Clinton administration.

Other key board members during the campaign were Dolores Sibonga, Maria Batayola, Jackie Der, Casey Bui, Pat Norikane Logerwell, Savitha Reddy Pathi, Gemma Valdez Daggatt, Larry Yok and Judy Tobin.

Jackie, a Chinese American from Oakland, worked for the UW Medical School. She traveled to Olympia to fight for affordable health care, a career path I followed years later. She married the love of her life, Alan Painter, a Franklin High graduate who served as district manager for Mike Lowry in the 1980s. Sadly, cancer claimed Jackie's life at the age of 61 in 2015.

Joy Shigaki, a Sansei with family roots in Seattle, became capital campaign manager in early 2004. She was a community liaison for King County Executive Ron Sims and had just completed a brief stint working for unsuccessful U.S. Presidential candidate Howard Dean. Joy was quick, disciplined and relentless. She researched donor prospects and held the campaign to an aggressive schedule.

We hired the Collins Group, a seasoned regional consulting firm that worked on campaigns for museums and nonprofit organizations, as our fundraising consultants. The Collins Group advised SCIDpda on the ID Village Square Project before being replaced by Ed Shumacher, a brilliant out-of-the-box consultant who provided a more suitable partnership for SCIDpda. I met Ed right after I was hired at the Wing Luke. In 1990, Ed prepared a report for the Wing Luke board, arguing that the museum's survival depended on deepening the engagement of the Asian American community.

Stuart Grover, a Collins Group principal, had worked with Kit Freudenberg on the museum's earlier $350,000 campaign to move from its tiny one-room storefront on Eighth Avenue South into the old China Garage in 1987. At the time, I was at the *International Examiner*. Stuart stopped by to ask me for the names of potential Asian American donors. I solicited him for ads for the paper. I found him to be a first-rate strategic thinker. He was erudite, but loved sharing groan-inducing corny jokes and witticisms.

I never imagined I would work directly with Stuart years later on a capital campaign, much less one of such magnitude.

The other Collins Group consultant who worked closely with us was JoAnn Marshall (now JoAnn Mills). JoAnn had worked as a psychotherapist for 15 years. Her calm, empathetic words helped power us through difficult moments.

Buttressed by a fundraising feasibility study I had prepared and the reputation of the Collins Group, I proposed a wildly ambitious $30 million capital campaign goal. That amount was later pared down to $23.2 million, but even that was a moonshot.

Our team got to work.

Once a month, Beth, Cassie, Joy and I dutifully trekked from the ID over to the Collins Group office on the second floor of an old brick building on East Pine Street. The board leadership team—Ellen, Paul, Helen and Gloria—joined us there. We met over lunch in a cramped conference room, a large bank of windows facing Pine Street. We celebrated our most recent gifts, agonized over the most recent rejections, and talked about upcoming solicitations. Our meetings were interrupted by the sirens of emergency vehicles screaming down the street, drowning out our voices at inopportune moments and punctuating the urgency of deadlines.

As we left, we paused and chatted in the lobby at the doorway of a new-age business called Travelers India Shop & Tea Company. The shop was filled with bright displays of candles, colorful scarves, shawls and saris. The scent of burning incense choked the air. It was a very odd transition—moving from the pressure cooker of campaign meetings into a post-hippie-era oasis on our way back to our pocket-sized community museum in the urban core.

At times, it felt like my life had devolved into an endless chain of back-to-back meetings, morning to evening, seven days a week. Capital campaign meetings, staff meetings, management team meetings, board meetings, donor meetings, community meetings, consultant meetings, and meetings to debrief what had happened at meetings.

I found it difficult to balance the competing demands of work and parenthood.

During museum board meetings, held in the tiny classroom at the back of the Wing Luke, Cian and Kino waited for me in the office. They played RuneScape and MapleStory on my computer while munching on Flamin' Hot Crunchy Cheetos and Big League Chew Bubblegum. Rus Bareng, a program assistant, bonded with my kids after he showed off his "strong" set of Yu-Gi-Oh cards. Gloria's two young kids, Brady and Lindsay, waited, too, along with Mimi Gan's two girls, Grace and Chloe. When I heard a loud noise from upstairs, I assumed it was my two boys creating mischief. I was less distracted if I knew that Rus was with them.

I couldn't wait to finish up, take my boys home, get them fed and put them to bed. My overtaxed brain had to shut off. I needed sleep. I knew the next day would be as relentless as the last. If I didn't pace myself, I wouldn't make it to the finish.

Chapter 64

Lobbying for Government Support

I WAS CONVINCED THAT A state appropriation would thrust the campaign forward. I knew that the Seattle Art Museum, Henry Art Gallery, Seattle Symphony and Seattle Opera had received state appropriations much larger than what we were seeking. I was determined to make sure that the Wing Luke Museum got its share.

Two newer board members—Doug Chin and State Representative Sharon Tomiko Santos—tried to dissuade me from going to Olympia to lobby. Governor Gary Locke didn't include our request in his budget, despite a face-to-face meeting with Gloria, Helen and me in his office. Doug and Sharon thought I was wasting my time. They resigned from the board.

Doug was a former *Examiner* board president who helped grow the newspaper through the strategy of creating special issues on topics such as employment and Asian American history. In a blunt email, he told me that in all his many years of working for the State of Washington, he had never seen a small group like ours get money if they weren't first included in the

Governor's budget. He reminded me that the state was facing a $2 billion shortfall. "There is zero chance you will get money from the state," he said. "Zero."

State Representative Sharon Tomiko Santos told me that she could not support allocation of funds to our capital project when many needy social service projects struggled to keep afloat in the faltering economy.

Their skepticism made me more determined to succeed.

Beth Takekawa suggested that I ask Sharon Maeda, who had just returned to Seattle in 2003 from a stint in New York working for the United Methodist Church, to help us lobby. Beth had previously worked with Sharon's consulting firm Spectra Communications. She pointed out that Sharon, who served under Housing and Urban Development Secretary Henry Cisneros in Washington, D.C., was a brilliant tactician.

"It sounds like a great project, Ron, and I'd love to help," Sharon told me. "But I've got to say no. Remember, I've never done this stuff before. I was in Washington, D.C. That's different from Olympia, Washington. But the biggest obstacle is that I don't have a car. I just got back into town."

Kevin Hughes, a seasoned arts lobbyist, inquired about working for us, but his fee was too high. Beth and I couldn't think of anyone else. Aware that the legislative session had already begun, I decided to go to Olympia myself.

Ruthann Kurose called to bolster me. "I know you can do it," she told me. "You know how to work the system. Don't listen to all those naysayers."

Her words heartened me. I didn't see Ruthann much anymore. She lived on Mercer Island, serving as a trustee of Bellevue College from 1996 to 2008, where she fought for diversity. We no longer got together for runs. She told me the lack of consistent exercise made it much harder to manage her diabetes. We wistfully recalled when we were both fit enough to run and talk during two full laps around Greenlake.

Ruth Woo also stood at my side. She made calls to powerful elected officials who respected her. Over the years, Ruth's husband Ben, a force in his own right, wryly introduced himself not as an architect or by a current job title, but with the cheerful exclamation, "I'm the husband of Ruth Woo!"

With the encouragement of Ruthann and Ruth, I tenaciously stayed the course in my quest for state dollars. I created a one-page "elevator statement," citing the uniqueness of the museum as the only pan-Asian American community-based museum in the country.

The Wing Luke was the first Smithsonian affiliate in the Pacific Northwest. I brandished this credential in front of legislators. In 2001, Franklin Odo, head of the Smithsonian Institution's Asian Pacific American Program, told me that the Smithsonian wanted to initiate collaborations to spread its artifacts and exhibitions into local communities. There was no fee to become an affiliate, nor was there any obligation to borrow artifacts or participate in specific programs. "It's a pretty sweet deal," he told me. "You can use our logo. That will help boost your fundraising." He was right.

Three times a week, I drove to Olympia in the predawn hours. I wore my "lobbying uniform"—a gray wool sports coat from Lamonts department store, one of several formal ties I had received as gifts from friends, and my father's old black wash-and-wear overcoat from JCPenney. My previous sports coat and two ties from Sears, tattered and stained, went to Goodwill. I carried a small sheaf of one-page project descriptions in a buff-colored manila folder and a stack of business cards in my pocket.

On Ellen Ferguson's advice, I attended weekly meetings of the Heritage Caucus, which convened promptly at 7 a.m. There, I met legislators interested in culture and history projects, along with preservationists and museum folks from around the state. I promote the Wing Luke Museum's effort.

I spent the rest of my day in Olympia visiting the offices of legislators, starting with my district representatives. In many cases, I found the legislative assistants more knowledgeable than their bosses. Several became friends. They took me to lunch. They strategized about how to get the key votes we needed to secure funding.

Back in Seattle, Beth, Cassie and others at the museum asked our community partners to make phone calls, write emails and letters, and meet with their legislators.

The tide turned by the time the House capital budget was prepared. "I've never seen anything like this," one legislative aide told me. "While the legislators are proposing huge cuts to the arts, your community has made funding for the new museum as high a priority as funding the social safety net."

Velma Veloria, enjoying her clout as the first Asian American woman in the state legislature, pushed our case as a member of the capital budget committee.

I sought help from Kip Tokuda, a former legislator and the older brother of my former schoolmate Marilyn Tokuda. Another sibling, Wendy, was a famous news anchor in San Francisco. Kip's mom, Tama Tokuda, volunteered as a docent during the *Executive Order 9066* exhibition.

Kip retired from politics the year before I approached him. He had a disarming laugh and a self-deprecating manner. He was well-liked by his former colleagues, Republicans and Democrats alike. He was a mentor and father figure to young legislative aides, including Nori Catabay and Hyeok Kim. He shored up their spirits after the disheartening passage of Initiative 200, which ended affirmative action in state and local hiring. Nori explained to me how Olympia worked, taking a full day to lead me around to the offices of individual legislators.

Kip reached out to his former colleagues. He called back to reassure me. He told me that Hans Dunshee, the chair of the House capital budget committee, phoned to say, "Every single Asian in the state of Washington has called me on behalf of the Wing Luke Museum—and a couple of honkies, too!"

When the session was over, we got $1.5 million from the state to purchase our building. It was a big breakthrough.

We scored an additional $3 million in the following biennial session. My relationships with legislators and their aides deepened. I learned the value of never looking past the low-paid staff who screen calls and messages, meet with constituents and provide daily briefings. They made sure our project wasn't ignored.

Senator Adam Kline, an unapologetic liberal firebrand who represented South Seattle, took me with him to buttonhole other senators, including conservative Republicans. Through Adam, I learned that despite strong public disagreements between Democrats and Republicans, it was possible to find common ground, especially if an issue was positioned as nonpartisan and beneficial to a very broad audience.

I went with capital campaign manager Joy Shigaki to Washington, D.C., to lobby for a federal appropriation. During one trip, Joy agreed to a side shopping excursion to help me find a new pair of dress shoes to replace the ones I had worn for the past 10 years. I had no sense of what was fashionable, but I knew that my old shoes wouldn't last much longer. We went to Filene's Basement, where I found a pair of black, square-toed slip-ons. The sale price was just under $30. Joy reassured me that this was very reasonable. I took the shoes home and wore them for the next several years, through the end of the campaign.

In May 2003, I was invited to a White House reception to celebrate Asian Pacific Heritage Month. I used the opportunity to continue lobbying in D.C. To my surprise, nearly all the members of Congress had gone home on recess except Hawaii Senator Daniel Inouye. His travel plans had fallen through. He agreed to a one-on-one meeting because he had plenty of time on his hands. "You're lucky you caught me here," he said.

I was truly lucky. Senator Inouye chaired the Senate Appropriations Committee and the Defense Subcommittee, which gave him enormous power over federal allocations. I knew that he got money for a huge expansion of the Japanese American National Museum in Los Angeles. Maybe, I thought to myself, he could help the Wing Luke, too.

Senator Inouye greeted me in the reception area, smiling warmly, shaking my right hand with his left hand. I remember learning in my Asian American studies class that he lost his right hand in a grenade explosion. Inouye, a decorated member of the Japanese American 442nd Infantry Regiment, was a larger-than-life figure to many Asian Americans like me who looked to him as a progressive political role model. During the Watergate hearings, I bristled along with every other Asian American when John J. Wilson, attorney for disgraced Nixon aide H. R. Haldeman, referred to Inouye as a "little Jap."

Senator Inouye's hair was black and his face was round and cherubic, with slightly puffy jowls. He looked two decades younger than his true age. He invited me to his office. He spoke in a relaxed, melodic baritone, his words slow and measured. I liked his plain-spoken manner and humility.

He explained that he was an ardent fan of museums. He revealed that he had been to the Wing Luke Museum and had many good friends in Seattle. He said he would be happy to work with Washington's U.S. Senators Patty Murray and Maria Cantwell to support the new Wing Luke Museum.

"But it's tough to get money for brick-and-mortar construction," he cautioned. "Have you thought about approaching the Taiwan government for a grant? Lately, they've been real interested in establishing a more favorable image in the U.S., so they're looking for ways to get involved in cultural projects."

I told him that I didn't have any relationships in Taiwan.

"How about permanent exhibitions?" he asked. "Are you planning anything on the Nisei veterans?"

I told him we wanted to incorporate portions of the *Executive Order 9066* exhibit into the museum's new space.

"Good," he said finally. "Let me see what I can do. In the meantime, keep me posted on the progress of your campaign. I'll work with you on this, but I need to stay behind the scenes." Because of Senate protocol, he said, "the girls"—referring to Cantwell and Murray—"will be the leads on this." I was momentarily taken aback by his use of the term "girls." In retrospect, I believe that he meant no disrespect. He was a full generation older than they were.

On September 26, Senator Inouye sent me a letter indicating that he would soon visit with Cantwell and Murray as "a follow-up to our discussions." He said that it was too late for a 2004 request but added, "for the next go-around, I will do my best."

In May 2004, I returned to Washington, D.C., to brief Senator Cantwell on the Wing Luke campaign. The museum worked with her staff to prepare a formal funding request. When I entered her office, Cantwell came out to greet me with news that "Danny" had just succeeded in getting the museum $1.5 million. He embedded the funds in a federal defense appropriation bill, among a hodge-podge of allocations for groups like the Daughters of the American Revolution. She was so excited that she jumped up and down and pumped her fist in the air. I was elated as well. "He came through!" she exclaimed. "He came through!"

CHAPTER 65

Finding Community Dollars

THE COLLINS GROUP COUNSELED US not to limit our fundraising to the public realm. They taught us that successful campaigns rely on a variety of sources—individual donors, foundations and corporations, and government. This was the classic "balanced" fundraising pyramid.

As activists in the civil rights era, our first thought was to turn to the government. We didn't think about putting in our own money and using community dollars to leverage other kinds of support.

"Each board member has to make a significant gift," Stuart Grover advised. "It starts there. Other potential contributors will look to see what they do. There's no other way you're going to reach your fundraising target."

Based on the size of our campaign, Stuart felt that the museum board needed to donate a total of $500,000. I thought about our 12 members. Most were community activists of limited means. I took a deep breath. "That's over $40,000 per person," I said. "Is that even possible?"

Stuart told me to think creatively. First, he said, gifts could be three- to five-year pledges. Spouses, siblings or other family members could pool their money to make memorial contributions to honor parents or grandparents. We could also add new board members.

Ellen Ferguson led the charge. Early on, she pledged $100,000. She contributed another $25,000 after the campaign stalled. She and Paul Mar had lunch with Ellen's dad, Hugh Ferguson, at Four Seas Restaurant to ask him for a gift. The next day, Ellen excitedly called to inform me that her dad decided to "do the big one," meaning a $1 million pledge. I gasped and nearly fell off my chair. When I shared the news with Beth, Cassie, Joy and other staff, the office erupted in cheers of joy.

We were so caught off-guard—and so inexperienced in donor stewardship—that we forgot to send flowers and a card to thank Ellen's father. It took Ellen to jolt us out of our bliss and remedy our big *faux pas*. I felt sheepish. Lesson learned.

In September 2004, Ellen's father hosted a donor cultivation event at his beautiful home and garden in Medina, a wealthy community on the eastern shore of Lake Washington. As with my foray into Laurelhurst with George Pillsbury years earlier, I got lost on the drive over.

Our other Wing Luke board leaders—Paul Mar, Gloria Wakayama, Helen Kay and Victor Mizumori—each came through with pledges of $50,000 to $100,000. Other board members stretched to make significant commitments as well.

Inspired by the leadership of the board, the Wing Luke staff team set its own ambitious goal of $50,000.

As the person leading the charge, I wondered what to do. I had little money. But I remembered that I had a joint savings account with my mother at United Savings and Loan. It came from my time as a busboy at the Hong Kong Restaurant. I hadn't touched it. The total swelled to $10,000, mostly through the accumulation of interest. I gave it all to the campaign. If I was to ask the Wing Luke board and staff to step up, I needed to as well. I still had time to rebuild a financial safety net.

I reflected on how I got the money. A portion came directly from my salary. But a portion also came from the waiters. At the end of each day, they gave the busboys a bonus for cleaning up their tables. My gift was a way to repay my father and the other men.

Our success in getting money from Olympia and Washington, D.C.—and the significant board and staff gifts—sparked a cascade of big grants. In 2004, we received $1 million from the Bill & Melinda Gates Foundation, $1.25 million from the Paul G. Allen Foundation for the Arts, $1.2 million from King County and $1 million from the Seattle City Council.

The Allen Foundation grant came about through the advocacy of Huong Vu, a young Vietnamese American program officer who visited the East Kong Yick Building on a hot July day with fellow staffer Peter Berliner. In advance of their tour, I called to reassure Huong that the dead pigeons had been cleared away. She thanked me. When Huong walked inside the old hotel, she got goosebumps all over her arms. "I think that was the presence of many generations that came before us," she told me later.

Huong became an ambassador for the Wing Luke cause. She was part of the Joy Bucks Club, an informal collective of Asian American women at charitable foundations across the country. Every year, they met at the Grantmakers in the Arts conference and pushed for funding equity.

Around this same time, I met Margot Copeland, a new executive at KeyBank Foundation. She supervised diversity initiatives out of KeyBank's corporate headquarters in Cleveland. I took her to lunch and on a tour of the East Kong Yick Building. An African American native of Richmond, Virginia, Margot had a luminous smile and a magnetic personality. We connected. Before she left, she looked me in the eyes and said, "This is significant. Ron, I'm going to do something big." She followed through with a six-figure gift.

Without knowing it, I had developed a reputation for being a fundraising whiz. I was considered a master schmoozer with an aptitude for converting lukewarm supporters into passionate donors. Uncle Bob Santos joked, "When people see you coming in a suit and tie, they know they better stay over on the other side of the street."

But fundraising didn't come easily. It took a lot of willpower to put on my public face and go out the door to sell the cause. An introvert by nature, I felt far more at home in my old skin as a low-key reporter, working behind the scenes to gather information for stories, unknown to others except for my byline.

One evening, in the midst of the campaign, I arrived at a political fundraiser at the home of Ben and Ruth Woo. Ben was lounging outside the front door, drink in hand. I heard boisterous chatter emanating from the house. Ben, cheeks noticeably reddened by the alcohol, asked me how the campaign was going. "It's tough," I told him. I explained that I didn't enjoy the glad-handing, the small talk and the countless community events. "It takes a lot out of me," I said. "I don't see how you and Ruth do this all the time." Ben turned to me with a wry expression and exclaimed: "What? You think I enjoy this stuff, Ron? I'd rather skip the dinners, write out a check and spend my time going off to hunt for mushrooms."

It didn't dawn on me until then that there were community

leaders that I looked up to who didn't relish fundraising either.

Tours of the vacant Kong Yick building were a fail-proof strategy. I teamed up with Paul Mar. We talked about the old bachelor apartments and our blueprint for turning the building into a modern paean to past and present generations. On the top floor, we carefully navigated around the carcasses of dead pigeons and layers of droppings encrusted into the wooden floor boards. Although the broken windows were secured with plywood, pigeons managed to find their way inside. Sometimes, a pigeon or two swooped in, startling visitors. One time, when I poked my head inside a doorway, a pigeon flew within an inch of my face. I skipped backward, my mind recoiling to a scene from the Alfred Hitchcock movie *The Birds*.

Beth Takekawa reminded me that I had spent my adolescence trying to catch pigeons in the Hong Kong Restaurant building; now I was trying to evict them from our future home. When I lived in the ID, I saw flocks of pigeons strutting near the dumpsters behind my apartment and in Hing Hay Park, softly cooing as they pecked at bread crumbs and rice spread out by elderly residents. Like other Chinatown denizens, I learned to avoid walking beneath the overhead telephone wires so I wouldn't be hit by surprise bird bombs.

By the third year of the campaign, the fundraising stalled. During our monthly meetings with the Collins Group, tensions rose. *Had we reached too high?* Stuart tried to provide reassurances. He cracked puns to lighten the mood. The puns were badly timed, making everyone cranky.

Even more challenging, personal losses were taking a big toll. In 2003, Beth's father died unexpectedly of cancer. The next year, Beth's mother also died of cancer. Gloria's mother passed away. Ellen's elderly father began going in and out of the hospital, suffering near heart failure.

I was floored by three unexpected deaths. Keith Wong, my pal from Franklin High and the Hong Kong Restaurant, died of a heart attack on August 27, 2003. He was only 52. My friend Karen Chinn, who moved back to Seattle with her husband Philip Lee to raise their young daughter, succumbed to cancer on November 18, 2003. She was 44. Their daughter Louisa—the spitting image of Karen—was in 3rd grade. Craig Shimabukuro, the chain-smoking radical, someone I had grown very fond of, died suddenly at his Beacon Hill home on March 16, 2004 at the age of 56.

I became blind in my left eye, the result of myopic macular degeneration. It became difficult for me to read prepared remarks in front of an audience. Beth began printing out my speeches in giant 16-point type. I gravitated toward memorization and ad-libbing.

Beth had her own physical challenge. She became deaf in her left ear three months after she was hired at the museum. Both of us made the best of our situations. We thought it was funny that the museum was being led by one person who could barely see and another who could barely hear.

In 2005, Loan and I divorced. It was a very trying, chaotic period. I was a single parent and primary caregiver to Cian and Kino. I also cared for my aging mother, living alone in the house after the death of my father.

Stuart Grover called us "the walking wounded." Still, we refused to succumb to the mounting fundraising pressure and "campaign fatigue." Beth believed that the secret ingredient that sheltered the campaign at its lowest moments was our unshakeable commitment to building a legacy. "We all drank the Kool-Aid," she cracked. "If there wasn't Kool-Aid drinking, nothing would ever happen in the world."

The news media kept a spotlight on us. On April 26, 2005,

the *Seattle P-I* featured a cover story, "Old Chinatown attracts new money." It highlighted the Wing Luke effort and developer James Koh's purchase of three historic buildings—the Milwaukee Hotel, the Mar Hotel and the Alps Hotel. There was a striking photo of me inside the East Kong Yick Building, clutching my two sons, Cian, 9, and Kino, 7, as an old window shutter rattled ominously from the wind.

In the summer of 2005, Paul Mar looked into the New Markets Tax Credit (NMTC) program as a source of equity funding. He discovered that the museum, located in an impoverished neighborhood, was eligible for this federal program. In late 2005, another party receiving NMTC funds had defaulted on its deal. The Wing Luke Museum was able to step into an arrangement that yielded roughly $2 million. The deal closed in the spring of 2006, thrusting the capital campaign one giant stride toward its final goal. We felt a new surge of hope.

Yet even with the New Market Tax Credit money, we had not closed the campaign. By 2006, we were at 70 percent of our fundraising goal and running out of time.

On October 9, 2006, the *Seattle Weekly* ran an article headlined, "A Wing Luke and a Prayer." The article noted that some in the arts community were "sniping," believing that I had overplayed my hand. The article quoted curator Matthew Kangas as saying, "It's laudable, but I'm skeptical." Kangas scoffed at the museum's community-based approach to exhibitions and programs. He added, "The great Asian art collectors here are white. Seattle's Asian-American community is not mature enough to support arts institutions."

Velma Veloria, in the same article, retorted, "Oh, that's bullshit! We'll be able to raise the money." Velma went on to say that traditional art collectors were "conservative and classist." Velma pointed out that art permeated the lives of Asian

American pioneers who lived at the Kong Yick. "Good God! Look at the art all over their walls! Look at Angkor Wat! Don't tell me that's not 'mature enough!'"

The article, describing me as a "steel-nerved gambler," pointed out that the museum still had millions to raise from small donors. "That's where the sledding becomes very, very difficult," I told the reporter. But I added that the museum was "The Little Engine That Could." I had been reading that Little Golden Book Classic to my children before bed.

Mayumi and her brother Gerard, an accomplished sculptor, helped raise $250,000 to establish the George Tsutakawa Art Gallery. The Cathay Post and the Alaskero Foundation each contributed $100,000 to restore two apartments to commemorate Chinese American veterans and Filipino cannery workers. The Alaskero Foundation was established with funds from the sale of the Local 37 union hall in Pioneer Square. Former Governor Gary Locke lent his name to the new Gary Locke Library and Community Heritage Center. A mezzanine meeting space was named in honor of Ruby Chow and her husband Ping. The welcome hall was named in honor of Ellen's parents, Hugh and Jane Ferguson.

An intimate 59-seat story theater was created on the first floor for small talks and film showings. I asked Althea Stroum, a local philanthropist, to donate a theatrical curtain from the Nippon Kan to serve as a backdrop for the new theater. Her family purchased the Nippon Kan from the previous owner, putting the curtain in storage. We hired a firm to clean and restore portions of the century-old fabric, which featured colorful advertisements from local Japanese American businesses.

With a $500,000 grant from the Atsuhiko and Ina Tateuchi Foundation, the theater became the Tateuchi Story Theatre. Ina and I served together on the Seattle Public Library

Foundation board during the Libraries for All Campaign. Ina's financial advisor, Dan Asher, brokered the gift. In 1995, Dan had helped the Wing Luke raise funds for *Visas for Life*, a traveling exhibit about Chiune and Yukiko Sugihara, a diplomatic couple who saved thousands of Jews in Lithuania from the Holocaust.

Paul Mar secured a $10,000 gift from the International District Rotary Club. In September 1986, the ID Club achieved notoriety when it admitted 15 women in violation of Rotary International's male-only membership clause. In 1987, the U.S. Supreme Court ruled against the restriction against women.

Despite my initial hesitation, the grand staircase to the second floor of the new museum was named in my honor as a way to attract additional dollars. The wood to construct the staircase came from joists on the first floor and from the mezzanine ceilings at Wah Young Company and three other former businesses in the building.

By the winter of 2007, we had raised $19.6 million. By fall 2008, the figure crept up to $21.5 million.

Vera and Joey Ing, seeing the campaign inch toward the finish, made a $100,000 gift. It was their biggest charitable donation. The Ings were dear friends of Ron Ho, a world-renowned jewelry artist and stalwart donor to the museum's annual art auction. I later learned that Joey and Ron were classmates at Roosevelt High School in Honolulu in 1954. Vera commissioned Ron to create three necklaces for her. The museum store became the Vera and Joey Ing Marketplace.

Bettie Luke invited me to speak at the annual New Year's banquet of the Luke Family Association at the Four Seas Restaurant. Bettie and her sisters Ruby Luke and Marguerite Young spearheaded a $100,000 campaign to claim a permanent meeting room in the new facility. They each pledged $10,000.

At the event, I saw Mrs. Bo Luke, an elderly sewing woman I interviewed for the *Tired Hands* project. Her nickname was *lai len vong* (拉鍊王) or "zipper queen" because of her incredible proficiency at sewing zippers on jackets. Mrs. Luke smiled as I talked about the value of gifts from ordinary people. At the end, dozens of people scrambled to my table with gifts of cash, checks and pledges of money written on torn scraps of paper. Mrs. Luke wrote a check for $500.

The Wing Luke campaign attracted 1,500 individual donors.

Debbie Louie contributed $2,500, her first-ever major charitable gift. Greg Tuai, who made an unprompted lead gift to help fund publication of the second edition of *Reflections of Seattle's Chinese Americans*, gave generously to the capital campaign, too. Greg's cousin Elana Lim, who grew up with her family in the Number 507 apartment upstairs in the East Kong Yick Building, made a substantial gift to honor her family.

My sister Linda gave $5,000 in memory of our parents.

In October 2017, nearly 10 years after the end of the campaign, I sat down for a bowl of noodles with Huong Vu at Phở Bac. It was one of the first *phở* restaurants in Seattle, located in a red, boat-shaped building at the corner of 14ᵗʰ Avenue South and South Jackson. "I don't know if you knew this," she told me, "but there was deep, deep skepticism from all the funders that you could pull this thing off. No one believed you could do it."

She recalled that after I took her and Peter Berliner on the Kong Yick tour years earlier, she struggled to prepare a report for the Allen Foundation. "It was six pages long, small 10-point type," she said. "I had to rewrite it a few times. I had never had to do this for any other arts group. I only needed a page and a half for groups like Bellevue Art Museum, Seattle Art Museum and Seattle Children's Theater. They received way more money for their capital campaigns. The Wing Luke was considered a high-risk grant. I was troubled by this."

I smiled coyly. "As you probably figured out, I'm not easily deterred."

Huong continued, "You don't know how gratifying it was when your project finished on time, on budget and turned out to be so successful."

After we finished eating, I gave her a ride back to her home in the Central District. I went back to Beacon Hill. Suddenly, I recalled all the gossip and cynical remarks that reached my ears after the fundraising began. I had pushed aside five years of it. But it all came flooding back, as if an old seawall had just crumbled against the onslaught of a tsunami. But I stood safely on high ground. The campaign was over.

Earlier that day, I watched *Breaking2*, a 55-minute documentary on Kenyan runner Eliud Kipchoge's epic attempt to complete a marathon in under two hours. He clocked in at a breathtaking 2 hours and 25 seconds, the fastest marathon in history. I was spellbound watching the uncanny determination in Kipchoge's face as he sped along the track in his red singlet, surrounded by half a dozen pacers. "I want to tell the world that no human is limited," he said, answering those who had said a sub-two-hour marathon was impossible. "It's not about the legs. It's about the heart and mind."

If the skeptics had turned out to be right and the Wing Luke campaign had fallen short, I would not have despaired. I tried my best. My board and staff did, too. We contributed everything. Our community friends didn't disappoint us. That's how miracles are born.

CHAPTER 66

Construction

THE COMMUNITY PROCESS THAT THE Wing Luke Museum pioneered for its exhibitions and programs also guided the remodel of the East Kong Yick Building. Cassie convened listening sessions with Wing Luke board, staff and community stakeholders. The findings became the basis of a visitor experience report in April 2002. Included were a story theater, community hall, special exhibition galleries, historical immersion exhibits, indoor sculpture garden, community heritage center, learning studios and a museum marketplace.

The meetings were held in the Pioneer Square office of Olson Sundberg Kundig Allen, the firm selected to implement our vision. Rick Sundberg was the lead architect.

Earlier, we had hired another local firm, Schacht Aslani Architects, to conduct a pre-design study to explore the feasibility of converting a historic hotel into a functional museum. Richard Rabinowitz, the national consultant who developed the history program at the Lower East Side Tenement Museum, collaborated.

Olson Sundberg's final architectural plan called for gutting much of the East Kong Yick Building's interior, including the mezzanine. But it also called for retention of exterior facades, the steep hotel staircase, two interior light wells, the Yee Family Association balcony and sections of the third floor.

Working with seven other artists, John Pai devised a master art plan. It called for multisensory installations employing sound, light, projections, moving air currents and fabric. "There's an opportunity to allow a true sense of the building to be revealed, as well as a true metaphoric story of the residents who walked these halls," John wrote.

We began construction in June 2006. Beth and Paul provided oversight. Marpac Construction served as general contractor. HomeSight, a community development nonprofit in Southeast Seattle, was project manager and finance consultant.

The first step was removing the pigeon droppings and demolishing walls dividing some interior spaces. We encountered several unforeseen problems. The most significant was the load-bearing columns in Wah Young Company. They were not anchored at all in the basement. The problem was corrected, but at a price.

We abandoned the original plan to build out the basement. We found it too costly, partly due to the need for "clear path" circulation to the elevators.

We took care to preserve the ornate Chinese family association room and protect the original tin ceiling with a temporary shield. We left intact the narrow corridors, the hotel manager's office, several apartments, toilets, shared kitchens, shower rooms, windows and doors.

The rough-hewn old-growth timbers in the light wells were stripped of their lath and plaster. The light wells were uncovered to let in natural light from above. Fir joists were recycled as stair treads. An old fire door was repurposed as the front counter in the lobby.

None of the unexpected construction issues were insurmountable. Paul Mar credited the solid working relationship between the architect, contractor and museum. No one had to call in attorneys, the bugaboo of many stalled projects.

The museum hired Ed Echtle, an independent contractor, to dismantle the Yick Fung store and reinstall it in the museum space, and to remodel a Canton Alley apartment already within the building. He did a magnificent job, finishing in July 2008, several months after the grand opening.

I first learned about Ed from Brian Lock. "You should meet this *lo fan* friend of mine," Brian said. "He helped develop a website for the Olympia Chinese community. It's pretty cool." Brian and Ed were small town boys who did a lot of hiking, fishing and camping. Ed was raised in Tenino. The two were born just days apart in the same hospital in Olympia.

I met Ed in person when he drove to Seattle to interview me for his master's thesis on the Wing Luke Museum. "Tenino?" I said, scratching my head. "Where's that?" He laughed. "It's small." He noted that Tenino's sandstone quarries had provided cut stone for many of Seattle's early buildings.

Ed and I discovered that we had many common interests. He had worked as director of the Bigelow House Museum in Olympia. He taught immigration and labor history at The Evergreen State College. Like Greg Tuai, he was a Renaissance man, armed with many different skills, including research, writing, photography, video, carpentry and construction.

Ed made his money as an independent contractor. I hired him to make upgrades to my house on Beacon Hill. He was amazingly adept at devising simple, low-cost solutions while respecting the integrity and character of the original structure.

I told Ed I wanted to preserve Jimmy Mar's store as a permanent feature of the new Wing Luke Museum. "Can this be done?" I asked. He responded without blinking, "Sure." Then—hoping to appeal to his appreciation for historic preservation—I added, "Do *you* want to do it?" He paused briefly, then declared firmly, "Sure."

We got to work. Bob Fisher, the museum's collections manager, hired a moving company to wheel the cabinets, shelves, walls and counters carefully across Canton Alley from 705 South King Street in the West Kong Yick Building to the east building. Ed methodically disassembled and reassembled the pieces, much like putting together a complex jigsaw puzzle. We retained everything—the potbelly stove, lights, cash register, scales, hand-written signs, wooden crates, floor boards, light fixtures and merchandise.

Three dozen vintage mason jars with metal twist tops that lined the shelves near the front counter made a safe journey over. These jars—filled with fresh ginger, mango slices, preserved plum candy and more—stirred sweet memories of my childhood visits to Uncle Jimmy's store.

Jimmy Mar continued to work in his little back office during the move. Ed noticed that his mood began to sour. Concerned, Ed gingerly approached him as he sat in his cubicle, his back turned away. "Is everything okay?" Jimmy didn't respond. But Ed heard him quietly sobbing. Ed left him alone.

As construction progressed—and Jimmy saw his old store re-emerge in the new museum—his upbeat demeanor returned.

After completing installation of Jimmy Mar's store, Ed moved on to the restoration of Canton Alley #6. This was Debbie Louie's childhood home. We wanted to use it for tours to illustrate family life in Chinatown in the 1960s.

Debbie spent her early years hanging out with Donnie

Chin and Dean Wong in the IDEC radio room just across the alley. She heard the coded chatter and beeping of the police scanner and monitored the security cameras. She listened to Donnie's boombox, which played the Temptations, the Spinners, the Commodores, Earth Wind & Fire, Gap Band, L.T.D., Brothers Johnson, Marvin Gaye, Stevie Wonder and Gil Scott-Heron. In nice weather, she and other kids sat outside in the alley and played *mahjong*, using Donnie's medical kits as stools. They took turns wheeling one another around on a hand truck.

The other kids who hung out at IDEC included the Lees from Ying Hei Restaurant—Jeannie, Angela, Chris and Diana. They played tag with Donnie's stun gun, pitched quarters in competitions, and played dodgeball behind the Chong Wa Benevolent Association.

When I first approached Debbie about resurrecting her former home, she balked. She did not want to relive the embarrassment of her impoverished past. Dean had captured a haunting portrait of Debbie as a four-year-old in glasses, the right lens covered with tape, staring out through the security screen mesh on the door of her residence.

But after I explained the significance of her experience, Debbie began to embrace her modest origins with swelling pride. Her mother donated a sewing machine, a table and other household objects. Shannon taped an interview with Debbie.

There was one difficult moment during the Canton Alley restoration. Construction crews demolished the space to make way for structural reinforcements to the back wall. But they didn't document the original location of the divider walls and the clawfoot bathtub, porcelain kitchen sink and toilet. Ed didn't know how to fit everything back together. He was thoroughly stumped.

Fortunately, there were photographs. Ed and Bob Fisher

figured out where everything belonged by closely scrutinizing the 12"x12" commercial floor tiles in the pictures.

Ed also helped reinstall trim in the third-floor hallways. When he ran out of tongue-and-groove fir flooring to finish a room, he drove to Second Use, a building materials salvage company south of downtown. He found boards that had been recovered from a Greenlake mansion owned by former Seattle Mayor Ole Hanson, who made his mark by fiercely opposing the Seattle General Strike of 1919. Ed relished knowing that he was using pieces of Hanson's lavish residence to reconstruct a laborer's hotel.

When Ed began working on the new museum, he couldn't understand why he felt such a strong sense of *déjà vu*. In 2017, it finally came to him. In 1985, he came to Seattle with friends to attend concerts at Gorilla Gardens, an underground music club which was the birthplace of grunge. It was located at 410 Fifth Avenue South, just four blocks from the East Kong Yick Building.

During that phase in his life, Ed was a drummer and played at house parties in Olympia. He lived with band members in a house known as "The Alamo," named by housemate Slim Moon, who later co-founded Kill Rock Stars Records. Grunge legend Kurt Cobain was a regular visitor. He was dating Tracy Marander, one of Ed's housemates at the time.

Luckily for me—and the Wing Luke Museum—Ed's interest in musical performance waned. He moved to Santa Cruz in 1989, where he apprenticed with a talented builder and re-modeler. He returned home with a new set of skills.

CHAPTER 67

Goodbyes

I FELT SAD THAT MY parents didn't live long enough to see the new museum open. My father passed away on April 23, 1996, at age 79 and my mother died on May 31, 2005, at age 86. They inspired me. They encouraged me. Their love sustained me through everything.

My friend Fran Matsuoka used to call weekly to share sightings of my father at the Beacon Hill Library. "He's very proud of you," she said. I didn't realize it at the time, but he scoured the newspapers for any mention of my name or the Wing Luke Museum. After he passed, I discovered a manila envelope stuffed with clipped news articles.

My mother frequently stopped by the museum. She parked her bright red 1979 Mercury Zephyr in front of the entrance. She shuffled to the doorway, dressed in an ultramarine blue jacket, a purple sweater vest, dark slacks and rubber-soled loafers. Smiling, she asked the front desk volunteers, *"Is Ah-lon dare?"* The message "Your mother is here" quickly reached me. Aware of her eroding eyesight and slow motor skills, I rushed down to greet her, looking to make sure she hadn't accidentally swiped her vehicle against the front facade.

I was grateful that my mother and father lived in the comfort of our Beacon Hill home until their final days. My father died in the hospital after a short bout of pneumonia. When he collapsed at home, I called Donnie Chin. Donnie arrived right away with an ambulance which transported him to Swedish Hospital. My mother suffered from failing kidneys and early-stage dementia in her final year. She faded quickly in her last two months and died at Providence Hospital.

About a week after my mother died, I had been scheduled to be in Washington, D.C., to deliver the keynote address at the annual conference of Smithsonian Affiliate organizations. Harold Closter, director of the Smithsonian Affiliates program, had invited me. I cancelled my travel plans and began working with Jimmy Mar on funeral arrangements.

I was also disappointed that Clifton Goon didn't live long enough to witness the opening of the new museum. He had been in an assisted care facility since 1998. He was struck by a vehicle while crossing the street in Chinatown. His body, ravaged by rheumatoid arthritis, deteriorated. He had trouble eating solid foods and talking. I kept him informed about the progress of the project. He could do little more than signal by shifting his eyes and mumbling. I could tell he was pleased. He passed away on December 30, 2006.

By early 2007, having reached my fundraising goals and broken ground for the new museum, I told my staff and board that I was leaving at the end of the year. This didn't come as a total surprise. I had announced at the beginning of the campaign that I was only going to stay through the fundraising. Still, many assumed that I might remain through the opening the following year.

In an April 2, 2007, letter to my board co-chairs Gloria and Ellen, I wrote: "It has been an honor beyond words—the highlight of my life—to have worked alongside both of you and the other members of the board in creating a cultural institution that now has so much meaning to so many people, anchored in its first permanent home in the neighborhood."

On my last day, I didn't have much to take home. I filled two cardboard storage file boxes with personal effects—a large bundle of cards and letters from friends, a few folders with work papers, and a dozen pictures that adorned the window behind my work cubicle which my kids, nieces and nephews had scrawled with crayons and colored pencils.

The August 16, 2007, edition of *The Seattle Times* proclaimed, "Head of Seattle's Wing Luke Museum to Retire." The story, which described me as "a self-taught curator who turned a rundown museum into a nationally acclaimed institution for Asian history and culture," didn't get it quite right. I wasn't retiring. Everywhere I went, I was asked what I intended to do during retirement.

The article stated that Beth Takekawa, CEO of the Museum, would take over as executive director. But she had already been functioning as both CEO and executive director during the campaign. My departure caused minimal disruption. Joy Shigaki stepped down as campaign manager and moved to New York to begin a new chapter. Charlene Mano helped close out remaining fundraising tasks.

By that time, invitations to speak had already begun to take me outside the U.S. I delivered keynote addresses at the British Columbia Museums Association conference on October 2, 2004, in Nanaimo and at the Canadian Museums Association on March 30, 2007, in Ottawa. I was invited by Joy Davis, a program director at the University of Victoria, to teach a week-long class for the cultural resource management program. The students were young aboriginal Canadians. I learned that the Wing Luke Museum, by Canadian definition, was a "community cultural centre," not a museum. I also learned that these cultural centres were pioneered by indigenous people who described themselves as "First Nation bands," not "Native American tribes."

The Wing Luke board hosted a farewell party for me at the House of Hong on December 12, 2007. I was touched when former *UW Daily* colleague Dean Paton took the mic. If life had dealt me a better hand, he told the crowd, I would certainly have joined several of our peers—Peter Rinearson, Tim Egan and Steve Miletich—in garnering a Pulitzer Prize nomination in journalism.

I appreciated Dean for standing by me during my discrimination complaint against the *UW Daily*. Through the years, we met spontaneously for dinners at the tiny Atlas Café (大來飯店) on the corner of Maynard Avenue South and South King Street. It was run by Louie Hong, a lean, spry old man who opened it in 1956. We sat on adjacent counter stools reminiscing about the Watergate era and the dystopian reign of "Tricky Dick" Nixon. He said that my story about Bill Wong, the waiter at Hong Kong Restaurant, helped him see beyond Chinese stereotypes. Dean stunned me in 2017 when he revealed that he had struggled with a debilitating stuttering problem his whole life. I had no clue. At the *UW Daily*, I had envied his brash, no-holds-barred investigative reporting.

I stayed away from the museum in the months before the opening. I knew there was much still to be done, but I was finished. Beth Takekawa was in charge. I was busy cobbling together a new career and a new life.

I came back for the Wing Luke annual art auction on

March 22, 2008. It was a "Hard Hat Gala" in the new community room. Beth welcomed the audience. Mary Nam, an anchor at KOMO 4 News, served as mistress of ceremonies. KeyBank was the title sponsor, and my old friend Margot Copeland was back in town. I hadn't seen her in over five years, but her warm presence lit up my heart that evening.

I returned to the museum again on Saturday, May 31, 2008, to speak at the grand opening. The program was held on a dais on King Street in front of the museum. There was a ribbon-cutting ceremony with U.S. Senator Maria Cantwell, U.S. Representative Jim McDermott, Governor Christine Gregoire, King County Executive Ron Sims, Seattle Mayor Greg Nickels and our museum leadership team.

The day's festivities included performances by the Filipino Youth Activities Drill Team, the Seattle Chinese Community Girls Drill Team, One World Taiko, Morning Star Korean Cultural Center and Ke Liko A'e O Lei Lehua Hawaiian group.

After the outdoor program, Wing Luke's sister Ruby Luke, decked out in a dress of green sequins and a white, feathered hat, took me by the arm and led me through the front doors so we could explore the new museum together. I wore the square-toed dress shoes I had purchased from Filene's Basement. The leather in the uppers was cracked and the soles were badly worn, but the shoes delivered me successfully through the end of my tenure at the museum. Beaming, Ruby told a newspaper reporter, "I know my brother would be very impressed."

I felt proud. The opening of the museum capped over a decade of dreaming, planning and hard work. I led a crusade that many skeptics had glibly discounted. Stuart Grover told us that based on the relative size of our annual budget and the size of our fundraising campaign, we had just completed the largest nonprofit fundraising campaign ever in the region.

The museum, rebranded as the Wing Luke Museum of the Asian Pacific American Experience—or "The Wing" for short—soon received several major honors, including the 2009 Great Places Award, the 36th International Design Award and the American Institute of Architects 2009 Honor Award.

On February 10, 2013, U.S. Secretary of Interior Ken Salazar and other officials—including U.S. Senators Patty Murray and Maria Cantwell, and U.S. Representatives Jim McDermott and Adam Smith—came to The Wing for a special ceremony announcing that the museum had been designated an "affiliated area" of the National Park Service. It was nice to be able to sit in the back of the room and not be the center of attention.

After I left the museum, I accepted a part-time position as "community scholar-in-residence" at the University of Washington graduate program in museology. I taught classes on fundraising and the community-based exhibition model.

I also became a consultant for the Gates Foundation, providing advice on the development of its new visitor center. Martha Choe was chief administrative officer and my former ID cohorts Annie Xuan Clark and Olivia Taguinod worked there, too.

I formed my own firm, Chew Communications, to publish community histories and to support emerging nonprofit cultural organizations. I teamed up with Ed Echtle and Debbie Louie to produce booklets for ICHS and Nikkei Concerns, both of which were celebrating 35th anniversaries. I produced three separate anthologies of senior stories for the National Asian Pacific Center on Aging.

Shannon Gee, who rose to senior producer at the Seattle Channel, became an associate of Chew Communications. She accompanied me to film two beloved Chinese institutions in their final days. In the fall of 2008, the Kong Sun Company and the Sun May Company closed in anticipation of a major rent increase by their new landlord James Koh.

The Kong Sun Company (江山公司) was operated by Carol Szeto. School kids on tours of the museum trekked there to buy rice candy, Chinese greeting cards and cheap mementos. Like me, Carol once worked at the Hong Kong Restaurant. We reminisced about the old days. She led Shannon and me down a flight of stairs to a dark basement to show us an ancient teller window. "Do you know what this was for?" Carol asked. I said no. But we all thought it would be a shame if it wasn't preserved.

At the Sun May Company, Donnie Chin began furiously packing up boxes of merchandise and hauling out antique cabinets. "This is so fucked up," he complained, shaking his head. "Take whatever you want. There's a lot of stuff I'm just going to have to dump." I salvaged an old wood-framed window that may have been part of the original store. I couldn't bear to see it go to a recycling station. I stored it outside on my back porch. Shannon took a few chairs, incense sticks and an antique artillery shell box, handy for storing digital video tapes.

Later that year, Kwan On Wing, directly across the street from Sun May and Kong Sun, also closed. Maxine Chan alerted me. I found out too late to bring in Shannon to videotape. Maxine's father Robert was a dear friend of David Louie, the proprietor who ran it with his wife May. Robert and David took English language classes together at Seattle Central Community College. Robert bought bean sprouts for his restaurant from Kwan On Wing. Shannon played basketball with David's daughter Vivian.

Kwan On Wing was the first Chinatown business to sell white sugar sponge cake (*bok hong go* 白糖糕) and rice noodle roll (*cheong fun* 腸粉). The batter for both was prepared over an old gas stove. The *bok hong go* was sweet, spongy and moist. The *cheong fun*—filled with dried shrimp, green onions and dried radish—was equally scrumptious; each roll was at least 18 inches long. At 50 cents a pop, it was the greatest lunch bargain in the city. My mother often dropped off a bag for me at the museum.

Suddenly, King Street was becoming a ghost town. One by one, flickering candles of the past were extinguished. Ying Hei was gone. King Café, Quong Tuck, Wah Young, Gom Hong and Wa Sang were gone. Now, Sun May, Kong Sun and Kwan On Wing joined the roster. At least Jimmy Mar's store was now safely ensconced inside the new museum.

Around this same time, Vera Ing was itching to write her autobiography. "It's not that simple," I warned. She scowled and crossed her arms. "Well, *of course!*" she said. "You have Chew Communications. *You're* going to help me." After looking over a few chapters she had written, Ed and I decided it would be more efficient to interview her and ghost-write other sections. Vera's book, *Dim Sum: The Seattle ABC (American Born Chinese) Dream*, was finished in 2010, four years before Vera passed away at the relatively young age of 73.

After tackling Vera's book, I felt ready to resurrect Gene's unpublished manuscript. I decided to finish it as part of a larger project that included oral histories of activists in the union reform movement. When I called Silme's widow Terri Mast for lunch, she had already read my mind. "Let's do it," she said. "It's time." The Alaskero Foundation provided a grant. Ed helped with research. Debbie designed the book. *Remembering Silme Domingo and Gene Viernes: The Legacy of Filipino American Labor Activism* was published in association with University of Washington Press in 2012.

In an article in *City Living Seattle* headlined "Three decades later, Ron Chew fulfills a promise to a murdered friend," I explained that my book was prompted by a visit to my house by one of Cian's friends, a young teen. When she told me that her last name was Doniego, I asked her whether she was related to Angel Doniego, a KDP activist who had worked with Silme and Gene. She was stunned. "Omigod! That's my father. Do you know him?" She knew nothing about his history.

At the February 2, 2012, book launch in the Wing Luke community hall, I spoke in public for the first time about my close connection to the cannery reform efforts. The next day, the pent-up emotions of 30 years broke free. I sat alone in my car in a parking lot in Chinatown, weeping. An enormous weight dissipated.

A year after the book's publication, Shannon completed an hour-long video documentary titled *One Generation's Time: The Legacy of Silme Domingo and Gene Viernes.* She put to good use much of the interview footage she gathered for the book.

Apart from my projects, I also found myself being asked to perform wedding ceremonies for friends and former work colleagues. I found it hard to say no. The one request I turned down was that of Dean Wong. He approached me when I was in the middle of my divorce.

On August 6, 2011, I served as the minister for Shannon's wedding to Ian Devier, another Seattle Channel producer. The outdoor marriage was held in a serene residential garden on Whidbey Island on a breezy, sunny day.

A year after I married Shannon and Ian, Debbie asked me to perform the marriage ceremony for her and her partner Pete Martone. They met at Microsoft and dated for four years, then moved to Morgantown, West Virginia, where Pete began a new job at West Virginia University. They came back to Seattle to get married. Like me, Pete didn't like to dress up. But he found a sports coat and slacks at Goodwill. I lent him my favorite yellow tie, left over from the capital campaign. Debbie wore a beautiful red Chinese gown her mom brought from Hong Kong when she first came to Seattle in 1964. I administered their vows on September 2, 2012, in a simple ceremony in my backyard.

When Shannon gave birth to a baby girl in early spring of 2013, she named her Lynne, after Shannon's late mother. But Shannon also wanted a Chinese name. I consulted with friends for suggestions. Lynne also became Gee Hoi-Chi (朱海慈). *Hoi* (海) means ocean or expansiveness. *Chi* (慈) means kindness or benevolence.

Aleta Eng and Dorothy Ng, the two young women who coordinated the Chinese heritage bus tour in 2010, also turned to me. I married Aleta and Matthew Gormley at the Rosehill Community Center in Mukilteo on February 10, 2012. I married Dorothy and her partner Richmond Wu on August 8, 2015, at Emerald City Trapeze Arts in SoDo.

In 2013, I was startled when the Franklin Alumni Association named me to the Franklin High School Hall of Fame. I was embarrassed to receive this honor because I had been such a mediocre student. The other inductees were King County Council member Larry Gossett (one of the Gang of Four) and the late Bill Speidel, founder of the Seattle Underground Tour.

The Hall of Fame event was held on May 16 at Mount Baker Community Club. Classmate Cindy Lee introduced me. My thoughts drifted back to high school. I remembered that my spacy friend Manuel Alinas used to have a huge crush on her.

Larry reminisced about the 1968 demonstrations at Franklin which led to his arrest. He noted that his current office was in the same location as the jail where he was held over four decades earlier.

Bill Speidel passed away in 1988. I used to see him nearly every weekend at the Hong Kong Restaurant. He came by to drop off free copies of the weekly *Seattle Guide*, pausing to exchange pleasantries with Uncle Alvin. When my father neared retirement, Bill's publication ran an ad with a sketch of my father in his waiter's uniform, noting that Hong Kong had been serving generations of Seattle families.

Bill's daughter Sunny accepted the award on her late father's behalf. Sunny and her husband Brian Haughton had taken over operation of the Underground Tour. I knew Brian from the *UW Daily*. He regularly covered my discrimination complaint. I was grateful to him for ensuring that coverage was always balanced and fair.

CHAPTER 68

A Trip to My Father's Village

IN HIGH SCHOOL, I WAS told that the Chinese who came to America were from Canton, the southernmost province of China. I assumed I was Cantonese. But when I heard true Cantonese people talk, I couldn't understand them.

My language was slower, more guttural and much louder—spoken in a shout. *Were we really Cantonese? If not, where did we come from?* I knew that we weren't northern Chinese. They spoke Mandarin. That sounded even stranger.

My mother explained that I was a *Hoy san nghin* (台山人), a person from Hoisan. We spoke *Hoy san wah* or Hoisanese (台山話), not Cantonese (廣州話).

She told me that we were from the four-county Sze Yip (四邑) region in the Pearl River Delta in Kwangtung Province. The four counties are Hoisan (台山), Yanping (恩平), Hoiping (開平) and Sanwui (新會).

My mother added that I was a *hoo ji how* (土紙頭)—an "earth paper head," an American-born person with a U.S. birth certificate. I wasn't a *hong san doy* (唐山仔), a kid from China.

Hong San (唐山) is what she and people from Hoisan called China. *"Doy"* (仔) was the word for boy.

During my childhood, my mother played a question-and-answer game to help me remember my Chinese roots. She supplied both questions and answers in a rhythmic, quick-paced Chinese call-and-response. My job was simply to listen. Over time, I was expected to provide the answers.

> *What is your surname?*
> *My surname is Chew.*
> *What is the name of your father's village?*
> *Fow Seck Village.*
> *What is your Chinese name?*
> *Jick Ping.*
> *What is your older brother's name?*
> *Jin Ping.*
> *What is your younger brother's name?*
> *Hep Ping.*
> *What is your sister's name?*
> *Thlew Ping.*
> *What is your father's name?*
> *Soo Hong.*
> *What is your mother's name?*
> *Wee Gam Har.*
> *What is the name of my village?*
> *Ai Gong Village.*

I woke up from afternoon naps on the living room sofa in our Beacon Hill home listening to my mother repeat this same Q&A. Over time, it sounded like a Chinese nursery rhyme. At first, I found it amusing. I played along, hardly conscious of what I was saying. But it stayed with me.

During my unruly adolescent years—when I began arguing loudly with my parents in English, often cursing at them—I feared that my mother would make good on her threats to bring all of us—my sister, brothers and me—to China. She said she could never accept living in a country in which children could shamelessly defy their elders. She added that we wouldn't survive more than a week in China because of our attitude and our inability to speak Chinese. "If you don't want to come with me," she added tearfully, "you can stay here. But don't ever call me your mother again."

These stormy episodes subsided as we grew up and each of us moved out to live on our own. My mother made peace with her Americanized children. Seattle became her home, even though she never shed her bittersweet longing for China. Broken English became her barely-mastered second language.

For me, the United States was my full world. As I matured beyond my parents' dominion, fluent English became my celebratory prize. My Chinese eroded. I didn't care to learn more about—much less travel to—Hoisan, a faraway land that existed only in the stories of my parents, especially my mother. I wanted to blend in and be accepted by others where I was.

But now that my father and mother were both gone, I yearned to see their first home. I wanted to unravel the mystery of who they were. I discovered that it wasn't enough just to know my Seattle origins or even to have lived in Chinatown in the shadow of my grandfather. I had to go to Hoisan.

Like me, my children uncritically embraced their American identity. But I didn't want them to someday wake up like me and find a key part of their history mired in mystery. Their mother agreed.

In December 2006, Loan took Cian and Kino to Vietnam with her extended family. The trip included stops in Hanoi, their grandmother's village in Yên Bái, Nha Trang (a small coastal town where Loan was born) and Saigon, which teems with over 12 million inhabitants.

In 2008, my sister Linda proposed a trip to China. My brothers Tom and Harvey didn't have time. They said no. I said yes. I wanted to see our father's village and to bring Cian and Kino. Linda wanted to attend the Summer Olympic Games in Beijing. She also wanted to visit other parts of China. On three separate trips, she had adopted infant girls from orphanages. Noel (楊英英) came from Yangzhou in Jiangsu Province. Her younger sister Emma (常秋葉) came from Changzhou, also in Jiangsu. The youngest, Kia (常曉粉), came from Luoyang in Henan Province. Now that they were older, she wanted to take them and their older brother Orion to see the orphanages and their country of origin.

I contacted our Seattle cousin, Sen Poy Chew, to see if he might help set up a visit to Fow Seck. He wrote to a 73-year-old childhood friend, Sen Nguk Chew (趙善玉), still living in the village. Sen Nguk Chew agreed to take us to our ancestral house and a cemetery where many Chew relatives were buried.

Working with a travel agent, Linda pieced together a packed itinerary for our nine-member group: the two of us, her four kids (Orion, Noel, Emma and Kia), her good friend Judy, and my two kids (Cian and Kino). We had three different interpreters for various legs of the journey.

In just 21 days, we managed to visit 11 cities and towns in seven provinces. It was the kind of vacation that only Linda—the most efficient and fast-paced person I know—would even dare to attempt. By the time we settled into one hotel, it was time to pack up, get on a plane or train and speed somewhere else. I realized that there was little point in unpacking more than a few toiletries at each stop. After we got back home, I spent two weeks trying to take another vacation to recover from the vacation.

The three orphanages we visited were Changzhou Children's Welfare Institute, Yangzhou Welfare Institute and Luoyang Children's Welfare Institute. It was moving to watch each of my nieces read heartfelt thank-you letters, composed beforehand, to the respective directors and staff who cared for them as infants. We examined the spare living spaces they had occupied as orphans and met other abandoned infants.

In between the far-flung orphanages, we made many other stops. We visited the 1,400-year old Buddhist temple of the Six Banyan Trees in Guangzhou. In Guilin, we took a cruise on the Li River and marveled at the majestic peaks in the distance. We saw the Temple of the Soul's Retreat with its rows of huge religious statues. We explored the famous Ling Yin Temple. We stayed at a lavish hotel filled with European boutiques and spent an evening watching *The Goonies* on HBO while the rain came down in torrents outside. We toured a comb-making factory and jade factory. We explored the 100,000 Buddhist figures that make up Dragon Gate Grottoes in Henan Province. We ordered two buckets of KFC chicken and four orders of french fries in Changzhou, then worked out with weights and on a treadmill at the fitness center in our hotel. We breathlessly climbed a towering section of the Great Wall in Beijing.

About a week into the trip, I realized that we hadn't visited a single museum. It didn't feel right. As the tour bus left the hotel, I turned to our tour guide and interpreter Wendy and asked, "Can we visit some museums today?" Wendy seemed perplexed. She huddled with the driver. The two spoke for nearly five minutes over the din of the kids in the rear of the bus. Wendy came back over and asked, "Why would you want to visit a museum?"

I paused. I didn't know what to say. Wendy did not know what I had done for a living. But why would that matter? Wouldn't a museum or two be part of any itinerary like ours?

I awkwardly answered, "Uh, I used to work for a museum in the United States." Wendy persisted, "But wouldn't you rather visit more of these interesting sites like the temples and the historic places?" I didn't know what else to say. She conferred again with the driver, then said: "The driver says there aren't any museums around here. We would have to drive far to find one, but we can if you like. How about later in the trip?"

The following week, we made our way to three museums: the China National Silk Museum in Hangzhou, the China Block Printing Museum and Yangzhou Museum. They provided a badly needed dose of air conditioning for our kids, who were withering in 100-degree temperatures. It was striking how sparse the crowds were. There were a handful of foreign tourists. The exhibitions were dull compared to the outdoor wonders. Wendy was right.

As we approached the Yangzhou Museum—a huge modern building—we couldn't figure out where to enter. The parking lot outside the towering block structure was nearly empty. There were no visitors to follow. We walked around the building, trying doors until we found one that opened.

There was no shortage of tourists when we arrived in Xi'an to see the ancient terracotta warriors. The site was wildly popular. I suddenly developed a splitting headache. I told the others to go ahead without me. I passed the time in a nearby café. Kino stayed to keep me company.

We concluded our journey in Beijing. The capital city had been completely made over for the Olympics. Over a million cars were removed from the streets and hundreds of factories closed. Everything was remarkably tidy and efficient. The air was clearer than usual. We watched a soccer match in a spectacular new stadium.

I was overwhelmed by the entire trip. It was too much to absorb in a short amount of time. Now, over a decade later, I can't recall much about the soccer game or even certain cities we visited.

But I'll never forget our brief foray into my father's village of Fow Seck at the beginning of the trip. It changed me forever.

We first stayed at the White Swan Hotel, a luxury hotel in Guangzhou overlooking the Pearl River. From there, we traveled by van to a smoky hotel in Kaiping (開平), the most convenient point for an overnight stopover before venturing into the village.

Our air-conditioned tour van took us into Hoisan. It was a long and tedious drive through the countryside along rural lanes to reach Fow Seck. Outside, the temperature climbed to a muggy, nearly unbearable 110 degrees. We passed shimmering rice fields filled with little green sprouts, water buffaloes, rows of trees, bamboo groves, lotus fields and noisy geese. There were few other vehicles on the road. I didn't see any working-age adults, just elderly people and young kids. Wage-earners had forsaken the land for factory jobs in overcrowded cities.

I wasn't accustomed to being surrounded by soil, greenery and quiet. My breathing slowed. My anticipation rose.

We first found our way to the home of Sen Nguk Chew and his wife. They waited at their front door. Sen Nguk approached first, greeting us with a smile and handshakes. He was a slender man with graying hair and a slight hunch. He blinked into the scorching sun through a pair of wire-rimmed glasses. He was dressed in a thin white polo shirt, black trousers and plastic sandals. His wife, who greeted us next, had similar salt-and-pepper hair. It was parted in the middle so that her hair draped over her ears like a helmet. She was stocky and more animated and expressive than her husband. She wore a white, patterned blouse. She had black trousers and plastic sandals like her husband.

We immediately discovered that our interpreter didn't speak or understand Hoisanese. Everyone turned to me. My rudimentary Chinese turned out to be a lifesaver as we made introductions and discussed the day ahead.

Sen Nguk told us that he had worked as an accountant but had been retired for over 10 years. Their three sons were also accountants. He took us on a brief tour of their modest two-story house, which looked eerily similar to my parents' house in Seattle. The kitchen tables were cluttered with foodstuffs, cans, jars and empty platters. The floors were lined with boxes, baskets and odds and ends. Chinese calendars and photos of relatives were pinned randomly on the walls. Sen Nguk said that he and his wife sometimes cared for a granddaughter but that it was usually just the two of them in the house.

After the tour, they joined us in the van as we continued to my father's ancestral home.

We drove for a while before passing through the gates marking the entrance to Fow Seck. We slowed as we made our way along narrow lanes past ancient brick structures. As we neared our final destination, our driver misjudged the width of our vehicle. Despite our entreaties, he tried to navigate through the tiny alley between two buildings. The van got stuck halfway through. We were wedged in, a huge rock scraping paint from the right side of the vehicle. After he backed out, we decided to walk the rest of the way.

I now understood how our Chinatown alleys—Canton Alley and Maynard Alley—came into being. They were modeled after the tight village access lanes that opened into resident living quarters. Western depictions of Chinatown alleys—as turf for sinister hitmen with long knives and hatchets—flouted these origins.

We stepped inside the open doorway of a small building. A storage basket hung from one corner of the ceiling. I wondered if this was what my mother called a *thloong lom* (餸籃) or storage basket for leftover food. In the days before refrigeration, my mother had told me, meats and leftover food were cured with salt and hung in these baskets. It made sense why we ate dried, salted and cured meats at mealtime with bountiful portions of plain steamed white rice. For poor people, this was a good meal. This was how my parents ate.

Our eyes were immediately drawn to one wall which held the family altar, framed by two wooden panels carved with Chinese characters. The altar was decorated with faded photographs, plastic flowers and sticks of incense. The photographs were Polaroid snapshots of my parents, Tom, Linda, Harvey and me growing up. They must have accompanied the letters that my parents dutifully sent back to China.

It was an especially poignant and nostalgic moment for Linda and me to have traveled thousands of miles to discover pictures of ourselves occupying a wall set aside for memory and worship.

An old woman—we called her *Ha Gu* or Auntie Ha—said the altar room used to be the living room. One room in the back was where Number One Uncle, Kin Hong, and his wife lived. A side room was where Number Two Uncle, Hung Hong, and his wife lived. Our mother stayed in a small house across a narrow lane, next to an outdoor kitchen, which had deteriorated into brick rubble.

Was this the primitive kitchen that my mother once described to me? My mother told me that after she got married, she was disheartened to see that her bedroom was a tiny section of a room below the dining area. "What a humiliating fate for the daughter of a village chieftain (*heung jeung* 鄉長)!" she lamented. She was especially proud of her father's eminent status.

The villagers led us through the ritual of paying respects to our ancestors. We each filled a little red cup with alcohol, clasped our hands together, bowed three times and poured the wine onto the rough-hewn tile floor near an old water pump.

Ha Gu asked me how our mother—"Fourth Auntie"—was doing. I told her my mother had passed away three years earlier. She held my gaze, nodded, then offered her condolences. Her expression hardly changed. She probably knew. The letters and remittances from America had ceased. Our return to this ancestral place restored the union between two separate Chew homelands, but only for this brief moment.

After the ceremony, our party from Seattle reboarded the bus and took a short drive to *Yeung-hang-san* (羊坑山), Fow Seck's northeast cemetery. The unmarked cemetery was hidden behind several rows of trees and brush. Arriving at a clearing, we spotted a cluster of Chew headstones. This was where my grandfather's two wives, Woo and Eng, were buried. The villagers arrived separately, bringing food from the ancestral house. We bowed and poured alcohol onto the ground in front of each grave marker. Incense was lit. A large tarp was laid over the ground and a roasted pig was chopped into small pieces with several cleavers. Flies swarmed over the meat, eliciting a few queasy groans from two of Linda's girls. The kids ate heartily despite their initial qualms.

In the smothering heat, I felt strangely at peace in this forested final resting place. The trees provided partial relief from the blazing sun. I sensed the presence of ancestral spirits. I shivered, despite the inferno. I wondered if the spirits of my father, mother, grandfather and uncles accompanied me on this journey home.

One of the older female villagers approached me. "You speak Chinese like someone from our village. You are from America. How did you learn?" I told her that my mother taught me and that I worked in a restaurant in Chinatown when I was younger. She added, "I can tell you're from Fow Seck because of the shape of your nose—it's tall—and by the shape of your jaw. You're definitely from Fow Seck." I, too, had noticed similarities in appearance and gait between my father, Linda, myself and some villagers. I marveled at the durability of genetic traits.

I asked the woman whether she knew about the famous Sunning Railroad and Chin Gee-Hee, the early Seattle pioneer who launched the project.

Surprised, she asked, "How do you know about him? This was a long time ago."

I told her that I had been director of a history museum in an old building built by Hoisanese immigrants and that some of Chin Gee-Hee's descendants lived in Seattle. I asked if any traces of Chin's railroad remained.

She said that when she was a young girl, she was told that the railroad was destroyed by the Japanese. If we had time, she said, she could take us to an area the railroad used to pass through. "It's not far," she said, pointing into the distance. She added that Japanese soldiers invaded the village, forcing residents to retreat to the mountains to hide.

I thanked her but declined. We had to leave soon. "I hope to return to Fow Seck someday to learn more history," I said. She frowned. "I'm 63," she said. "By the time you come back, I may not be here to help you."

We finished our meal and hurried back into the van. We felt the refreshing blast of the air conditioner, which had been running while we were paying our respects at the cemetery. But as soon as we tried to take off, the engine sputtered, then died. It got hot very quickly inside the bus. The villagers, most of whom were older and skinnier than us, lined up behind the vehicle, pushing to get the engine restarted. Linda and I joined them. The kids—city-bred and softened by the easy life in America—stayed on the bus, afraid to face the heat again. With the help of our village clan, we were soon on our way.

After we returned home from China, I kept in touch by email with a young school teacher I met at Fow Seck Elementary School and a college student who approached us in Guangzhou. Both spoke rudimentary English. For several years, they patiently responded to my continuing questions about China. I told them I was an avid gardener. They sent snapshots of native plants and blooming flowers. I answered their questions about Seattle and sent pictures of my backyard garden. This correspondence kept my passion alive to one day return to China.

Linda has talked often about another trip; Tom, too. But in 2017, Sen Nguk passed away. Next time, we'll have to rely on others to take us into the village. I hope my father's old home will still be standing.

CHAPTER 69

Running Toward Health

I N 2012, I TOOK UP running again at age 58. It was the hardest time of my life. I was trying to recover from my divorce and the Wing Luke fundraising campaign. I was also trying to manage the daily pressures of being a single parent to Cian and Kino, both of whom had burst into adolescence.

After school, Cian and Kino came home with a pack of kids from the neighborhood, and I cooked mounds of *ngook beng, chow mein*, broccoli and *fung cheng* to feed them all. After helping my kids with homework and scooting them off to bed, there was little time for anything else.

Two years earlier—on September 27, 2010—I started a new job as director of the International Community Health Services (ICHS) Foundation. I was back in fundraising. Teresita Batayola, CEO at ICHS, was shoring up the agency during a very tough economic time. She pleaded with me to return to community work and help her. She explained that ICHS might lose most of its state funding, raising the possibility that the ID clinic would have to shut down. She was persuasive.

In addition to being Nancy Lim's best friend and Maria Batayola's older sister, I knew Teresita as an exceptionally dynamic leader. She was as tiny as her mentor Ruth Woo, but when she spoke, her words had weight and purpose. Teresita was the only leader I felt I could work for if I returned to the nonprofit sector. Teresita joined ICHS in 2005 after a brief stint as chief of staff to David Della, who was elected to the Seattle City Council in 2003.

When she approached me about joining ICHS, I was already well acquainted with the agency's vital services. In its early years, the clinic provided low-cost health care to the waiters at the Hong Kong Restaurant and garment workers like my mother.

I remembered when it opened on November 3, 1975, in a one-room storefront at 416 Maynard Avenue South, next door to the Kokusai Theater. Bruce Miyahara was the clinic's first director. He was a Sansei with thick, long hair, a walrus mustache, big tinted glasses and platform shoes. Sister Heide Parreño, a young Catholic nun, worked as the clinic's first nurse practitioner. I interviewed the two—and Uncle Bob, the clinic's most ardent political ally—for *Examiner* stories during the agency's early fights for public funding. I hung out there with Susie Chin and Donnie Chin.

After my mother retired—and ICHS moved into the ID Village Square—I took my mother to the clinic to check her blood pressure. She went several times a week. The staff took time to explain the many government forms and bills she stuffed in her handbag. In my mother's final months, Dr. Kimo Hirayama, a doctor who treated many of the Chinese patients, prescribed medication to lessen her suffering. The compassion of "Dr. Kimo"—and his skill with end-of-life situations—eased the enormous burden on me and my siblings.

I knew many of the employees at ICHS. Maxine Chan was the marketing and events specialist. Aleta Eng's mother, Linda Eng, was eligibility coordinator. May Sheung Chan, the mother of Wing Luke staffer Vivian Chan, greeted and checked in patients at ICHS's Holly Park clinic. I knew Kuei Lan Lin, an ICHS pharmacy cashier, from our days at the Hong Kong Restaurant. She worked as a bar waitress when I was a busboy.

After I joined ICHS, I began to doubt my decision. I didn't know how skillfully I could balance my new job responsibilities with an equally demanding personal life. I wasn't fully confident I could re-stoke a passion for fundraising.

Although both my parents had been gone for years, my heart still ached. The house at 1919 South College Street was sold. When I drove past College Street on my way to work, I'd think about checking on my mother. But then I'd remember that she was gone. It was an impulse I couldn't shake.

To quiet the cacophony in my head, I returned to running. I hadn't jogged in nearly 20 years. I bought a pair of cheap gray sweatpants and sneakers from JCPenney. At 4:30 a.m., I ventured out, gingerly navigating over the potholed sidewalks on Beacon Avenue South. At first, I couldn't go more than a block without stopping and gasping for air. It gradually got easier. Each time, I came back feeling better than when I left.

I thought about a scene from the movie *Forrest Gump* when Forrest explains why he had just spent the last three years, two months, 14 days and 16 hours on an epic, long run: "My mama always said, 'You've got to put the past behind you before you can move on.' And I think that's what my run was all about."

As I became fitter, I signed up for a few 5Ks. My first was a Halloween race at Seward Park. There were several hundred participants. Many wore ghoulish costumes and painted their faces. I saw several super-skinny elite runners at the front. They wore singlets, compression tights and feather-light racing flats. They zoomed out of sight with a few giant spider strides. I was glad I didn't see anyone I knew. I feared that I might drive myself too hard and collapse near the edge of the road, waking to the smell of the half-digested *mapo tofu* I had unwisely eaten an hour earlier.

I replaced my worn sneakers with a new pair from the clearance rack at Big 5. I snagged a red Adidas waterproof training jacket for less than a dollar at Goodwill Outlet.

In 2011, ICHS launched a capital campaign to raise money for a new medical-dental clinic along Aurora Avenue North in the city of Shoreline, just north of Seattle. It would be the first nonprofit clinic there. Teresita asked me to head up the effort.

In the middle of one morning run, I thought to myself: *What if I commit to running at least a mile each day until I finish the fundraising? That would push me to work harder and finish earlier. A mile isn't that far.* I had read about "streakers" who sustained far more ambitious running streaks than mine, lasting for decades. My goal seemed doable.

I began to count down the days. On January 2, 2013, I wrote a humorous piece for the *Examiner* about my rediscovered interest in running. The article mentioned my pledge to run every day until I completed the $12.8 million fundraising campaign for the Shoreline clinic, scheduled to open in 2014. I had already run over 300 days in a row.

In early 2013, Teresita and I began to discuss naming the new Shoreline clinic in honor of Ben and Ruth Woo, our two favorite unsung heroes. Over the years, they eschewed recognition. Ben passed away in 2008. He requested that there be no memorial service and that his ashes be spread over Lake Washington. Shortly after his death, Sharon Lee, director of the Low Income Housing Institute, proposed naming a housing project in South Lake Union in Ben's honor. Ruth curtly told her, "No. The only thing you can name after Ben is a mushroom."

Undeterred, Kip Tokuda and I conspired with Jennifer Belcher, former Washington State Public Commissioner of Lands and a close friend of Ruth, to try to talk Ruth into agreeing to the idea. I asked Ruth if the three of us could come over to her house to strategize about a state appropriation for the Shoreline clinic. I didn't mention the real reason for our visit. Ruth listened stoically while we explained how using her name and Ben's would aid the fundraising. Ruth pushed back with a stern, "Over my dead body."

After this meeting, I spotted Kip eating *dim sum* alone at Four Seas Restaurant. I stopped at his table. "Hey, Ron," he said. "Was that you I saw running up on Beacon Hill the other day? What were you doing out so early? Are you crazy or something?" He made a face. We both laughed. "Crazy?" I responded. "Yes, Kip. Guilty as charged." I explained my plan to run every day until I finished raising money for the Shoreline clinic. "You should be out there with me," I insisted. He smirked. "No way, Ron," he said. "I'd rather eat my greasy *dim sum* meal." We again brainstormed about how to get Ruth to lend her name to the Shoreline clinic. We discussed the urgency of taping an interview with her and celebrating her legacy while she was still alive.

Several weeks later, I was horrified to learn from his cousin Ann Fujii that Kip had died of a heart attack on a fishing trip at Deer Lake on Whidbey Island. He was only 66.

In July 2014, I signed up for the Skagit Flats half-marathon in Burlington. I had never raced that distance. It was scheduled for September 7. The opening date of the clinic was September 15, 2014.

The race was billed as "very flat." I reasoned that without

having to navigate hills, I could conclude my streak without subjecting my weary joints to any further indignities.

Two weeks before this race, my streak almost ended prematurely. During a training run in the morning darkness, a car's headlights blinded me. I ran smack into a thick tree trunk. I tumbled to the ground. My fall was cushioned by grass, but the impact bent the frame of my glasses and left me with a bloody nose. My left knee ballooned, turning blue and purple. I limped home. When my doctor at Group Health examined me the next day, she told me the injury wasn't quite as bad as it looked. The tissue above my patella had been damaged, but not the knee itself. If I was careful, I could go ahead with the half-marathon. I was relieved. I continued to train.

The following week, I tweaked my left knee again. I was helping the staff at the *Examiner* move file cabinets, chairs and tables from their old office on South Washington Street into a new, smaller office on the second floor of the Bush Hotel. The knee swelled after I went home. Icing my leg daily, I continued to run—slowly and warily. I kept my mileage to a minimum, tapering as race day approached.

The race was grueling. As promised, the course was flat. But the weather was hot. It got more sultry after the sun burned away the clouds. Waves of heat rose from the paved and gravel roads. There were no trees. I faded to an anemic slog during the last three miles. I was surprised that I finished third among the 60- to 64-year-olds. My time was just under 1 hour and 45 minutes. I received a medal and posted a picture on Facebook.

I was jubilant. I could now take a break from running. Earning my first black toenail made me feel like a real runner. The following week, the sparkling new three-story, brick-clad Shoreline clinic opened for business just north of 165th Street on the busy Aurora Avenue North corridor.

In December 2014, I met a tall, angular Chinese American runner at a holiday race in Kent. He was bespectacled like me. His hair was neatly combed straight back. His cheeks were flushed from a warm-up; his expression was intense. Terry Wong was his name. He had been running seriously since age 49, when he began training for the Seattle marathon for his 50th birthday. He had a dental practice in the old Main Street School Annex on Sixth Avenue South, next door to the building where Dr. Ernest Ching had his office.

Terry's parents owned the American Noodle Manufacturing Company at 675 South Weller Street. His father sometimes delivered fortune cookies, noodles, wonton and egg roll wrappers to the Hong Kong Restaurant. "Small world, huh?" I said to Terry.

At the 2015 Seafair Torchlight run in downtown Seattle, I met another Chinese American peer, Sherwin Eng. We were in the same class at Mercer Junior High. He worked for Evan Pilchik, the photography company hired for the event. Three days before the July 26 race, Donnie Chin was murdered. Sherwin was still in shock. We consoled each other. His voice broke and he sobbed. I gently embraced him. His grandparents' home was at 611 Eighth Avenue South, just inches away from the spot where Donnie's car crashed after he was shot.

I dedicated my run to Donnie. Sherwin wished me luck. I told him I had been thinking about launching a Lunar New Year run to support ICHS. "Ron, if you need a photographer, you just tell me where and when," he said. "I'll be there. It'll be for Donnie." True to his word, Sherwin has donated his photo services for all three Lunar New Year 5Ks, the first in Bellevue in 2016 and two in Shoreline in 2017 and 2019, raising over $90,000 for charity care for needy patients.

I've kept up my devotion to running. Every morning, I

look forward to going out alone for an hour or two on Beacon Hill. This ritual helps me stay sane and healthy.

I coordinate my racing schedule with my sister Linda. She started running two years after me. Linda and I discovered that we're part of a larger community. In 2009, Jerry and Betty Dietrich, a couple from Gig Harbor, formed the Silver Striders, a support group for senior runners in Washington state. They publish an online magazine with weekly race reports and results, highlighting top finishers in five-year age categories from 50 to 95. Linda and I often see our names on the list. Terry Wong's name is there, too. At Silver Strider races, we enjoy chatting with our amicable running foes and vying with them for ribbons.

In 2016, the Silver Striders sponsored the inaugural ICHS Lunar New Year 5K run as part of its year-long Grand Prix competition. The event took place on Sunday, February 7, at Mercer Slough Nature Park in Bellevue on a windy but clear day. The majority of runners were over 50.

As I set up the registration table, Bruce Fisher, official photographer for the Silver Striders and husband of Judy Fisher, a perennial top finisher in her age group, tapped me on the arm. "Hey, Ron," Bruce said, scowling. "How come you're not suited up?" I explained that I was too busy overseeing the event to participate.

In the distance, I saw several other Silver Strider aficionados approaching to pick up their race bibs. I also saw Al Sugiyama, in the midst of his uphill battle with cancer, arriving with a small a circle of friends, eager to support the ICHS cause.

I felt a startling moment of bliss. My two separate worlds had converged.

CHAPTER 70

My Garden Retreat

I BECAME AN AVID GARDENER several years after my divorce. For years, I ignored the shabby tangle of plants, weeds and patchy lawn in the front and back of my Beacon Hill home. Meanwhile, Kim, my next door neighbor, spent every waking moment obsessively nursing and pruning her flowers and shrubs.

Kim and her non-gardener husband John were home all the time. They retired after closing Asian Furnishings, an antique furniture business in Pioneer Square. They first opened it in Bellevue. It went under after the Nisqually Earthquake in 2003.

Kim's real name was Yun-Hee Kim. Kim was her surname, but she asked all the neighbors to call her Kim. She was born in South Korea in 1942. She and John met in the early 1960s when he was stationed at the U.S. Eighth Army base in Seoul. John was from Winona, Minnesota. At the time, Kim worked as a portrait painter. They married in Seoul in 1965.

I watched Kim propagate new plants from cuttings. She

hired day workers to move soil, rocks and pavers in and out of her yard. She created a garden paradise that sprawled inside and outside the ramshackle house that she shared with John. Kim's handiwork drew the rapt attention of passersby who stopped by during the summer to gawk at her colorful, spiky dahlias.

As my kids got older and more self-sufficient, I became intrigued with what Kim was doing. One day, I asked her for help. A friend had given me a spider plant. The leaves were wilting and turning dark brown. It appeared to be dying. "Nothing wrong," she said. She yanked out the dead leaves, put it in a larger pot with more soil and gave me a few basic pointers. She said she learned gardening from her grandmother in Korea. She gave me another spider plant and a jade plant. "These are easy," she said, "but make sure to water every couple days."

I met Eiric, a yoga instructor on Beacon Avenue South, who stopped by Kim's house to talk about gardening. He was nearly as avid about plants as Kim was. I hired him to remove my front lawn and design a low-maintenance garden and a stepping-stone walkway in its place. Over several seasons, he did this for both my front and back yards. We went to several local nurseries together to pick plants and haul stones.

I asked him how I would care for the plants after he was gone. He reassured me. "I can come back and help you prune," he said. "Treat them like furniture. You can always move them to a different spot."

I became an early morning regular at the gardening department at Lowe's, Home Depot and McLendon Hardware. I looked for weekend sales on hardy shrubs, dwarf evergreens, flowering perennials and groundcovers. I watched YouTube videos about indoor and outdoor plants. I even bought a subscription to *Cottage Living* for more ideas about plants and landscaping.

I sprinkled plants inside the house. I set them in aged terra-cotta pots from Goodwill Outlet and rummage sales. Brian Lock gave me two palms that he grew from cuttings from a very old plant at the Ming Tree Restaurant when his family owned it. Another friend gave me a small bush with variegated leaves, which my good friend Lorraine Sako, a landscape architect, helped identify as a schefflera.

At first, I didn't quite grasp Kim's obsession, but one day it made perfect sense. "Ron, it's my therapy," she proclaimed as she finished watering the last of her outdoor blooms for the day. The sun was fading quickly from the sky. A hummingbird buzzed past us. A mournful Korean folk song played from a CD inside Kim's house. She flexed her back and wiped her muddy hands on her apron. Then she stood straight up to ponder her surroundings. She looked into the distance. It dawned on me that I had become a gardener to heal from the trauma of divorce. What demons were Kim trying to keep at bay? I was afraid to ask.

One day, I called Lorraine on the phone and yelled, "Fatsia Japonica!" Laughing hard, she asked, "What? Why are you calling? Is this Don Knotts?" She knew that he was my favorite actor. I repeated myself. I said I had figured out the name of a big-leafed mystery plant near my front door. "It's called Fatsia Japonica. Are you impressed?" She was. She knew me when the only plant I could identify was a dandelion.

During spring and summer, my yard overflows with showy lavender bushes, trim boxwoods, clumps of fragrant pale-pink winter daphnes, slim stalks of blue and white bellflowers, mounds of purple heather, trailing rosemary, snow-white candytuft, dainty sweet alyssum flowers, and wide carpets of blue star creeper, phlox, periwinkle, sweet woodruff, Japanese spurge, salal and creeping thyme.

I moved the plants that Eiric had set in the ground to better locations, observing sunlight, shade and wind conditions. I killed a few plants, but I soon got the hang of it. I learned patience. I studied Pacific Northwest natives, including azaleas and rhododendrons similar to those I had seen during my China trip. I realized that nature was not as big a mystery as I once thought.

I was drawn to the simple beauty and shape of old rocks and stones, weathered by long exposure to the elements. I discovered listings for free rocks on Craigslist. I drove around the city to snatch up the largest ones I could lift and haul back home in my Toyota Camry.

Where had all these rocks come from? The plants in my garden had to be thriving in places other than commercial garden centers. I felt an intense longing to journey beyond Beacon Hill and the big city.

I turned to Ed Echtle and Brian. They took me on road trips to small towns and abandoned settlements in South Puget Sound. Ed was the driver and tour guide, tossing out fascinating little factoids as effortlessly as the fishmongers throw salmon at Pike Place Market. He kept me spellbound. Carlos Smith, Susie Chin, Steve Goon and Laura Wong-Whitebear often came with us.

I brought Cian, Kino and their friends on weekend hikes to lookouts on Mount Rainier and to nearby scenic trails. We slept overnight in a heated yurt at Seaquest State Park, explored Ape Cave (an underground lava tube near Mount St. Helens), and waded in the refreshing still waters of Snow Lake in Snoqualmie Pass.

On a trip to Dewey Lake near Mount Rainier, I saw a spectacular alpine meadow overflowing with bright lavender wildflowers. I felt like I had been transported into the middle of the poppy field from the classic movie *The Wizard of Oz*. I couldn't resist the urge to plop down on my back and stretch out my arms. I gazed up at the cloudy blue sky. I didn't want to leave.

On one steep hike, Ed and Brian noticed that I was struggling to keep my balance over some of the uneven trails lined with massive bulging tree roots, dead branches and huge boulders. "We've got to get you some hiking boots, Ron," Brian pronounced. "You can't be climbing up and down these big-ass mountains in those street shoes."

They introduced me to G.I. Joe's in Lakewood. I bought a pair of my very first waterproof hiking boots on sale. The place reminded me of Chubby & Tubby. It had the same crowded, haphazard displays, old-store aroma and dusty corners. The boots were a no-name brand, but I was startled by how much more relaxed my feet felt during subsequent hikes.

In November 2007, Ed and Brian took me to the Staircase region of Olympic National Forest for a lowland hike. It was a brilliant, clear day. They noticed animal droppings on the ground and taught me a new word—"scat." They warned me to look out for cougars. We hiked along a picturesque forested loop trail, passing over a wooden bridge which took us over the Skokomish River. Brian spotted a long steelhead hiding under a log in the river. Ed told us he caught his first fish there at the age of five.

On our drive back home, we stopped for a bite at the Ming Tree Restaurant in Shelton. Outside was a weathered neon sign with *chop suey* lettering. Brian's dad had recently sold the restaurant, but he was still helping part-time in the kitchen. Jeannie Ellingsworth, an elderly waitress who helped care for Brian as a child after his mother passed away, served us. I thought fondly of other Chinese American *chop suey* diners I visited during the Chinese heritage tour over a decade earlier.

During these hikes, I fell in love with moss. It brightens shady areas of the forest, drapes tree trunks, and softens rock ledges, fallen logs and the edges of streams. *How did this weird plant survive without stems or roots?*

I began scooping up moss from street crevices for my garden. I used Go-GURT to glue them to the top of my large rocks. I found a very lush patch on the cracked pavement near Yasuko's Teriyaki on Capitol Hill. During a morning run on Beacon Hill, I passed the home of a Chinatown waitress who was a friend of my mother. She sawed down a big tree in her backyard. She was getting ready to dump several big sections. I hauled them home to use in the garden as faux tree stumps and fallen logs. I used them to cultivate moss.

During the spring and summer of 2007, Ed helped me construct a tiny backyard cottage with an adjoining porch. I dreamed of having a small rustic sanctuary that could double as a fun play space for Cian and Kino. After Ed patiently listened to me describe my vision, he made a quick sketch on a napkin. "Is this what you want?" He nailed it. "Yes!" I exclaimed. "Can I hire you to do it?" He said yes. I was ecstatic. He told me he had built a similar structure before, inspired by U.S. Forest Service cabins.

Ed researched city regulations. We didn't need a permit if the structure didn't exceed 120 square feet. Ed removed a small pear tree from a corner of the backyard. He leveled the ground and fashioned a plywood floor on concrete blocks. He then put up the walls, rafters and a pitched roof. We made many trips to Home Depot and Lowe's to pick up building materials. He added vintage windows and an old glass-paned door. He finished in just two months.

To furnish the cabin, I found a loveseat sleeper at Salvation Army for $50, then scored an upholstered rocking chair for

$5 and a small table and a schoolhouse chair for $1 each at Goodwill. I bought a set of white lace curtains from Ikea, a floral hurricane lamp from Grocery Outlet, and a seagrass carpet from Lowe's. Steve Goon gave me a honey-colored drop-leaf secretary desk and a brass floor lamp. I converted several salvaged crates into bookshelves and filled them with books from childhood, including my Scholastic paperbacks.

The only thing I was missing was artwork.

One day, I had lunch with Jill Chan Rinearson and her cousin Sally Yamasaki. We shared funny parenting stories. Jill was a former *Examiner* contributor. Her father was former Superior Court Judge Warren Chan. Jill said she had taken up watercolor painting. I asked her if she would sketch a portrait of me for my cabin. She balked. "Me? I'm no artist!" In the 1980s, when I had mentored her as a writer, I noticed a similar lack of self-confidence, despite her considerable creative talent. Several weeks later, I found a wooden frame at Goodwill for a dollar. I called her. "Here you go, Jill," I said. "Make it fit inside this." She relented, taking photos of me sitting in various seated positions inside my cabin for the sketch.

I also approached my friend Mizu. I remembered several pieces she made for a 2004 exhibition on race at the museum. After attending a Wing Luke family art program with her six-year-old son Bryan, she started designing family-story collages. "Can you do something like that for me?" I asked. I gave her a batch of old photos of my father, mother, me and my two sons. She then took pictures of objects in my house. Several weeks later, she returned with several gorgeous collages of my parents.

I was now set. My home was complete. I had a garden. I had a garden retreat. I had art. I could quiet my mind, read, nap and rest my soul.

In 2012, *The Seattle Times* featured my cabin and garden

in its Sunday *Pacific Northwest Magazine.* I found it ironic. I once cynically told Dean Wong—when we both worked at the *Examiner*—that I wasn't a "nature person." I told him I had no interest in exploring hiking trails. He felt the same way. I joked that I didn't want to "accidentally step into a big pile of deer crap and get my street shoes dirty."

When I'm in my garden on warm summer days, I like taking off my shoes and kneading the soil with my bare toes. I lie on a small patch of grass in the middle of this paradise and gaze at drifting white clouds, just as I did when I was a child. Daydreaming, I feel my breathing slow. My home beckons.

CHAPTER 71

Still Not Retired

M OST OF MY PEERS HAVE retired. They're seeking new adventures. I envy their freedom. I want to revive Chew Communications, pursue my own projects, write and travel while I'm healthy.

In 2012, Dale Hom left the U.S. Forest Service. In 2016, he created *Walk Don't Run: Growing Up Asian in Seattle*, a graphic novel about a Chinese American kid on Beacon Hill. In 2015, Gary Iwamoto collaborated with Bob Santos to produce *Gang of Four*, the story of the enduring friendship between Bob, Larry Gossett, Roberto Maestas and Bernie Whitebear. In 2016, Dean Wong fulfilled a dream by publishing *Seeing the Light: Four Decades in Chinatown*, a collection of his best photos and personal essays.

Mayumi Tsutakawa said goodbye to the Washington State Arts Commission in January 2016 after 14 years. Diane Narasaki retired in October 2018 after 23 years at the helm of Asian Counseling and Referral Service. Sue Taoka celebrated her retirement from Craft3, a nonprofit financial institution, at the Four Seas Dynasty Room on May 15, 2019. Her husband Dicky Mar announced plans to step down as president of the International District Emergency Center board after nearly 30 years, clearing the way for others to reimagine its future without Donnie Chin. On June 14, 2019, Lori Matsukawa anchored her final 11 p.m. news broadcast at KING 5 TV, capping an illustrious 36-year run at the station.

On the final day of 2017, Steve Goon retired from the U.S. Postal Service. We celebrated at my house. I made *ngook beng* and broccoli with zucchini and onions. His hearty appetite hadn't left him. He filled his plate with several extra helpings of rice. We reminisced about our parents, Keith Wong, Donnie Chin and Uncle Bob. I noticed that his baldness had caught up to mine. His forehead showed new crinkles. He's thicker around his middle. He still exercises, but he traded in his running shoes for a bicycle and laps in the swimming pool.

Steve had taken over his parents' old home on South Forest Street, just three blocks from my own house. Ed remodeled the kitchen. Steve is gone often. His sweetheart Laura lives in Barcelona. His 95-year-old uncle Harry Choi moved to Hong Kong.

I lunch every few months at a Chinatown restaurant with old friends from the *Examiner*—Serena Louie, Michelle Kumata, David Takami, Ken Mochizuki, Jeff Hanada, Mayumi Tsutakawa, Cliff Louie, Pat Norikane Logerwell, Ann Fujii Lindwall, Sumi Hayashi, Dean Wong, Bob Shimabukuro and Greg Tuai. We call ourselves the "ID *lunchee* bunch," harkening back to our rambunctious lunches at Ying Hei. It's nice to see who's still around and catch up. We order lots of dishes and exchange silly banter. For the past several years, I've served as president of the *Examiner* board, mentoring young writers and helping raise money.

On August 15, 2019, Ken explained to the *lunchee* bunch that he was writing a graphic novel for the Wing Luke Museum. It features a few local heroes who aided Japanese Americans during wartime incarceration. Gary Iwamoto interrupted by asking, "What's a graphic novel?" Ken and I were surprised. We translated: "It's a comic book, Gary. It's not called that anymore." I chuckled silently to myself. That term went the way of the rotary phone, rolodex and slide projector.

In May 2018, Debbie Louie returned to Seattle to work at ICHS. Her husband Pete remained in Morgantown, West Virginia to finish his graduate studies. Debbie is a tenant at Steve's house. She walks to work every day. I talked her into participating in a few charity 5Ks at Seward Park. She's getting faster.

These days, I leave the recalcitrant political battles to the younger ones. I offer support and words of advice when asked. Otherwise, I slip into the background. It's their time, just as it once was mine. I'm buoyed by their optimism. I try to ground them in community history.

I'll retire from ICHS after I'm done fundraising for a new program to support frail seniors who want to grow old at home. It's a partnership between ICHS and Kin On. Teresita approached Keiro Northwest, which manages the Keiro Nursing Home, to join the endeavor, but they declined. Sadly, the financially-strapped nursing home closed at the end of 2019 after 41 years.

The new senior program will be on Beacon Hill next to Pacific Tower. Heidi Wong, former development director at Kin On, directs the fundraising campaign, and Tagoipah Mathno, a Cham-Muslim American who graduated from Franklin High School in 2008, provides support.

Heidi was born in Seattle but spent nine years in Hong Kong before returning to Washington at age 11. She lives in

Bellevue but seems more like a Beacon Hiller to me. She is a longtime member of the Seattle Chinese Baptist Church. Tagoipah grew up in Rainier Beach. She lives on Beacon Hill. Her family came as refugees from Vietnam. She is passionate about sharing the story of her Cham people and fighting back against the web of unjust social structures in this country. She hopes to produce a graphic novel.

Like me, Teresita wants to retire after the Beacon Hill senior program is up and running. She's a few months older than me. She foresees traveling more and volunteering in the ID. "Maybe I'll grow chickens with Dionnie," she quips.

Of the many friends, family and colleagues I've lost, the death that still haunts me is that of Lorraine Sako. She died on April 4, 2019, after a gutsy three-year battle with glioblastoma, the same aggressive cancer that claimed the life of U.S. Senator John McCain. She was only 62. My heart aches for her husband John Pai and their daughters Mirabai and Naima.

I still think about Nancy Lim even though she's been gone since 1993. She died on Chinese New Year. Teresita's daughters are friends with Max, Nancy's politically active son, who's now in London. If Nancy had lived, ICHS would have captured her heart. She'd be at ICHS with Teresita and me, and a bit cynical like us. We might all retire at the same time.

It's been years since I've attended the annual pig roast potluck in the Danny Woo Community Garden. Teresa Woo faithfully attends because her family donated the land. But she doesn't stay long. Her knees—and now her feet—groan from arthritis during the hill climb. "Uncle Bob is gone," she laments. "It feels very different. I'm a stranger. There's more white people than Asians. They ask, 'Who are you?' They don't have a clue."

On June 15, 2019, I saw Selena Dong (now Selena Dong

Epley), my former student intern, at a funeral service for her uncle Bruce Dong at the Seattle Chinese Baptist Church. He was featured in the *Reflections* book. Selena's father was Vincent Dong, one of the founders of the U.S. Forest Service's Asian Pacific American Employee Association. Vincent worked with Dale Hom.

Selena arrived late with her brother Braden, sliding quietly into a folding chair next to me. We were surprised to see each other. She's a parent like me and has been a superior court judge in San Diego for five years. We joked about the carefree days at the Commission on Asian American Affairs. She confirmed that she still loves greasy noodles.

I told her and Braden to come back to Seattle to see the Wing Luke Museum. I promised to show them around. Selena said she'll bring her daughter Sophia. I reminded them that the Dongs were early pioneers who helped make Seattle. I sensed their pride.

Selena told me that when she was sworn in as a judge, she shared these words: "My dad was my first and best example of intellectual curiosity, quiet leadership, kindness and humility, and if I strive to follow his example every day, I will never be led astray."

Selena's words touched me. There's no greater gift to the world than children. Parents can help their children soar. I've tried to do my best for Cian and Kino. I can only hope.

Orion Burt, my sister's son, married Josie Pratt on June 29, 2019, near Santa Fe, New Mexico. He's the first of my nieces and nephews to tie the knot. I attended, along with Cian and Kino, Linda's extended family, and Tom's kids Andreas and Emily Chew. The ceremony was held outdoors in Chimayó, a tranquil old village nestled in the Sangre de Cristo Mountains, 25 miles north of the city.

I stayed in an Airbnb in Santa Fe with Cian, Kino, Andreas and Emily for four nights. Cian and Kino didn't remember much about our earlier trip to Santa Fe in 2005. They didn't recall the visit to the Indian Market outside the Palace of the Governors. At the time, Kino, riding atop my shoulders, had pointed to the long row of Native American artisans seated on the ground with their wares and asked, "Papa, how come there are so many homeless people?" He made me wonder why the artisans hadn't been given better accommodations. Nothing seems to have changed since then.

Kino arranged Uber drivers for our jaunts around town. Our first driver was Karla, a pleasant silver-haired artist. Her hair was pulled back tightly with hairpins. She wore tinted glasses, silver hoop earrings and a gauzy, black tunic. As she piloted us toward the Famous Plaza Café for lunch, she pointed to structures built by the Pueblo people and early Spanish missionaries. She recounted episodes in the city's history. She said she was from San Francisco but had spent the past 50 years in Santa Fe. She built her own adobe house 35 years ago with help from local Pueblo friends.

As we neared our destination, she turned and asked, "Where are you folks from?"

"Seattle," I said.

Her face brightened. "The last time I was there, I visited the Wing Luke Museum. It was around Christmas. It was snowing. The museum was closed. I saw an older gentleman shoveling snow outside. I think his name was John. He was very nice. He was kind enough to let me come inside and look around. I liked the museum. It was alive. Going through the hotel made me feel like I was in my grandparent's home in Imperial Valley. Walking through the past is a rare treat."

"What a coincidence!" I exclaimed. "I used to work there.

That person must have been John Hom."

"Yes. I think that was his name."

My heart surged. My mind flashed back to a previous life. I peered over my shoulder at Andreas and Emily, both seated behind me, and gave them an emphatic thumbs-up. That day's lunch with the kids was especially satisfying. We had much to talk about.

CHAPTER 72

COVID-19 and George Floyd Murder

IN EARLY MARCH 2020, THERE was panic in the International District. At the International House Apartments, at 607 Maynard Avenue South, an employee tested positive for the fearsome novel coronavirus responsible for the COVID-19 pandemic. Two other employees were in quarantine.

The building housed over 100 non-English-speaking seniors. I remembered when the International House project first broke ground. I wrote about it in the November 1978 edition of the *Examiner*. The Milwaukee Hotel was reeling toward closure. But new low-income housing—and hope—had finally arrived. Tomo Shoji became a resident. A wide-grinning old-timer from Fow Seck—a dear friend of my father—moved into a modest unit with his garrulous wife. They lived there until they passed away.

Now, current residents needed to be quickly informed and tested. I worried about one of my mother's old sewing factory buddies, an ICHS patient. She was a longtime resident, one of the last of my mother's hardy counterparts.

Responding to the crisis, Teresita and other ID nonprofit leaders met with Dicky Mar at the International District Emergency Center (IDEC) on March 16. The following day, ICHS and IDEC set up a drive-through COVID-19 testing site in front of ICHS's ID clinic. Dicky mobilized volunteers—old hands like his wife Sue Taoka, Melvin Inouye and Kerry Taniguchi—to set up tents and coordinate logistics. The public health department provided 200 test kits. In the first week, ICHS staff administered 96 tests; results for 16 came back positive for the virus.

"Hey, I thought you were retired, Dicky," I said. He laughed. "No, I'm still around. These things happen, and your first thought is, 'What would Donnie do?' He'd be out here trying to help."

I understood his response, as did Teresita, who began directing the agency through the most harrowing period in its 47-year history. As the pandemic roared through Seattle, ICHS operations were brought to a near halt. Forty percent of the staff were furloughed, Teresita and myself included. We desperately looked for protective masks, gowns, medical supplies and financial support. Like drought-weary farmers, we waited for word of funding in the emergency stimulus package approved by the U.S. Congress.

Washington Governor Jay Inslee, responding to the soaring number of fatal infections, ordered the temporary closure of nonessential businesses. Restaurants and shops throughout the International District were shuttered. Those over 60—a high-risk population—were urged to "shelter in place" at home. Teresita was 67. In two months, I would turn 67, too. We continued to come in to work at the clinic, but took precautions.

Kerry was 65. Dicky was 68. Sue was 70. Melvin was 77. They stood under a blue IDEC canopy in the blustery wind and hard rain, directing traffic in front of ICHS. Their faces were obscured by surgical masks, but I recognized them right away.

I hadn't seen much of Melvin since he retired six years ago as a Metro bus driver. I remembered him from the Milwaukee Hotel fire watch. He did the 10 p.m. shift. When I was at the Wing Luke Museum, he helped move heavy objects during exhibit fabrication. Melvin was born in the Japanese American internment camp at Minidoka, Idaho in 1943. A few days before the drive-through testing began, his mother passed away at the age of 100 at Madison House, an assisted living facility in Kirkland.

I chatted with Kerry. He had been retired for four years. During the holidays, he plays Santa Claus at the Wing Luke and Tai Tung Restaurant. Donning a red costume to match his white flowing beard, he gleefully doles out fortune cookies and candy to kids. He knew Donnie from Bailey Gatzert Elementary School.

Donnie's sister Connie chided Kerry for going out. He's not in great health.

"But I'm old school, you see," he said. "If Donnie was around, he'd be out here. He'd ask, 'What are you doing sitting around? How come you're not stepping up?' I'm that way, too. I'm not going to run from a good fight. If I die, I die."

Kerry is hardcore, just like Donnie was. Donnie's ghost has risen. Maybe it's been here all along. Donald Trump talks about the "Chinese virus," pandering to xenophobes. On March 26, vandals smashed a window at Jade Garden restaurant in Chinatown. On April 12, three men plastered alt-right white supremacist stickers near Asian businesses. On May 11, Viet Wah supermarket was burglarized. I've been harassed on my morning runs. Debbie has, too.

In April, the *International Examiner* decided not to print for the first time in its 46-year history. There was no place to drop off papers. With the spike in anti-Asian sentiment, distribution became risky. For the next several months, Editor-in-Chief Jill Wasberg chose to keep the news flowing online only.

The Earth shook again in the weeks following the May 25 murder of George Floyd, an unarmed African American in Minneapolis. A white police officer pressed his knee on Floyd's neck for nearly nine minutes. Three other officers abetted. I was horrified. The incident ignited outrage across the nation and around the world. It was long overdue. For days, thousands of demonstrators marched through Seattle streets, demanding an end to police brutality and deep systemic change.

During the protests, over 100 businesses in the city were vandalized and robbed, 20 of them in Chinatown. Jade Garden was struck again. The area looked like a scarred war zone. After surveying the damage, community volunteers went up and down Weller, King, Jackson and Main streets, removing debris and covering storefronts with sheets of plywood. The ICHS clinic got the same protective makeover.

Over the next week, young artists painted the plywood with beautiful Asian murals and words of inspiration. My jaw unclenched. On Sixth Avenue South, Donnie's likeness appeared in the boarded-up window at Maneki, a Japanese restaurant dating back to 1904. Next door was the figure of a black hand with the words "Black Lives Matter." I smiled. Donnie would have been proud of the juxtaposition.

"I think we'll bounce back," Jamie Lee told me. "It'll take a long time though. Some small businesses will survive. Some will not. My hope is that this new energy and care for the neighborhood continues after this is over. We'll become a new version of ourselves."

After we spoke, I went to Tai Tung, the oldest Chinese restaurant in the International District, to order crispy almond chicken from owner Harry Chan. He prepares it just like the Hong Kong Restaurant once did. Tai Tung was established by Harry's grandfather Quan Lee in 1935. I'm confident the business will be around through another generation.

Like Jamie, my spirit holds strong. Maybe I'm witnessing the rebirth of the International District and the civil rights movement at the same time. It sure looks like it. I bet Jill could use another reporter.

Acknowledgments

I FEEL BLESSED. THIS BOOK would not have been possible without the encouragement and active contributions of many individuals and organizations.

First, I thank my lead collaborators: Debbie Louie for layout, design and editing; Ed Echtle for research; Diane Wah and Gary Iwamoto for final copy editing and proofreading; Dean Wong, Dorothy Ng, Han Eckelberg, John D. Pai, Karen Ducey, Rick Wong and Shannon Gee for photography; and Jeff Hanada for cover design.

Second, I thank the following individuals for sharing stories, photographs, documents, fact-checking and helping in countless other ways: Frank Abe, Ruth Abram, Karen Maeda Allman, Nellie Fujii Anderson, Melanie Apostol, Nobuko Awaya, Bill Backus, Russel Bareng, Maria Batayola, Teresita Batayola, John Bisbee, William Satake Blauvelt, Paula Bock, Linda Chew Burt, Orion Burt, Emma Catague, Cherry Cayabyab, Ching Chan, Harry Chan, Maxine Chan, Vivian Chan, Katherine Cheng, Benjamin Chew, Sen Poy Chew,

Susan Chew, Sylvia Chew, Bill Chin, Dr. Henry Chin, Susie Chin, Wilson Chin, Barbara Chinn, Cassie Chinn, Glenn Chinn, Kathryn Chinn, Binko Chiong-Bisbee, Fabiana Chiu-Rinaldi, Martha Choe, Janine Chu, Anne Xuan Clark, Michelle Corsilles, Leslie Cossitt, Diane Cowles, Anne Crisey, Jade D'Addario, Cynthia del Rosario, David Della, Greg Della, Mark Della, Jerry Dietrich, Dovan Do, Howard Dong, Aleta Eng, Gilbert Eng, Selena Dong Epley, Teresa Fang, Ellen Ferguson, Bob Fisher, Michael Flor, John Foz, Ann Fujii-Lindwall, Robbie Fujino, Theresa Fujiwara, Sandra Goong Fukuhara, Jeni Fung, Mimi Gan, Steve Goon, Sumi Hayashi, Dale Hom, Faye Hong, Doug Honig, Alina Hua, Sat Ichikawa, Tom Im, Melvin Inouye, Francisco Irigon, Ray Ishii, Alice Ito, Sue Karren, Leslie Katsman, Helen Kay, Elaine Kitamura, Frank Kiuchi, Michelle Kumata, Ruthann Kurose, Francesca Lacagnina, Tracy Lai, Julia Laranang, Alan Chong Lau, Angela Lee, Cynthia Lee, Jamie Lee, JoAnne Lee, Patricia Lee, Fran Levine, Thomas Lew, Kuei Lan Lin, Henry Liu, Brian Lock, Maxine Loo, Serena Louie, Shuet Louie, Bettie Luke, Randy Luke, Sharon Maeda, Connie Chin Magorty, Andrea Mano, George Mano, Irene Mano, Mark Mano, Charlene Mano-Shen, Dicky Mar, Paul Mar, Terri Mast, Fay Chew Matsuda, Leslie Matsuda, Melissa Szeto Matsuda, Lori Matsukawa, Calvin Matsuoka, Janice Matsuoka, JoAnn Mills, Paul Mitchell, Victor Mizumori, Ken Mochizuki, Karen Moon, Cindy Chu Mori, Tomio Moriguchi, Paul Murakami, Rick Nagel, Kazuko Nakane, Diane Narasaki, Phil Tajitsu Nash, Assunta Ng, Duy Nguyễn, Khanh Nguyễn, Loan Nguyễn, Arnie Ohashi, Arlene Oki, Lorraine Pai, Artis Palmer, Heidi Park, Judy Pigott, Jesse Reyes, Mimi Roberts, Mika Kurose Rothman, Peggy Saika, Edna Sawyer, Marjorie Schwarzer, Karen Seriguchi, Joy Shigaki, Stan Shikuma, Bob Shimabukuro, Jasbir Singh,

Jasmit Singh, Molina Singh, Connie So, Sheryl Steiffel, Mizu Sugimura, Ed Suguro, Olivia Taguinod, David Takami, Beth Takekawa, Kerry Taniguchi, Sue Taoka, Jack Tchen, Tony To, Marilyn Tokuda, Wendy Tokuda, Leeching Tran, Mayumi Tsutakawa, Greg Tuai, Deborah Uno, Pradeepta Upadhyay, Velma Veloria, Stan Viernes, Steve Viernes, Ruth Vincent, Huong Vu, Gloria Lung Wakayama, Sam Wan, Ben-Ling Wong, Terry Wong, Laura Wong-Whitebear, Teresa Woo, Vicki Woo, Sally Yamasaki, Fred Yee, Larry Yok, Teresa Yoneyama, Joan Yoshitomi, Marguerite Young, Erin Younger and Cai Zeng.

Third, I thank the following organizations for photos and documents: El Centro de la Raza, Inlandboatmen's Union, International Community Health Services, International District Emergency Center, International District Improvement Association, *International Examiner*, Seattle Civil Rights and Labor History Project, Seattle Public Library, University of Washington Libraries Special Collections, University of Washington Press and Wing Luke Museum.

Finally, I thank the following for their generous financial support: Historic South Downtown, International District Improvement Association, Nellie Fujii Anderson and Linda Chew Burt.

Index